Spirit and Life

The Four Gospels For Awakening

Spirit and Life
The Four Gospels For Awakening

A Practical Commentary on the
Life and Teachings of Jesus Christ

Volume 1
The Way of Illumination

"The words that I speak unto you, they are spirit, and they are life."
(John 6:63)

Swami Nirmalananda Giri
(Abbot George Burke)

Light of the Spirit Press
Cedar Crest, New Mexico

Published by
Light of the Spirit Press
lightofthespiritpress.com

Light of the Spirit Monastery
P. O. Box 1370
Cedar Crest, New Mexico 87008
OCOY.org

Copyright © 2025 Light of the Spirit Monastery.
All rights reserved.

ISBN-13: 978-1-955046-36-7 (paperback)
       978-1-955046-37-4 (ebook)

Library of Congress Control Number: 2025943193
Light of the Spirit Press, Cedar Crest, New Mexico

   Bisac categories:
1. REL006020   RELIGION / Biblical Commentary / New Testament / Gospels & Acts
2. REL067030   RELIGION / Christian Theology / Christology
3. OCC010000   BODY, MIND & SPIRIT / Spirituality / General

First edition, (August 2025)

Cover painting: The Sermon on the Mount by Carl Bloch
Front plate: Face of Christ from Christ and the Rich Young Man by Heinrich Hoffmann
Interior paintings based on the paintings by Heinrich Hoffmann by Luke Chatsworth for Light of the Spirit Monastery

11182025

Contents

Preface vii
Introduction ix
Christ the Word 1
The Annunciation to the Virgin Mary of the Birth of Jesus 23
The Birth of Jesus–1 29
The Doubt of Joseph and It Resolution 39
Further Assurance by the Angel to Saint Joseph 53
The Prophecy of Isaiah.. 61
The Birth of Jesus–2 66
Revelation to the Shepherds 69
The Presentation in the Temple and Prophetic Witness of Simeon and Anna............. 74
The Magi Visit the New-born King of the Jews.................................... 80
Herod's Anxiety... 92
Herod Consults the Magi Who Find the Child Jesus........................... 100
The Child Jesus is Found 103
The Child Jesus is Taken to Egypt and Later Returned........................ 115
Jesus in the Temple 117
The Appearance and Teaching of John the Baptist 121
John Denounces The Religious Hypocrites 149
John Foretells the Advent of Jesus.. 164
The Baptism of Jesus by John.. 169
The Temptation of Jesus 175
John the Baptist Witnesses to Jesus... 190
Jesus Meets and Calls His First Disciples 193
More Disciples Come to Jesus... 196
Jesus Performs His First Public Miracle 200
The First Cleansing of the Temple at Passover..................................... 203
The Insight of Jesus 207
Nicodemus Speaks With Jesus... 209
John the Baptist Speaks to His Disciples About Jesus 223
Spiritual Wisdom of John the Baptist 227
Jesus in Samaria Meets a Former Disciple.. 233
Jesus Returns to Galilee and Heals 246
More Disciples Are Called... 249
In the Synagogue at Capernaum 254
Jesus Heals the Sick... 259
Jesus' Ministry in Galilee Continues... 260

A Leper is Healed	265
Return to Capernaum	269
The Calling of Levi	276
Fasting	279
Wisdom in the Spirit	281
Healing Waters	286
The Way Things Are	293
Truth: The Call to Life	299
The Two Resurrections	301
The Right Self-perspective	303
The Wrong Way To Go About It	308
The Effects of Ignorance and Ego	312
Testing the Testers	315
Jesus' Ministry Continues	318
The Ordaining of the Twelve	320
Healing	322
The Wisdom That Heals	325
Spiritual Salt	340
The Light of the World!	348
Spiritualizing External Laws	352
The Golden Rule	379
Go Within!	382
The Lord's Prayer	387
The Secret, Hidden Life of the Spirit	393
Wise Judgment	401
Change Yourself	406
Caution and Prudence	409
Rules For Living in the Spirit	413
The Two Gates and Ways (Paths)	416
Be Cautious, Be Wary	422
False and Real Discipleship	425
Being Worthy of Healing	429
From Death To Life	435
Message to John the Baptist	437
The Greatness of John the Baptist–Elijah Reincarnated	441
Mercy and Love	447
The Friends Of Jesus Think He Is Insane	451
The Kingdom of God is Come Unto You	452
The Blasphemy Against The Holy Spirit	455
Evil Or Good	458
The Power Of Every Spoken Word	460
The True Family Of Jesus	462
The Field Of The Heart	465
The Seed In The Heart	471
Light In The Heart And Mind	478
Ears To Hear	480

The Field Of The Soul	481
The Pearl of Great Price	485
Revealing That Is A Concealing	486
The Kingdom Of Heaven Within	487
The Storm And The Calm	490
Encounter With Possessing Demons	492
Healing Touch	495
Death, Blindness and Muteness Vanquished	498
In The Synagogue at Nazareth	501
Sending The Apostles On His Mission	504
Wisdom To The Wise	507
The Way of Discipleship	512
The Death Of John The Baptist	517
The Word Goes Out	520
Compassion And Care	522
Storm and Doubt	525
Continuing Grace	528
Some Plain Speaking	529
Glossary	535
About the Author	552

Illustrations

The Face of Christ	xiv
The Annunciation	22
The Revelation to the Shepherds	68
Jesus Among the Doctors	118
The Miracle at Cana	201
The Samaritan Woman at the Well	240
Jesus Healing	258
Jesus Teaches the Beatitudes	324
The Lord's Prayer	386
Jesus Raises the Widow's Son	434
Jesus Teaching by the Seaside	465
Jesus in the Synagogue at Nazareth	500

PREFACE

This is not a commentary on the four Gospels individually, but on a harmony of the Gospels: one continuous narrative as found in *A Harmony of the Gospels For Students of the Life of Christ* by A. T. Robertson (published by Harper and Row).

To me, the text commented on here is not a mere biography but a spiritual revelation consisting of both the life and the teachings of Jesus. Naturally, as someone who has a background in both Christianity and Hinduism (Sanatana Dharma), my analysis is a synthesis of western and eastern perspectives which I believe that Jesus himself possessed as I have explained in my book *The Christ of India*. (Which I am pleased to say has been publicly endorsed and recommended by the Shankaracharya of Puri–Govardan Math.)

Introduction

When studying the Gospels we have to keep in mind these four things:

1) We are only being given fragments of Jesus' teaching, fragments that seemed the most significant to the authors, but nonetheless only fragments. Because books had to be handwritten, and because the original Christians were vegetarians and would not use animal skins (parchment) that could be made into long scrolls, but rather only used papyrus which was greatly limited in its length, the evangelists were constrained to write as economically (briefly) as possible. So the Gospels had to be short, and only what seemed to the evangelists the most salient of Jesus' words could be set down.

2) Although there are early Gospel fragments, they are few and just that: fragments. The complete texts date from around the beginning of the fourth century. This means that they were likely edited to fit the theological alterations of three centuries from their original composition. This applies also to the "original Aramaic" text used by George Lamsa, which is really only the Peshitta text which was totally overhauled in the fifth century to conform to the theology of the state religion of the Byzantine empire–for example, turning the Holy Spirit from a "She" into a "He."

Here are two examples of how Jesus' words were changed to fit the new Christianity of that time. In a very early Aramaic version of the Gospels, the Cureton Gospels, in Luke 21:34, which the King James Version (which is based on the "official" Greek text) has as: "Take heed to yourselves, lest at any time your hearts be overcharged with surfeiting, and drunkenness," an exhortation to "moderation." But the Aramaic text has: "See that you never make your hearts heavy by drinking wine or eating meat." Not moderation but total abstinence. Then in John 14:1 the KJV has: "Let not your heart be troubled: ye believe in God, believe also in me." The Cureton is: "Believe in God, and you *are* believing in me." There is no "also" about it.

If we go through the Gospels and Epistles we find a verse here and a verse there that express the real teachings of Jesus, the wisdom he learned first from the Essene teachers and then from the yogis of India. (See *The Christ of India*.) Jesus taught totally within the context of the wisdom of the East–India specifically. That is why a Saint Thomas Christian priest from South India once remarked to me: "You cannot understand the teachings of Jesus if you do not know the scriptures of India, especially the Upanishads." Although there are profound metaphysical/spiritual principles in these fragments of Jesus' teaching in the Gospels, to discover his meaning we must approach them in the same context within which he gave them: that of the wisdom of the Eastern sages, including Lao Tzu. Consequently I will be trying to rescue the meaning from some passages, as well as commenting on their surface appearance.

3) The material selected to include in the Gospels was done so for symbolic reasons as much as for historical and doctrinal presentation. Therefore we should also consider what might be the hidden symbolism in the incidents and teachings. The early Christians considered that the Gospels were a kind of mystery-drama portraying the spiritual journey of each spirit as it progresses to Christhood. So the study of the Gospels should be both objective and subjective.

4) The incidents and teachings of the Gospels are intended to be interpreted in various ways, all of them legitimate. Paramhansa Yogananda insisted that all scriptures should be studied with the understanding that they have three levels of meaning: physical, mental, and spiritual. So we should be intent on discovering the wealth of wisdom contained in even the simplest words of the Gospels.

For a completely straightforward historical account of Jesus and his teachings I recommend that you study *The Aquarian Gospel of Jesus the Christ* by Levi Dowling, upon which I have also written a commentary, *The Aquarian Gospel For Awakening*.

In this commentary I will be using the King James Version text. Though this is not usually a favored translation at this point in time, it has been preferred by those of more esoteric understanding, including Paramhansa Yogananda and Eastern Orthodox Christians. The esoteric understanding, of course, will be up to us.

Jesus did not speak Greek, he spoke Aramaic. The Gospel of Matthew was written in Hebrew, and the other three were written in Greek. Saint Luke, author of his own Gospel, translated Saint Matthew's Gospel into Greek. Why? Because as a philosophical language capable of great nuance and subtlety Greek was unparalleled in the Mediterranean world. Also, through Greek the evangelists could reveal the inner meaning, the inner thought, of Jesus. So in this commentary I will do quite a bit of analysis of the Greek words of the text, for they will reveal profound aspects of Jesus' teachings. I will also be using a great deal of Sanskrit words, so I am including a Glossary at the end of this book.

Wherever I have put words in brackets in the Gospel text these are variant or supplemental words that are indicated by the Greek text which has been consulted throughout using Strong's *Concordance*.

I have only commented on those parts of the Gospels which are relevant to spiritual life, especially yoga sadhana, and what applies to the life of a sadhaka. I recommend that you read my book *The Unknown Lives of Jesus and Mary* to fill out the historical and esoteric picture. And for a very detailed account of Jesus' divine life, see the *Biblical Revelations* of the holy stigmatist Anne Catherine Emmerich (available from Amazon and other sources).

Perhaps the most important thing I should say is this: In these pages you will find the teachings of Jesus, Isha Nath, the divine yogi, presented in the perspective of his adopted religion: Sanatana Dharma–Hinduism. (For information on that subject see my book *The Christ of India*.)

Christ the Word

In the beginning was the Word, and the Word was with God, and the Word was God. The same was in the beginning with God. All things were made by him; and without him was not any thing made that was made. In him was life; and the life was the light of men. And the light shineth in darkness; and the darkness comprehended it not.

There was a man sent from God, whose name was John. The same came for a witness, to bear witness of the Light, that all men through him might believe. He was not that Light, but was sent to bear witness of that Light.

That was the true Light, which lighteth every man that cometh into the world. He was in the world, and the world was made by him, and the world knew him not. He came unto his own, and his own received him not. But as many as received him, to them gave he power to become the sons of God, even to them that believe on his name: Which were born, not of blood, nor of the will of the flesh, nor of the will of man, but of God.

And the Word was made flesh, and dwelt among us, (and we beheld his glory, the glory as of the only begotten of the Father,) full of grace and truth.

John bare witness of him, and cried, saying, This was he of whom I spake, He that cometh after me is preferred before me: for he was before me.

And of his fulness have all we received, and grace for grace. For the law was given by Moses, but grace and truth came by Jesus Christ.

No man hath seen God at any time; the only begotten Son, which is in the bosom of the Father, he hath declared him. (John 1:1-18)

In the beginning was the Word. In India when you come across a Christian church or institution you usually find somewhere on the building or on a sign in front one or both of two Gospel verses: "I am the way, the truth, and the life: no man cometh unto the Father, but by me" (John 14:6), or the opening verse of Saint John's Gospel: "In the beginning was the Word, and the Word was with God, and the Word was God." Of course this is to get "the poor heathen" to convert and join them.

But what they do not know is that this first verse of Saint John's Gospel is really a quotation from Vedic texts. The original Sanskrit is: *Prajapati vai idam agra asit. Tasya vak dvitiya asit.* "In the beginning was Prajapati [the Creator], and with him was Vak [the Word]." It is no amazing coincidence, either. Saint John is citing these words that are found in three different Vedic texts: Krishna Yajurveda, Kathaka Samhita, 12.5 and 27.1; Krishna Yajurveda, Kathakapisthala Samhita, 42.1; and Jaiminiya Brahmana II, Samaveda, 2244. These are from the Yajur and Sama Vedas respectively. They were written down long before the Hebrew nation even existed.

How did Saint John know this verse and consider it of such prime authority that he would begin his Gospel with it? Either through his Essene background (for the Essenes did keep and study oriental scriptures–see *The Christ of India*) or from the teachings of Jesus given to his disciples. Chances are, it was from both. So putting this verse on signs outside churches is just a proof of how little the Churchians know of Jesus and his authentic teachings.

"In the beginning was the Word" means that the Word was already in God at the beginning of the projection of relative existence/creation. It was with God and was God. But what is the Word? The Greek word *Logos* means something spoken or thought, reasoning (intelligence), communication, revelation, speaker, speech, utterance, work and word. This is a great deal, and all of it meaningful when we realize that the Word is Ishwara, the Lord, an expansion or projection of the Absolute, Brahman, the transcendent Reality that encompasses the entire range of being and existence.

Before we analyze these meanings of Logos, we need to consider the triune concept of the Absolute that Jesus found in the scriptures of India during his so-called "lost years" which are described in *The Christ of India*. God is often referred to as Satchidananda: Existence, Consciousness and Bliss. Sat is Brahman, Chit is Ishwara, the guiding consciousness within creation, and Ananda is the creation: Divine Vibration or Outbreathing–itself.

In the Bhagavad Gita we find the three monosyllables Om Tat Sat that express the same thing Jesus meant when he spoke of the Father, Son and Holy Spirit. Sat means Reality, Tat means That, and Om is the Cosmic Vibration, the Holy Breath (*Agia Pneuma*). Sat is the Father, Tat is Ishwara the Son, and Om is the Holy Spirit. So the subject of these eighteen verses is Ishwara, who is also called the Only Begotten of the Father, since he is the direct and only emanation of/from Parabrahman, the Father.

The great error of exoteric Christianity is to identify Jesus of Nazareth with Ishwara and claim that he is the Only Begotten of the Father and the creator of the world. We will have more to say on that later.

Now we should return to the subject of Logos, the Word, as its various meanings give us a hint of the nature of Ishwara.

Logos means intelligence, and Ishwara is the Intelligence, the Intelligent Witness-Power behind/within everything. Logos means an impelling force, and Ishwara is the Projecting Power and the Consciousness that stimulates all relative beings to evolve. Cause is another meaning of Logos, and Ishwara is the cause all creation. Logos is also communication, and it is Ishwara that develops and opens our minds to realize that there is a transcendent reality, and thus Ishwara leads us to the realization of Brahman. Logos means that which reveals, and Ishwara reveals the higher realities to us.

The most important meaning of Logos is: something that is spoken. Being the emanation of Brahman, Ishwara is "spoken" by Brahman. And so is every sentient being. We are all "words" of Brahman, spoken–willed into manifestation–by Brahman. Every one of us is an actual and potential Word of God. That is, we are already one with Brahman, but we are evolving through rebirth and yoga sadhana to become a perfect objectification of that eternal nature.

Therefore, when in this opening section of Saint John's Gospel Jesus is also spoken of as the Word, it is in the sense that as a perfected, liberated being, or mukta, he is a perfect "speaking" of God. Anyone who becomes totally purified, evolved and established in the consciousness of oneness with Brahman is a Word of God. Jesus is not unique. In all the cycles of creation, Sons and Words of God are manifested. I have already cited that Jesus said to his disciples: "Believe in God, and you are believing in me." The fact is that if we truly believe in God in the fullest sense we shall also believe in our divine Self. In *The Aquarian Gospel* by Levi Dowling, it is made clear that Ishwara alone is the archetypal Christ, and that Jesus is *a* Christ, not *the* Christ. Moreover, he was/is not unique. God is revealed in all the liberated masters and avatars. But there is only the one Absolute God: Brahman.

Logos is derived from *Lego*, which means a revelation, a conveying of some truth or knowledge. I have already pointed out that this is true of Ishwara, but if we consider Saint Paul's words: "God, who commanded the light to shine out of darkness, hath shined in our hearts, to give the light of the knowledge of the glory of God in the face of Jesus Christ" (II Corinthians 4:6), we will realize that God is revealed in Jesus as a perfect reflection. And in that context alone did Jesus say: "I am the way, the truth, and the life" (John 14:6). Jesus and all siddha purushas are embodiments and communications of the Divine Consciousness that is revealed in them. In them "dwelleth all the fulness of the Godhead bodily" (Colossians 2:9), yet Brahman/Ishwara alone is THE Way, Truth and Life.

Lego also means a call. Every siddha purusha is a call to humanity to follow his example and become one in consciousness with Brahman. That is why Swami Nikhilananda said: "You cannot accept Christ and reject Krishna, and you cannot accept Krishna and reject Christ." Of course he meant the true Christ, not the false mythical Christ of exoteric Christianity.

And the Word was with God, and the Word was God. The same was in the beginning with God. Although Ishwara is an emanation of Brahman, Ishwara did not at any time "come into being," but as Brahman Itself was inherent in Brahman, and like the creation is manifested in cycles. Because Brahman/Ishwara is beyond description and speech I am having to speak in approximations so our human intellects can at least somewhat comprehend these mysteries.

Ishwara is really Brahman and therefore absolutely eternal. At the same time, all sentient beings were with/within Brahman, and although we have come into manifestation cyclically as does Ishwara, we, too, are eternal, always with and within Brahman. This is indicated by Krishna in the Bhagavad Gita: "For me great Brahma is the womb, and in that do I place the seed. The origination of all beings comes from that. Whatever be the forms produced within all wombs, the great Brahma is their womb, and I the seed-casting Father" (14:3-4). We are all seed-words of Brahman.

All things were made by him; and without him was not any thing made that was made. The word translated "made" is *ginomai*, which does not mean to make or create from nothing as exoteric Christianity claims, but means to be generated: emanated, just as was Ishwara. Ishwara manifests us, but we are eternal, individual spirits within Him: jivas within Shiva.

Ishwara being divine, perfect and all good, so is all of relative existence. What we call evil is a distortion or deformation of good. Distortion and deformation of good comes from ignorance (avidya), which itself is corrected—and the original perfection and good restored—by knowledge (jnana). Therefore nothing is ever "lost" or "damned" or any such foolish epithets. Maya is the whole drama in which sin and evil appear, and when maya is totally dispelled from our mind our innate knowledge arises and the drama is ended, the theater is closed and we all go home and experience the fulfillment of the prayer of Jesus: "O Father, glorify thou me with thine own self with the glory which I had with thee before the world was" (John 17:5), which proves that Jesus was and is "one of us" in the sense that all of us are essentially Brahman.

In him was life. The word *zoe* simply means life, for Ishwara is the life principle itself.

Ishwara is the very principle of consciousness within all beings. Wherever there is consciousness, there Ishwara is present as enlightener and manifester. Furthermore, Ishwara in time reveals to the inmost consciousness of every sentient being their purpose for being in manifestation. It is Ishwara who calls us back to Brahman in transcendental union. No wonder, then, that Patanjali said of Ishwara: "He is guru even of the ancients" (Yoga Sutras 1:26).

And the life was the light of men. The word translated "men" is *anthropos,* which means a human being, but the words from which it is derived give some interesting implications. One root is *eido,* which means to be conscious, to be aware, and to understand, and also to possess the power of will. Another root is *optanomai,* which means focussed awareness and self-assertion. *Orao* means to learn, to understand. There are several other root words, all of which mean to be intelligently conscious. Thus, to be a human is to have fully developed consciousness and intelligence. Some of the root words emphasize that the awareness is not passive but active and intentional. So the sum if it all is that a human being is fully awake and aware. Ishwara is the light of human beings because each is conscious within the consciousness of Ishwara and ultimately of Brahman. The individual spirit (jivatman) is essentially consciousness, and the Supreme Spirit (Paramatman) is Consciousness Itself.

And the light shineth in darkness. We have not considered the meaning of light, which is the translation of the word *phos*. *Phos* comes from the no-longer-used word *phao,* which means both to shine and make manifest or appear. That in turn comes from *phaino* and *phemi,* which mean to reveal oneself as well as one's thoughts. From this we see that Ishwara is the power of manifestation, of creation, and that creation is really light, not "solid matter" as we think it is. It is also the revelation of Divine Thought. To understand this well, the seeker must turn to the writings of Paramhansa Yogananda who, as far as I can determine, is the only one who has written fully on this matter from a truly spiritual standpoint. Chapter Thirty of *Autobiography of a Yogi,* entitled "The Law of Miracles," is very helpful in understanding the divine, creative nature of light.

"Darkness" is the translation of *skotia,* which means dimness or obscurity. That comes from *skotos,* which means to be in shadow: *skia.* In Greek all these words are both literal and symbolic and can therefore mean external darkness or obscurity in the mind. They are the counterpart of maya (illusion) and avidya (ignorance). In other words, "the shadow of death" which appears nineteen times in the Bible. And that is samsara, the world of ignorance, illusion and death.

All things are formed of the Light of God, but maya and avidya cover that over, cloud our minds and make us see only darkness, though we call it light and life.

And the darkness comprehended it not. Katalambano means to vigorously seize something, to apprehend or attain it as well as perceive or comprehend it. Maya/avidya cannot touch the true Light, much less understand what it really is. Therefore, just like human beings who are in that darkness, maya/avidya detests, yes even hates, the Light and is the enemy of the Light. Such aversion is at the root of active denial of the existence of God and Truth, which is why Max Heindel wrote in *The Rosicrucian Cosmo-Conception* that such denial is the most negative condition the human being can fall into. That is why Jesus said: "Ye cannot serve God and mammon [maya/samsara]" (Matthew 6:24; Luke 16:13).

There was a man sent from God, whose name was John. We will be considering the Gospel accounts of Saint John the Forerunner (the Baptist) later on.

The same came for a witness, to bear witness of the Light, that all men through him might believe. He was not that Light, but was sent to bear witness of that Light. This was put in by Saint John the Evangelist to affirm that Saint John the Forerunner was not the Messiah. This statement was relevant at the time because there were very many who believed that the Forerunner was actually the Messiah instead of his cousin, Jesus. Even though Saint John himself declared Jesus to be the Messiah, these people refused to accept that and clung to their belief that John was the Messiah. This is so typical of "cult religion" that it is almost comic. No matter who the religion is named after and how exalted they claim him to be, they only accept his teachings which please them. One of the first things that I had to acknowledge in my own life was the fact that the "one, true church" I belonged to was no such thing, and that its members had simply decided on what they wanted to believe or not, and then combed through the Bible to find passages that would support them, or at least be made to seem to support them.

"And when the people saw that Moses delayed to come down out of the mount, the people gathered themselves together unto Aaron, and said unto him, Up, make us gods, which shall go before us; for as for this Moses, the man that brought us up out of the land of Egypt, we wot not what is become of him. And Aaron said unto them, Break off the golden earrings, which are in the ears of your wives, of your sons, and of your daughters, and bring them unto me. And all the people brake off the golden earrings which were in their ears, and brought them unto Aaron. And he received them at their hand, and fashioned it with a graving tool, after he had made it a molten calf: and they said, These be thy gods, O Israel, which brought thee up out of the land of Egypt. And when Aaron saw it, he built an altar before it; and Aaron made proclamation, and said, To morrow is a feast to the Lord. And they rose up early on the morrow, and offered burnt offerings, and brought peace offerings; and the people sat down to eat and to drink, and rose up to play. And the Lord said unto Moses, Go, get thee down; for thy people, which thou broughtest out of the land of Egypt, have corrupted themselves: They have turned aside quickly out of the way which I commanded them: they have made them a molten calf, and have worshipped it, and have sacrificed thereunto, and said, These be thy gods, O Israel, which have brought thee up out of the land of Egypt" (Exodus 32:1-8). Most religion is a calf of gold being worshipped instead of God.

That was the true Light, which lighteth every man that cometh into the world. The True Light is God Who *is* Light (I John 1:5). And that Light came into the world in the incarnation of Jesus, "For in him dwelleth all the fulness of the Godhead bodily" (Colossians 2:9). This does not mean that Jesus was the Second Person of the Trinity, the Only Begotten of the Father: Ishwara and Brahman respectively. Rather, being a fully liberated and perfected spirit, a mukta and a siddha-purusha, Jesus was absolutely one with God. In his entire being God was made manifest. To see him was to see God, to speak with him was to speak with God. Therefore Jesus said: "He that hath seen me hath seen the Father" (John 14:9). Not that he was "swallowed up" in God or overshadowed by God in some mediumistic or puppet-like manner, but rather that the eternal Unity which is the potential of every individual spirit was perfectly realized and shown forth in him. When he told his hearers: "Be ye therefore perfect, even as your Father which is in heaven is perfect" (Matthew 5:48), he was calling them to the exact same realization and spiritual status which he had attained. That is why he said in Revelation: "Him that overcometh will I make a pillar in the temple of my God, and he shall go no more out" (Revelation 3:5, 12). Having attained full enlightenment there is no more need for incarnation in any of the worlds, from lowest to highest. That is the state which is *theosis*–deification–not as exoteric Christianity conceives of it, but the state of liberation (moksha) as understood by the sages of India, at whose feet Jesus both learned about and attained that divine condition.

It is imperative that we pause here to discover the real meaning of that spiritual state to which Jesus called his disciples. The Beloved Disciple John in his epistle speaks of those that overcome the world (I John 5:5-5), and in dictating his experience on Patmos he relayed these words of Jesus in the book of Revelation: "To him that overcometh will I give to eat of the tree of life, which is in the midst of the paradise of God.... To him that overcometh will I give to eat of the hidden manna" (Revelation 2:7, 17).

First we must understand these words in their intended yogic sense. The paradise of God is the illumined Sahasrara chakra of which the brain is the material manifestation. The tree of life is the Spirit itself, the Chidakasha (Ether of Consciousness) which is in the midst of the Sahasrara. The hidden manna is the Word of God, Soham, which imparts the direct experience and communication/union of the spirit with God by which Jesus says we shall live (Matthew 4:4; Luke 4:4). (See *Soham Yoga, the Yoga of the Self*.) The spiritual nature of these promises is shown by the next verse: "And he that overcometh, and keepeth my works unto the end, to him will I give power over the nations" (Revelation 2:26). Obviously this is not a promise of universal rulership of the earth, but the mastery of all the facets, faculties and powers of the individual person's makeup which are symbolized more than once in the Bible by the word "nations." In sum: "He that overcometh shall inherit all things" (Revelation 21:7), just as did Jesus.

Saint Paul had this understanding also when he expressed the hope and intention "that I may win Christ,… if by any means I might attain unto the resurrection of the dead. Not as though I had already attained, either were already perfect: but I follow after, if that I may apprehend that" (Philippians 3:8, 11-12). If he had meant the resurrection of the physical body that exoteric Christianity teaches will occur at the end of the world, he would naturally have said that he had not already attained it. But he was speaking of the resurrection into God Consciousness, into God whose perfection would then be his as a Son of God. Therefore he continued: "I count not myself to have apprehended: but this one thing I do, forgetting those things which are behind, and reaching forth unto those things which are before, I press toward the mark for the prize of the high calling of God in Christ Jesus" (Philippians 3:8-14), the call that comes to all who have "ears to hear" (Matthew 11:15).

Affirming this we have the words of Saint John: "Beloved, now are we the sons of God, and it doth not yet appear what we shall be: but we know that, when he shall appear, we shall be like him; for we shall see him as he is. And every man that hath this hope in him purifieth himself, even as he is pure" (I John 3:2-3). We must heed the words of the Bhagavad Gita: "Therefore be a yogi" (6:46).

I do not want to weary the point, but since what I am saying is so different, even contrary, to the beliefs of ordinary Christianity (Churchianity), I want to consider one more example, also from Saint Paul. "Let this mind be in you, which was also in Christ Jesus: who, being in the form of God, thought it not robbery to be equal with God.... He humbled himself, and became obedient unto death, even the death of the cross. Wherefore God also hath highly exalted him, and given him a name which is above every name: that at the name of Jesus every knee should bow, of things in heaven, and things in earth, and things under the earth; and that every tongue should confess that Jesus Christ is Lord, to the glory of God the Father" (Philippians 2:5-11).

Let this mind be in you, which was also in Christ Jesus. The word translated "mind" is *phroneo*, which means thinking, resolving and seeing (understanding). The idea is that we should think, will, see and understand things exactly as did the Lord Jesus himself. Saint Paul further said: "Who hath known the mind of the Lord, that he may instruct him? *But we have the mind of Christ*" (I Corinthians 2:16). Here the word translated "mind" is *nous*, the entire mind of a person, encompassing knowledge and understanding. It also means awareness and perception. Therefore we are told that we can have the same mind as Christ Jesus. That is why the very word "Christian" means "another Christ." It was first used by the unbelievers to mock the followers of Jesus because at that time the original Christians believed that the very purpose of their religion was to enable them to become other Christs: "Till we all come in the unity of the faith, and of the knowledge of the Son of God, unto a perfect man, *unto the measure of the stature of the fulness of Christ*: that we… may *grow up into him in all things*, which is the head, even Christ" (Ephesians 4:13, 15).

Who, being in the form of God, thought it not robbery to be equal with God. Being in the image and likeness of God–as are we, also–Jesus aspired to divinity. The word *morphe* translated "form" does not just mean outer shape, but *nature*. Jesus had learned in India that although he was finite and God was infinite, yet he could realize and manifest fully that divine nature and likeness. Saint Paul was simply transmitting the teaching of Jesus when he told the philosophers on Mars Hill regarding God: "In him we live, and move, and have our being;… *For we are also his offspring*" (Acts 17:28). As said before, Ishwara is *the* Christ, and Jesus became *a* Christ–as shall we, persevering yogis, become.

He humbled himself, and became obedient unto death, even the death of the cross. Wherefore God also hath highly exalted him. Uperupsao means to elevate or raise to the highest position. Can the eternal God, about whom we sing: "Glory be to God in the highest," be elevated or raised to any degree? Of course not. "God also hath highly exalted him" could never be said about the Only-Begotten of the Father, the Second Person of the Trinity: Ishwara. Jesus attained that position through his self-purification as a yogi, culminating in his voluntary sacrifice on the cross. That is why Jesus himself said in Revelation: "To him that overcometh will I grant to sit with me in my throne, *even as I also overcame*, and am set down with my Father in his throne" (Revelation 3:21).

Those who through yoga sadhana overcome all obstacles to the manifestation of their innate divinity will be like Jesus and will be established ("sit") with him in the same exalted status which he attained before us. Saint Paul wrote about Christ that God "raised him from the dead, and set him at his own right hand" (Ephesians 1:20). And it shall be the same with all who resurrect into divine consciousness like Jesus.

The difficulty with these various passages I have cited is the mixture of terminology that at one time implies Jesus is absolute divinity, and then in another place that he attained to his deification. This is why it is so important to realize that Jesus lived most of his life in India as a yogi before returning to Israel and beginning his ministry, and that after three years he returned to India. The historical records show that Jesus was a yoga siddha, an adherent of Sanatana Dharma. We can only have an accurate perspective on Jesus if we realize this to be true.

Now back to our analysis of Saint John's words about the Only-Begotten, Ishwara.

He was in the world, and the world was made by him, and the world knew him not. Ishwara is not in the world just as an invisible presence. Rather, the world itself is the visible presence of Ishwara. At the beginning of a creation cycle, when relative existence begins, there is *the idea* of an emanation from Brahman, the Absolute, although there is no actual emanation or any kind of action or development within Brahman, Who is essentially unchangeable. Since in relative existence duality is an absolute necessity for its realization, consequently at the very moment of the extension/emanation of Brahman it becomes dual: consciousness and vibration, God and Matter. Ishwara is the inner Guide, and vibratory creation–MahaShakti, Prakriti or Pradhana–is the Guided. We can think of Ishwara ("Christ Consciousness") as the screen, and Creation as the play of light and shadow projected onto it. But we must never lose sight of the fact that the two are One.

Therefore Ishwara is in the world as its inner existence (antakharana), being its projection. Since the material world is itself vibration, ideation, it cannot conceive or "know" Ishwara. And that is why people whose consciousness is submerged and confined in materiality cannot conceive or believe in God as He is. As the great Christian philosopher Origen said, they are merely material bodies (somas), not conscious beings or spirits (pneumas) at all. Of course, he meant that from a practical standpoint, not as an absolute principle, for everything is Spirit, including us.

Just as matter cannot know either itself or its origin, neither can those people who are (truly) imprisoned in the body. Only through evolution does matter start to be revealed as consciousness (spirit), and it is the same with sentient beings. "Know Thyself" is the primary impulse of the universe. But Self-knowledge is no simple thing, and requires a great deal of evolution to even intuit, much less realize and manifest. So neither the world nor the worldly know either Ishwara or their true Self.

He came unto his own, and his own received him not. God comes to sentient beings every day and they do not perceive him. At best some humans have a theory about him. But full knowledge of God, Brahmajnana, is beyond most at the present. Yet hints and fragments are there, even if only subliminally as a vague intuition which can, if fostered, develop into an increasingly defined understanding and eventually into spiritual realization.

In my childhood I listened on the radio to a program hosted by Tom Brenneman who also had a magazine. In one issue of his magazine I read an article by a man whose sister and her husband had decided that their son should have no contact with religion, and who had commanded all their friends and relatives that nothing about religion or God was ever to be spoken in from of him. And so it was. When the boy was five or six years of age, the man was asked to stay in their home and look after their son while they went on a trip. During that time he noticed that if the boy did anything "bad" he would keep saying something under his breath for a while. Finally the man realized that he was whispering "The Bipper, The Bipper," over and over. So he asked him, "What is 'The Bipper?'" The boy looked at him in surprise and asked, "You mean The Absolutely Bipper?" "Yes," replied his uncle. "Well," began the boy, "the Absolutely Bipper is everywhere and knows everything. And he doesn't like it when I do something wrong. And when I do, I just keep saying, 'The Bipper' over and over until I feel all right." The uncle was amazed: his nephew knew about God and his relation to human beings. And that knowledge had come to him from within his own Self. So it has been through the history of humanity: people have intuited the Infinite Consciousness pervading everywhere and within them.

Sometimes that inborn awareness comes out in strange ways. I knew a minister who was once harangued by a self-styled atheist who spent about an hour expounding the "truth" of atheism and the folly of theism. When he was finished the minister said: "There are two points about all that you have just said. One: it is complete nonsense. Two: you do not believe a word of it yourself." The man put his right hand up in the air and declaimed: "I swear to God in heaven that I *do*!"

Once I was watching the news. A clip from a speech by Kruschev before the Supreme Soviet was shown in which he said, "My conscience is clear before God and man." Whoops! That was not the way a true Communist-atheist spoke. But awareness of God is at the core of our being, and if it is not intentionally and insistently blocked it must come out onto the conscious level.

But as many as received him, to them gave he power to become the sons of God, even to them that believe on his name. Happily, in time all consciously become aware that there is a Greater Being. At first they are in awe of Infinite Existence, but if they follow through on their conviction, living accordingly, that insight develops in scope and they come to realize that their very being comes from the Infinite. And if that is not inhibited, it grows into the realization that they are part of God, that they share the identical essence. When they come into contact with the wisdom of the Indian seers (rishis), then they find out and recognize what they have always known: they and God are one. This is "receiving" God.

Worshipping God as far away in the heavens or in any way separated from him is only believing, not receiving. When someone wants to know about God, that is good; but wanting to know God Himself is the ripening of wisdom. Blessed are they that come to hear the inner impulse from their own Self, saying with Krishna in the Bhagavad Gita: "Therefore be a yogi" (Bhagavad Gita 6:46). That is why Paramhansa Yogananda often said: "Yoga is the beginning of the end."

Knowledge is power. Therefore when God is "received" by insight and understanding, the powers of the inner Self begin to come forth through awakening which really is the action of God within the individual. The "power to become the sons of God" is within us, and both we and God together bring that onto the conscious level. This happens in many ways according to the karma and mentality of the individual. Then our work begins. And since it is also God's work, it must come to perfection. But faith (belief) is a prime factor for success, since true faith is not simple intellectual belief or conviction, but a deep-based intuitive knowing that only comes about when the person is truly "ready."

Yoga is the way of "becoming." But what is God's name? A name in a very high sense is the designation of a person's nature. But in the highest sense it *is* a person's nature. The yogis of primeval India revealed that highest name in the two oldest upanishads, the Isha and Brihadaranyaka. "O Pushan, the sole seer, O Controller, O Sun, offspring of Prajapati, spread forth your rays and gather up your radiant light that I may behold you of loveliest form. I am that Purusha [Spirit-Self]: I am Soham [*Soham asmi*]" (Isha Upanishad 16; Brihadaranyaka Upanishad 5.15.2). The Sanskrit text is: *Yo sav asau purushah; soham asmi. Soham asmi* literally means "I Am That I Am," which is exactly what God told Moses was his Name (Exodus 3:14). "In the beginning this [world] was only the Self [Atman], in the shape of a person. Looking around he saw nothing else than the Self. He first said, 'I am Soham [*Soham asmi*]'" (Brihadaranyaka Upanishad 1.4.1).

Soham is the name of both Ishwara and the individual spirit or jiva–for the two are one, as can be realized and experienced. (Again, see *Soham Yoga, the Yoga of the Self*.) Thus Soham is the "first speaking" of the Absolute Itself: the expression of the knowledge and knowing of the Self. Soham is the Name (Embodiment) of the Primeval Being, the Self of the Universe and the Self of our Selfs. Soham is the Consciousness of Brahman and of the Self of each one of us. We, too, are Soham.

Which were born, not of blood, nor of the will of the flesh, nor of the will of man, but of God. In relative existence everything proceeds from something. Something never comes from nothing. Therefore those who are awakened in their consciousness and are increasingly revealing the divine image and essence within themselves do not just appear suddenly, but are the evolutes of a great chain of already-existing elements. Actually everything comes from a single element, Brahman, but Brahman manifests in a stream of increasingly evolving states and entities.

I am always amazed that anyone can seriously say, "My father made me," or that a man will say that he "made" his children. That is an absolute impossibility. God is the sole factor in all existence, and no creation or manifestation is itself a creator or manifestor in the truest sense. God alone is Father and Mother. To make this clear, Saint John is telling us what is not our origin, what did not produce or manifest us. There are three things on the list: blood, will of the flesh and will of man.

"Not of blood." The word translated "blood" is *haima*, which means the living, red blood of animals and human beings. Our physical blood comes from our earthly father, but Jesus, having no human father, did not have human blood, but divine consciousness itself manifesting in his body as blood. In the same way the awakened sons of God have divine consciousness alone as their enlivening and evolving element or spiritual "blood."

We often hear of people getting religious after having a spiritual awakening through some kind of trauma or pain, such as the death of someone or a manifestation of their own mortality, etc. Although this is a viable change, it is purely in the mind and intellect, and is not in any way of the spirit, though it can lead to awakening in the spirit–but not necessarily. Also, a lot of people have some unusual experience which their ego and its ignorance inflates to cosmic proportions when in reality it is hardly a speck of dust.

Liberated consciousness only proceeds from the Ever-free Consciousness that is Brahman. It cannot be manufactured or dreamed up and somehow objectified. But what about yoga sadhana, yama-niyama and purification of the yogi's makeup? All necessary; but as Sri Ramakrishna continually pointed out, all that, including meditation, is karma yoga, the yoga of action. It produces the highest form of spiritual karma without which nothing can be attained by us, but there is a point where karma (action) leaves off as the dream it is, and Reality dawns–and dawns of itself. For nothing leads to the Eternal but the Eternal.

Nothing external, no action, can bring about the Divine Vision. However, those who walk the right path attain the Goal that has always been there waiting. Enlightenment cannot be produced, but it can be revealed. That is what true yoga is all about.

To see yourself in a mirror presently encrusted with dust and dirt you must do something: clean the mirror until nothing that can cloud it remains. Then without effort you will see your face. The work is not the seeing, but the seeing is made possible by the work. Cleaning in no way changes the essential nature of the mirror. It just reveals it. We must hold this perspective in mind at all times. The knowledge of the Way enables us to reach the Goal. But the Goal is at all times right at hand.

Those who think they must go from one point to another will only keep wandering in illusion. This is why Saint John wrote to spiritual aspirants: "Beloved, now are we the sons of God, and it doth not yet appear what we shall be: but we know that, when he shall appear, we shall be like him; for we shall see him as he is. And every man that hath this hope in him purifieth himself, even as he is pure" (I John 3:2-3). We already are what we are. Anything else is illusion and delusion. Yet we do not at this moment experience our true being, "what we shall be." But when we gain the knowledge, the vision of God, Brahmajnana, Atma Sakshatkara, Self-Realization, then we shall see both Brahman and ourselves as we really are: One. First we must purify ourselves—we must clean and polish the mirror. "Therefore be a yogi" (Bhagavad Gita 6:46).

"The will of the flesh." The word translated "will" is *thelema*, which means both will and desire. The word translated "flesh" is *sarx*, which means specifically animal flesh with the implication of something external as well as simple humanity. We can consider their significance in turn.

First, the birth into the divine consciousness of the atman-self cannot and does not ever come from the externals of human life. No one is "driven into the arms of God" by misfortune, pain or sorrow. Only the eternal impulse for conscious union with the Absolute impels us toward It. Implicit in this is the important truth that the motive for liberation into Spirit can never come from material or external factors. For such things are alien to the spirit, and indeed conceal from us the very life/existence of the spirit. So nothing of human, external existence and the state of mind they create in us can even conceive of the holy birth into God, much less be "fulfilled" in God. Rather, they will be eliminated by the entry into divine consciousness. They cannot exist together with it in any degree.

Nothing of our human nature incites us to seek higher life. Only from our true Self-nature as sons of God within God can the urge to transcend relativity and enter into eternity arise. And it arises from within us, not from without. Liberation into Infinity is antithetical to the motivations of earthly existence, for it dissolves them and frees us from them absolutely.

"The will of man." Usually the word translated "man" is *anthropos*, which means humanity in general. But here the word is *aner*, which means a male human being. Females conceive and give birth, but only males make conception possible. So here "will of man" means all those things which bring about, foster and perpetuate our imprisonment in the delusional material consciousness which arises from our experience of human existence which is fundamentally unreal. So nothing in our relative, human makeup can ever be an effective element in our prodigal self's awakening, arising and returning to its origin which is God alone.

"But [the will] of God." It is the will of God both within us as our true Self and outside us as the evolving universe that brings us to the status of sons of God, born of God alone. God sends us forth from the depths of his Being into relative existence, and God calls us back into his pure Being when the evolutionary cycle is completed.

We can see, then, that all the exoteric or externalized religions which arise or arose from earthly consciousness not only do not motivate or facilitate spiritual awakening and growth, they are its enemies. For the ways and means of genuine spiritual evolution bring about the annihilation of the illusions of "blood," "flesh" and "man" in us on which they are based and without which they could not exist.

But Sanatana Dharma is another thing altogether, because it can lead the questing individual spirit-Self to become itself sanatana: eternal spirit.)

And the Word was made flesh, and dwelt among us, (and we beheld his glory, the glory as of the only begotten of the Father,) full of grace and truth. In the person of all truly perfected beings or siddha-purushas the Word, the will and purpose of God, is incarnated. Thus they are avataras, "descents" of the Divine, total revelations of the Ultimate Reality. They live among human beings whom they have come to call to the same divine status they have attained. And those who are sufficiently evolved in their own consciousness do in truth behold their glory and recognize it as the Divine Glory, Ishwara, that is now revealed in them. And in that "grace and truth" they follow after them and their examples and likewise return to the bosom of the Father and fully enter into the boundless kingdom of infinite Being and Consciousness. As Buddha said: "Birth is ended, the holy life fulfilled [has been lived], the task done. There is nothing further for this world."

John bare witness of him, and cried, saying, This was he of whom I spake, He that cometh after me is preferred before me: for he was before me. This has more than one meaning. Jesus came after John because he was conceived and born after John was conceived and born. But most important, though John was only a few months older than Jesus, even as children John was like a spiritual teacher to Jesus. After John was led into the desert by an angel and shown where he should live and engage in spiritual discipline, he likewise took Jesus into the desert, instructed him in spiritual practice, and they spent much time together in the desert. That is why in the Greek text he says that before Jesus came to the Jordan to be baptized by John he had been John's disciple. "He was before me" can be equally correctly translated, "before [this] he was mine." For the word translated "me" is *moo*, which also means both "mine" and "my own." As Yogananda revealed, John was the guru of Jesus, and that was why Jesus was baptized by John at the time of his revelation as the Son of God, although as a Nath Yogi his sadguru was Chetan Nath, while earlier John was his upa (auxiliary or secondary) guru. (See *The Christ of India*.)

And of his fulness have all we received, and grace for grace. This is an incredible assertion by Saint John the disciple, the author of the Gospel. When as a young boy I read the book of Acts and learned that the shadow of Saint Peter could heal the sick (Acts 5:15) and that cloths simply touched by Saint Paul could heal the sick and exorcise evil spirits (Acts 19:12), I understood absolutely that they had not just been "saved" and lived good lives as Christians, but that Jesus had transformed them into a completely other kind of being than they had been before. They were no longer human, but something greater. And I realized that everyone had to pass into that higher mode of being. I then took a vow at 4:00 p.m. on Friday, July 6, 1955, to not give up until I learned how that could be done. After some years of search and struggle I read the Bhagavad Gita and *Autobiography of a Yogi* and discovered that yoga was the way and that Jesus himself had been a yogi.

Through yoga meditation the fulness of divine consciousness can be attained by the yogi. The word translated "fulness" is *pleroma*, the same word that the Christian Gnostics used as a synonym for the the Godhead, the fullness of Divine Being. The disciples received/attained the same total spiritual perfection/realization that Jesus had attained. Pleroma means filling, what is filled and the act of filling. This corresponds to the yogis' declaration that for the adept yogi knowing, knower and known become one.

The word translated "grace" is *charis*, which means favor, gift and grace–all with the implication that it is something which is given and actively received. It is also a supernatural ability indicated by our word "charism" which is really a form of *charis*. The idea in Saint John's statement is that the disciples received as a gift the fulness of Divine Being, the fulness of the Divine Spirit, the fulness of God, into their own essential being or Self. "For in him dwelleth all the fulness of the Godhead bodily. And ye are complete in him, which is the head of all principality and power" (Colossians 2:9-10).

For the law was given by Moses, but grace and truth came by Jesus Christ. The real part of us, the spirit-Self, has passed through millions if not billions of external entities or bodies in succession. They were all matter, whereas we are spirit. So the bodies were our prisons. Even though they were meant for our advancement and evolution, still they were prisons like the schools we endured in this life. They were burdens and obstacles. And this is because the material and the spiritual are antithetical to one another. As Saint Paul (Galatians 5:17) tells us, the flesh wars against the spirit and the spirit wars again the flesh: by their nature they oppose one another. When the external life is in the ascendent it destroys our spiritual awareness, and when the spirit life is dominant it dispels our identity with the material.

In the same way, external religion actually opposes spiritual life, and religion based on internal awareness opposes much of material life. The law given by Moses was a signpost to higher realities, but a sign cannot take us to our desired destination. It only points the way. Jesus brought both the knowledge of the indwelling spirit and the way to free it from external domination. As he said (Matthew 5:17), he came to fulfill the law–to enable human beings to follow the principles that before were beyond their ability to fulfill. He brought grace and truth to make possible the purpose of the law. "For I say unto you, That except your righteousness shall exceed the righteousness of the scribes and Pharisees, ye shall in no case enter into the kingdom of heaven" (Matthew 5:20). Freedom of–and in–the spirit is the Gospel of "Christ in you the hope of glory" (Colossians 1:27). Christ came into the world outside us so we might discover the Christ within us, our own eternal Christ nature.

No man hath seen God at any time; the only begotten Son, which is in the bosom of the Father, he hath declared him. As long as we hold in our consciousness the delusion that we are mortal, external beings and not ever-free spirits, then we are only human beings and the vision of our god-nature is impossible for us. But when we enter into our eternal consciousness that is Christ in us the hope of glory, then we "hear" the Gospel of Christ, awaken into our true nature, and our inner Christ will itself be our savior. This alone is Christianity–the religion which reveals the inner Christ-nature of each person. But externally-oriented Christianity denies our Christ-nature, while Sanatana Dharma, Hinduism, affirms it. So when I became a Hindu, like Jesus, then I truly became a Christian.

The Annunciation to the Virgin Mary of the Birth of Jesus

The angel Gabriel was sent from God unto a city of Galilee, named Nazareth, to a virgin espoused to a man whose name was Joseph, of the house of David; and the virgin's name was Mary.

And the angel came in unto her, and said, Hail, thou that art highly favoured, the Lord is with thee: blessed art thou among women. And when she saw him, she was troubled at his saying, and cast in her mind what manner of salutation this should be. And the angel said unto her, Fear not, Mary: for thou hast found favour with God. And, behold, thou shalt conceive in thy womb, and bring forth a son, and shalt call his name JESUS. He shall be great, and shall be called the Son of the Highest: and the Lord God shall give unto him the throne of his father David: And he shall reign over the house of Jacob for ever; and of his kingdom there shall be no end.

Then said Mary unto the angel, How shall this be, seeing I know not a man?

And the angel answered and said unto her, The Holy Ghost shall come upon thee, and the power of the Highest shall overshadow thee: therefore also that holy one which shall be born of thee shall be called the Son of God. For with God nothing shall be impossible.

And Mary said, Behold the handmaid of the Lord; be it unto me according to thy word. And the angel departed from her (Luke 1:26-35, 38).

In my book, *The Unknown Lives of Jesus and Mary*, a compendium of very old writings which were read by the early Christians for information about Jesus and his Mother long before the Bible was compiled, many more details can be found. Although it was decided that only the writings of the Apostles, Saint Luke and Saint Paul would be included in the Bible, these early texts were considered as authoritative as those. (No one at that time was so deluded as to believe that the Holy Spirit had "written" the books of the Bible.)

And the angel came in unto her, and said, Hail, thou that art highly favoured, the Lord is with thee: blessed art thou among women. And when she saw him, she was troubled at his saying, and cast in her mind what manner of salutation this should be. For me, the saddest and most disturbing aspect of today's "yoga world" and its citizens is the prevalence of utter delusion which grips the more ambitious among them. Any strange experience is touted as a revelation or proof of Self-realization or evidence of their being high souls and marvels to the angels. Quite a few have written to me to inform me of their exalted status–often that they have discovered they are Jesus reincarnated.

The Virgin Mary was not just some nice little Jewish girl that God chose at random from many to be the mother of the Messiah. She was a fully perfected being, a siddha-purusha, an avatara, as was her Son. She was the Mother of the human race, Eve who had been beguiled by Lucifer the Archangel in Paradise. He had spoken very pleasant words to her there, and she was naturally put on her guard by the words of Gabriel, lest another attempt was being made to deceive her and again prevent her spiritual destiny from being fulfilled. (For more on this see *Robe of Light*.)

Her example is of great value. We should always have a healthy doubt or skepticism regarding our spiritual experiences. We should question and analyze and keep a sensible perspective on ourselves as persons and yogis. For the Lucifer of ego is always present to not just fool but to destroy us if it can. We must always examine ourselves and see if the experience or insight has increased our understanding and confirmed us in our search for liberation. Are we a better yogi from it? Do we see more clearly in spiritual matters? If not, it is worthless and an ego-based maya: an illusion.

The subconscious mind cannot reproduce the form and presence of a great Master in the dream state because it cannot relay his form and presence. There are two basic tests: did the holy one really look like himself, and what was our consciousness during and after the dream–which would reveal if it was a real superconscious vision. One of my yoga friends who eventually "crashed and burned" often said to me, "I dreamed of N. last night." When I would ask, "Did he/she look like themselves?" she would reply, "No. But I know it was really him/her." So she deluded herself and eventually destroyed herself. As Sri Ramakrishna was wont to say: Sadhu [Sadhaka] Beware.

Then said Mary unto the angel, How shall this be, seeing I know not a man? I once read a very interesting essay about the foolishness of Victorian and Edwardian society which considered that if a young lady blushed and "became confused" at the merest hint of something "improper" it was a sign of her innocence and purity. But it was just the opposite: a totally innocent person, male or female, would not understand what was said and would only be puzzled and no doubt ask for clarification! And the author cited the Virgin Mary. She asked the Archangel a very savvy and informed question showing that she did not think babies were found under cabbages. Purity is not ignorance. A yogi is not a childlike "innocent" who is so busy "loving God" that he does not know the nature and way of this world. He does. That is why he is a yogi: he does not want to get entangled in the ways of the world and its life, which he knows and understands very well and therefore avoids. Devotion is not dimwittedness. Yogananda said that stupid people cannot find God. The prime qualification for a yogi is a fully operative observant intelligence. Sri Ramakrishna used to say: "Be a devotee, but why a fool?"

And the angel answered and said unto her, The Holy Ghost shall come upon thee. We begin our evolutionary journey in relative existence with the simplest of forms and spend ages, even creation cycles, evolving to the human level. And from there we spend countless incarnations until we evolve to the point where we can begin consciously accelerating our rate of evolutionary development. In the beginning this just involves ethical behavior and development of the capacity for kindness, love, respect for others and even self-denial or sacrifice for the benefit of others. Naturally, the scope of who we relate to in a higher and more refined or subtle manner is at first very limited, but expands throughout our subsequent lives. Eventually we begin to move into higher awareness. And if we progress steadily onward, the time comes when the Holy Spirit "comes upon us." At first this will be a keen awareness of our own spiritual existence, especially our immortality. But then the time comes when we are aware to some degree of the all-pervading Spirit and at least intuit that our finite being exists within Infinite Being in some manner. At first this is quite vague, but if it is not interfered with by negativity on our part it becomes more and more a part of our conscious awareness. And all this development is possible because of our eternal existence within the Infinite.

And the power of the Highest shall overshadow thee. Eventually a moment comes where there is not just awareness of the all-encompassing Spirit, there is a definite moment when communication of Spirit with our spirit begins to occur. This is very tenuous, even fragile, and that communication may be disrupted and dispelled many times before it becomes established as a steady condition. There is not just Presence at this point, but now Power begins coming into play. And if nothing is done on our part to retard or halt it, there is a continual growth in the scope (breadth) and depth of that profound interaction. At this point conscious spiritual life begins and ripens into an intelligently ordered ascent in our spiritual evolution. The individual becomes and remains a yogi.

Therefore also that holy one which shall be born of thee shall be called the Son of God. From the first moment the yogi begins to apply himself to the practice of authentic meditation and consciously living the yoga life, the process of enlightenment begins which culminates in atjmajnana–the consciousness of our true Self as a "son" of God, the Supreme Self. I have to use the qualifying word "authentic" because we can waste lifetimes in the pursuit of false, ignorant and ultimately destructive "yoga." And this is compounded when we are wasting our lives in misplaced loyalty to a false, ignorant and ultimately destructive "guru" or an organization operating in the guru's name.

Nevertheless, when we are practicing real yoga in the correct manner, having ordered our life to conform to the principles of yoga sadhana–the observance of yama and niyama–every step taken is a step forward on the journey to the Divine. Then everything will take place exactly when and as it should, and our success will be assured.

For with God nothing shall be impossible. Through genuine yoga sadhana we are with God on the path "that shineth more and more unto the perfect day" (Proverbs 4:18). The beginning yogi can have no idea what his life shall be from that point on. It truly will progress "from glory to glory" (II Corinthians 3:18).

But first he must understand what is necessary for his success in yoga, what is required of him: the full price. "For which of you, intending to build a tower, sitteth not down first, and counteth the cost, whether he have sufficient to finish it? Lest haply, after he hath laid the foundation, and is not able to finish it, all that behold it begin to mock him, saying, This man began to build, and was not able to finish. Or what king, going to make war against another king, sitteth not down first, and consulteth whether he be able with ten thousand to meet him that cometh against him with twenty thousand?" (Luke 14:28-31). This is a tremendously serious matter.

Yogananda said in a talk that the persevering yogi will find as time goes by that all around him his fellows yogis will be falling on the spiritual battlefield, "and some will come to the door and fall asleep." I am extremely sad and grieved to tell you that every one of my early yogi friends failed to persevere in the yoga life. Most quite overtly walked away one by one, and others kept up a pretense of fidelity but their lives revealed the falsehood of their pretense. In the beginning I had believed absolutely that they would be faithful all the way and the light of the Self would be revealed in them. But it was not so. Some sank into the swamp of moral depravity, alcohol and drug addiction and materialism. Others just became mediocre non-entities, devoid of any spiritual consciousness or conscience.

They did not even pretend. Spiritual amnesia became their lot. And it was totally willful on the part of all of them. They turned away and went into the shadow that soon became total darkness. "If therefore the light that is in thee be[comes] darkness, how great is that darkness!" (Matthew 6:23).

And Mary said, Behold the handmaid of the Lord; be it unto me according to thy word. The word translated "handmaid" is *doule*: a female slave, but it has the connotation of being so voluntarily. The Virgin Mary was committed from birth to fulfill the will of God. So though she was faced with the prospect of being mocked, despised and considered a blaspheming liar, as well as a woman deserving legal condemnation to death for adultery according to the Mosaic Law, she agreed to pay the price. It was in consideration of the sacrifices of Jesus and Mary that Saint Paul wrote: "Ye are bought with a price: therefore glorify God in your body, and in your spirit, which are God's" (I Corinthians 6:20). And: "Ye are bought with a price; be not ye the servants of men" (I Corinthians 7:32). We belong to God, not to the world or any other human being, and the yogis who think and live accordingly will one day be revealed as "words of God"–themselves embodiments of the spoken will of God. That is how Jesus became the Word of God. And so shall we.

And the angel departed from her. But the will of God which she made her own never departed, but became revealed in her to perfection.

The Birth of Jesus–1

Now the birth of Jesus Christ was on this wise: When as his mother Mary was espoused to Joseph, before they came together, she was found with child of the Holy Ghost (Matthew 1:18).

Now the birth of Jesus Christ was on this wise. All the details of Jesus' birth should interest us because they are symbols of the elements that produce Christhood. Nobody is conceived haphazardly, it happens in a very exact way. If a single element is omitted there will be no conception. Here, too, there is a precise order of things. Even though each birth is unique, each one is also alike.

The first element of the birth of Jesus was the birth of his mother. In Paradise Adam and Eve were to produce children in a manner unknown on earth. By an act of will they were to project light from their bodies. This light would combine, and the two polarities would amalgamate to produce a fully-formed body for a soul that would instantly inhabit it. And that would be the birth into Paradise. (See *Robe of Light.* The scriptures of India give instances in which great sages and their wives conceived children in this way during meditation.)

The virgin mother of Jesus was conceived in just this manner. As Saints Joachim and Anna stood in the passage beneath the Ark of the Covenant the astral light of their auras merged and a ray of light that was the spirit-soul of Mary came from the Ark above. In that instant the New Eve was conceived. (See *The Unknown Lives of Jesus and Mary.*)

After the Lord Jesus' ascension, the Apostle James the Great became the spiritual head of Christianity and the bishop of Jerusalem. Some years later he wrote a letter to the Christians of the Mediterranean world, for they were all his spiritual children. In that letter he told them: "A double minded man is unstable in all his ways.... Wherefore purify your hearts, ye double minded" (James 1:8; 4:8). He had heard Jesus himself say that "No man can serve two masters: for either he will hate the one, and love the other; or else he will hold to the one, and despise the other. Ye cannot serve God and mammon" (Matthew 6:24). The word translated "double-minded" is *dipsuchos*, which literally means "two-spirited." We see ourselves trying to be two contradictory things at once rather than eliminate that which conflicts with our highest nature. The word also means vacillating–swinging back and forth from light and dark, from positive and negative, being a spiritual schizophrenic. That is why we are in this lunatic asylum called "the world." Yogananda said that human beings are all crazy, and people of the same craziness band together and call their insanity "normal." But all are crazy. Yoga is the only effective psychotherapy.

If we divide our consciousness between God and anything else, the conception of the inner Christ cannot come about, for we are engaging in spiritual adultery. One of the Gnostic books in *The Nag Hammadi Library* speaks of the soul falling into material existence and going around committing fornication with all it met. The idea is that the soul enters into union with material objects and either identifies with them or has its consciousness utterly shaped by them. For that very reason, severe as it sounds, Saint James further wrote: "Ye adulterers and adulteresses, know ye not that the friendship of the world is enmity with God? whosoever therefore will be a friend of the world is the enemy of God" within himself (James 4:4). These are words addressed to genuine aspirants to higher consciousness.

"[Know that] all this, whatever moves in this moving world, is enveloped by God" (Isha Upanishad 1). It is usually thought that the enlightened person sees God inside all things, but this verse from the oldest of the Upanishads says it is just the opposite. We should not first see an object and then see into it and behold God. Rather, we should be seeing God at all times first and then see all objects *within* God. For God is not inside the universe, the universe is inside God. And so are we. We should be seeing God all around us as well as within us.

In that soul which has no contact with anything else but God, which lives touching nothing but God, the conception of the Christ-consciousness takes place. Does this mean that to bring forth Christ-consciousness we must see, hear, touch, taste or smell nothing? Both Yes and No. It means that we maintain contact with God and experience all things objectively, not allowing ourselves to be seized and controlled by that experience. Rather, we keep ourselves focused on God alone. How? Through meditation centered on the consciousness of spirit.

We must ourselves be like the icon of the Virgin Mary known as The Sign of Salvation. She has her hands raised, both in prayer and to indicate that she is "touching" no earthly thing. Within the center of her breast is the Christ Child, blessing. We, her children, shall become like her if we persevere.

No man, angel, archangel, or any of the great bodiless powers made the Virgin Mary pregnant. God, the Holy Spirit, alone did so. Similarly, nothing in any of the many realms of existence can conceive Christ-consciousness in us. Only the Holy Spirit, overshadowing us through meditation, is capable of doing so. No good deeds or spiritual observances can produce the Christ-consciousness in us. No worship, pilgrimage, study of holy books or even association with holy people can engender the Christ-consciousness in us, because they are outside us, in the world. We should believe Jesus when he tells us that the kingdom of God is within (Luke 17:21).

One of the favorite activities of spiritual butterflies in India is to challenge a spiritual teacher, saying: "We have visited so many mahatmas [great souls] and listened to their words, and yet we do not have peace of mind." The teacher then says some silly platitude about perseverance, faith or some such. Really they should say: "Of course you are not gaining peace of mind. Your mind is inside and the mahatmas and their words are outside. Until you forget external sources and turn within yourself through faithful meditation, peace is impossible."

"Beloved, now are we the sons of God, and it doth not yet appear what we shall be: but we know that, when he shall appear, we shall be like him; for we shall see him as he is. *And every man that hath this hope in him purifieth himself, even as he is pure*" (I John 3:2-3). To manifest Christ-consciousness we must purify our lives, turning from that which is destructive to higher consciousness and its development. What is that necessary purification? First the adoption of a vegetarian (preferably vegan) diet and abstinence from addictive substances such as alcohol, nicotine and drugs. That will bring about purification of the body.

At the same time there must be adherence to strict principles of morality and the observance of yama and niyama.

Yama consists of: 1) ahimsa–non-violence, non-injury, harmlessness; 2) satya–truthfulness, honesty; 3) asteya–non-stealing, honesty, non-misappropriativeness; 4) brahmacharya–continence; 5) aparigraha–non-possessiveness, non-greed, non-selfishness, non-acquisitiveness. These five are called the Great Vow (Observance, Mahavrata) in the Yoga Sutras.

Niyama consists of: 1) shaucha–purity, cleanliness; 2) santosha–contentment, peacefulness; 3) tapas–austerity, practical (i.e., result-producing) spiritual discipline; 4) swadhyaya–self-study, spiritual study; 5) Ishwara-pranidhana–offering of one's life to God.

That will purify the mind and will.

True spiritual life is thoroughly practical, and so must the reordering of our life be in order to live in the spirit. Until this complete restructuring is done nothing will produce a lasting positive effect in our life. The Bible likens spiritual life to the preparation of a field before sowing the seed: "Break up your fallow ground, and sow not among thorns" (Jeremiah 4:3). "Sow to yourselves in righteousness, reap in mercy; break up your fallow ground: for it is time to seek the Lord, till he come and rain righteousness upon you" (Hosea 10:12). Otherwise nothing is gained. Purification of life is necessary, for only in the purified life and mind will the pure light of our inner Christ shine forth.

The divine spirit is always in us, but just as a sooted lamp gives no light, however brightly the flame may be burning within, unless we cleanse our hearts, thoughts and deeds no light will shine into our darkness, revealing the inner Christ. "Blessed are the pure in heart: for they shall see God" (Matthew 5:8).

The Gospel says about the Virgin Mary that "she was found with child." The Virgin had Christ within. So it is with us. The Christ of our own divine nature is within us eternally, but we do not realize it until a certain level of evolution is reached. Actually, the very concept could not be understood by us if the Christ was not already beginning to be born in us. The Christ is always present within, so in one sense we are always pregnant with Christ, even from the moment we come into relative existence. But we do not know it until spiritual awakening begins in us spontaneously after untold lives.

The divine Christ has always been in us potentially from eternity. Inside every single atom Christ-consciousness is present as its essential nature. The atoms will evolve and change perpetually, but that divine essence will never change, for that is immortal and eternal. In time it will manifest, and that is the message of the birth of Christ from Mary. For it is not enough for the Christ-consciousness to be within, innate, it must be brought forth and manifested. This objectification of Christ can be greatly advanced by our consciously setting in mind that the Christ is inherent in everything and determining to look at all things in that perspective.

However we must keep in mind that within relative existence, Christ is only *inherent* in all things, including all people. Until the advent, the revelation, of the Christ in them takes place we should look upon them only as what they are at the moment. Nobody takes a tomato seed and a lettuce seed and tries to make salad with them. They have to be planted, cultivated and given time to grow. So it is with all things and all people. Their potential Christ must become manifest.

But if we will look at all things as *potentially* Christ it will help us to act in a more realistic manner toward them. How differently we would treat the world around us if we understood that Christ is within the heart of all matter. And we would certainly see people differently if we kept in mind that they are evolving Christs. Who would eat the flesh of animals if they realized that they, too, are striving up the evolutionary ladder toward the status of Christ? There is a basic reverence that should be shown to all things, for all things are manifestations of the primal force that is the Holy Spirit. Those who seek for the revelation of their own Christhood will be benefited if they adopt such a viewpoint. What a glorious thing to realize that we are living within the greater life of God at all times. "For in him we live, and move, and have our being;... for we are also his offspring" (Acts 17:28).

God is woven into the fabric of the universe, actually *is* the fabric of the universe. The wonderful truth is that perfection is potential in all things and its actualization is absolutely inevitable. And how even more wonderful it is to live with that in our consciousness. For real spiritual life is a world-view. It is also discovery, and that is why we have the term Self-*realization*.

When she was espoused (engaged) to Saint Joseph, Mary was found to be pregnant. When we attempt to link our consciousness with God we find out that we are already joined to God. When the spiritual awakening comes that we might call the espousal to God, we discover that we are even now eternally wedded to God. Then we have to get busy and actualize that insight. Through the unfoldment produced by meditation the truth of our unity with God is revealed. Meditation is the means by which the inmost Divine Consciousness within us is quickened into life and manifestation.

"Then said he, Unto what is the kingdom of God like? and whereunto shall I resemble it? It is like a grain of mustard seed, which a man took, and cast into his garden; and it grew, and waxed a great tree; and the fowls of the air lodged in the branches of it" (Luke 13:18-19). Everything grows from the seed, and not just the one plant but all that will descend from it, for they are even now inherent in the seed. It is incredible to think that in the seed the entire plant is already present, as well as all plants that will be engendered from it. The roots, the branches, the leaves, the fruits, the seeds of untold millions of plants are held in our hand in the form of what looks like a tiny fragment of stone. But when planted it becomes a source of virtually infinite life. Experience reveals it to be so.

It is the same way with meditation. Practice, not talk, reveals all. The seed must be planted and given the right environment; then it grows. So it must be with us. Meditation must also be supported by a mode of life, thought and behavior that is conducive to its pursuit. "For thus saith the Lord, Break up your fallow ground, and sow not among thorns. But sow to yourselves in righteousness, reap in mercy; break up your fallow ground: for it is time to seek the Lord, till he come and rain righteousness upon you" (Jeremiah 4:3; Hosea 10:12). However unlikely it might seem that such a simple thing as meditation can produce infinite consciousness and perfect realization in those who apply it, "he that ploweth should plow in hope" (I Corinthians 9:10). It is all in the "plowing" and the "sowing."

Meditation is both the true spiritual conception and the seed from which Christ Consciousness grows within us. Meditation is also our spiritual espousal within which the Holy Spirit overshadows us that we may in time through earnest application bring forth the Christ within. "And the angel answered and said unto her, The Holy Ghost shall come upon thee, and the power of the Highest shall overshadow thee: therefore also that holy thing which shall be born of thee shall be called the son of God" (Luke 1:35).

Saint Matthew's statement that the Holy Spirit was the source of the conception of Christ indicates that however much we may intellectually understand about our innate divinity, we must do more than just believe it. It must be demonstrated by its actualization, otherwise it is all just empty talk.

In ancient India they used a very good simile. Fire is latent in wood, but it has to be evoked by the friction of rubbing two sticks together. This produces heat, and from heat the spark is produced that can ignite the fuel. With this in mind, the Indian sages spoke of spiritual practice as tapasya, the production of heat (tapa). The breath of the Holy Spirit fans the innate spark into divine fire. And that is the conception of Christ in us, the hope of glory.

First the Holy Spirit acts outside us, evolving the various forms in which we spend countless lives for many cycles of creation. Then when we reach the human level and have ripened enough, the Holy Spirit begins to work *inside* us, and that is the conception of our Christhood, the beginning of the end. That is why Jesus told his disciples that the Holy Spirit "dwelleth *with* you, and shall be *in* you" (John 14:17).

When as his mother Mary was espoused to Joseph, before they came together, she was found with child of the Holy Ghost. That is, before there was any physical affinity or union between them that would produce the conception of a child, Mary was found to be of child by the Holy Ghost. This is important, because the implication is that no human being, human agency or material factor can produce the Christ. Even more truly, no external factor can produce the Christ. This is one of the great principles expressed by the symbology of the virgin birth. Why? Because you and I come from God alone; we do not come from matter or from any earthly agency.

And when we desire enlightenment we can do no external thing to attain it, even though certain outer disciplines and observances can purify and prepare us for the search. Rather, we turn inward and seek the inner light, the light that "shineth in darkness" (John 1:5) always. For there is only one thing that transforms, and that is God. Therefore the conception of the Christ has to come from within. That is why the prophet sang: "O my dove, that art in the clefts of the rock, in the secret places of the stairs" (Song of Solomon 2:14). We cannot meet the Beloved anywhere except in the secret place of ascent in our inmost being. No one else can witness that meeting, for it is a totally interior event.

"A garden inclosed is my sister, my spouse; a spring shut up, a fountain sealed" (Song of Solomon 4:12). So God speaks of the individual spirit. The beloved of God is an interior being, accessible to him alone. He speaks of the spirit as "my sister, my spouse," and this has profound meaning. First of all, God the Absolute, God the Father, the Transcendent, the impersonal God, dwells in silence and never speaks. When there is "speaking" it emanates from the Only-begotten Son, the immanent divinity, the personal God.

How are we his "sisters" and "spouses"? Long ago in India the poet-saint Mirabai went to see a great saint in the holy city of Vrindavan. As a monk, it was the saint's discipline to never see or speak with women. When she was told this by one of the saint's disciples, Mirabai answered: "I thought there was only one Man in existence, and that we were all women beside him," making a play on the words *purusha* and *prakriti*, person and matter in the sense of creator and creation, the divine masculine and the divine feminine. Since our consciousness is completely drowned in and identified with matter, we are, in the functional sense, creatures and therefore feminine in nature.

But we are not only "sisters," we are also "spouses" since we are destined to attain to union with him and then, through him, to pass back into the infinite transcendent being of the Father. "I am the way, the truth, and the life: no man cometh unto the Father, but by me" (John 14:6).

In the mystery-drama that was the earthly life of Jesus we are shown that only the virgin spirit can give birth to the Christ, that we must be enclosed, shut up and sealed to all that is not spirit, that is not us. Therefore only spiritual virginity is spiritually fruitful. In the real world of God, physical union is sterile and abstinence from that union is fruitful. This is what we are taught by the fruitful virginity of the Virgin Mary. Solomon's father, David, speaking of the virgin soul, said: "The king's daughter is all glorious within" (Psalms 45:13). The "espoused" spirit is the in-turned spirit.

Although in truth Christhood is always within us, yet in our present condition it is lost to us and so we must seek for it. Although it is already ours, we have to make it our own in a practical way. We may own a car, but if we do not know how to drive it, it is not fully ours. Only when we master the art of driving and caring for the car will it be ours in the complete sense. This is why Jesus said: "From him that hath not shall be taken away even that which he hath" (Matthew 25:29), strange as it sounds to us. The same is true of our own inner divine spirit. We have to make it ours through spiritual practice. The food outside us is meaningless if we do not perceive and assimilate it. Our inner Christ is valueless if we do not perceive and manifest it. We sometimes have to act as though God is far away before we can discover that God is near. Spiritual life is more a matter of realization, of recognition, than attainment.

Odd as it might seem, spiritual life is very much like the play therapy employed in psychology. By acting out imaginary situations we reveal the real status of things. And then we can drop the play-acting. But first we need it. It is the result that justifies its use. Building a case for or against something in spiritual matters has no value. It is *use* that shows us the viability of a spiritual approach or discipline. As a Pogo character once said: "Cut the philosophy and *run!*" Sometimes we need the play therapy, pretending that we (and God) are something we are not, yet enabling ourselves thereby to discover what we really are. Illusion sometimes reveals truth to the illusory mind.

The mind is thoroughly turned outward and has lost touch with inner realities. Its whole life is absorbed in the perception of objects and it is completely unaware of itself as a subjective reality. Just as a therapist has to sometimes go along with the patient's delusions, we have to do the same with the mind. It demands something to "do" and something to "see," so we give it the process of meditation to "do" and our own inner consciousness to "see." And that inner consciousness, like a seed, through the practice of meditation is enabled to develop into Divine Consciousness. Through meditation Christ grows within us, just as in the Virgin Mary, and in time manifests and becomes our Savior.

The Doubt of Joseph and It Resolution

> Then Joseph her husband, being a just man, and not willing to make her a publick example, was minded to put her away privily. But while he thought on these things, behold, the angel of the Lord appeared unto him in a dream, saying, Joseph, thou son of David, fear not to take unto thee Mary thy wife: for that which is conceived in her is of the Holy Ghost (Matthew 1:19-20).

The mysteries and ways of the spiritual life are not only hard to understand, they often are impossible to understand. Saint Joseph was a man of purified intellect, capable of communication with the higher worlds, yet he could not comprehend the mode of the Virgin's conception. Despite being a just and good man, he had no understanding of what was happening. In the same way the interior life is not always comprehended by us. What Saint Joseph thought was a sign of irregularity, even of evil and disgrace, was in fact a sign that things were going right, that the advent of the Messiah was approaching. He simply had no way to judge the situation. If a holy man, possessing such a clear and pure mind, could not comprehend such matters, how can we? Few things are more puzzling to the earth-conditioned mind than the life in which the Christ is to be revealed.

Nothing is trivial in the Gospels. Every detail contains profound meaning. Saint Joseph is described as being just, *dikaios*, which means innocent, holy and righteous as well as just, which also means "right living." There are many people who observe the rules, but they do so from wrong motives, such as fear or pride or the desire to impress others. Such persons are not just. Only those who observe the spiritual laws because they truly wish to attain higher consciousness are like Saint Joseph.

As a child I continually heard people saying that something was not wrong because it would not send them to hell. I realized their motive was to escape punishment, not to cultivate virtue. Such people were not really moral, they were a sham. I also used to hear it said that if human beings were not immortal then moral observation would be useless since we would have no eternal reward or punishment. This attitude itself is utterly immoral. That is why "the good" so often turn out to be very bad. Most religious people are scabs on the body of religion.

Being religious counts for nothing in the lives of most people. They really do not have a conscience, a sensitivity, in relation to God, man and the world around them. Most people are externally alive and internally dead. They are very sensitive to external things, but the inner things of the spirit mean nothing to them, so they either ignore or express contempt for spiritual matters, branding genuine aspirants to Christhood as fools and fanatics. "God doesn't expect all that!" they declaim, as though they have either spoken to God or read his mind to know that. It is with both the lax and the painfully rule-abiding in mind that Jesus said: "Except your righteousness shall exceed the righteousness of the scribes and Pharisees, ye shall in no case enter into the kingdom of heaven" (Matthew 5:20).

In the Gospels (Luke 18:9-14, Matthew 19:16-22) we find two people who kept all the law: the Pharisee of the parable and the young man who came to Jesus seeking eternal life. They both lacked the dimension of spiritual consciousness, so their goodness counted for little. Therefore Saint Matthew wants us to know that Saint Joseph did not keep the observance of the Mosaic Law in a mechanical way because his ancestors had done so or because he hoped for a reward, but rather because he had an inner awareness, a spiritual responsiveness that motivated him to observe it.

"The Lord said unto Samuel, Look not on his countenance, or on the height of his stature;... for the Lord seeth not as man seeth; for man looketh on the outward appearance, but the Lord looketh on the heart" (I Samuel 16:7). Simply observing external behavior tells us nothing about the real nature of a person, and may even deceive us as to their true character, since we cannot perceive their motive. There are people who do good to others because they have a merciful heart, and others who do so because they want to be thought of as a philanthropist or gain influence that way. The same is true of religious observance.

Saint Joseph was not merely acting like a just man, he *was* a just man. And he was minded "to put her away privily," to quietly send Mary away, back to Saints Joachim and Anna, without any fuss or public notoriety. He wished to dissolve the espousal contract and cut off from her completely. Otherwise he would be either denying the fact of her seeming wrongdoing or condoning it. That is the way just people act. They banish from their life sphere all that is wrong or even tainted with wrong. Never will they be cruel or speak cruelly to the person, or about them, but they will firmly eject all wrong, and wrongdoers, from their lives. For "what communion hath light with darkness? And what concord hath Christ with Belial? Wherefore come out from among them, and be ye separate, saith the Lord, and touch not the unclean thing; and I will receive you. Having therefore these promises, dearly beloved, let us cleanse ourselves from all filthiness, perfecting holiness,… hating even the garment spotted by the flesh" (II Corinthians 6:14-15, 17; 7:1; Jude 1:23). It is a sure principle that those who do not eliminate from their lives the evil, the corrupt and the doubtful are themselves evil, corrupt and doubtful, if only in their hearts. Such persons should be avoided, especially if they pretend to be teachers of religion and spiritual life.

One time I visited a monastery whose abbot and brotherhood were very friendly and, since I was a monk, they seemed to think of me as a family member. In speaking with me they happened to tell me of a man whose conduct in the monastery had been extremely bad. "You will no doubt meet him, he usually visits on the weekends," they told me. This surprised me. Why would they allow such a person to ever step on the monastery grounds? Then I decided that they were being merciful and hoping for his reformation; and I reprimanded myself for being incompassionate. Upon meeting the man I saw that he was utterly corrupt and unfit for secular life, much less monastic life. So I decided that they were being unwisely kind in letting him visit and unwisely hopeful in thinking that he might eventually change his ways. Later I came to understand the true character of the situation. The monks, including the abbot, were secretly as fully depraved as that young man. The only difference was that they were willing to pretend piety and he was not. But they were cut from the same cloth. How could they reject someone just like themselves? As Jesus said, a house divided against itself cannot stand (Matthew 12:25).

As a rule corrupt people foster others that are corrupt like themselves. Birds of a feather do flock together. I could cite other examples, but the principle is simply this: Those who allow negativity into their life situation are themselves negative. All the excuse-making we can come up with for them does not change the facts. Those who do not reject the evil that is external to them are definitely not rejecting the evil that is within them. Their seeming mercy and compassion are but a cloak, a non-verbal admission of their own state.

But Saint Joseph was truly a righteous, just man cognizant of the obligations spiritual life lays upon the individual. He had always put away from himself that which was wrong, and it did not matter that Mary had been a temple virgin from the age of three or that she was the one who wove both the purple and the scarlet into the veil of the Holy of Holies. That meant nothing to him in the face of what he thought was evidence of her wrong-doing. And though he was mistaken, the scriptures and the saints have never condemned his attitude or his decision. On the contrary they have praised him above any other man. Being kind, he did not want to publicly disgrace her or cause her any suffering. Yet being a just man, he could not live with her.

A minister I knew once gave a sermon on traffic signs and their meaning for spiritual life. At one point he told of being given a ticket for driving through a Stop sign. "But I slowed down," he protested to the policeman. "The sign does not say *Slow*, it says *Stop*," came the reply. He got the ticket, and rightly so.

Many times we try to make peace with the very things with which we should be warring, to slow instead of stop, to have "peaceful coexistence" with evil. Not being pure like Saint Joseph, how do we expect to have the Christ in our lives? Does darkness remain at the advent of light? Saint

Joseph has shown us the right mode of behavior. That which was in error or appeared to be wrong could not remain in his life. That is the way it must be for us, too. Otherwise we will fail in spiritual life.

It is not without significance that Saint Joseph was not going to run away, just disappear from Nazareth and avoid having to do anything overtly about the Virgin's situation. We like to do this avoidance ploy a lot; but not Saint Joseph, who knew before Jesus ever said it, that our Yes has to *be* Yes, and our No has to *be* No (Matthew 5:37). Nothing in between, no "gray area" here.

Sometimes we think, "Oh, I'll just pull back. This thing attracts me and leads me into negativity, so I'll just pull back and avoid it," or, "I have this negative psychic mechanism in myself. I'll just disengage from it, unmesh the gears." This is a skillful ploy of the ego because the negative thing is still there to go back to. Once a man called on the phone and announced that he wanted to become a monk because he and his wife had "realized" that they were at a point where they needed to go their separate ways. When I asked if they were going to divorce, he was indignant and said: "I *love* my wife. I could *never* divorce her." That man was no Saint Joseph.

We all must be Saint Josephs as well as Virgin Marys if we are going to find the Christ being born within us. We are to be the whole Holy Family. We need to study the lives of all three to understand how to maintain spiritual life.

Saint Joseph did not want to make a fuss about his problem. Those who lead a spiritual life do it quietly, in silence. They keep everything inward, as did the Virgin Mary. ("But Mary kept all these things, and pondered them in her heart" Luke 2:19.)

Saint Joseph's decision shows his kindness and mercy. He did not want to embarrass Mary or her family. So he was intending very privately and discreetly to put her away from him.

But while he thought on these things, behold, the angel of the Lord appeared unto him in a dream, saying, Joseph, thou son of David, fear not to take unto thee Mary thy wife: for that which is conceived in her is of the Holy Ghost. Saint Joseph was pondering the matter of what to do concerning Mary, and how to do it. He was a resolute person, but he was not a hasty person.

Emotion did not rule him, but wisdom arising from within. Even in sleep this problem was before his mind. In his humility he did not have over-confidence in his own judgment. And because of this humility God sent him the guidance he needed. And the "angel" of guidance which we need is our own innate wisdom revealed through the intuition that is born of meditation.

Joseph, thou son of David. Why does the angel call Joseph "son of David"? Jesse, the father of David, had several sons, but David was chosen by God to be the King of Israel. Here is the account:

"The Lord said unto Samuel, Fill thine horn with oil, and go, I will send thee to Jesse the Bethlehemite: for I have provided me a king among his sons…and thou shalt anoint unto me him whom I name unto thee. And Samuel did that which the Lord spake, and came to Bethlehem. And he called Jesse and his sons. And it came to pass, when they were come, that he looked on Eliab, and said, Surely the Lord's anointed is before him. But the Lord said unto Samuel, Look not on his countenance, or on the height of his stature; because I have refused him: for the Lord seeth not as man seeth; for man looketh on the outward appearance, but the Lord looketh on the heart. Then Jesse called Abinadab, and made him pass before Samuel. And he said, Neither hath the Lord chosen this. Then Jesse made Shammah to pass by. And he said, Neither hath the Lord chosen this. Again, Jesse made seven of his sons to pass before Samuel. And Samuel said unto Jesse, The Lord hath not chosen these. And Samuel said unto Jesse, Are here all thy children? And he said, There remaineth yet the youngest, and, behold, he keepeth the sheep. And Samuel said unto Jesse, Send and fetch him: for we will not sit down till he come hither. And he sent, and brought him in. And the Lord said, Arise, anoint him: for this is he. Then Samuel took the horn of oil, and anointed him in the midst of his brethren: and the Spirit of the Lord came upon David from that day forward" (I Samuel 16:1, 3-1). David represents the inmost, subtle life that is the spirit.

Although the Lord Jesus said: "Seek, and ye shall find" (Matthew 7:7), if we do not seek in the right manner or use the right means we shall never find. Buddha gave a whole discourse on this truth. He said that no matter how sincerely a person wanted milk, if he just pulled on the cow's horn he would get no milk. Conversely, even if he did not want milk, if he pulled on the cow's udder he *would* get milk. Then he points out that no matter how fervently or sincerely we churn water, we cannot get butter. But if we churn milk, we shall. Right Effort is one component of the Aryan Eightfold Path. And that effort must be centered in consciousness, nowhere else.

We also have to seek in the right place, among the right things. "Not by might, nor by power, but by my spirit, saith the Lord of hosts" (Zechariah 4:6). This is extremely important, for most of so-called "spiritual" life is all bound up in power and phenomena that are touted as both spiritual life and the evidence of spiritual life. But they are not. Not realizing this, seekers wander throughout lifetimes in the labyrinth of relativity, never getting anywhere. Insight into this dilemma was given to me by a visitor who said of a mutual acquaintance: "I have heard him speak at length on the trappings of religion, but I have never heard him speak about religion." It is easy to get lost in a sea of religiosity, obsessed with the externals of religion, but few gain insight into the true nature of religion: the union of the individual consciousness with the Universal Consciousness.

David demonstrated this principle. In the seventeenth chapter of First Samuel we are told that the armies of Israel and the Philistines were gathered facing one another. A giant named Goliath challenged the Israelites, saying that he would fight anyone in single combat, and that if he lost the Philistines would become their slaves, but if the one fighting for Israel lost, then the Israelites would be the slaves of the Philistines. So terrible was Goliath that no one would accept the challenge, day after day.

David, who was not considered old or strong enough to fight, came to bring his brothers some provisions from home. He saw that not only would no man of Israel accept the challenge, everyone ran and hid when Goliath came forth. He reproached his brothers and the other soldiers nearby, and then went to King Saul and said that he would fight Goliath. The king put his own armor and helmet on David, but David took them off and went forth clad only in his ordinary clothing, carrying a simple staff and armed with a slingshot and five stones he took from a brook.

Goliath was furious and considered the Israelites were mocking him, and said: "Am I a dog, that thou comest to me with staves? And the Philistine cursed David by his gods. And the Philistine said to David, Come to me, and I will give thy flesh unto the fowls of the air, and to the beasts of the field. Then said David to the Philistine, Thou comest to me with a sword, and with a spear, and with a shield: but I come to thee in the name of the Lord; and I will smite thee, that all the earth may know that there is a God in Israel. And all this assembly shall know that the Lord saveth not with sword and spear: for the battle is the Lord's, and he will give you into our hands. And it came to pass, when the Philistine arose, and came and drew nigh to meet David, that David hasted, and ran toward the army to meet the Philistine. And David put his hand in his bag, and took thence a stone, and slang it, and smote the Philistine in his forehead, that the stone sunk into his forehead; and he fell upon his face to the earth. So David prevailed over the Philistine with a sling and with a stone, and smote the Philistine, and slew him; but there was no sword in the hand of David" (I Samuel 17:43-50).

To be a descendant of David in the spiritual sense is to be rooted in higher consciousness, to be thoroughly oriented toward that consciousness and away from the delusions of material consciousness. For it is consciousness alone that conquers *un*consciousness. It is spirit alone that frees from the bonds of matter, however gross or subtle, the transcendent alone that delivers us from the relative. We must begin with spirit if we would end with spirit. That is why meditation–genuine, authentic meditation, Soham sadhana–is both the beginning and the end of the matter.

As already mentioned, Abraham was the first ancestor of Jesus that consciously sought God, and for that reason Saint Matthew begins his genealogy with him rather than Adam, as does Saint Luke. Jesus had lived before he was born of Mary, and one of his previous lives had been as Abraham. Although he had lived before that, it was as Abraham that he really began the journey that would end in his Christhood. His life as Abraham was his spiritual "ancestor." We, too, are the "descendants" of our previous lives, of the many faces we have put on as we played so many parts on the stage of earthly life. Just as we inherit our physical characteristics from our physical parents, so we inherit our psychic characteristics from our previous personalities. Fortunately, our spiritual character comes from God, ensuring that our divine qualities can be hidden but can never be erased or diminished. We have a divine genetic structure, and our destiny as gods is assured. It can be helpful to recall our past lives, but the best memory is of the glory which we had with God before relative existence ever came to be. "And now, O Father, glorify thou me with thine own self with the glory which I had with thee before the world was" (John 17:5).

When we have a viable spiritual ancestry, a viable spiritual background, then there is a possibility of our being wedded to the life that will in time bring forth our own Christhood. Every time we sit for meditation we are creating the needed genealogy for that possibility.

The genealogies given in various scriptures, including those of India, also indicate that spiritual unfoldment comes in orderly steps, that there is a sequence of development in the journey Godward. This, then, necessitates the application of spiritual methodology, for there is nothing haphazard or whimsical in spiritual life, neither on our part nor on that of God, although most religion acts as though God is an erratic tyrant that is the sole element in our "salvation." Catch Him on a good day and you are saved; catch Him on a bad day and you are damned. Please Him and you go to heaven; anger Him and you go to hell.

Joseph, thou son of David, fear not to take unto thee Mary thy wife. Sri Ramakrishna said there are two things that destroy spiritual life: shame and fear. And he said uncompromisingly that no one will find God who has these things in his heart. Therefore the angel says, "Joseph, fear not."

Fear is the ego's ploy. It is also a demonic strategy. Evil people traffic in fear, and foolish people give in to it. So nearly everyone works with fear because that is how life is sustained on the earth: fear of pain, fear of deprivation, fear of isolation, fear of death.... But President Roosevelt was right: the only thing we have to fear is fear itself. Therefore those in spiritual life cannot be cowardly. And if we are afraid, we must squelch it and be courageous.

When Jesus was arrested the apostles ran away and locked themselves in the upper room for fear of the Judean authorities. But Saint John, even though he was known to the high priest to be Jesus' disciple (John 18:15), went right in when Jesus was taken to the high priest's palace, and he stood next to the cross on Golgotha (John 19:25-26). This has a practical lesson for us. All the other apostles died martyrs' deaths, but Saint John did not. Why? He had already lain down his life for Christ. The Lord Jesus said to Pilate, "Thou couldest have no power at all against me, except it were given thee from above" (John 19:11). If we have that perspective we will realize that if heaven wills it, if our higher consciousness has so ordered it in the framework of our karma, then so be it. "Nevertheless not my will, but thine, be done" (Luke 22:42). Therefore we must eliminate in ourselves the very capacity for fear or shame. And that is done by living in God and moving in God and fixing the mind on God, especially by meditating. We must ever be like Saint Joseph and heed the words of the angel: Fear Not.

Fear not to take unto thee Mary thy wife: for that which is conceived in her is of the Holy Ghost. Why should we not fear to take up the life of the spirit that will give birth to spirit consciousness? Two reasons are given, one not readily understood and one easily comprehended.

In the King James version the angel refers to the Virgin as "Mary, your wife," but the word in the Greek text is *gune*, which was used to denote any female of any age, whether unmarried, married or a widow. We have already noted that the Virgin Mary was never formally wedded to Saint Joseph, but only the espousal ceremony took place. In Israel, though, such a ritual was considered absolutely binding and therefore the two persons were looked upon as fully married, at least in the potential sense. To be espoused was to be married. And so it is with us. We are already in union with God. If we were not, we could not even aspire to that state, we could not covenant and "espouse" ourselves to God. To even reach out for God is the evidence of our already being with God. We just need to dispel the illusion of separation.

God is already our "spouse" irrevocably. So there is no need for fear. We shall come at last to that glory which we had with Him originally (John 17:5). We may lose our awareness of God, but we cannot lose God. We cannot ever be either separated from God or be rejected by God. We do not have to win God over, the estrangement is our doing alone. We closed our eyes to God, but He did not go away. Now we seek for Him by stumbling around in the dark instead of intelligently figuring out how to open our eyes and see Him. As Buddha said: "Turn around and behold! the other shore." There is really nowhere we need to go. We just need to open our eyes and see where we have always been.

For that which is conceived in her is of the Holy Ghost. The spiritual life is itself the fruit of the Holy Spirit within us. It just needs some time to bring forth that which we seek: the illumined consciousness that has its origin in God and is an extension of the Divine Life that is our life. Therefore we need never fear or have any doubts.

That which is illusory in us does indeed fear that which true spiritual life bears within itself, for that will be the dispelling of all illusions, including the ego, the master illusionist. So people become afraid: "Will I go crazy? Is this all just a fool's parade? Will the Devil get me? What will happen to me? Will I dissolve, be snuffed out like a light?" But these are only the antics of the threatened ego. We, our true self, need not be afraid for a moment. "Ye are of God, little children, and have overcome: because greater is he that is in you, than he that is in the world" (I John 4:4). "The word of the Lord came unto Abram in a vision, saying, Fear not, Abram: I am thy shield, and thy exceeding great reward" (Genesis 15:1).

Just as Saint Joseph continued to live with the Virgin Mary in his house, so our spiritual quest must become integrated into our life, which in turn must be oriented to our spiritual quest. If we would truly be sons of David, other Josephs, then we must completely assimilate the spiritual life, it cannot be just on loan or lease to us: we have to possess it.

Sad to say, a lot of "seekers" are really accomplished bonsai gardeners of the spiritual life. They manage to keep trimming and cutting at the roots so that the tree never grows to the size it should, but just stays a decorative little ornament. This we must be warned against. There are many people who want to appear spiritual, but they do not want the result of spiritual life: real change. They want God to come down and make this world a happy place for them and make them a success. They want to say, "Ever since I gave my life to God, my business has increased and my crooked toe has straightened out," and suchlike. They want God to *descend*, but they do not want to *ascend* in response.

In spiritual life there are times when we have to take the advice of the angel to not be afraid, but go ahead and do it, and see what happens. People who really do not want to do something sit around and go around, saying: "But what about this? But what about that? What if this happens? Oh, what will I do then?" It is really just their way of saying: "I don't want to do it; and I won't." In the thirty-fourth Ode of Solomon we find this:

> There is no hard way where there is a simple heart,
> > Nor any barrier where the thoughts are upright.
> Nor is there any whirlwind
> > In the depth of the illuminated thought.
> Where one is surrounded on every side by pleasing country,
> > There is nothing divided in him.

"It is too hard, I am not ready," shrieks the ego (and those ruled by it), but the Lord Jesus said: "My yoke is easy, and my burden is light" (Matthew 11:30). For "there is no hard way where there is a simple heart." But if the heart is divided, or united in negative will against spiritual action, the yoke is hard, even unbearable, for "a double minded man is unstable in all his ways" (James 1:8). If the thoughts of the heart are upright and not crooked and low, then the way is not hard to walk. But for the crooked and the self-degraded, it is an impossible ascent.

When the mind shines with the light of spirit there are no whirlwinds to confuse, disturb, worry, bother or deflect us. But many little tempests in teapots arise when we are desperate for an excuse to evade real spiritual life. When the landscape of spiritual life pleases us then we have no conflict in living it, not with ourselves or with others, including those who would oppose us. Like a ship in a good breeze, we sail on steadily, undisturbed and unhindered. The person who continually asks: "How am I going to do that?" does not really want to "do that" at all.

Spiritual life is not for the fearful or the hesitant. In speaking of the necessary spiritual conquest, Jesus said: "The kingdom of heaven suffereth violence, and the violent take it by force" (Matthew 11:12). That is, we storm the citadel and seize it. No hanging back and no trying to avoid pain. Spiritual life is not for weaklings. "Strive to enter" the kingdom, is his counsel (Luke 13:24). The word translated "strive" is *agonizomai*, from which we get the English "agonize." Jesus further said regarding the kingdom of heaven: "The law and the prophets were until John: since that time the kingdom of God is preached, and every man presseth into it" (Luke 16:16). Kick down the door, rush in, grab it and make it yours. Obviously the matter of "pressing into" the kingdom is no easy weekend project.

My maternal grandmother was a great spiritual clairvoyant, healer and visionary. Life was extremely hard for her. Like so many healers she had very poor health, and she was often emotionally assailed by negative people. One day she felt utterly exhausted inwardly and outwardly and decided that she was going to have to slack up a bit in her spiritual endeavors. Immediately the room vanished and she saw a huge old hound dog lying in the sun. A voice spoke and said: "Any old dog can lie around waiting for a better and easier time. Are you one?" The vision vanished and grandmother got up and went on as usual, laughing at God's sense of humor.

A Thai Buddhist meditation master has told about the first day he went to study with the Venerable Acharya Mun, the greatest spiritual figure to arise within Thai Buddhism in many centuries. He was lying down, idle, when suddenly Acharya Mun appeared and shouted: "Are you a pig to lie around that way? This is no pig-stye, and I do not keep pigs here. Get up!" And he did; and he never forgot.

Saint Paul characterizes spiritual life as that of a soldier, a warrior, saying: "Finally, my brethren, be strong in the Lord, and in the power of his might. Put on the whole armour of God, that ye may be able to stand against the wiles of the devil. For we wrestle not against flesh and blood, but against principalities, against powers, against the rulers of the darkness of this world, against spiritual wickedness in high places. Wherefore take unto you the whole armour of God, that ye may be able to withstand in the evil day, and having done all, to stand. Stand therefore, having your loins girt about with truth, and having on the breastplate of righteousness; and your feet shod with the preparation of the gospel of peace; above all, taking the shield of faith, wherewith ye shall be able to quench all the fiery darts of the wicked. And take the helmet of salvation, and the sword of the Spirit, which is the word of God: Praying always with all prayer and supplication in the Spirit, and watching thereunto with all perseverance" (Ephesians 6:10-18).

We must neither fear nor hesitate to, like Saint Joseph, take up the way of life in which the Christ is conceived, is already present, and to say: "Yes. Henceforth this is *my* way of life." When we plant an apple seed we know we are going to get an apple tree; we do not say: "Oh, I hope this does not come up a peach tree." In the same way we cannot plant God in our life and it not bear God as its fruit. Spiritual life is absolutely ours by nature, for it is our nature to be with God, to be free.

We do not reluctantly take up spiritual life like bad-tasting medicine. We take to it like life itself, for it is. When someone has been under the water a long time, when they come up their lungs are as if bursting. Does anybody have to say to them, "Quick, breathe! Quick, breathe!"? No; they breathe, and gratefully, too. When we have come alive in God, nobody will have to tell us to keep on living the life in God, pushing us and poking us. We will not need all kinds of encouragement and assurance. We will move right along. "And it came to pass after these things, that God did tempt [test] Abraham, and said unto him, Abraham: and he said, Behold, here I am" (Genesis 22:1). No hesitation, no doubt, no confusion and delay. "And the Lord came and called, Samuel, Samuel. Then Samuel answered, Speak; for thy servant heareth" (I Samuel 3:10). Jesus said: "Behold, I stand at the door, and knock: if any man hear my voice, and open the door, I will come in to him, and will sup with him, and he with me" (Revelation 3:20).

The angel then told Saint Joseph:

Further Assurance by the Angel to Saint Joseph

And she shall bring forth a son, and thou shalt call his name Jesus: for he shall save his people from their sins (Matthew 1:21).

True spiritual life unerringly brings forth increasingly higher life in us, unlike false spiritual systems and fake yoga methods that are nothing more than false pregnancies–nothing ever comes of them. The sons of God are never stillborn; the spiritual life, symbolized by the Virgin Mary, always brings forth living children. The spiritual life is not an external object that we can put away somewhere to occasionally bring out, admire and show to others as proof of our rightness or goodness. It is not a trophy, it is the contest itself. Most people prefer holy things to the holy life. They obsess on supposedly spiritual books or sacred, semi-magical objects that have "power" of some kind. And they equate this clutter with spiritual life. Being basically material in consciousness, they go after material expressions of what cannot be expressed.

"And he spake a parable unto them, saying, The ground of a certain rich man brought forth plentifully: and he thought within himself, saying, What shall I do, because I have no room where to bestow my fruits? And he said, This will I do: I will pull down my barns, and build greater; and there will I bestow all my fruits and my goods. And I will say to my soul, Soul, thou hast much goods laid up for many years; take thine ease, eat, drink, and be merry. But God said unto him, Thou fool, this night thy soul shall be required of thee: then whose shall those things be, which thou hast provided? So is he that layeth up treasure for himself, and is not rich toward God" (Luke 12:16-21). This is a picture of someone with materialistic, externalized religion. More and more he gathers up "stuff," congratulating himself on the depth and growth of his spiritual life. Satisfied with himself, he tells himself he has great merit or good karma or virtue accruing to him, so he can be at ease. But eventually the summons comes: his soul is required of him and he leaves this world and all his external holiness behind. False religion lays up treasure for the ego and its puppet, our conditioned personality, and not for God–either the God within or the God without. To those who follow such deceptive religion shall come the indictment: "Thou sayest, I am rich, and increased with goods, and have need of nothing; and knowest not that thou art wretched, and miserable, and poor, and blind, and naked" (Revelation 3:17).

She shall bring forth a son. The spiritual life brings forth living children, as has been said. And we are told that those children are *sons*. How is this? In the esoteric tradition of both India and Christianity, spirit/consciousness is masculine and energy is feminine. The Creator is male and His extension as the Creation is female. As His living images we are both polarities, though usually in men the divine male aspect is dominant and in women the divine female aspect is dominant. Both are divine and neither is superior to the other, since they are ultimately one. Whatever the sex of the body, from an esoteric perspective those who are more centered in spiritual consciousness are "male" and those who more centered in material consciousness are "female." There was a great saint in Alexandria, Egypt, named Mother Sara. She often rebuked shallow monks, saying: "*I* am a man, and *you* are women." A contemporary saint of Egypt, Abdul Messia, used to point at bishops and say to the monks: "Stay away from those women!" meaning that they were not truly *pneumatikos*, spiritual.

We are all negatively polarized ("feminine"), but once we are processed through the womb of spiritual life we shall come forth positively polarized ("masculine"), whatever the gender of our physical body. This is why Saint Teresa of Avila used to reprimand the nuns, saying: "Sisters, you are acting like *women!*" She was not speaking of the bodily condition, since "there is neither male nor female: for ye are all one in Christ Jesus" (Galatians 3:28).

"Simon Peter said to them: Let Mary go forth from among us, for women are not worthy of the life. Jesus said: Behold, I shall lead her, that I may make her male, in order that she also may become a living spirit like you males. For every woman who makes herself male shall enter into the kingdom of heaven" (Gospel of Thomas 114). We are all females who need to become males. We are brides of God that need to become grooms through transmutation into gods. This is the meaning of the words: "As many as received him, to them gave he power to become the sons of God" (John 1:12).

There is another aspect to this: "male" symbolizes consciousness. Hence the idea is that spiritual life gives birth to consciousness, nothing else. This is extremely important, for no matter how much yogis like to say that psychic powers are distractions, they continually cite them as evidence that someone has spiritual attainment. The stories may be very noble, such as someone knowing the troubles of another or even giving help to someone whose need they perceived clairvoyantly. But still all this phenomena is in the realm of the Maya Machine, the Realm of Illusion, and the gears of the machine may grab us, grind us up and assimilate us so that we are more bound than ever. Seen as symbols, the miracles of Jesus (including his resurrection) are meaningful, but in themselves they are nothing but "special effects" in the cosmos, in the prison of ignorance.

Yet it is definitely true that as we advance in our development certain intuitive capacities develop and sometimes even the ability to do "miraculous" things may arise. But this is not the goal, and should be treated like distractions in meditation: adamantly ignored. Every religion, and sects within the religion, have miraculous "proofs" that supposedly it alone is "the truth." Healings, visions, prophecies (that often do not really come true), revelations and a host of material advantages, all are trotted out by them to demonstrate that not only is God with them, God is not with anybody else. At one time in my life I belonged to a little Christian group that claimed to be the only true Christian Church. They could quote the Bible, of course, but they could also cite miracles and visions that led people to them as the true Church. But miracles happen in other groups, and when they heard of them they glibly cited: "They are 'the spirits of devils, working miracles' like it says in Revelation (16:14)." They had it all neatly worked out.

Just as social action and theology are used as substitutes for religion in modern times, so also is the miraculous part of the costuming and illusion in the more metaphysical or mystical religions. But it is all part of the show, a continuation of the circus. *Where is liberation?* This is the question we must ask. Otherwise, like Omar Khayyam in the *Rubiyat*, no matter how many holy people we visit we will still go out the same door we came in.

Some types of yoga or esoteric practices, particularly, are attractive traps, for they give experiences and confer some psychic abilities, but produce no change in the fundamental consciousness. The result is the same: bondage. People waste lifetimes in spiritual pursuits while remaining as ensnared as they were when they pursued material things. False religion produces incredible glorifications of the ego and the mind, spectacular illusions of greatness and godliness and godlikeness. "But one thing is needful" (Luke 10:42), the liberation of the spirit. If that is not accomplished, then all is in vain.

"It shall even be as when an hungry man dreameth, and, behold, he eateth; but he awaketh, and his soul is empty: or as when a thirsty man dreameth, and, behold, he drinketh; but he awaketh, and, behold, he is faint, and his soul hath appetite" (Isaiah 29:8). Various cultures have stories of those who have been given a treasure by spirits only to later discover that it was only stone, or lead or water. This has been our story in our religious involvements for many lives. What about this present life? Is it the same old story again?

At the time of Gautama Buddha there were several schools of yoga. He learned the practices of all of them and attained perfection in them, being declared liberated by his teachers, most of whom wanted him to be their successor. He could do amazing things in the realm of supernormal accomplishments, but he was not liberated. He was bound just like the rest of ignorant humanity. So he decided to strike out on his own and seek liberation, and became enlightened. May it be so with us, too.

Healings, miracles, visions and suchlike are all material things, and have only a material effect. (They usually have material causes, too.) The subtle astral and causal realms are still material, and part of the net of relative existence and duality. All phenomena are external and therefore, from the spiritual perspective, in the realm of the unreal. The more we have to do with them the more unreal we become in our consciousness. The more we divest ourselves of such things the more real we will become. The spiritual search is the search for pure consciousness. And it is in meditation that we find what we are seeking, for that alone will give birth to the positive polarity of pure consciousness, pure spirit.

And thou shalt call his name Jesus: for he shall save his people from their sins. Throughout the world it is known that a person's name has a deep-rooted connection with him, almost being inseparable from his life. A word can be a mere designation of an object or it can be a revealing of that object's nature or character. So the angel told Saint Joseph to call Mary's Son *Yahoshua*, The Lord Shall Save, "for he himself will save his people from their sins." Jesus, *Yahoshua* in Hebrew and *Yeshua* in Aramaic, means Savior, and that is what the consciousness born of meditation is all about: liberation. Nothing more or less than that. So that is the test of true religion and of true spiritual life.

The two key words here are sozo, "save," and *amartia*, "sin."

Sozo means to save in the sense of both delivering and protecting. It also means to heal, preserve and make whole. There is no way it can be applied to being saved from going to hell, or saved from the consequences of our wrongdoings. Rather, it means a spiritual healing and restoration.

Amartia literally means "to miss the mark," to fail, to err. And that is it–nothing about breaking God's law, angering God, being alienated from God or any such thing. It means to fail to realize and manifest the truth of our eternal, divine nature. That is very serious, because it results in great suffering and bondage for those that fail/fall. So it is no light matter, something to be shrugged off. It should be taken seriously, in the light of our divine sonship. Our interest in no longer failing must be intense interest in manifesting ourselves as spirit.

We are to be saved, liberated, from our sins, from our falling short of our potential divinity. Many "saved" fundamentalists talk about how they no longer lie, steal, cheat, etc. But that is not being saved; that is just not doing something wrong. Real salvation is dynamic. It is *being* something: being a liberated son of God, having attained that state "when the morning stars sang together, and all the sons of God shouted for joy" (Job 38:7).

What is it to be saved? It is be living consciously in the fulfillment of the prayer recited daily in India:

> Lead me from the unreal to the Real.
> Lead me from darkness to the Light.
> Lead me from death to Immortality.

We are to be delivered from weakness and failing, not to continue in them and have it glossed over, as is common Christian thinking. Jesus said: "If the Son therefore shall make you free, ye shall be free indeed" (John 8:36). Not just partially free, or obliquely free, or symbolically free, or potentially free: we shall be really, functionally, free.

The angel did not say Jesus was to save the world, but rather that he would save "his people." In the closing hours of his life Jesus said an astounding thing in a prayer: "I pray not for the world, but for them which thou hast given me" (John 17:9). He did not pray for those who are either too undeveloped or too addicted to ignorance to even think about wanting to think about being free from bondage. Just the opposite; they seek after even more bondage and revel in it.

A busybody once demanded of Buddha why he lived in the forest and did not go into the large cities and preach to the people. Buddha asked his critic to go into a very large city nearby and ask every single person, including the children, what they most wanted. After weeks the man returned and reported that they all wanted short-term material things. "Who wanted liberation?" Asked Buddha. "No one," the man replied in disgust. "Why, then, do you want me to force on them something they do not want?" asked Buddha. And the man understood.

Therefore Jesus was not interested in those who were not interested and whose interest could not be awakened in this life. But he eagerly sought out those in whom the spark of spiritual awakening, however dormant, could be found. Those whom God had given to him were those he saved. They were his destiny.

The disciples of Christ are those in whom the Christ-nature is being brought forth within the depths of their being. It is they who are capable of being saved, none others. Consequently we must make sure that we are "his people" through observance of his precepts and the practice of meditation.

He shall save his people from their sins. It is the revelation of our own Christhood that alone can save us. Only we ourselves as Christs can save ourselves. Even God does not do so, though He *is* our salvation. There are no intermediaries in this matter. Saints, angels, prayers, doctrines, rites, pilgrimage, virtues, good deeds and so forth can help us, but they will not save us. That comes from within, from our true Self. The path to salvation, then, is the inner path. We must never lose sight of this and allow ourselves to become caught in the web of externalism, however sacred it may seem to be.

When Sri Ramakrishna was striving for the Supreme Consciousness, his meditation was continually interrupted by the appearance of the goddess Kali whom he had worshipped so many years and had seen and spoken to countless times. Finally, in his mind he cut her form in two with the sword of inner discrimination and his mind soared to the heights of non-dual consciousness. It was not that he ceased to believe in Kali, or had come to have an aversion for her. He knew that in essence she was the Parabrahman he was seeking to experience. But it was his perception of her as relative being that was holding him back, not the Mother herself. Sometimes we have to reject that which we have long revered to reach the truly holy. So much that we cling to in spiritual devotion is really an extension of our ego, though we deify it. Our problem is that we *like* God rather than *love* him. Or, as has been said more than once: Most religious people prefer to talk about God rather than to be with God.

Guru Nanak in his hymns often speaks of "the Godwards." That is what we must be in an uncompromising manner, rejecting all that would come between us and God, however much it may pretend to lead to God. No thing, person, concept or feeling can take us to God. That is done by us in silence, in the depths of meditation.

We do not need to be saved from the sins of others, only our own. The concept of original sin, that we are all guilty of Adam's sin, is the maximum absurdity. So also is the idea that the evil or karma of anyone else is harming or even hindering us. The only way that can happen is when our own sins and karmas match those of others and they come together like a magnet because of their affinity. And even then, it is our own negativity that is making the connection. And most importantly: *no person can "take on" our karma, or delete our karma or change or mitigate it in any way.* It is ours, and we alone can deal with it. And we have the power to do so. We need only know the way. (See *Soham Yoga: The Yoga Of The Self.*) It is the action of God both inside and outside us.

The Prophecy of Isaiah

>Now all this was done, that it might be fulfilled which was spoken of the Lord by the prophet, saying, Behold, a virgin shall be with child, and shall bring forth a son, and they shall call his name Emmanuel, which being interpreted is, God with us. Then Joseph being raised from sleep did as the angel of the Lord had bidden him, and took unto him his wife. And knew her not till she had brought forth her firstborn son: and he called his name Jesus (Matthew 1:22-25).

All these things took place, not because the prophet spoke it, but the prophet spoke it because he perceived the divine pattern. All that was happening was the manifestation of the divine eternal plan, which "verily was foreordained before the foundation of the world, but was manifest in these last times" (I Peter 1:20). And although prophets were the messengers, "the mouth of the Lord hath spoken it" (Isaiah 40:5).

Behold, a virgin shall be with child, and shall bring forth a son. Only in the virgin soul is God conceived, only in that enclosed garden, in that sealed fountain (Song of Solomon 4:12), does God begin to work to bring forth life. The Bhagavad Gita (5:10) speaks of lotuses floating on water and not getting wet. The idea is that because of our karmas we may have to interact with the things of this world and with the world itself, but we can remain untouched by it. We touch it, but it does not touch us. "Pure religion and undefiled before God and the Father is this: to keep oneself unspotted from the world" (James 1:27). How can we do this? Through the consciousness that is cultivated within meditation. There comes a time when we do not "come out" from meditation at all, but remain in that inmost state of clear peace.

The virgin brings forth a son. That which is brought forth in us is the consciousness, the full awareness that God *is* with us. And that comes from direct experience. It is no theory or hope, but a present reality that we are at all times intimately in communication and communion with God. "He who sees me everywhere, and sees all things in me–I am not lost to him, and he is not lost to me," says Krishna in the Bhagavad Gita (6:30). This is not an intellectual opinion, but a living condition. True spiritual life opens in us the consciousness of God. "In that day there shall be a fountain opened to the house of David and to the inhabitants of Jerusalem for sin and for uncleanness" (Zechariah 13:1). That fountain is not external, but internal. "He that believeth on me, as the scripture hath said, out of his belly [inmost being] shall flow rivers of living water" (John 7:38).

And they shall call his name Emmanuel, which being interpreted is, God with us. The child's actual, proper name was Jesus; Emmanuel was his spiritual title that expressed his purpose in being born. Emmanuel can mean two things:

1) Through him God is being made present. That is, spiritual life makes the Spirit present in our consciousness.

2) Through him we come to know that God is already, and always, present with and within us. That we are never really estranged or separated from Him.

Inner, spiritual life is the true Emmanuel. We recover our lost awareness through meditation, and that awareness pervades our whole life, flowing "rivers of living water" through our expanding consciousness. The essence of spiritual life is the realization of God as ever-present.

We should not become spiritual junk collectors. A lot of people in their spiritual life just collect external and irrelevant holy junk, both physically and metaphysically, until they are weighed down with it and consequently think they are deeply religious and spiritual when they are really only spiritual scavengers. They cram all kinds of "spiritual" things into their lives and minds, but are never conscious of God or the path to God. There are people who build huge temples and decorate them lavishly. Whenever they enter, they feel material, egoic and emotional satisfaction and upliftment, but they never experience God there, only themselves. We must avoid becoming spiritual bag people. There is no point in gathering the accouterments of a wedding if the marriage never takes place.

Many people become so involved with seeking and walking the path that they lose all interest in arriving at the goal. They are rather like those who make great amounts of money doing medical research: if they discovered a cure they would be out of work. Seekers usually do not want to be finders. We must be careful that we do not become so pleased with being religious and dedicated that we lose all interest in truly knowing God.

Then Joseph being raised from sleep did as the angel of the Lord had bidden him, and took unto him his wife. Why? because "now it is high time to awake out of sleep: for now is our salvation near" (Romans 13:11.) We need to hear the call: "Awake to righteousness" (I Corinthians 15:34). "Wherefore he saith, Awake thou that sleepest, and arise from the dead, and Christ shall give thee light" (Ephesians 5:14).

Only those who are awakened from the sleep (unconsciousness) of ignorance can hear and follow the call to supernatural life, to superhuman evolution. We may hear a multitude of lectures and read a mountain of books on spiritual topics, but it will mean nothing if we still spiritually sleep. Therefore David prayed: "Lighten mine eyes, lest I sleep the sleep of death" (Psalms 13:3).

Many "spiritual" people are walking in their sleep and assume they are awake. Sleepwalking is actually an interesting simile of many seekers' condition. Sleepwalkers are both dreaming and at the same time perceiving their external surroundings to a dim degree as part of the dream. That is why they will open and walk through doors, not walk up to a wall and try to go through, and just stand there. They are more asleep than awake, yet they are somewhat awake. In the same way, at one point in our evolution we are partially awakened into the realm of spirit, but at the same time we are immersed in the sleep of earthly existence. We are not fully in or out of either state, and consequently are doubly confused and at the same time doubly aware. This state cannot continue for long, though, and we will either awaken or fall back into complete sleep. Most people fall back asleep and dream they are awake. Only those who rouse themselves and diligently apply themselves to meditation and reformation of their life to conform to the principles of awakening will succeed in remaining truly awake.

Sometimes sleepers slightly wake up, stretch, snort a bit, yawn, and turn over and go back to sleep. Practically speaking, this is no awakening at all. Yet many people do just that in the spirit, and then congratulate themselves for the rest of their life, thinking they are awake and moving. It would have been of no use for the angel of the Lord to come to Saint Joseph if he had not awakened, gotten up, and done something. To be roused from sleep is not a simple thing, it is something for us to work toward. Those who wish to heed the command of the holy angel of their own inner intuition-wisdom, and thereby do the will of God, must be awakened from their habitual lower consciousness "into his marvellous light" (I Peter 2:9), into "the light of life" (John 8:12).

And took unto him his wife. Saint Joseph received the Virgin Mary into his home. Saint Joseph did not just get a message; he *acted* on it. He did something personal. For to be truly awakened is to do something, even if much of that something is internal.

And knew her not till she had brought forth her firstborn son: and he called his name Jesus. The idea here is that we do not impinge on spiritual life and make it ours, instead our spiritual life extends from within us and makes us its domain. The Virgin did not become Saint Joseph's wife and build her life around him, he reshaped his life around the Virgin. One of the reasons nearly everyone fails in spiritual life is the way they try to accommodate it to their ego-mind. "Will remodel to suit tenant" is their motto. But this does not work. It is not spiritual life that is to undergo the change: *we* are. Yet we are constantly hearing about adapting the eternal ways of the spirit to "the times," "the situation," "the culture," "the people," "modern science," "modern psychology," etc., etc., etc. There is no end to the adaptations (that are really compromises) demanded of those who seek to live a truly spiritual life. But what a howl goes up when it is suggested that the things of material life are supposed to be eliminated or adapted to the principles of spiritual life. "Fanaticism," "anachronism," "obscurantism," "harshness," "rigidity," "backwardness," "antiquation"–these are but a few (and the milder) of the screeches that arise. The truth is the truth: we do not change the rules of spiritual life; we live them and they change us. The definitive non-dual philosopher, Shankara, said it all when he wrote: "O Lord, You do not belong to me; I belong to You." Saint Joseph had the right perspective on things. Spiritual life does not conform to us. We conform to spiritual life. Otherwise we have no spiritual life at all, just our own ego game.

Saint Matthew tells us that Saint Joseph lived with the Virgin in absolute continence, "and knew her not," to underscore that he lived a virgin life. He also points this out as a symbol that spiritual life cannot be hazy or fuzzy, sometimes lived and sometimes not, or that we can compromise or fudge in any sense. Either we are living the spiritual life or we are not. Spiritual life is absolute by its very nature, for it is the path to the Absolute. We should not deceive ourselves in this. One reason Saint Joseph was worthy was that he was fully and totally what he was. We must be the same.

There is a point we should look at here. The Virgin Mary only had one child: Jesus. No other. It is the same with spiritual life: it only brings forth spiritual consciousness, not improved health, material prosperity, influence with others, a positive self image or any such egocentric goals. Fake religion will accommodate the fake ego and give all those things away like a frantic game show on television. But real spiritual life will not. So we should not expect it or even want it to. We must not turn the house of God into a place of worldly commerce. "And Jesus went into the temple of God, and cast out all them that sold and bought in the temple, and overthrew the tables of the moneychangers, and the seats of them that sold doves, and said unto them, It is written, My house shall be called the house of prayer; but ye have made it a den of thieves. And the blind and the lame came to him in the temple; and he healed them" (Matthew 21:12-14). "Know ye not that ye are the temple of God, and that the Spirit of God dwelleth in you?" (I Corinthians 3:16). When we cast out the ways of the greedy and selfish ego, then all that is blind and lame in us can approach Christ and be healed. Otherwise we remain sick within.

The Birth of Jesus–2

> And it came to pass in those days, that there went out a decree from Caesar Augustus, that all the world should be taxed. And this taxing was first made when Cyrenius was governor of Syria (Luke 2:1-2).

The life of Jesus was looked upon by the early Christians as a kind of divine mystery drama, profoundly symbolic of spiritual principles. Yet it was known to be a genuinely historical event as well. Saint Luke chose to give us these practical points so we will know that Jesus was a fully historical person. Also by telling us that he was born in the reign of Caesar Augustus during the governorship of Cyrenius in the region of Syria (which was much larger than the present country of Syria), we can know the general time of his birth.

> And all went to be taxed, every one into his own city (Luke 2:3).

That is, everyone went to be registered (for a census was being made as well as a tax roll) at the place of his birth.

> And Joseph also went up from Galilee, out of the city of Nazareth, into Judaea, unto the city of David, which is called Bethlehem; (because he was of the house and lineage of David:) to be taxed with Mary his espoused wife, being great with child. And so it was, that, while they were there, the days were accomplished that she should be delivered. And she brought forth her firstborn son, and wrapped him

in swaddling clothes, and laid him in a manger; because there was no room for them in the inn (Luke 2:4-7).

Jesus was born in a cave and resurrected from a cave because a cave represents the heart, the *hridaya guha* (cave of the heart) of an individual in which dwells his eternal spirit-Self which is consciousness. Christhood, perfect liberation of the spirit, is present with us at all times. It is not attained, but revealed. It is awakening into our eternal being after having slept the dream illusion of relative existence for countless ages. Nothing "makes" us a Christ, because that is our essential nature. Religion cannot do it, nor can philosophy or "right living." Most that is called yoga is equally worthless, but real yoga sadhana does the needful. Why, then, are not multitudes of people flying to the Infinite throughout the world? First, because they do not really want to trade the finite for the Infinite. They would rather lose themselves, literally, than let go of the illusions of finite, relative existence. Second, because they will never agree to follow the yoga life, without which yoga sadhana simply cannot be done. (See *Living the Yoga Life: Perspectives on Yoga*.)

There was no room for the Virgin Mary in any inn, because nothing of earth-bound deluded consciousness is compatible with divinity.

Revelation to the Shepherds

And there were in the same country shepherds abiding in the field, keeping watch over their flock by night. And, lo, the angel of the Lord came upon them, and the glory of the Lord shone round about them: and they were sore afraid. And the angel said unto them, Fear not: for, behold, I bring you good tidings of great joy, which shall be to all people. For unto you is born this day in the city of David a Saviour, which is Christ the Lord. And this shall be a sign unto you; Ye shall find the babe wrapped in swaddling clothes, lying in a manger. And suddenly there was with the angel a multitude of the heavenly host praising God, and saying, Glory to God in the highest, and on earth peace, good will toward men (Luke 2:8-14).

And there were in the same country shepherds abiding in the field, keeping watch over their flock by night. The Bhagavad Gita tells us: "The man of restraint is awake in what is night for all beings. That in which all beings are awake is night for the sage who truly sees."(2:69). Because the shepherds were awake when everyone else slept, the angels came and told them of the birth of Christ. Only those who are inwardly awake while others inwardly sleep will be visited by the messengers of intuition which will point them to the paths to higher life. Just to take up real yoga requires a great deal of awakening, and to persevere in that yoga eventually requires total awakening.

When things began happening for me spiritually I knew I had to get out of the dead world into which I had been born and go to where I could learn sadhana and benefit from the company of other yogis. So I moved halfway across the country. There I met other yogis that became my real friends. As I have said before, sadly they all faded away eventually and left the yoga life. Why did this happen? Naturally karma and samskara were determining factors, but there was a common denominator to all of them. They had read or heard about yoga, learned to meditate and settled down to be members of a group and were faithful to an organization. In other words, the mode of life they had led as members of a Christian church was just continued, though with different beliefs and with meditation. For they never pushed their frontiers any further. They were like the caveman I once saw in the comic strip "BC." He climbed up a high mountain, looked in all four directions and climbed down, saying: "So much for the whole world." They had found their spiritual niche and just sat there being faithful and believing until eventually they drifted away.

Life does not stand still. Those who do not "keep on keeping on" and move ever forward will find their spiritual aspirations diminishing until they are just rote yogis, and then after another "while" they are just what they were before. They will have come full circle. They began with nothing and end with nothing. Some of my friends kept a token "yogi identity" but it was nothing but just an identity–no reality.

A yogi must be like the explorers in early America such as Daniel Boone. He must continually move into new territory and find new vistas and never be satisfied to settle down in one spot and vegetate. Sri Ramakrishna used to tell the following parable:

"Once upon a time a wood-cutter went into a forest to chop wood. There suddenly he met a brahmachari. The holy man said to him, 'My good man, go forward.' On returning home the wood-cutter asked himself, 'Why did the brahmachari tell me to go forward?' Some time passed. One day he remembered the brahmachari's words. He said to himself, 'Today I shall go deeper into the forest.' Going deep into the forest, he discovered innumerable sandal-wood trees. He was very happy and returned with cart-loads of sandal-wood. He sold them in the market and became very rich. A few days later he again remembered the words of the holy man to go forward. He went deeper into the forest and discovered a silver-mine near a river. This was even beyond his dreams. He dug out silver from the mine and sold it in the market. He got so much money that he didn't even know how much he had. A few more days passed. One day he thought: 'The brahmachari didn't ask me to stop at the silver-mine; he told me to go forward.' This time he went to the other side of the river and found a gold-mine. Then he exclaimed: 'Ah, just see! This is why he asked me to go forward.' Again, a few days afterwards, he went still deeper into the forest and found heaps of diamonds and other precious gems. He took these also and became as rich as the god of wealth himself. Therefore I say that, whatever you may do, you will find better and better things if only you go forward. You may feel a little ecstasy as the result of japa, but don't conclude from this that you have achieved everything in spiritual life."

> And it came to pass, as the angels were gone away from them into heaven, the shepherds said one to another, Let us now go even unto Bethlehem, and see this thing which is come to pass, which the Lord hath made known unto us. And they came with haste, and found Mary, and Joseph, and the babe lying in a manger. And when they had seen it, they made known abroad the saying which was told them concerning this child. And all they that heard it wondered at those things which were told them by the shepherds.
>
> But Mary kept all these things, and pondered them in her heart.
>
> And the shepherds returned, glorifying and praising God for all the things that they had heard and seen, as it was told unto them (Luke 2:15-20).

We know the shepherds really believed the message of the angel because they got up and went to see for themselves the reality of the angel's words.

Dead faith is that which is simply stored up in the mind, but never acted upon, and absolutely never becomes a meaningful part of the person's life. Millions of people in the East believe in oneness of the Self with the Absolute and believe in the possibility of realizing that divine Self. But they do nothing about it. They just go to temples, make pilgrimages, do a bit of worship and read holy books. But it never crosses their mind to become yogis and know the Self. They convince themselves that it will be many lifetimes before they can take up sadhana and know the Self. But that is contradicted by all the scriptures, Taoist, Hindu or Buddhist. They all say with Saint Paul: "Behold, *now* is the accepted time; behold, *now* is the day of salvation" (II Corinthians 6:2). The word translated "accepted" is *euprosdektos*, which means "favorable." Right now, this very day, the path to realization of the Self can be taken up and followed and produce results. There will be no better time or situation. The tomorrow of the procrastinator never comes.

> **And when eight days were accomplished, his name was called JESUS, which was so named of the angel before he was conceived in the womb (Luke 2:21).**

I have already pointed out that a person's name is intimately connected with him and his life itself. This is why a person may be asleep and impossible to rouse with any words or shaking, but when his name is called he readily awakes. We are deeply identified with our name on the subtle levels of our being.

The name of Jesus expressed his destiny. Before we were conceived our destiny was already determined, as was that of Jesus. "Why am I here?" is a most intelligent question, but it is hard to find the answer. Jesus came into this world for a reason, and so did we.

One of my close friends was a psychologist whose classes I attended in college. We often talked together, and he had a supply of psychologist/psychiatrist jokes. One he told me was about a minister who sometimes went on Sundays to a mental institution and gave sermons. One Sunday he asked the rhetorical question, "Why are we all here?" Immediately one of inmates called out, "Because we are not 'all there'!" Simple as it is, that is exactly why we are here: because we have not prepared ourselves, have not cultivated our consciousness so we could even enter the realms of higher consciousness, much less live and function there. It is all a matter of the condition of our inner bodies. Our Self is always perfect and can dwell at peace anywhere. But our inner levels are not evolved enough to enter into the states of consciousness that transcend this world and those worlds between here and the There which we are intended to inhabit.

Yoga is the door, the key, the path and the goal.

The Presentation in the Temple and Prophetic Witness of Simeon and Anna

And when the days of her purification according to the law of Moses were accomplished, they brought him to Jerusalem, to present him to the Lord; (As it is written in the law of the Lord, Every male that openeth the womb shall be called holy to the Lord;) And to offer a sacrifice according to that which is said in the law of the Lord, A pair of turtledoves, or two young pigeons (Luke 2:22-24).

For forty days after giving birth, a woman was to remain quiet and isolated. Foolish people (men) thought this was because she was "unclean," when it was actually a sensible rule to enable her to regain her health and strength after the ordeal of childbirth.

The Jewish priesthood was usually drawn from the tribe (clan) of Levi, but it was also the rule that if a firstborn child was a male he could also function as a priest if he desired. This is why Jesus could teach in the synagogue (Luke 4:16).

Therefore Mary and Joseph went to offer Jesus as a Levite. (Regarding the symbolic nature of the sacrifices, see *The Christ of India*.)

And, behold, there was a man in Jerusalem, whose name was Simeon; and the same man was just and devout, waiting for the consolation of Israel: and the Holy Ghost was

upon him. And it was revealed unto him by the Holy Ghost, that he should not see death, before he had seen the Lord's Christ.

And he came by the Spirit into the temple: and when the parents brought in the child Jesus, to do for him after the custom of the law, then took he him up in his arms, and blessed God, and said, Lord, now lettest thou thy servant depart in peace, according to thy word: for mine eyes have seen thy salvation, which thou hast prepared before the face of all people; alight to lighten the Gentiles, and the glory of thy people Israel (Luke 2:25-32).

About 250 B.C., the Greek Pharaoh of Egypt, Ptolemy, was determined to make the library of Alexandria a repository for all the knowledge of the Mediterranean world. To accomplish this he sent to every country for books. He also commissioned translations of many books into Greek, for at that time Greek was the language of learning. Through such translations scholars of many nationalities could come to Alexandria and find all the books of wisdom accessible–such was his aspiration.

Representatives of Ptolemy wrote to Jerusalem, to the Temple, requesting a copy of the Hebrew sacred books. A reply was sent immediately, stating that the scriptures of the Israelites were for them alone, not for perusal by Gentiles. Ptolemy then requested a translation of the scriptures, if the Hebrew originals were to be refused him. Again the answer came that such things were for the people of the Covenant alone. This displeased Ptolemy greatly, but he set about figuring a way to get the Hebrew holy writings. At that time there were more than twenty thousand Jewish slaves in Egypt, so Ptolemy sent word to Jerusalem that he would have all of them set free in exchange for a Greek translation of the Hebrew scriptures. After consultation the Jewish elders decided that for the sake of the enslaved Hebrews they would assent to Ptolemy's request for a translation.

Upon receiving word of this agreement, Ptolemy was elated. But his advisors expressed the opinion that since the Jews (Judeans) were so reluctant to give out their scriptures they might produce a concocted fraud instead of a translation of the real scriptures. Ptolemy saw the logic of this, so he sent to Jerusalem asking that a team of translators be sent to Egypt to produce the translation under his supervision. The Jewish elders chose seventy-two scholars, six from each of the twelve tribes, and sent them to Alexandria. There Ptolemy had constructed a small city for their accommodation across the Nile from his palace. To make sure that there could be no collaboration in either producing a false text or a collusion to leave out any parts of the holy books, Ptolemy arranged that the translators should live in separate houses—two in a house, working together. Nor were the teams of translators permitted to communicate with one another.

On the first evening the translators were brought across the Nile to present their day's work. Thus thirty-six translations were presented. Upon examination it was found that all of them were identical word-for-word! Each day this phenomenon was repeated. The Egyptians considered this a miraculous proof of the divine character of the Hebrew scriptures, and as a result many of them converted to Judaism. Even today the Christians of the Eastern church use that very translation, called the Septuagint, for the Old Testament. In time the Septuagint came to be used by all the diaspora Jews who could not read Hebrew. At the time of Christ there were several synagogues in Jerusalem that used it, as well. The Gospel authors quote the Septuagint in their references to the Old Testament.

Although the translators were kept separated on the days of translation, on the Sabbath they were allowed to be together. When the time came for the translation of the book of Isaiah, one of the translators—Simeon—told the others that he felt the part about a virgin conceiving and giving birth should be omitted or changed, for the Egyptians would only laugh at the Jewish religion if they knew such a thing was written in their scriptures. (So Ptolemy's advisors were right.) Moreover, he said that he himself could not believe such a thing as Isaiah had written. His colleagues, however, were offended at his suggestion and expressed their disapproval of his words. That night when he was alone, an angel appeared to him and told him that because of his unbelief he would not die until he saw the virgin and her child of whom Isaiah had prophesied. At that time Simeon was already nearly one hundred years old.

On the next Sabbath Simeon told his fellow translators of this angelic visitation, and when they returned to Israel upon completion of the Septuagint, this was made known. Since the child of the virgin was to be the Messiah, all the people came to believe that Simeon would not die until the Messiah was born. Every year at Passover inquiry would be made as to whether Simeon was alive. As the years passed it became evident that Simeon's longevity was an undisputed miracle.

At the time of Jesus' presentation in the Temple, Simeon was three hundred and fifty years old–a great sign indeed. After declaring to all present that Jesus was the fulfillment of the angel's prophecy, he peacefully died soon after. So we see that all Israel knew of this Child and his destiny.

> **And Joseph and his mother marvelled at those things which were spoken of him. And Simeon blessed them, and said unto Mary his mother, Behold, this child is set for the fall and rising again of many in Israel; and for a sign which shall be spoken against; (yea, a sword shall pierce through thy own soul also,) that the thoughts of many hearts may be revealed (Luke 2:33-35).**

Whenever any force for good comes into the world it is immediately opposed, because duality is the nature of the world itself. Jesus was the fall and the rising of many. Those who welcomed and accepted him and his teachings were lifted up, but those who detested and rejected him plunged themselves down into darkness. God did not put them into darkness: they did it to themselves.

I knew a very outstanding minister, remarkable in many ways, a true light in the world. I well remember the time she came to the church in my little hometown and preached a sermon entitled: "Will You Be Drawn Or Will You Be Driven?" Her thesis was quite simple: people are either drawn to God and spiritual life or they are repelled by it and evade it. This is determined by their own inner state and ultimately is a matter of choice. And it is essential that a spiritually intelligent person make a very conscious choice in his life to draw near to God and never turn away.

From the time of his conception, which was considered illegitimate, until this very moment, Jesus is for many "a sign spoken against." He is a diagnostic element: those who are true in heart and soul accept him, and those who are false in heart and soul reject him and anyone like him. The mind is a field of vibrating energy that is also magnetic. It is attracted to those things which vibrate compatibly with it, and repulsed by those things which vibrate with an incompatible magnetism. Those of a positive vibration respond positively to Jesus, and those of a negative vibration respond negatively to Jesus. Positive people accept truth and negative people reject it. In this way, "the thoughts of many hearts may be revealed."

There is oftentimes a price to be paid for taking something into our life, and the Virgin Mary paid a great price, being mocked and scorned as a liar and immoral by those who did and do not believe in Jesus' divine conception through these last two thousand years. And the crucifixion of Jesus was truly a sword thrust through her very soul. Yet, as she prophesied, the true of heart and soul throughout all generations have called her blessed (Luke 1:48).

> **And there was one Anna, a prophetess, the daughter of Phanuel, of the tribe of Aser: she was of a great age, and had lived with an husband seven years from her virginity; and she was a widow of about fourscore and four years, which departed not from the temple, but served God with fastings and prayers night and day. And she coming in that instant gave thanks likewise unto the Lord, and spake of him to all them that looked for redemption in Jerusalem (Luke 2:36-38).**

So these two supremely purified and illumined souls were drawn by the very presence of the infant Jesus to honor and speak of his spiritual glory and significance to those assembled in the temple.

All of Israel knew about Saint Simeon and the promise made to him by the angel, so at every Passover they made inquiry as to whether he was still living. In this way the true of heart knew that Jesus was indeed the

Messiah when they learned of Simeon's witness to Jesus and his subsequent departure from this world.

The Magi Visit the New-born King of the Jews

> Now when Jesus was born in Bethlehem of Judaea in the days of Herod the king, behold, there came wise men from the east to Jerusalem, saying, Where is he that is born King of the Jews [Judeans]? for we have seen his star in the east, and are come to worship him (Matthew 2:1-2).

Bethlehem is known as the "City of David" (Luke 2:4, 11). Although Joseph and Mary were living in Nazareth, it was divinely ordained that the Messiah should be born in Bethlehem, the ancestral home of Saint Joseph. The meaning is that Christ Consciousness can dawn in us only when we are at the source, at the core of our being. This is borne out by the fact that Jesus was born in a cave, in the depths of the earth. For liberated consciousness can only arise from the inmost depths of our being, from the "cave of the heart," the core, of our existence. When through meditation we reach the "point of light within the mind of God" from which we have originated, then the Christ becomes manifested in us.

Bethlehem literally means "House of Bread." This is particularly fitting, as Jesus referred to himself as "the bread of life" and "the living bread" (John 6:35, 48, 51). Of course he was speaking of his consciousness as a Messiah, a Christ, an anointed son of God, as are we all, but he had realized and manifested it, and had come to help us do the same. This is the true Good News (Gospel) of Christ.

King Herod was abhorrent to the Israelites for four reasons: 1) He was half Gentile in his ancestry; 2) he was totally Gentile in his thinking, having been brought up in the household of the Roman Emperor, and was a servant of Rome; 3) he tried to impose Roman culture (and even religion) on the people of Israel; 4) he had rebuilt the Temple in Jerusalem in a completely Roman style, violating the symbolic pattern given to Moses. In short, Herod was the enemy within, attempting to destroy the civil and moral character of Israel.

Symbolically, Herod represents the spiritual state already discussed as a kind of sleepwalking. He was neither Hebrew nor Gentile, yet his entire inclination was toward things Gentile. This perfectly reveals our own dilemma. We are seemingly half spirit and half material, but the material eclipses the spirit and overshadows every aspect of our thought and action. This is not a happy picture, but it is heartening to know that Christhood can be born in us even while were are in this state. However, the inner Christ will not grow "in wisdom and stature" (Luke 2:52) and "be made manifest to Israel" (John 1:31) at the declaration of our divine sonship: "This is my beloved Son, in whom I am well pleased" (Matthew 3:17), until the Gentile side of us has been completely eliminated through assimilation into the Israel side, making us truly "all one in Christ" (Galatians 3:28).

It is not enough to say: "Christ is within all of us" if that Christ is not brought forth consciously and developed to full potential in order to be our savior and deliverer. Nor is it sensible to say: "Oh, there is still so much bad in me that spiritual life is not for me right now." Or: "I still have a lot of negative stuff to work through before I can think about meditation and spiritual life. After all, I don't want to be a hypocrite." Jesus was born right in Herod's back yard. Eventually Herod died and Jesus lived. The same can happen with us. Even in the territory of the ego our inner Christ can appear and in time survive the Herod-ego. "For with God nothing shall be impossible" (Luke 1:37).

The wise men came not from Persia as is mistakenly thought, but from India, and they represent the wisdom of India, the place where the sun of divine illumination first shone out from within the liberated sons of God, and it is from there that all spiritual knowledge arose and spread throughout the world. Wherever the light of spiritual consciousness, and even civilization, is found, its roots are in India. Pythagoras, Apollonius of Tyana, and Jesus were all messengers of the Light of India to what was then the Western world. Apollonius and Jesus became martyrs of that Light, and Pythagoras was greatly persecuted, as well, having to live on an island to escape being killed. Mahendranath Gupta, the author of *The Gospel of Sri Ramakrishna*, said that undoubtedly there are good people in all countries of the world, but they have their faces turned toward India, for India draws the awakening soul.

When the Christ is born, wisdom arises from the depths of the spirit to reveal and manifest that Christ, "the dayspring from on high [which] hath visited us" (Luke 1:78). In other versions the word used is Orient rather than dayspring. "The east" symbolizes the east of the spirit as opposed to the west of the outer layers in which our spirit is covered, and also the intuitional right brain as opposed to the discursive-thinking left brain. The inner light shines upon us from the core of our being and is interpreted to us through our intuition. It is those that dwell in the east of spirit-consciousness that seek and find the Christ.

This being so, we must consciously cultivate the eastern awareness through meditation. Actually, being right-brained and spiritually oriented is what being oriental means. It is not geographic. After all, to the Japanese and Chinese the United States is the East. For them Paris would be the Far East. So to be Eastern is to be intuitional and spiritual. To be Western is to be just the opposite. It is a matter of the polarization of consciousness. We must all become oriental in the spiritual sense, for the sun only rises from the east, never from the west.

It is true that all human beings have the Christ (or Buddha) Nature, but only the eastern wisdom of the spirit can perceive and ultimately reveal it. Even though it is equally present to the western part of us, it still remains in darkness, turned away from the inner sun-rising. Herod and his cohorts never found Jesus. They could not: it was antithetical to their nature which was to kill the Christ, not to worship him. In the same way, our Herod ego and his henchmen, our mind, emotions, body and all that is outer, have only one capability: the destruction of Christ Consciousness. They are all the enemies of Christ, many antichrists of whom Saint John the Apostle wrote (I John 2:18). As wise men of the east we must outwit them as did those first wise men from the east.

The journeying of the wise men from the east to the west has a profound significance: there must be a transfer of the inner spiritual consciousness into the outer part of our being and life. The west must become the east in a unification of consciousness. Until then we are spiritual schizophrenics, "a house divided against itself [that] shall not stand" (Matthew 12:25). Meditation is the only way this transformation can take place. And when it does take place there will be a great change in us. Meditation that only produces pleasant or egoically-satisfying experiences but has no effect on our outer, ordinary life is false and should be discarded. When sugar is dissolved in water all the water tastes sweet; likewise, Right Meditation causes the perception and manifestation of spirit to be present in every atom of our life.

Even the Bible says that we are judged by our works, not by our intentions, not by what we think about it, but by what we do about it. Why? Because what is done is the real manifestation of what is going on inside. The thirty-fourth Ode of Solomon expresses it this way: "The likeness of that which is below is that which is above. For everything is above, and below there is nothing, but it is believed to be by those in whom there is no knowledge." That which is going on outside is first going on inside, for the inner is the sole source of the outer. This is indicated by Jesus when he says: "The Son can do nothing of himself, but what he seeth the Father do: for what things soever he doeth, these also doeth the Son likewise" (John 5:19). That is, only what "takes place" in the transcendent Godhead can take place in the immanent Godhead and be manifested through the creation. The Ode goes even further and says that things only occur "above," and that "below" is only a reflection. So in certain instances we *can* judge a book by its cover. Since this is the truth, we can see that meditation is only viable when it has an external effect. Furthermore, the character and duration of that effect will reveal whether the meditation is worthwhile or not.

We have seen his star in the east, and are come to worship him. As soon as the star rose, they started on the journey. It is popularly thought that after spiritual consciousness arises we can dawdle around before acting on it. But that is supremely chancey, almost a guarantee of failure. The people who are going to attain in spiritual life are those who, the moment they learn about the path to God, say: "That is for me," and start traveling it. Whatever form it may take, they make a beginning and keep it up, not making excuses or telling themselves that later on they will start. Such delays can carry over into another lifetime, for the cycles of spiritual growth do not last forever in the life of the individual, but are like the tides of the ocean.

Jesus gave this parable about excuse-makers: "A certain man made a great supper, and bade many: and sent his servant at supper time to say to them that were bidden, Come; for all things are now ready. And they all with one consent began to make excuse. The first said unto him, I have bought a piece of ground, and I must needs go and see it: I pray thee have me excused. And another said, I have bought five yoke of oxen, and I go to prove them: I pray thee have me excused. And another said, I have married a wife, and therefore I cannot come. So that servant came, and shewed his lord these things.... And the lord said unto the servant,... none of those men which were bidden shall taste of my supper" (Luke 14:16-21, 23-24). By delaying they wasted an entire incarnation and established the habit of putting off spiritual life, a habit that can persist for many lifetimes of neglect. Of this be assured: spiritual *life* and spiritual *practice* are the same thing.

Three areas of excuse are shown in this parable: 1) The addiction and distraction of material possession ("I have bought a piece of ground, and I must needs go and see it..."). 2) The addiction and distraction of the body and the five senses ("I have bought five yoke of oxen, and I go to prove them..."). 3) The addiction and distraction of "personal relationships" ("I have married a wife, and therefore I cannot come..."). Which ones do we use? They are the seal of death upon us, the stone of the tomb, that must be broken and taken away if Christ is to be revealed in us resurrected. Otherwise we do not merit being taken seriously in regard to spiritual life. The wise ones start the journey the moment the inner star rises–and persevere.

The wise men coming from the east indicates that when we begin to dwell primarily within as a result of meditation, the wisdom of the spirit will arise in us in the form of intuitional insights. We will begin to be guided from within rather than from without. If meditation does not enable us to know the way for ourselves, what is its value? "If the Son therefore shall make you free, ye shall be free indeed" (John 8:36). "For as many as are led by the Spirit of God, they are the sons of God" (Romans 8:14).

A great spiritual renaissance took place in Thailand during the twentieth century, stemming from the Thai Buddhist Master, Acharya Mun, who restored the "forest monk" tradition which was centered on the practice of meditation. The following conversation, taken from *The Venerable Phra Acharn Mun Buridatta Thera, Meditation Master* by The Venerable Prha Acharn Maha Boowa Nyanasampanno, took place between Acharya Mun and a Buddhist monk-scholar.

"**The Monk:** You have always preferred the solitude of the wilds. What do you do when questions or doubts arise? I am here in Bangkok surrounded by the Scripture and scholars and yet there are times when I am at my wit's end. You are known to be alone most of the time, with no access to Scripture or to scholars. What do you do for help when doubts, questions or obstacles arise?

"**The Venerable Acharya:** May it please your eminence. I have been studying and listening to the dharma throughout my waking hours, day and night. Never during my waking hours has the mind been disassociated from dharma, by which all doubts have been cleared up and all problems dealt with, one after another. In such a way are the defilements counteracted, fought against and eradicated. It is in the mind that all problems, obstacles and defilements occur, be they external or internal, crude or subtle, far or near, great or small. It is also in the mind that all these things are conquered. There is no need to worry about turning to anyone for help when such difficulties occur. From my experience, there is no better weapon with which to fight against defilements and to solve problems, and this is also in complete accordance with the Buddha's saying: *Atta hi attano natho*—one is the master of oneself—the truth of which has been all this time evident to me. It is the dharma or well-developed mindfulness-and-wisdom which always comes to my rescue, always functioning promptly and effectively.

"In some cases it took an unusually long time before some hurdles could be crossed, but in the end it was never beyond the power of mindfulness-and-wisdom which had to be developed specially for such particular occasions. This is why I always prefer the seclusion of the wilds, where I can come to grips with all problems through self-help.... Often an aspirant feels he is groping in the dark and is always wasting time due to trial and error. It is through steadfastness of aim and dedicated effort that I have achieved what I have, crossing one hurdle after another."

Commenting on this conversation, at which he was present, the Venerable Maha Boowa says: "The Monk appeared to be greatly interested and impressed in the Venerable Acharya's explanation, giving his whole-hearted appreciation that the Venerable Acharya was indeed a competent bhikkhu [monk] able to help himself in the seclusion of the wilds. He agreed with the Venerable Acharya that the dharma recorded in the Scripture and the dharma taking place in the mind were on far different levels. Even the dharma as recorded in the Scripture cannot be as absolutely reliable now as it had been in the early centuries after the Buddha's complete passing away. With the passage of time there were bound to be deficiencies due to the defilements of the later compilers of the texts. Such being the case, the dharma in the Scriptures and the dharma in the mind are sure to be on different levels."

Saint Paul expressed the same inner confidence, saying: "Not that we are sufficient of ourselves to think any thing as of ourselves; but our sufficiency is of God; who also hath made us able ministers of the new testament; not of the letter, but of the spirit: for the letter killeth, but the spirit giveth life" (II Corinthians 3:5-6).

This does not mean that we should ignore scriptures, spiritual writings and spiritual teachers. It is only wise to learn from them and keep their precepts in mind. But none of these are legitimate if they try to bind us into dependence on them, particularly through fear or a feeling of our personal inadequacy.

The wise men made their way to Jerusalem, asking: "Where is he that is born King of the Jews [Judeans]? for we have seen his star in the east, and are come to worship him."

They did not wander around the countryside asking everyone they met about the Christ. No; they went directly to Jerusalem to make inquiry. Jerusalem is also a symbol of spiritual consciousness, for there the Divine Presence dwelt unalloyed within the Holy of Holies of the Temple. We cannot seek for spiritual light among the sooted-up lamps of the senses and intellect. We must seek for the pure light of the spirit, the light of "Christ in you, the hope of glory" (Colossians 1:27). And that quest is meditation.

They asked only about the Christ, nothing else. Many people think that meditation should reveal to them their past lives, give them psychic powers and experiences and a host of other totally ego-oriented things. But the wise care nothing for such, seeking only the liberation of Nirvana. The spiritual quest is just that: the quest for the *spirit*, not anything else.

Those who are addicted to externalism will demand uplifting sermons and inspiring rites and impressive buildings in which to enjoy them, but the wise will seek the Christ directly, and that is an exclusively inner search. When the women came to the tomb of Jesus, the angels asked them: "Why seek ye the living among the dead?" (Luke 24:5). The outer world is dead, whereas the inner world is alive. The Living Christ, like his kingdom, can only be found within. However sacred external objects, places and acts may actually be, they are as dead as anything else in the outside world if they do not awaken the awareness of spirit within us. If we seek life among them we will not only be foolish, we will be failures in our search. But those who prefer the dead will heap up idols to themselves from among the external rubble and be pacified. Religion involved in externals is also dead, and all its piety is nothing more than the dead burying their dead (Matthew 8:22) deeper in materiality.

Elijah stood on Mount Horeb "and, behold, the Lord passed by, and a great and strong wind rent the mountains, and brake in pieces the rocks before the Lord; but the Lord was not in the wind: and after the wind an earthquake; but the Lord was not in the earthquake: and after the earthquake a fire; but the Lord was not in the fire: and after the fire a still small voice" (I Kings 19:11-12). God was in none of the phenomena, but in the unmoving silence he spoke within the heart of Elijah, not outside.

When the wisdom arises from the east of spiritual awakening it directs us within. We must mistake no external or internal phenomena as being spiritual, for they are not. Only God-consciousness is truly spiritual. And God is beyond the reach of the senses, physical, astral or causal. Only in the spirit will we truly "see." No phenomena in meditation are truly spiritual. In fact, truly spiritual meditation eventually cuts off phenomena. What, then, is real meditation? It is a single thing: the cultivation of *consciousness*. That is why Jesus continually exhorted his disciples to watch, to simply be silently aware in the depths of their being (Matthew 21:42; 25:13; 26:41). He also used the simile of people waiting with burning lamps (Luke 12:35) to give the idea that we are not silent in a negative or blank sense, but are conscious, even alight with consciousness. And consciousness is silent.

"Commune with your own heart, and be still" (Psalms 4:4). "Be still, and know" (Psalms 46:10). "The Lord is in his holy temple: let all the earth keep silence before him" (Psalms 46:10). "And when he had opened the seventh seal [of the highest state of consciousness], there was silence" (Revelation 8:1).

One of Yogananda's most advanced disciples, Sri Durga Mata, told me that once a man came to see her because he felt he was getting nowhere in meditation. When she questioned him she discovered that he was meditating perfectly and reaching great depths of awareness. But because he expected flashing lights and ringing bells and all kinds of yogic thrills he did not realize that he was on the right, and only, track. He was entering into the heart of God and did not know it because he expected lesser things, the toys of the ego-mind. But when the wise seek they continually question: "Does this give me the consciousness of spirit?" If the answer is Yes, they keep it in their life and cherish it. If the answer is No, they eliminate it from their life. They arrange and live their life according to the single standard of consciousness.

Where is he that is born King of the Jews [Judeans]? Both Bethlehem and Jerusalem represent the higher consciousness within all of us. Our spirit is his kingdom. And that is what the wise men of the East seek, for Jesus said, "My kingdom is not of this world… my kingdom [is] not from hence" (John 18:36).

All the devout of Israel went to Judea, to Jerusalem, for the Passover. In the same way, if we wish to accomplish the true Passover, the passage from the darkness of material slavery into the freedom of spirit, we must journey into the consciousness that is spirit. There are many other kingdoms we must pass by or through to get to that sacred kingdom, and we must make sure we never get caught up in them. There are people who get totally caught up in the kingdom of their mind, the kingdom of emotions, the kingdom of health and food, and the kingdom of sex and consequently never reach the heavenly kingdom that lies beyond them all. "Turn away mine eyes from beholding vanity; and quicken thou me in thy way" (Psalms 119:37), should be our daily prayer.

For we have seen his star in the east. As I already pointed out, these wise men of the East did not delay. When they saw the star rise, immediately they set out to find the Christ. That is why David said: "O God, thou art my God; early will I seek thee" (Psalms 63:1). "My voice shalt thou hear in the morning, O Lord; in the morning will I direct my prayer unto thee, and will look up" (Psalms 5:3). And God has said: "Those that seek me early shall find me" (Proverbs 8:17).

The moment we learn of our inner Christ, at that very moment our search should begin. As soon as we hear of the possibility of union with God we should start seeking him. Upon learning that liberation is possible we should commence walking the path to freedom. Those who dilly-dally, discuss, think it over, decide to learn more about it, consider all the angles and wait till "the right time" will never make the pilgrimage.

When Saint Paul spoke to the Roman governor of Judea, we are told the governor said: "Go thy way for this time; when I have a convenient season, I will call for thee" (Acts 24:25). But he never called and so never entered the gates of righteousness (Psalms 118:19), for the "convenient" time for his ego never came.

And are come.... They did not just have a vision and spend the rest of their lives bragging about it. Nor did they speculate about what it might be like to behold the King. Neither did they go on and on about how they wished they could go to see him. They *did* go. They acted. They could say with Saint Paul: "I was not disobedient unto the heavenly vision" (Acts

26:19). In other words, true spiritual experience has a practical effect. It is lived out. What is experienced in the inner world is made manifest in the outer world. So again we are learning the traits of the wise men: they translated their inner vision into outer action.

Although it was rather unsophisticated, the old American folk hymn "How Far From God" gives a good idea about this. It begins: "I looked down the road and I wondered just to see how far I was from God. And I buckled up my shoes and then I started walking." We seriously look into our spiritual status and as a result put on our "walking shoes" in the form of self-purification and meditation and start walking on the path to God. Like Saint Paul we say, "I was not disobedient unto the heavenly vision" (Acts 26:19). And like the Prodigal Son: "I will arise and go" (Luke 15:18). The observance of yama and niyama is the arising, and meditation is the going.

This awakening and arising and going is what we really mean by spiritual evolution. Evolution is the entire process by which we return to the Infinite Spirit from which we originally came. That is why Saint Paul (Romans 8:19, 22) says the whole of creation is literally in birth pangs, and is in labor for the manifestation of the sons of God: for us to emerge through the self-evolution of yoga sadhana and stand outside of all limitations and bonds, free in the Light that is God (I John 1:5), that is our own true being. So the wise consciously evolve themselves through yoga sadhana, heeding the exhortation: "Work out your own salvation" (Philippians 2:1) "as workers together" (II Corinthians 6:1) with God.

...to worship him. The Greek word *proskuneo* literally means "to bow down before." But it comes from the root word *pros*, meaning "to draw near to," the word that is usually translated as "worship." The wise men wanted to come near to the Christ in humility, in simplicity of heart, which is what it means to be poor in spirit (Matthew 5:3). In meditation we divest ourselves of everything–visual images, emotions, memories, thoughts, intentions and aspirations–and approach our inmost consciousness in complete freedom of spirit. In this way alone can we draw near to the inner Christ.

Religion comes from the Latin word *religere* which means "to bind back" in the sense of returning something to its original place and establishing it there so it strays no longer. So religion is the process of returning to God and uniting ourselves permanently with him. "Him that overcometh will I make a pillar in the temple of my God, and he shall go no more out" (Revelation 3:12). "For in him we live, and move, and have our being… for we are also his offspring" (Acts 17:28). Having come from God, we shall return to God. In this perspective it becomes quite clear: meditation is the true religion, and those who seek their Source through meditation are the truly religious.

In the Yoga Sutras of Patanjali, the fundamental text of yoga, ten necessary elements are set forth, without which there can be no success in the search for God. The tenth element is *Ishwarapranidhana*, which means "offering the life to God," but not in the sense of simple dedication to God or the resolve to "serve" God. Instead, it means to pour out our life into the greater Life that is God; to merge the little wave of our life into the great Ocean of God; to become irrevocably one with him; to hear the Cosmic Voice saying: "Son, thou art ever with me, and all that I have is thine" (Luke 15:31). This is the real way to worship God.

Herod's Anxiety

> When Herod the king had heard these things, he was troubled, and all Jerusalem with him. And when he had gathered all the chief priests and scribes of the people together, he demanded of them where Christ should be born. And they said unto him, In Bethlehem of Judaea: for thus it is written by the prophet, And thou Bethlehem, in the land of Juda, art not the least among the princes of Juda: for out of thee shall come a Governor, that shall rule my people Israel (Matthew 2:3-6).

The ego and all its satellites become "troubled," stirred up like a nest of disturbed hornets or as water on the boil. They are agitated indeed, sensing the loss of their grip on us and their eventual dissolution. The ego and its cohorts have no objection to philosophy, religion or even ineffective disciplines as long as it leaves their kingdom intact or even strengthens it. But when the real thing starts to come about they swing into action, battling for survival. So it is not just a matter of being a little bit discomfited and jittery. When we begin authentic spiritual life it is a declaration of war.

A council of war is then needed. You have to know the enemy. And the ego does. The ego wants to cut off all possibility of spiritual realization at the very root: the state of consciousness in which Christ-hood can be born. So it finds out what conditions make Christhood possible, where Christhood is first conceived, and where it will be born. Then it begins to block and destroy.

Why did not Herod go to Bethlehem? Because he could not. Only the wise could find Jesus. The ego cannot search out the Christ, in fact it *will* not, because if it did it would dissolve. The ego can know about God, but the ego cannot go to God.

There is another aspect to this. The knowledge of the scriptures and their meaning did not enable him to find Christ. In the same way, the knowledge of scriptures or the knowledge of the words of the wise mean nothing if we ourselves have not seen within the star of Christ at its rising. There are many who study philosophy, religion and scriptures, but nothing ever comes of it because they are not wise men from the East of the spirit; they are foolish men from the West of mere egoic intellect and material consciousness. Religion causes so much misery in the world because the people in it are Herods. It is not religion that is at fault, it is the unfit and unworthy people who are in religion, using it for their own wrong ends.

Moreover, intellectual knowledge of what is true and right does not produce results. It is only intuitive insight and inspiration that enable us to undertake our spiritual search in the Judea of the higher reaches of our consciousness. And the place where he is born is Bethlehem, the House of Bread, for he is the Bread of Life, the Bread of Heaven–the true Staff of Life.

Out of thee shall come a Governor, that shall rule my people Israel. To be of Israel, to be of God, we must be governed by Christ–our lives are to be reshaped and ordered completely according to the principle of divine consciousness, the real Christ that is within. If we are truly God's people, we are ruled by Christ in all things. But this is not an authoritarian type of rule. Rather, it is a reflection of our Christ nature in all parts of our life that ultimately becomes a transformation of our entire nature into Christ. The conquered become the conqueror. We lose nothing, but gain everything. This is no tyranny, but the only real freedom. Through meditation we polish the mirror of our consciousness so that it can become the perfect image of the infinite Christ. It is of meditation that Saint Paul is speaking when he says: "But we all, with open face beholding as in a glass [mirror] the glory of the Lord, are changed into the same image from glory to glory, even as by the Spirit of the Lord" (II Corinthians 3:18). Meditation is both the search for Christ and the finding of Christ.

But the Christ within us comes forth to govern and to rule. Therefore the whole purpose of the pursuit of truth, if we want to think of it in a philosophical way, is the governance, the changing, ordering and disciplining, of our lives. The inner light of Christ is invoked so our illumined will can govern all of our life. This is what all viable spiritual practices accomplish: the divine rulership, the giving of the scepter into the hand of Christ by taking it out of the hand of Herod, the ego. For the spirit is to reign, to have mastery over ourselves and our life, "that God may be all in all" (I Corinthians 15:28).

The ego and its agents, the body, the senses, the mind and the emotions, cannot really find the Christ. Herod and his advisers knew where Christ was to be born, but they were incapable of going there to find him. The ego and the spirit are by their natures antithetical. If they touch, the ego is dissolved. And the spirit cannot enter into that which is not also spirit. Oh, yes, the spirit can momentarily become fascinated by the ego and its illusions, and can even mistake the ego for itself. Yet this state cannot continue forever, even though like the Prodigal Son "he would fain have filled his belly with the husks that the swine did eat" (Luke 15:16). But he could not, so he "came to himself" and turned his thoughts toward his true home. It must be the same with the spirit. It must turn away from the ego and come to know itself.

The ego is always seeking to extend its territory, so naturally in time it begins looking into religion and its possibilities. It may even become a student of mystical theology and write books on "spirituality." For the ego needs to always be an authority to others. If mysticism is a fertile realm of influence and control of others, the ego becomes a mystic, complete with mystic visions and "powers." Since its motivation is itself, all it can ever really do is keep leading itself and its dupes back to itself. And it usually only talks about and expounds one thing: itself. No matter what the subject of a lecture is supposed to be, those in the grip of ego will spend most of the time on the fascinating subject of "me." They will use themselves to illustrate any points they wish to make, their main point being themselves. We will hear all about their past and what they have been thinking about lately, and may even get a commercial or two about their latest project or triumph. And if anyone has praised them we will get a word-for-word relay of that. "Aren't I great?" is the sum total of all their words and deeds.

Surely we have all seen a little child visiting someone and saying it wants to take home everything that appeals to it, often to the embarrassment of the host. It is the same with the ego-centered. If they read the life of a saint they immediately want to be able to shine with light, float in the air, heal the sick and be sought out by hundreds and thousands of admirers. But they in no way wish to love God with the self-forgetful love that is the prerequisite of holiness. They may decide to take up (or appear to take up) a showy form of asceticism if that impresses the crowd, but real sacrifice and denial for the love of God does not even cross the stage of their holy show. Once such a person wrote me a letter in which he expounded to me the need for the two of us to accept the bitter prospect of the world never knowing about our spiritual struggles and successes. Indeed! Just add ego and stir. Other egotists will love it and keep coming back for more. That is the bottom line of their religiosity.

"How art thou fallen from heaven, O Lucifer, son of the morning! how art thou cut down to the ground, which didst weaken the nations! For thou hast said in thine heart, I will ascend into heaven, I will exalt my throne above the stars of God: I will sit also upon the mount of the congregation, in the sides of the north: I will ascend above the heights of the clouds; I will be like the most High" (Isaiah 14:12-14). This is the character of religion when it is the ego and not the spirit that is involved. When the ego pretends to be spiritual, metaphysical and mystical, then it becomes Herod inquiring after Christ. But it never finds him.

Meditation is the way to Bethlehem. Other things may help greatly in preparing us for the journey and in keeping up our strength along the way, but meditation is the actual going. A seeker in the grip of ego will not meditate. He will worship, study, "praise the Lord," discuss on and on about spiritual topics, practice self-denial and sacrifice (at least in front of others), and missionary (*especially* missionary). But he will *not* "be still and know" (Psalms 46:10). Rather, he will talk and do and appear to know. Now he may claim to meditate ("I just get lost for hours in meditation," when no one is around), and he may sit with closed eyes in public meditations. But he will not be meditating, although afterward he will claim to have been having visions and profound insights all the while. Some are even able to sleep sitting bolt upright for hours. But the real thing will not be happening; not at all. I have known a couple of others that claimed they could not meditate because they would get in such a high state of consciousness that they couldn't function for days, their minds would go so high or deep. Some do not meditate, but they *teach* meditation.

We can test our seeking with the same criterion: meditation. How much do we meditate, and how much does meditation recreate our hearts, minds and lives? The answer will tell us whether we are real gold or fool's gold. And nobody fools God, for He it is that "placed at the east of the garden of Eden Cherubims, and a flaming sword which turned every way, to keep the way of the tree of life" (Genesis 3:24). Meditation is the flaming sword that both guards and leads to the Tree of Life: the inner Christ. And those who meditate enter Paradise and partake of Life.

Can the ego engage in religion? Yes, it can, feeling (and showing) how holy it is, filled with self-satisfaction and egoic confidence.

Can the ego engage in theology? Yes, it can, vaunting its "rightness" of belief, "proving" what is "the truth" and warning those "astray" in "heresy" as to their soul's danger in not agreeing with its orthodoxy.

Can the ego engage in external worship and prayer? Yes, it can, displaying itself with beautiful ceremonial, music, impressive trappings and inspiring words of prayer and praise.

Can the ego engage in study of scriptures? Yes, it can, priding itself on its scholarship and profound insights, writing books and articles to share its wisdom.

Can the ego engage in speaking of spiritual things? Yes, it can, uplifting and inspiring its hearers with "the truth" and memorable thoughts of goodness.

Can the ego engage in the doing of virtuous deeds? Yes, it can, "helping others" with its caring love (which usually turns a profit or wins a government grant), impressing them with such dedication and unselfishness.

Can the ego engage in the observance of religious disciplines? Yes, it can, "keeping the feasts and the fasts" like a true Pharisee, doing what "must be done" and avoiding what "must not be done." And never consorting with those who do otherwise unless it be to admonish them with self-satisfied smugness or righteous indignation.

Can the ego engage in authentic meditation? *No, it cannot.* But it can most certainly try to talk us out of meditating or talk us into taking up a worthless, false form of meditation.

"Like the sharp edge of a razor, the sages say, is the path. Narrow it is, and difficult to tread!" (Katha Upanishad 1:3:14). Meditation is the only safety net we can provide for ourselves as we walk the razor's edge to the Eternal. Meditation is like the water Dorothy threw on the Wicked Witch of the West: it melts and dispels the ego in just the same way. Meditation is the Red Sea in which the Pharaoh of the ego and all its army is drowned and swept away (Exodus 14:21-28). It is through meditation that we are enabled to say with Saint Paul: "Not I, but Christ liveth in me" (Galatians 2:20).

So we must not believe the ego-Herod when it pretends to have spiritual interest and spiritual life. Like Herod it has no intention of worshipping the Christ, but rather wishes to destroy the Christ and maintain its ages-long rule. Therefore we must base our spiritual life dead-center in meditation. It must be the hub, the spokes and the wheel of our spiritual practice. Otherwise the ego will manage to slip in and cunningly subvert us so the sad words of Jesus can be applied to us: "Whither I go, ye cannot come" (John 8:21). If, however, we persist in meditation, and the way of life which supports meditation, it will be said of us by the angels: "These are they which follow the Lamb whithersoever he goeth" (Revelation 14:4).

One of the major reasons meditation is safe and reliable is the fact that it is an inward, private, even secret, matter with no scope for egoic display. All spiritual reality is inward, or rather, the perception of spiritual reality is inward, since spiritual reality embraces (and is) all things. Meditation being an inward process, it puts us into alignment with spiritual reality and banishes all illusion, including its source: the ego. For this reason it is imperative to base our life upon meditation.

Each one of us is a living temple of God. "Know ye not that ye are the temple of God, and [that] the Spirit of God dwelleth in you?" (I Corinthians 3:16). "What? know ye not that your body is the temple of the Holy

Ghost [which is] in you, which ye have of God, and ye are not your own?" (I Corinthians 6:19). The external Temple in Jerusalem was a symbol of the human being's spiritual anatomy. The Ark of the Covenant represented the core of our being, the pure consciousness that is our spirit, our reality. Consequently it was kept hidden within the Most Holy Place. "And thou shalt hang up the veil under the taches, that thou mayest bring in thither within the veil the ark of the testimony: and the veil shall divide unto you between the holy place and the most holy" (Exodus 26:33).

The mind is the veil that divides the body from the spirit. That is why Saint Paul describes human beings as threefold: body (soma), mind (psyche), and spirit (pneuma). It is imperative, not optional, that we center our consciousness in spirit. "Walk in the Spirit, and ye shall not fulfil the lust of the flesh.... If we live in the Spirit, let us also walk in the Spirit" (Galatians 5:16, 25). For David, describes the spiritually-centered individual as "all glorious within" (Psalms 45:13). Jesus prayed: "O Father, glorify thou me with thine own self with the glory which I had with thee before the world was" (John 17:5). The wise seek to re-attain this glory, the glory which actually *is* God.

"Behold, the kingdom of God is within you" (Luke 17:21). The Lord Jesus not only told us that the kingdom of God is within us, he also told us how to enter that inner kingdom: "But thou, when thou prayest, enter into thy closet, and when thou hast shut thy door, pray to thy Father which is in secret; and thy Father which seeth in secret shall reward thee openly" (Matthew 6:6). The Fathers tell us that "the closet" is our heart, our spirit, and the door is our mind with its various senses. In the closet-spirit alone can we be purified from all outer darkness, praying with David: "Create in me a clean heart, O God; and renew a right spirit within me" (Psalms 51:10). And with David we must resolve: "I will walk within my house with a perfect heart" (Psalms 101:2). That is, even in our outer activities we will remain centered in the inner consciousness of our spirits, the centering that is accomplished through meditation.

"Then the spirit entered into me, and set me upon my feet, and spake with me, and said unto me, Go, shut thyself within thine house.... And I will put my spirit within you, and cause you to walk in my statutes, and ye shall keep my judgments, and do them" (Ezekiel 11:19; 36:27). For as David said to God: "Behold, thou desirest truth in the inward parts: and in the hidden part thou shalt make me to know wisdom" (Psalms 51:6). It is for this reason that the images of the Cherubim in the Most Holy Place were facing inward, not outward. "The wings of these cherubims spread themselves forth twenty cubits: and they stood on their feet, and their faces [were] inward" (II Chronicles 3:13). Another metaphor of inner-directed consciousness is given in the book of Revelation wherein the most highly-evolved beings in the cosmos are described as being "full of eyes within," their entire awareness being both complete ("full") and within spirit alone. "And the four beasts [literally: "living creatures"–not animals] had each of them six wings about him; and they were full of eyes within: and they rest not day and night, saying, Holy, holy, holy, Lord God Almighty, which was, and is, and is to come" (Revelation 4:8).

God dwells in the hidden depths of existence. "The secret things belong unto the Lord our God" (Deuteronomy 29:29), for "he made darkness his secret place" (Psalms 18:11). Knowing this, David wrote of those who seek God: "Thou shalt hide them in the secret of thy presence… thou shalt keep them secretly" (Psalms 31:2). "He that dwelleth in the secret place of the most High shall abide under the shadow of the Almighty" (Psalms 91:1). And Saint Paul tells us: "Your life is hid with Christ in God" (Colossians 3:3). The real life in God is a hidden, inmost life.

Herod Consults the Magi Who Find the Child Jesus

> Then Herod, when he had privily called the wise men, inquired of them diligently what time the star appeared. And he sent them to Bethlehem, and said, Go and search diligently for the young child; and when ye have found him, bring me word again, that I may come and worship him also. When they had heard the king, they departed; and, lo, the star, which they saw in the east, went before them, till it came and stood over where the young child was (Matthew 2:7-9).

There is a valuable lesson in the foregoing. When the ego cannot keep us from taking up a viable form of spiritual life it attempts to derail us in two ways. One is to make us over-exacting and anxious about doing everything right. Relentlessly the ego hounds us with the need to be correct and not go wrong. Of course, it does not want us to do well in spiritual life; rather it is attempting to overwhelm us with doubts as to the rightness of what we are doing and to tie us in knots with anxiety and over-scrupulousness. It wishes to confuse and harass us so much that we will throw up our hands and give up and drop spiritual life altogether, or adopt a "safe" mediocrity that will leave the ego intact. (This latter is the state of most members of all religions.) "Go and search diligently for the young child," said Herod. "You've got to do this right!" insists the ego, until in frustration we stop doing it at all.

The other way involves the same pressure and paranoia-producing badgering, but this time the intention is for us to go so hard and heavy at the right thing, overdoing it so intensely, that we will, like a meteorite entering the atmosphere, simply burn out, leaving nothing behind but a vapor trail. Both ploys have the same goal: the destruction of all attempts to attain our inner Christhood.

But the usual strategy of the ego is to make us think that we need do nothing at all, or else that we can manage by just moseying and dawdling along the way, so that finally life will end and we will have attained nothing.

Another way the ego tries to trip us up is through getting us to be over-cautious. This is especially the way of religion that makes everything "of the devil" and consequently of great danger except for what they approve or desire. Instilling great fear in their adherents, they keep them from thinking or doing anything not prescribed for them by the supposed guardians and teachings of "the truth."

On the other hand, when the ego wants us to do something it is presented as easy, beneficial, and fun. And anything the ego hates is presented as deadly dangerous, hazardous and difficult to an indescribable degree.

This is particularly seen in the matter of contemporary "spiritual" philosophies and teachers. Outrageously dishonest, power-mad, foolish, outright-stupid, and colossally evil ideologies and persons are adulated and accepted without question by multitudes. But the same dupes, upon encountering even the simplest truth or honest teacher, become suspicious, draw themselves up sharply and begin warily questioning, investigating, and worrying. "I'm not so sure about this" say those who a few days or weeks ago were romping around at the latest profit-centered seminars and retreats, unquestioningly doing the most idiotic acts and glorying in the most idiotic ideas that were being enunciated by A Messenger. Finally they will turn away from spiritual reality, saying that it disturbs, worries or frightens them. If that makes them feel guilty, they will then claim stridently that what they are rejecting is really "negative," "evil," "cultish," "arrogant" and "deception." Then they resume their eager and exuberant consumption of whatever spiritual swill comes floating down the polluted rivers of their lives.

I knew a Christian woman who was told by an Indian "seer" to abandon her husband and two young children, convert to Islam, and become the third wife in the harem of a rich man in Kashmir. She did so without questioning. When the man threw her out because the other two wives threatened to kill her (they did poison her unsuccessfully), she came back to her family and continued to dress in a semi-Moslem manner and freely tell people about her escapade without the least touch of guilt at what she had done. But whenever she met any real teaching or teacher, she would begin to carry on about how for all she knew they were "of the devil" and sent to destroy her soul by getting her to "deny Jesus my Savior." By the way, without the least bit of doubt she still kept going to consult with the false seer that had told her to leave her family and renounce Christianity.

When the wise men left Herod's presence they saw the star, and it led them to Christ. In the same way, when we move out of the orbit of the ego and its instruments we will find ourselves able to make inner contact with the true Christ-self.

The Child Jesus is Found

> And, lo, the star, which they saw in the east, went before them. When they saw the star, they rejoiced with exceeding great joy. And when they were come into the house, they saw the young child with Mary his mother, and fell down, and worshipped him: and when they had opened their treasures, they presented unto him gifts; gold, and frankincense, and myrrh. And being warned of God in a dream that they should not return to Herod, they departed into their own country another way (Matthew 2:9-12).

We cannot have a static spiritual life, for real spiritual life keeps leading us onward, ever onward, like the star of Christ. There are fish that must continually keep swimming, otherwise they will suffocate. It is the same with us who wish to lead the life of the spirit: we have to keep on moving, going forward to the goal. When we examine the lives of great Masters, we find that they moved from stage to stage without halting for a moment. Stagnation mistaken for stability is a mark of dead religion which starts out and ends in the identical spot, no change, no growth, no evolution, no difference, because it is just that: dead.

When they saw the star, they rejoiced with exceeding great joy. When true spiritual life begins to manifest in us and intuition begins to function within us as it should, we become aware of the eternal call into the eternal kingdom. It is indeed a happy thing. "Let the heart of them rejoice that seek the Lord" (I Chronicles 16:10). Those following a genuine spiritual path are basically cheerful, hopeful people. As Saint Paul says, they "rejoice in hope of the glory of God" (Romans 5:2),… the hope of "Christ in you, the hope of glory" (Colossians 1:27),…." "the hope of salvation" (I Thessalonians 5:8).

If we hope in and look to our limited, presently ego-gripped selves to find the Christ, we are doomed to failure and despair. But if instead we are always "looking for that blessed hope, and the glorious appearing" (Titus 2:13) of Christ, an appearing that must occur when we leave Herod and journey to the Bethlehem within, we shall always be filled with hope and "exceeding great joy," rejoicing at the mercy and grace of God.

"Again, the kingdom of heaven is like unto treasure hid in a field; the which when a man hath found, he hideth, and for joy thereof goeth and selleth all that he hath, and buyeth that field" (Matthew 13:44). Joy is the motivation for all spiritual life. Where you find gloom, there the spirit is absent. We are even told by Saint Paul that joy was the sole motivation of Jesus when he underwent his sufferings. "Looking unto Jesus the author and finisher of our faith; who for the joy that was set before him endured the cross, despising the shame, and is set down at the right hand of the throne of God" (Hebrews 12:2). Gladness is the secret of spiritual life.

In *The Scent of Water*, Elizabeth Goudge wrote about a medieval thief who reformed and became a hermit. He helped build a church and did all the wood-carving himself. At the back of the church he carved his self-portrait showing himself wearing a crown of thorns. But the observant saw that there was a gap between the thorns and the surface of the carving, and when they put their fingers inside, by touch they could tell that beneath the crown of thorns he was really wearing a crown of roses. That was his secret. The world saw him as penitent and self-denying, but in reality he was crowned with joy.

"Peace I leave with you, my peace I give unto you: not as the world giveth, give I unto you," said Jesus (John 14:27). It is the same with the joy spoken of by Saint Matthew. The Greek word is *khara*, which means gladness and calm happiness, calm delight. The ancient Christian writers, as well as the later writers on mystical life, insisted that to be in the spirit is at all times to be *apatheia*, passionless. Unfortunately our English word apathetic means indifferent, flat, or inwardly unresponsive. What *apatheia* really means is freedom from the agitating egoic emotions. Very deep feelings rising from the spirit may be experienced by the spiritually evolved, but they are not the inner storms that materialistic people undergo. Those in tune with spirit experience the *phos ilaron*, the "gladsome light" of the Eastern Christian hymn, the "light of mellow joy" of which Yogananda wrote. So even though the spiritual person's joy is, like that of the wise men, "exceeding [*sfodra*] great [*megas*]," it is deep like the ocean, totally calm, and always under control.

The star led the wise men to the place where Christ was to be found. But the star did not show them Christ. Rather, they had to enter the house, for Christ is always to be found within. That is why Jesus warns us that whenever anyone says: "Here is Christ" or "There is Christ," pointing us to some person, some thing, or some place that is external to us, we should not believe them, for Christ and his kingdom are within each one of us. "Neither shall they say, Lo here! or, lo there! for, behold, the kingdom of God is within you" (Luke 17:21). "Then if any man shall say unto you, Lo, here is Christ, or there; believe it not" (Matthew 24:23). "And then if any man shall say to you, Lo, here is Christ; or, lo, he is there; believe him not" (Mark 13:21). It is the Christ that is within us that is our hope of glory. There is no other Christ.

Earlier I mentioned the style of icon called "The Sign of Salvation" which shows the Christ Child within the center of the Virgin Mary's breast. The idea is that Christ Consciousness is at the center of material creation symbolized by the Virgin Mother. Since we are images of the divine order, to find Christ we have to get to the center of our own being and enter into the depths of our own spirit, at the core of which is God, the Source of all being. We must find ourselves before we can find God. That is why Saint Paul told the Athenians during his first discourse on Mars Hill that the very purpose of God's creation of human beings was his intention that "they might feel after him, and find him, though he be not far from every one of us: for in him we live, and move, and have our being… for we are also his offspring" (Acts 17:27-28). Our success is assured: we need only seek. "Ask, and it shall be given you; seek, and ye shall find; knock, and it shall be opened unto you: for every one that asketh receiveth; and he that seeketh findeth; and to him that knocketh it shall be opened" (Matthew 7:7,8).

The wise men entered into the house, and we must make the same entry if we are really going to find the Christ. Unlike the popular, sentimental (and manipulative) view, we cannot find Christ in others, in community, in relationship, in nature or even in dogmatic truth. We can only find Christ in the depths of our own spirit. Then, it is true, we will be able to find the Christ everywhere, within and without. "I am the door: by me if any man enter in, he shall be saved, and shall go in and out, and find pasture" (John 10:9). But first the inner search and finding is necessary.

They saw the young child with Mary his mother. Jesus had an origin, a "point of entry" into this world: the Virgin Mary. The wise men found the Divine Child seated on the lap of his Mother. This is the pose that we see in icons called "the Throne of Heaven" which depict the Virgin Mary seated facing out with Jesus, the King of Heaven, on her lap because she is the Throne of Christ. That is why those who are truly going toward Christ are very intent on the Mother of Christhood, the Holy Power, the Holy Spirit. The Maronite Christians sing:

> Let us always remember
> > on whose lap our Lord is seen.
> With the Lord of salvation
> > will be found Salvation's Queen.

For us the symbolic message is that our inner Christ rests upon, is supported by, the Holy Spirit Mother, by the living Presence within us that has given us spiritual birth into the inner kingdom. It is the divine evolutionary power, the Holy Spirit, which enables us to evolve to the point where we can realize the Christ within. She is the light that illumines for us the way to Christ-realization. The wise seekers, when they begin to have an interior life, discover the treasure that is the Mother–Mahashakti. For just as Jesus was conceived and born through Her, so must we be conceived and born of Her. Jesus came into this world through Her, and we enter the divine kingdom through Her.

It has been discovered that when a newborn child is placed on its mother's chest, its heartbeat will synchronize with hers. In the same way the spiritually reborn will have hearts synchronized with their Cosmic Mother.

And fell down, and worshipped him. The first reaction of the wise men upon seeing Jesus was to bow down before him in reverent worship. This was their intention, having told others: "We have seen his star in the east, and are come to worship him." They knew that no words of praise were worthy of the Child, but they knew that reverence was appropriate. The spiritual life of those that seek God is one of worship and adoration. For by that means they draw near to God and eventually come into union with him. And meditation is the supreme worship of God.

And when they had opened their treasures, they presented unto him gifts; gold, and frankincense, and myrrh. We must open the treasure chests of our hearts to bring forth the gifts that are appropriate offerings for God and his Christ.

Gold represents the consciousness that results from spiritual evolution through purification. "And he shall sit as a refiner and purifier of silver: and he shall purify the sons of Levi, and purge them as gold and silver, that they may offer unto the Lord an offering in righteousness." (Malachi 3:3) It is the "gold tried in the fire, that thou mayest be rich" spoken of by Jesus in Revelation 3:18.

Frankincense represents prayer and spiritual aspiration. That is why David sang: "Let my prayer be set forth before thee as incense" (Psalms 141:2). In the book of Revelation we find this: "And another angel came and stood at the altar, having a golden censer; and there was given unto him much incense, that he should offer it with the prayers of all saints upon the golden altar which was before the throne. And the smoke of the incense, which came with the prayers of the saints, ascended up before God out of the angel's hand" (Revelation 8:3, 4).

Myrrh is the symbol of love for God, as in the Song of Solomon: "I rose up to open to my beloved; and my hands dropped with myrrh, and my fingers with sweet smelling myrrh, upon the handles of the lock.... His cheeks are as a bed of spices, as sweet flowers: his lips like lilies, dropping sweet smelling myrrh" (Song of Solomon 5:5, 13).

These treasures are not the tawdry imitations that are manufactured by the ego and matter-oriented mind. They are the inner realities that can only be accessed through meditation, and which are an inherent part of our eternal being. They need not be cultivated, only uncovered and freed for offering unto God in the highest form of worship: meditation. Just as purification of the ore brings forth the gold, but does not create it, so meditation and a life ordered according to spiritual principles purify us so the hidden gold of the spirit can manifest. The same is true of the other gifts of the wise.

All the esoteric traditions of the world say that everything is hidden in man, who is a miniature universe. Paradise and heaven itself are within all of us. We are journeying toward the infinite glory of God, but first we must discover our own inner glory, and see its identity with the glory of God. We belong with, and in, that glory. With this in mind Jesus set the example for us by praying: "O Father, glorify thou me with thine own self with the glory which I had with thee before the world was" (John 17:5). God does not bestow the glory on us; we have had it from eternity, but we have forgotten it and need to recall and reclaim it. Part of true spiritual life, of the journey back to God, is the inner discovery and the inner awakening and manifestation of that glory which is within us. This innate glory is the "wedding garment" of the soul (Matthew 22:11-12), the pledge of our spiritual union (marriage) with God in total and irrevocable union.

"A voice came out of the throne, saying, Praise our God, all ye his servants, and ye that fear him, both small and great. And I heard as it were the voice of a great multitude, and as the voice of many waters, and as the voice of mighty thunderings, saying, Alleluia: for the Lord God omnipotent reigneth. Let us be glad and rejoice, and give honour to him: for the marriage of the Lamb is come, and his wife hath made herself ready. And to her was granted that she should be arrayed in fine linen, clean and white: for the fine linen is the righteousness of saints. And he saith unto me, Write, Blessed are they which are called unto the marriage supper of the Lamb" (Revelation 19:5-9).

By meditation we open our treasures and clothe ourselves in the wedding garment of the spirit.

And being warned of God in a dream that they should not return to Herod, they departed into their own country another way. When we sleep, our consciousness withdraws into our astral bodies. Our dreams are the pictures that are the thoughts of our astral brain, the subconscious, for the subconscious does not think in words but in pictures, which is why verbal affirmations are of relatively little effect in comparison to the effect that visual phenomena have on us. Dreams may also be communications from our own higher self. God, the saints, and angels can communicate with us through dreams that are really visual interpretations of the ideas being imparted. It is important to know this, for when we have spiritual dreams we often take them at face value rather than analyzing them to see if the dream pictures were concept-messages from the higher realms.

Dreams need to be analyzed as symbols to determine whether or not they are viable communications from higher worlds. Not everyone can have spiritual dreams, because most people's astral bodies are coarsened and darkened by the thoughts, words and deeds of their waking life–and to a tremendous degree by their diet. But those who purify their thoughts, words, deeds and diet and practice meditation will so cleanse their subconscious levels that their dreams can be instructions or revealings of spiritual principles as well as practical advice for their life, as it was in the case of the wise men. On the other hand, we must not become obsessed with our dreams and think that every one of them is a divine revelation.

Where do these spiritual dreams come from? Sometimes from our own true Self, sometimes from holy beings, and sometimes from God. But what matters is discerning the meaning, whatever the source.

As the subconscious is opened up through meditation, and that which is subconscious becomes more and more conscious, then we will receive intuitional inspiration from the deeper (higher) levels of our being. This opening of the subconscious by meditation is referred to by Jesus when he said: "There is nothing covered, that shall not be revealed; neither hid, that shall not be known" (Luke 12:2).

There is another side to this, however. Many people get very frustrated when they sit to meditate and all kinds of thoughts and impressions start flooding into their mind. But this is supposed to happen. This is the subconscious being revealed. This is not failure, but success in meditation. It is not entertaining and it certainly does not flatter the ego, but that is good, too. Meditation makes us increasingly aware of all the nooks and crannies of our minds, aware of the inner workings and the inner ways of our minds. But beyond the convolutions of the subconscious are the "mansions of light" of the superconscious. They, too, are revealed through meditation when we persevere.

Because the wise men were wise in the truest sense, in the spirit, they could be warned of the treacherous intents of Herod. Consequently, "they departed into their own country another way." The spiritual meaning of their not going back to Herod but returning to their country by a completely other road than by which they came is incredibly important for us. Marcus Aurelius wrote that a mind expanded by an insight or understanding could never again return to its former narrow state. This is simple, but true. We cannot encounter wisdom and then return to the ways of ignorance and be as we were before. We can certainly turn back to the darkness we came out of, but whereas before it was an unease for us it shall now be a disease and a torment. Saint Peter puts it very graphically, saying: "If after they have escaped the pollutions of the world through knowledge… they are again entangled therein, and overcome, the latter end is worse with them than the beginning…. But it is happened unto them according to the true proverb, The dog is turned to his own vomit again; and the sow that was washed to her wallowing in the mire" (II Peter 2:20, 22). Jesus put it more mildly, saying: "No man putteth a piece of new cloth unto an old garment, for that which is put in to fill it up taketh from the garment, and the rent is made worse. Neither do men put new wine into old bottles: else the bottles break, and the wine runneth out, and the bottles perish: but they put new wine into new bottles, and both are preserved" (Matthew 9:16-17).

The idea is this: It is absurd to practice spiritual discipline and seek higher consciousness while believing that we can continue on as we always have been. For when that consciousness really dawns it will change us. And, just as an adult has no interest in the things so loved by children, that which before was valued by us may no longer be of any interest to us. Not only will our minds change, so will our lives. It is a matter of evolution. "Walking the Path" is a journeying *from* something *to* something;

and it is supposed to be permanent. There is no return ticket for the wise. To suppose that we can enter the realms of light and then go back to the realms of darkness without grave harm is a sad misconception. We must go forward, not back and forth.

"When that which is perfect is come, then that which is in part shall be done away. When I was a child, I spake as a child, I understood as a child, I thought as a child: but when I became a man, I put away childish things" (I Corinthians 13:10-11). To think and act as a child is normal and right for a child. But for an adult to revert to childish thoughts and ways is never right. No wonder so many religious people are confused in the spiritual sense. They keep going around and around, up and down, frustrating their souls. "And Jesus said unto him, No man, having put his hand to the plough, and looking back, is fit for the kingdom of God" (Luke 9:62). This is the simple, discomfiting truth. Continuing in our old ways and associations after having come to higher understanding is truly to sin against the light, to sin against ourselves.

The wise men were told not to return on the road they had taken, even though it had led them to Christ. This is a dramatic underscoring of what I have been explaining. The infant feeds from the breast and bottle, but must, after attaining some growth, leave them behind and begin eating other nourishment. The breast and bottle were not evil, but they have become irrelevant, and will be detrimental if the child reverts to them and refuses to eat other food. No matter how necessary the nest is, the bird must leave it. We must abandon limitations and broaden our consciousness day by day.

You do indeed catch more flies with honey than with vinegar; and you catch more flies with garbage than with vinegar, too. But the truth is, even if the path we walked did eventually bring us to the chance for higher awareness, it is no longer legitimate for us; it may even be poisonous to us now. We have indeed passed through many phases as we journeyed to this point, but they must now be left behind. They may have been very good for us then, but they are no longer any more meaningful to us than the food we ate last week. Press on! There is a time in development when even that which was good and helpful, if still clung to, will be a hindrance or even harmful; and therefore it must be left off. Like Saint Paul, we must not be "disobedient unto the heavenly vision" (Acts 26:19).

They departed into their own country another way. We came from God and we return to God; but the paths by which we leave and by which we return are not the same. One is the taking on of illusion and the other is the divesting of illusion. One is the downward-going path of increasing involvement in ego and material consciousness and the other is the upward-going path of decreasing involvement in ego and material consciousness. One is the path of unconscious involution and the other is the path of conscious evolution. Both are necessary, first the downward path and then the upward path, but they are mutually exclusive of one another, antithetical to one another. We cannot have one foot on the downward path and the other on the upward path, for they lead in opposite directions. "No man can serve two masters: for either he will hate the one, and love the other; or else he will hold to the one, and despise the other. Ye cannot serve God and mammon" (Matthew 6:24).

Now that is the part that sometimes unsettles and pricks us, but there is another aspect to the matter that is so wonderful, hopeful and positive that it takes away all the discomfort we may be feeling. And that aspect is the wonderful truth that there really is a road that leads back to our original home, back to God. Our return to God is not haphazard or whimsical on the part of either us or God, but is a definite, precise, and methodical route to divine consciousness. That is why, when preparing to return to the Father, Jesus told his disciples: "Whither I go ye know, and the way ye know" (John 14:4). To know the way to God—what a wonderful thing! To no longer wander in a vague search, either not knowing the way or thinking that a false way is the true way. There is a path that is "the way of holiness," a spiritual "highway" to the Infinite (Isaiah 35:8).

The return of the wise by another way is a symbol of the fact that all the good in us which brought us to the point of meeting our inner Christ must become transmuted and spiritualized, renewed in order for us to be able to "walk in newness of life" (Romans 6:4). "And he that sat upon the throne said, Behold, I make all things new" (Revelation 21:5). "Therefore if any man be in Christ, he is a new creature: old things are passed away;

behold, all things are become new" (II Corinthians 5:17). This is very important, for since we are in the grip of ego we like to hold on to the past good of which we are proud, and want to keep running in the same tracks as before. It is necessary for us to realize what a total revolution, inner and outer, is required before we can begin to hope for real spiritual attainment. Spiritual life is ultimately a total re-creation of ourselves by ourselves.

All our faculties which enable us to function intelligently must also be returned to their correct orientation of spirit; they must be taken from their present status of serving our ego and given back to their rightful owner, our divine spirit. It is evolution from life to life on this earth that has brought us to this point. And that was good. But now we must aspire to evolve henceforth into the higher realms of being. The blind, haphazard seeking that we engaged in through past lives was not without benefit; but now it must be abandoned. From now on we must seek in a careful, intelligent, and systematic manner. We must be yogis.

The very purpose of finding the Christ within is to enable ourselves to return, like the wise men, into our own country, the place of our origin. This is a most important fact, for when we realize that we are going back to where we came from, that it is our nature to be there, our perspective on the matter is greatly affected, for we realize:

1) We do not need to become something other than what we really are, we do not need to make ourselves into something else. So much of the struggle that we see virtually all religions engaging in is absolutely unnecessary, even detrimental to attainment of the true goal. By misapplied understanding and application religion binds us and keeps us from knowing our true selves just as much as any of the other evils of the world. Yes, erroneous religion is one of the evils of the world. For we need to regain our eternal status, praying: "O Father, glorify thou me with thine own self with the glory which I had with thee before the world was" (John 17:5).

2) We do need, however, to stop trying to be what we are not and never can be. Once we do that, we shall automatically become what we are. When we endeavor to stop the age-old delusions, though, we discover that we are not passively in ignorance. Instead, we are frantically applying all our energies to create and maintain our ignorance and illusion. Since this is

not a conscious process on our part we do not realize what we are doing. Authentic meditation reveals this situation to us right away, however, and we go on from there. Meditation, then, is not just a doing but a stopping.

3) Since Self-realization is our essential nature we need not doubt the possibility of our return. For "no man hath ascended up to heaven, but he that came down from heaven" (John 3:13). The very fact that we can ascend means we have first descended. We have already gone half the journey!

4) Our return is inevitable, having been eternally predestined for us. "Then shall the King say unto them on his right hand, Come, ye blessed of my Father, inherit the kingdom prepared for you from the foundation of the world" (Matthew 25:34).

It is also necessary for us to realize that spiritual experience or awakening is not the goal: it is only the beginning. The wise men did not stay with Jesus in Nazareth. They had to go back home. It is the same with us. No matter how wonderful our spiritual awakenings and experiences may be, we have to turn from them and be about our "Father's business" (Luke 2:49) of return.

The wise men went home, and we, if we are wise, will also go home. We must understand that true religion is not just pleasing or placating God, or even the emotional idea of loving God–it is returning to God. It is getting up and getting out of here. As it says in the *Constitution of the Apostles*: "May grace come to us and may this world depart from us." We do not belong here; we never have.

We must know that we came from God and must use every waking moment of our life to return to God, otherwise we are not wise, but foolish. We have to get away from the land of Herod, away from the land dominated by the alien powers of the Romans, and go back to where God is the heart of everything.

The Child Jesus is Taken to Egypt and Later Returned

And when they were departed, behold, the angel of the Lord appeareth to Joseph in a dream, saying, Arise, and take the young child and his mother, and flee into Egypt, and be thou there until I bring thee word: for Herod will seek the young child to destroy him. When he arose, he took the young child and his mother by night, and departed into Egypt: And was there until the death of Herod: that it might be fulfilled which was spoken of the Lord by the prophet, saying, Out of Egypt have I called my son.

Then Herod, when he saw that he was mocked of the wise men, was exceeding wroth, and sent forth, and slew all the children that were in Bethlehem, and in all the coasts thereof, from two years old and under, according to the time which he had diligently inquired of the wise men. Then was fulfilled that which was spoken by Jeremy the prophet, saying, In Rama was there a voice heard, lamentation, and weeping, and great mourning, Rachel weeping for her children, and would not be comforted, because they are not.

But when Herod was dead, behold, an angel of the Lord appeareth in a dream to Joseph in Egypt, saying, Arise, and take the young child and his mother, and go into the land of Israel: for they are dead which sought the young child's life. And he arose, and took the young child and his mother, and

> came into the land of Israel. But when he heard that Archelaus did reign in Judaea in the room of his father Herod, he was afraid to go thither: notwithstanding, being warned of God in a dream, he turned aside into the parts of Galilee: And he came and dwelt in a city called Nazareth: that it might be fulfilled which was spoken by the prophets, He shall be called a Nazarene. (Matthew 2:13-23)

There is no special or esoteric symbolism in these accounts, but they prove that the ancient prophets did truly see into the future and spoke in very specific details about the life of Jesus as the Messiah.

> **And the child grew, and waxed strong in spirit, filled with wisdom: and the grace of God was upon him (Luke 2:40).**

Jesus was a perfect siddha-purusha, one with the infinite Absolute. What really is described here is the emergence of his divinity. In *The Unknown Lives of Jesus and Mary* you can read a great deal about his childhood and the revelation of his omnipotence and omniscience. He *was* the grace of God in the world.

Jesus in the Temple

Now his parents went to Jerusalem every year at the feast of the passover. And when he was twelve years old, they went up to Jerusalem after the custom of the feast. And when they had fulfilled the days, as they returned, the child Jesus tarried behind in Jerusalem; and Joseph and his mother knew not of it. But they, supposing him to have been in the company, went a day's journey; and they sought him among their kinsfolk and acquaintance. And when they found him not, they turned back again to Jerusalem, seeking him.

And it came to pass, that after three days they found him in the temple, sitting in the midst of the doctors, both hearing them, and asking them questions. And all that heard him were astonished at his understanding and answers.

And when they saw him, they were amazed: and his mother said unto him, Son, why hast thou thus dealt with us? behold, thy father and I have sought thee sorrowing. And he said unto them, How is it that ye sought me? wist ye not that I must be about my Father's business? And they understood not the saying which he spake unto them. And he went down with them, and came to Nazareth, and was subject unto them: but his mother kept all these sayings in her heart.

And Jesus increased in wisdom and stature, and in favour with God and man (Luke 2:41-52).

When Christianity was adopted as the state religion of the empire, the Gospels were edited to conform to the theology preferred by the ruling powers. Certain historical facts were also altered. For example, Anna Catharine Emmerich saw in her visions that until the last week of his life Jesus never went to Jerusalem, but only to the tabernacle of the Essenes on Mount Carmel. This is supported by the verse in Saint Matthew's Gospel: "And Jesus went out, and departed from the temple: and his disciples came to him for to shew him the buildings of the temple" (Matthew 24:1). If he had gone to the Passover in Jerusalem throughout his childhood, Jesus would not need to be shown the buildings of the temple. So if we accept the assertions of Anna Catharine Emmerich (which I do), this incident really took place on Mount Carmel where the Essenes worshipped in the tabernacle that was made according to the instructions given to Moses.

Contact had been kept with the wise men–the rishis of India who had come to find Jesus after his birth–and Jesus was preparing to depart on his journey to India where he would be living with them and traveling in India for the next eighteen years. He wanted to make it very clear to the Essene community that the Essene teachers had nothing to teach him–just the opposite: he could teach them. So this incident took place in which it was demonstrated that the Essene masters were far behind Jesus in his understanding and knowledge.

When the Virgin Mary reproached him for not telling them he would be remaining for a while longer on Mount Carmel, he asked how it was that they did not know his purpose. So he must have at least hinted about it before they went there. Furthermore, the "Father's business" was obviously his proving of the inadequacy of the Essene teachings and his subsequent journey to India and the years he would spend there. In my opinion anyone who wants to "be about the Father's business" should follow Jesus' example and seek out and learn the same wisdom which he learned from the sages of India. As I mentioned before, a priest of the Saint Thomas Christian Church told me over thirty years ago: "You cannot understand the teachings of of Jesus if you do not know the scriptures of India."

Jesus left for India when he was thirteen, so when he got back to Nazareth he made the preparations, including finding a trade caravan to

India in which he could travel. For it was in India that "Jesus increased in wisdom and stature, and in favour with God and man."

Earlier I told you the sad fact that all my yogi friends eventually fell by the wayside and left the yoga path. They all had one thing in common: they never fully adopted and followed Sanatana Dharma–Hinduism–and identified with it in their daily life. One time after I had spoken at the Hollywood Vendanta Society, in the informal satsang in the bookstore building that followed, I was introduced to a very impressive young woman. "Sing your song for Swamiji," said one of the people there. So she sang for me a song she had composed: "Jesus Made Me A Hindu." She was right.

The Appearance and Teaching of John the Bapstist

Now in the fifteenth year of the reign of Tiberius Caesar, Pontius Pilate being governor of Judaea, and Herod being tetrarch of Galilee, and his brother Philip tetrarch of Ituraea and of the region of Trachonitis, and Lysanias the tetrarch of Abilene, Annas and Caiaphas being the high priests, the word of God came unto John the son of Zacharias in the wilderness. And he came into all the country about Jordan, preaching the baptism of repentance for the remission of sins (Luke 3:2-3).

And saying, Repent ye: for the kingdom of heaven is at hand. For this is he that was spoken of by the prophet Esaias, saying, The voice of one crying in the wilderness, Prepare ye the way of the Lord, make his paths straight (Matt. 3:2-3).

Saint John the Baptist specifically represents the aspiring will, the call to Christhood: the awakening and stirring of the consciousness to reach out for the Christ, not as an external savior, but as an inner state of salvation. The very arising of that state is an announcing of the advent of Christ, both as a potential and as an actuality. For this reason Saint John is also called the Forerunner of Christ.

In the first chapter of Saint Luke's Gospel we see that Saint John, like the Virgin Mary, was supernaturally conceived, the idea being that even the forerunners and foreparents of Christ are supernatural in character, that natural things cannot lead to the supernatural, to the consciousness of Spirit. When the forerunners arise in us, then the Christ is not far behind. The supernatural life, manifesting as spiritual aspiration and the application of spiritual will, must begin before the appearance of Christ.

When Saint John was a very small child an angel appeared to him and led him out into the wilderness and showed him a cave in which he should spend much of his time doing spiritual discipline–meditation. And he did so. If we, too, would have the word of God come to us, we must be dwelling in the inner wilderness, having our attention all within and caring nothing for the clutter and clatter around us in the deceptive world which is not only worthless but harmful to our spirit-souls.

After John was led into the desert by an angel, he likewise took Jesus into the desert and instructed him in spiritual practice, and they spent much time together in the desert. Therefore John was the first spiritual teacher of Jesus. Together they prepared themselves for the fulfillment of their destinies. We should follow their examples.

Israel was a very small country populated by people very closely knit by their spiritual heritage. And the expectation of the Messiah had for generations caused everyone to look avidly for his coming. Every year at Passover time in Jerusalem a crop of Messiah-claimants would appear and eventually disappear, coming to nothing. But this in no way diminished the hopeful eagerness of the people to behold the Lord's Anointed. Neither Jesus nor John sprang up overnight like mushrooms in the popular view. Over thirty years reports of these two had persisted. The remarkable accounts of them found in *The Unknown Lives of Jesus and Mary* were overwhelming in their implications that one of these two was surely the Messiah and the other his Forerunner, as prophesied.

Baptist means Immerser, for the awakening of the spirit and the putting forth of the will is that which immerses the material in the spiritual, eventually transmuting it into spirit. To be baptized/immersed is to have become spirit-oriented in thought, word, and deed. This orientation is produced by immersion in the Jordan River of meditation, for the chief characteristic of spiritual awakening is the practice of meditation. It is this immersion that washes away sins: neutralizes the negative karmas and habit patterns of our past and present lives. It is not enough to merely aspire. Everything in our life, inner and outer, must be baptized (purified) through the practice of meditation. It is through meditation that every bit of us is Christed.

John the Baptist came preaching "in the wilderness of Judaea." This is because Jerusalem was the spiritual heart of Israel, and Judaea was the district surrounding it. This indicates that the awakening and functioning of the spiritual will can only take place when we are in the territory of the spirit by our thoughts, words, and deeds.

But Saint John does not preach in the crowded city of Jerusalem nor in the towns of Judaea, but in the wilderness, the solitary uninhabited places. What is indicated here is that no matter how holy the crowd may be, the true awakening of spirit cannot be found there. Many of us fill our lives with holy paraphernalia, material and immaterial, but have no interest in the direct experience of God. Some people's hearts and lives are crammed with holy things, but the Holy God is absent. For true spiritual life we must leave all things behind and be alone with God in meditation. Then the divine message can come to us. In daily meditation we must lay aside all material and objective consciousness and seek baptism in the spirit.

The word *eremos*, translated "wilderness," means a place that is solitary and empty in the sense that there is simply nothing there of humanity or its civilization. So it means that our interior life must be empty of all the clamor of this world, including our own ego and the chatter of our minds. In meditation our minds must be divested of all things. Like the Psalmist we must be able to say: "I am like a pelican of the wilderness: I am like an owl of the desert. I watch, and am as a sparrow alone upon the house top" (Psalms 102:6-7). That wilderness is found deep within, in the silence accessed by meditation. Only in the heart cleared of earthly debris can that voice be heard. Buddha dwelt away from the busyness of towns in the solitude of the forests, and those who desired his wisdom had to seek him out there. The Samaritan woman did not meet Jesus in the town where she lived, but outside the town at the well, which symbolized the need to draw the water of life from the inner depths (John 4:5-42). Saint Paul points out in the thirteenth chapter of Hebrews that Jesus went "outside the gate" to open the path of redemption for us, and concludes by exhorting us to "go forth therefore unto him" as well. Of course the going forth is really a going within.

"The wilderness" also means the undiscovered parts of our being, those areas that we must explore and claim for our own if we would be real masters of the spiritual life. The subconscious and the superconscious must be entered into and made conscious, present to our awareness. Meditation alone can do this. In the wilderness, in the high places of solitude and silence, is the voice of the spirit really heard. Jesus still says to his disciples: "Come ye yourselves apart into a desert place" (Mark 6:31).

> **As it is written in the book of the words of Esaias the prophet, saying, The voice of one crying in the wilderness, Prepare ye the way of the Lord, make his paths straight. Every valley shall be filled, and every mountain and hill shall be brought low; and the crooked shall be made straight, and the rough ways shall be made smooth; and all flesh shall see the salvation of God (Luke 3:4-6).**

Those who were in the uninhabited region of Judaea heard this message: "Repent ye: for the kingdom of heaven is at hand." Every word of this is significant, so let us analyze them.

"Repent" is a very poor translation of the Greek word *metanoeo*. It is a fusion of two words, *meta,* which means a complete change, a total turning around, and *noieo*, which means perception and understanding, the state of consciousness. So *metanoeo* really means a complete turning around, a revolution, of consciousness. Saint John was exhorting people to a drastic change of mind and will, a complete turnabout from their usual material orientation to the awareness of spirit and spiritual values and laws. This has nothing to do with being sorry for and bewailing our sinfulness. There is no connotation at all of negative emotionality or self-condemnation. Rather, it means an intelligent and clear-sighted awareness that something is not right, and the desire to change the status, to reverse the current of our lives and minds.

The Prodigal Son (Luke 15:11-24) is a perfect example of what is meant by repentance. He asked his father for his inheritance and went to a foreign land where he wasted it all in foolish living and was reduced to such poverty that he became a worker with pigs and wanted to eat their swill, but being a human could not. Then, Jesus says, "he came to himself" and remembered his home and his father. So he determined to return home, which he did, and he was received with great love and rejoicing. What a positive picture Jesus gives us, wanting to inspire us with confidence and hope. There is no fear or condemnation here, but rather assurance of God's bountiful love and mercy. These are the real teachings of Christ. The Prodigal may have wasted his inheritance, but he could not cancel his sonship. He still belonged at home with his father, and was no less his father's son than if he had never acted foolishly. It is important for us always to keep in mind that it is our nature to be perfect and with God. Sin and separation from God is not real, but an illusion which we must wake from and shake off.

The Prodigal did not wail and denounce himself. Rather, he "came to himself" and remembered who he really was and where his true home was. So he got up and went home, a reasonable action that few of us do. We need to take stock of our situation, see that it could be much better, and then go ahead and make it better. "Get up and go" is the primary requisite for successful spiritual life. Anything that does not produce the needed change is either a sham or so weak that it might just as well be.

In all my life I have bought only one thing from a "thrift" store: a juicer. It was cheap, and it should have been. Not only was it worn out, the store's "fixers" had switched the wiring so it ran backwards and would not juice a thing. We are like that. Our machinery has been wired wrong, and we run backwards instead of forwards according to the divine plan. But if we rewire ourselves and reverse our spiritual polarity everything will work just fine. (That was not the solution with my juicer. No simile is perfect!)

We need a change of mind that changes our consciousness and our life. We must not only change our mind, our consciousness and our whole perspective on life, we must change our entire mode of living, as well. This is not just recommended, this is necessary. Every aspect of our life must be looked at and diagnosed as to whether it promotes spiritual life or hinders or even destroys or prevents it. And that which goes against spiritual life must be changed or gotten rid of. Those are the facts.

We are so weary of "spiritual authorities" fussing at us and demanding that we conform to their ideas that we shy away from anyone telling us what we should or should not be doing. But we do need to tell ourselves what to do, and then act on it. Most religious people live in a totally delusive way, just like everybody else, the difference being that they engage in religious acts which make them feel good, uplifted, virtuous or whatnot, but produce no real change in them. This is true of those with a more metaphysical bent, too. It matters not how exalted or inspirational the words, it is our daily life that matters. In past centuries Europeans hardly ever bathed. Instead they just kept dousing themselves with perfume to cover up the awful smell of their filthy bodies and clothing. A lot of religion and philosophy is like that—just a cover.

However, the change of life Saint John is talking about is an ordering of our life so Divine Consciousness can manifest. It goes far beyond the naughty-or-nice morality of Santa Claus religion. What is needed is a way of life that repolarizes the consciousness, or assists in that repolarization. Acts and thoughts that further our spiritual perfection are good, and those that hinder or reverse our spiritual perfection are bad. It is just that simple.

In the childish mishmash that is commonly thought to be Christianity it is supposed that nothing more is needed than the following of "do" and "don't do" rules. Consequently many brag about how close they are to God just because of what they do or do not do. But this is only a veneer; it has no heart, so it is dead. What Jesus intended for his disciples was a total change of consciousness, for if the consciousness changes, the life changes; but if the life changes and the consciousness does not change, then nothing is accomplished. It simply means that for a certain period of time the distortions of consciousness are not allowed to manifest. But they will come out, either in overt actions or in mental wrinkles and glitches. If it does not come out, then it will in future lives, just as seeds thousands of years old found in Egyptian tombs have grown when planted.

"Whosoever is born of God doth not commit sin; for his seed remaineth in him: and he cannot sin, because he is born of God" (I John 3:9). To simply say "I no longer do that" matters but little. What does matter is the change of the mind which renders that action no longer possible for us. That state alone is true free will, the free will of God. Consciousness is not only the root of things: consciousness is everything. Therefore if we do not deal with consciousness we deal with nothing.

Religion should not be a simple rearrangement of mental furniture, but the repolarization, a complete turnabout, of consciousness. Otherwise, since we will be facing away from God, every step we take, however religious, will take us away from God. That is why religions have perpetrated so much evil and confusion in the world. They were facing the wrong way! The more their adherents tried to walk the path, the further they got from God, and they adjusted their teachings to fit and perpetuate their alienation. Eventually they began telling people that the alienation was right and good, and what God intended–just as long as they followed the religious authorities everything was just fine. But they were lying. They took the words of their original wisdom and degraded them into nothing. They took faith and degraded it to superstition. As a result, the more religious many people are, the farther they get from God, because they pursue the wrong direction.

The consciousness must be changed and turned around utterly, and then each step we take will lead us toward God. Even the practice of a divinely-established religion is of little value if the consciousness is not turned inward through meditation, for that is the true way of repentance, the inner path which leads to God.

We must also note that Saint John tells us to turn ourselves around, not to be turned around by anyone else, not even by God. Our self-effort is needed to develop the will that is required for success in spiritual life. How will we manage all this? Again: by meditation, for meditation is the surest changer of the mind and the conduct. And why should we do all this? "For the kingdom of heaven is at hand." Right here and now. As Buddha said: "Turn around, and lo! the other shore."

Basileia Ouranos: the Kingdom of Heaven. *Basileia* means both the active ruling of a king and the realm in which he rules. *Ouranos* is the sky, the symbol of the infinite unconditioned all-pervading Consciousness that is God. Thus the Kingdom of Heaven is the active manifestation of God's Presence. It is not an isolated point in time or space, but Divine Infinity Itself. The Kingdom of Heaven is God. Our destiny, if we believe Saint John and Jesus rather than the "Christian" nay-sayers, is to live consciously in God. "The saints of the most High shall take the kingdom, and possess the kingdom for ever, even for ever and ever" (Daniel 7:18). To possess the Kingdom is to possess God. Truly, "Eye hath not seen, nor ear heard, neither have entered into the heart of man, the things which God hath prepared for them that love him" (I Corinthians 2:9). For it is *Himself* that He intends to make our "exceeding great reward" (Genesis 15:1).

And this Kingdom "is at hand." Again, see how positive and encouraging is the message. The Kingdom of God is not some far away place that must be won by perilous journey and grinding endeavor. *It is near and soon to appear to us.* We need only keep watching (Mark 13:37) through meditation.

Let us consider a bit more about "heaven." It is a basic fact of cosmic existence that anything which has a beginning must eventually come to an end. The Kingdom of Heaven, then, is the beginningless and endless Being of God himself. At the same time, there are many levels of existence. As Jesus said: "In my Father's house are many mansions" (John 14:2). There are many worlds, higher and lower, astral and causal, to which we can go after death. The astral worlds are indescribably beautiful and impart great enjoyment. The causal worlds are worlds of wisdom, and even more appealing to those that have evolved intellectually. But we must not remain in any of them, because there was a time when they did not exist, and there is coming a time known as the Mahapralaya (Great Withdrawal) when they will cease to exist until the next creation cycle. We have to be like the dove of Noah: "He sent forth a dove from him, to see if the waters were abated from off the face of the ground; but the dove found no rest for the sole of her foot, and she returned unto him into the ark, for the waters were on the face of the whole earth: then he put forth his hand, and took her, and pulled her in unto him into the ark" (Genesis 8:8-9). We can come to rest only in the depths of God. Everything else passes away.

One Pentecost I was visiting the Coptic monastery outside Frankfort, Germany. In his sermon the abbot, Father Matthew, explained to the people that they were greatly mistaken if they planned to go to heaven forever. "God has something much better than that," he told them. "He intends for us to enter into the great Light of God, into Himself." His words were certainly true, and prove that in Egypt some of the monastics have kept the true, original perspective of Jesus' teachings.

We came from that Light; we will go back to that Light; and we never really were outside of it. Where would we go to get outside of God? But that is our illusory experience, brought about by our looking outward instead of inward. The moment the illusion is removed from our mind we will discover we have always been in the Kingdom. That is why David sang: "When I awake, I am still with thee" (Psalms 139:18). And: "I will behold thy face in righteousness: I shall be satisfied, when I awake, with thy likeness" (Psalms 17:15). We need only awaken in God. It is very meaningful that David does not say that when he awakens "I *shall* be with Thee," but: "I *am* with Thee." It is a matter of eternal nature. No matter how long we may sleep in delusion, God is always with us, as we shall find when we awake.

The kingdom of God is not even a billionth of a hair's breadth from us. So it is not to be sought in the ordinary sense, as we would look for an external object like Ponce de Leon trying to find the fountain of youth, but it is to be *realized*, to be experienced. The finding, the discovering is not from a movement outside ourselves, but rather from an interior recognition and experience.

All true religious and spiritual life consists of that inner knowing, for "he is not far from every one of us: for in him we live, and move, and have our being" (Acts 17:27). This is why right meditation can immediately begin this awakening process, can right away give us some experience of the pure consciousness that is the Kingdom. We do indeed need a great deal of that experience, but right meditation does not lead up to it, it *begins* with it and ends with it, as it would have to, given the nature of both ourselves and God. This is a very important point, an essential understanding, for it reveals that most spiritual endeavors, including many forms of meditation, are utterly beside the point and incapable of ever leading to and revealing the Kingdom. They may produce experiences that fill volumes and lifetimes, but they cannot by their very nature reveal the Divine.

"For this is he that was spoken of by the prophet Esaias, saying, The voice of one crying in the wilderness, Prepare ye the way of the Lord, make his paths straight" (Matthew 3:3). There is meaning in this: Within us are the seeds of everything that shall come to be, the seeds of our ultimate destiny. At the very beginning the end is already present in potential form. We truly are embryonic gods. "Beloved, now are we the sons of God, and it doth not yet appear what we shall be: but we know that, when he shall appear, we shall be like him; for we shall see him as he is" (I John 3:2). This potential "Christ in you, the hope of glory" (Colossians 1:27) is what God, his saints and his angels see in us. And that is why they love us.

We, too, know the whole story even before it begins, for we are the ones that have determined it and written the script, not God. We are in no way bits of psychic driftwood being heaved up and blown about by the ocean and winds of God's capricious "providence." We have set our destiny long ago, and now we are busy fulfilling it. We may botch our lines in the many acts of the drama that is our unfolding evolution, but they are still *our* lines, no one else's. In one sense we are fully dependent on God, and in another sense we are not. People love to create a false dependency on their vague and erroneous idea of God and refuse to take charge of their lives and assume responsibility for themselves. However, that, too, is written into the script and it is none of our business to try and correct them, unless we wrote that into *our* script!

Those who are absorbed in the "reality" of external phenomena think that the prophecies of Jesus by various prophets are proofs of his divinity and his messiahship. They are no such thing: they are something much more. They are demonstrations of the truth I have just been outlining. Just as Jesus was "the Lamb slain from the foundation of the world" (Revelation 13:8), we, too, have eternal destinies, "things which have been kept secret from the foundation of the world" (Matthew 13:35), that we are working out right now. The kingdom of God is eternally destined for us, for "then shall the King say unto them on his right hand, Come, ye blessed of my

Father, inherit the kingdom prepared for you from the foundation of the world" (Matthew 25:34).

The love of God for us is also eternal, "For thou lovedst me before the foundation of the world" (John 17:24). "According as he hath chosen us in him before the foundation of the world, that we should be holy and without blame before him in love" (Ephesians 1:4).

Although we experience our life as unfolding bit by bit through innumerable ages and incarnations, "the works were finished from the foundation of the world" (Hebrews 4:3), at least in seed form, as it was with Jesus "Who verily was foreordained before the foundation of the world, but was manifest in these last times for you" (I Peter 1:20).

Moses spoke in a prayer of "Thy book which Thou hast written" (Exodus 32:32), for ultimately all things are the act of God, even though for our evolution we need to act seemingly on our own to develop our potentially divine will. As David sang: "Thou tellest my wanderings: …are they not in thy book?" (Psalms 56:8). And even more to the point: "Thine eyes did see my substance, yet being unperfect; and in thy book all my members were written, which in continuance were fashioned, when as yet there was none of them" (Psalms 139:16). God is the sole power behind all power. Consequently our determination of our destiny is his determination as well, making us all his "fellow labourers, whose names are in the book of life" (Philippians 4:3). In our superconscious minds we all know our future, and hints of it often filter down into our earthly consciousness. For example, a friend of one of my university professors had an obsessive hatred of taxis, and waged a one-woman campaign for years to ban them from New York City, an absurd and impossible goal. How did she die? By being run over by a taxi. My paternal grandmother held no superstitions, but freely admitted that she disliked Friday, and would never begin anything on that day. Even though she herself thought it was silly, she had a strong aversion to Friday the thirteenth. Will you be surprised when I tell you that she died on a Friday, the thirteenth of that month? What we think are baseless fears are often well based on our inner mind.

We all know our future because it is our creation. This is important to realize, because we alone can change our direction if we wish to. We need not bother God about it. Yet, if we empower our wills through drawing near to God by means of meditation, we will be assured of success. So we both "need" God and do not need him. Reality is always contradictory.

The awakening of spiritual will through meditation is the forerunner of Christ, for its purpose and effect is to "prepare the way of the Lord" and "make his paths straight." According to the prophet Isaiah when this is done, "Every valley shall be filled, and every mountain and hill shall be brought low; and the crooked shall be made straight, and the rough ways shall be made smooth; and all flesh shall see the salvation of God" (Luke 3:4-6). Meditation enters into the wilderness of our heart and mind, especially, and "works the works" of Christ in us. ("I must work the works of him that sent me." John 9:4) That is, what is lacking in us is supplied, and what is superfluous and distracting is removed. Unity and homogeneity will be established inwardly, and all inner kinks and obstacles will be removed so the Way of Christ may be lived as easefully as possible. When this occurs, not only the inner but the outer "flesh" shall be transmuted, and "all flesh shall see the salvation of God." This is why the saints shine with spiritual light and often are incorrupt after death.

It will be informative for us to consider the meanings of the various terms used in Saint Matthew's and Saint Luke's quotations of Isaiah, as they reveal the qualities that should be found in both our attitude toward spiritual life and our meditation

1) Crying. This word (in Greek: *boao*) means to shout for help or call out in a tumultuous way. The idea conveyed is that our spiritual life must be pursued with a sense of urgency and with great intensity (but *not* tension). "Lord, I cry unto thee: make haste unto me; give ear unto my voice, when I cry unto thee" (Psalms 141:1).

2) Prepare. This is a very interesting word: *etoimazo*. It means to prepare (make ready), provide what is needed as preparation, to make fit (capable) or adjusted, and to make something ready to hand. This tells us a lot. First, it does no good to sit around and aspire in an abstract manner, to think and even pray without putting forth our will and *doing* what is needed. Second: we need a lot of *change*. And that is accomplished by us, no one else. Third, we need to gain what we presently do not have. That is, we

must enlarge the dimensions of our life and consciousness and gain the evolution needed to successfully seek God. Fourth, we have to straighten ourselves up and make ourselves fit for and capable of divine experience. Fifth, we must be conformed to the divine image as Saint Paul counsels: "Be ye transformed by the renewing [renovation] of your mind" (Romans 12:2). And sixth, the consciousness of Spirit must always be right at hand, never far from our awareness. Like David we must say: "I have set the Lord always before me: because he is at my right hand, I shall not be moved" (Psalms 16:8). Meditation enables us to do all this.

3) Way (*odos*). Just as there is a path by which we go to God, there is a path by which God comes to us. And since the kingdom of God is within (Luke 17:21), both of these are *inner* paths, and ultimately are the same path. And that path is revealed and travelled in meditation. *Odos* means a definite route, not just a spontaneous or haphazard wandering, as spiritual life is usually thought to be. Instead, the Way is methodical and precise. I will never forget the intense relief I felt when, after years of struggle and searching without any real direction, I learned that the Way was knowable and practicable, because it was exact and methodical, that yoga meditation was the simple and sure key to it all. *Odos* also means a mode of travel, a means to reach the goal. Again: meditation is the thing, the journey to liberated consciousness.

4) Lord (*kurios*). Kurios means one who is both supreme in authority and in actual power, in the sense of rulership. In the context of the quotation from Isaiah, this means the absolute necessity for us to realize that God is the center of the whole matter, that the divine perspective must be the deciding factor in every phase of our life. That is why Saint John the Baptist said of Jesus: "He must increase, but I must decrease" (John 3:30).

5) Paths (*tribos*). There are channels by which God comes to us, such as the company of other seekers, the study of holy scriptures and the writings of saints, devotional music and worship. The most effective channel, of course, is meditation. But let us look a little more at this word, *tribos*, because it has an interesting and practical implication. One of its meanings is a track that has been worn deep, a groove. The message is that we must cut grooves in our spiritual bodies by repeated and prolonged practice, that

the advent of Divine Consciousness is not just for the asking, nor is it a quick matter, either. There are stone stairs in old monasteries that have have been worn down over the centuries to almost half their original thickness by the continual passing of the monks up and down them as they went to their spiritual exercises and duties. That is how our minds should be.

6) Straight (*euthus*). Although translated as "straight," the word actually means *level*. In other words, there should be no unevenness, no ups and downs, but all should be smooth and uniform. This is a symbol of the equanimity needed in spiritual life. Although we hear from all sides that it is normal for our spiritual life to move in cycles, to have upswings and downswings, mountaintops and valleys, it simply is not true, not if the seeker is meditating correctly according to the correct method. (For this, see *Soham Yoga: the Yoga of the Self*.) One of the first symptoms of right meditation is the cessation of such fluctuations. One's karma may move in cycles, making the external life more and less turbulent, but the yogi does not experience the inner roller-coaster effect that is usual for the non-yogi. This cannot be emphasized enough. The path of God is a level path. The Bhagavad Gita spends quite a bit of time insisting that the person on the right spiritual path is even-minded. False meditation and false religion do indeed produce a manic-depressive spiritual state, but not the Way of Christ. That Way is also level because the worthy seeker constantly and steadily maintains his spiritual practice.

Another meaning of *euthus* is "true" in the sense used in architecture. That is, a wall is "true" when it is perfectly perpendicular, with no deviation from straight up and down. An angle is "true" when it is exactly of the prescribed degrees. A stone is "true" when it is perfectly square in all its angles. Again we see the necessity for our path to conform totally to the measurements of God, not to our arithmetic of confusion and delusion.

Also, the path is straightforward, none of the meanderings or ambiguities which must result when we try to fudge and not be true in relation to God and spiritual realities. Therefore Jesus said: "Let your communication be, Yea, yea; Nay, nay: for whatsoever is more than these cometh of evil" (Matthew 5:37). And Saint James affirmed that, saying: "Let your yea be yea; and your nay, nay; lest ye fall into condemnation" (James 5:12). Our reaction/response to anything must be either Yes or No. Not Maybe or Sometimes. Every thing must be either In or Out of our lives and thinking.

Euthus also implies a *direct* path, one that has no twistings, turnings, backtrackings, or delayings. The path to God is not a roundabout matter, but moves straight toward God. It may take a while to travel it, but there is no wasting of time going over the same ground twice.

7) Every (*pas*). Now the prophet is going to talk about symbolic valleys, mountains, and hills that we need to deal with. And we must work with *every single one* of them. That is the idea of this word. *Pas* also means "the whole thing." Since we are striving to move from the fragmentation of multiplicity into the perfection of unity, we must be truly wholistic in our spiritual life. All fronts should be covered. This alone is mastery. All of us goes to God, or nothing of us goes.

8) Valley (*pharagx*). *Pharagx* is not the gentle pretty valley we usually think of. Actually a better translation would be "gap" or "chasm," in other words a break in the terrain, a discontinuity. A little introspection reveals that we have a lot of interior breaks. No wonder we are bundles of spiritual static sometimes. Far from being whole, we are really all broken up with gaps that need to be filled.

9) Filled (*pleroo*). *Pleroo* means to fill up so completely that everything becomes level all around. Not a dent or dimple remains. We need to fill ourselves with God-consciousness, with the direct perception of our spiritual nature. Then we will be made whole. Interestingly, the word also has the connotation of making something complete and fulfilled. We must be able to say to God as did Jesus: "I have glorified thee on the earth: I have finished the work which thou gavest me to do" (John 17:4). And that work is our Christing, our union with God.

10) *Mountain* (*oros*). This word means something that has been lifted up from the level, or has lifted itself up. Isaiah uses it to mean something that is unnecessary or superfluous, something that has been deliberately, and foolishly, intruded into our minds and hearts. There are a lot of those! Just as the chasms need to be filled, so the mountains need to be removed, completely obliterated from our inner landscape. We have a great deal of excess baggage to get rid of on our pilgrimage back home to God.

11) Hill (*bounos*). We cannot help but face the truth that the mountains we have raised up all over have got to go, but how inclined we are to let the little hills remain? "It is such a little thing," we protest. Yet it is "the little foxes, that spoil the vines" (Song of Solomon 2:15). With this in mind Jesus stated that "he that is faithful in that which is least is faithful also in much: and he that is unjust in the least is unjust also in much" (Luke 16:10). The little things do matter, in spiritual life just as much as they do in art, architecture, mathematical calculations, medicine and everything else that is vital to us. "Whosoever therefore shall break one of these least commandments, and shall teach men so, he shall be called the least in the kingdom of heaven: but whosoever shall do and teach them, the same shall be called great in the kingdom of heaven" (Matthew 5:19).

12) Brought low (*tapeinoo*). We have really covered this already. Part of the idea of this whole clause is that we overemphasize and underemphasize, overvalue and undervalue, put too much attention on some things and too little attention on others, thus putting ourselves in an unbalanced and confused state. Clear-sightedness and correct evaluation is needed.

13) Crooked (*skolios*). This word has two basic meanings: warped and crooked. Something which is "out of true" as already discussed is warped. One the best examples is that of a warped mirror such as is found in carnival fun houses. Because of the warping it gives a distorted, and therefore erroneous, reflection or impression. Yet, if it is returned to its original correct status the impression will be accurate. Our minds, especially, are very much like mirrors, and easily get out of true. Putting them back to rights is not so easy, but it can be done by meditation. To be crooked is to be out of phase, out of sync with our divine nature and the divine plan for that nature's elevation to divinity.

The *making* of the crooked straight and the rough smooth is expressed through the verb *eis*, which carries with it the idea of a perpetual process.

We should keep in mind the words of Christina Rossetti's poem "Up-Hill":

Does the road wind up-hill all the way?
  Yes, to the very end.
Will the day's journey take the whole long day?
  From morn to night, my friend.

We never stop until we are done. The auctioneer's expression: "Going... going... gone!" is quite apropos.

14) Rough (*trachus*) means both rough in the usual sense and also rocky, the idea being that alien elements are mixed into the ground, making it uneven. It also means land made jagged by rents or small chasms. All unevenness in the sense of inconsistency must be eliminated for us. So also must any alien elements, particularly those that come pushing up from the subconscious just as rocks are pushed up from far beneath onto the surface of the ground. *Trachus* also means rocky in contrast to soft and fertile earth in which the divine seed can sprout and bring forth the fruit of spiritual realization.

15) Smooth (*leios*) means level, and we have already covered the symbolism of that.

16) The flesh (*sarx*) that shall see the salvation of God is our humanity itself, that does indeed at the moment include the physical body. The totality of our being participates in the process of salvation, it is not a matter of the abstract spirit alone. Body, mind and spirit must work together in harmony for our liberation. This is why discipline and purification must take place on all these three levels. The bodies of many saints have not decayed after death because in life they became so spiritualized that they partook to some degree in the immortality of the spirit. Some great ones have even dissolved their bodies into light, as in the case of Saint John the Apostle and Saint Andrew of Constantinople. (In the Taoist tradition this "transmogrification" is the sign of perfect liberation.) However interesting and significant such phenomena may be, the idea we must keep concentrated on is the need for us to "work out our salvation" (Philippians 2:12) on all levels of our existence simultaneously.

17) Salvation (*soterion*) has several meanings, all significant for us: defence, deliverance, and health. First we arm ourselves against all those

things that are inimical to our ascent to higher consciousness. Purification, ascetic discipline and mastery of the straying mind are essentials of salvation. When we are perfectly defended by our own efforts and not those of any external source, we shall then rise above the enemies of the spirit and be delivered from them. But that is only a negative state: to be rid of the bad is not the same as attaining the good. We must continue on in our quest and become healed, restored to the glory which we had with God before ever the world was (John 17:5), before ever we entered into relative existence. But we do not simply return to Square One. Having developed the ability for greater and greater consciousness as we ascended the ladder of spiritual evolution, we return to God as gods: participants in the divine Omnipotence, Omniscience, and Omnipresence.

18) God (*theos*) is our goal, for it is union with God that is salvation. *Theos* basically means the Infinite. Infinite Consciousness is our goal; attaining it is our salvation.

How much is contained in that short quotation from Isaiah!

We must be our own John the Baptizer. By the power of our illumined will, which he symbolizes, we must systematically go through our whole life and baptize every bit of it, immersing it in the Water of Life (Revelation 22:1), the Consciousness of God. If there is something in our life that cannot be baptized because of its irrevocably negative or foolish nature, we must eliminate it completely. The folly and weakness of most religion is its insistence that someone other than ourselves should do this. So interference and coercion become the main activities of those religions. (At least they have an ideal, even if they go about it in a mistaken way. The "be comfortable and feel good" religions are the real "opium of the people.") It must all be done by us.

Every step of the path must be walked by us, every step being an act of conscious will and intention. If others attempt to do it for us we will just become victims, hypocrites or slaves. Those who have not evolved to the point where they have the good spiritual sense to see the need for the baptizing, and enough desire for the goal to be motivated to do it, should then occupy themselves with something else. Just as the fruit must ripen on the tree, so must each individual ripen inwardly to the point where the upward path is the only reasonable path to take. Jesus said: "My yoke is easy, and my burden is light" (Matthew 11:30). Yes, a yoke is very light to an ox since it is so strong, but it will break the back of a dog. So the matter of ease and lightness depends completely on our level of development.

A time comes when no denial, no discipline, no effort is too much for the questing soul. Saint Paul tells us that Jesus, "for *the joy* that was set before him endured the cross, despising the shame, and is set down at the right hand of the throne of God" (Hebrews 12:2). The joy, the infinite bliss of God, made even the cross seem like a small thing to endure. When we see things as Christ did (and we shall in time), then nothing can deter us from pressing on and winning the heavenly prize. "I press toward the mark for the prize of the high calling of God in Christ Jesus" (Philippians 3:14). "To him that overcometh will I grant to sit with me in my throne, even as I also overcame, and am set down with my Father in his throne" (Revelation 3:21).

I would like to pause here and give some attention to the subject of what constitutes a worthy teacher and a worthy teaching. Kenneth Wuest made an expanded translation of the New Testament in which he put a lot of the literal meanings of the Greek words, even if it came out sounding strange and overloaded. His translation of Matthew 3:1 is: "Now, in those days there makes his public appearance John the Baptizer, making a public proclamation with that formality, gravity, and authority which must be listened to and obeyed."

Formality, gravity and authority–these are the qualities to be found in the manner of those who are authentic spiritual messengers or teachers, as well as in their teaching *and* in those who respond to that teaching. These qualities are so important that it is worthwhile to stop and consider them well.

Formality. Formality does not mean stiffness, stuffiness, or snobbishness, but orderliness, decorum, and propriety.

A teacher worth hearing is clear in his thinking and his expression, he is methodical in presentation and communicates his ideas easily and clearly to his hearers, to whom he shows respect (this, too, is implied by formality) and a belief in their spiritual capacity.

A good teacher believes in his students as much as he believes in his teachings. Consequently he does not hesitate to tell them the full truth and the highest truth. He assumes they can handle the truth, which may contradict all they ever heard before or may go against the grain of their lower natures. He never treats them as though they are mere children or as mentally or morally deficient. This being so, he does not hesitate to challenge them and set before them the highest ideals. They may choose to not follow what he presents, but he knows they can understand and act if they will to do so.

The viable teacher never plays Daddy or Mommy, though this is very popular, since so many people are seeking a substitute for unsatisfactory parents.

And his conduct is always ethical towards his students, based on his respect for them and his own self-respect. He never lies to them or seeks to please them by being less than what he should be or teaching on a lesser level than he should. He is not pompous or bombastic, but he is definitely dignified and straightforward, even when friendly and casual. All these qualities are seen in the teachings he gives, as well as in the qualities of those who can truly "hear" them and follow them. These are not just high ideals; I have met teachers who possessed all these qualities, even though a far greater number did not have even one of them.

Gravity. Heavy, ponderous, turgid, pompous, conceited, severe, humorless, or grim–these are *not* what the word means in the Gospel. What is indicated is that a worthy teacher is serious, and he takes his teaching and his students very seriously because he values them. He does not see his hearers as only so many chair-fillers or sources of income or notoriety. He believes in them as completely as he believes in what he has to teach them. On the other hand he never adopts a meddling or Mother Hen attitude toward them. He is earnest in his attempt to open higher realms of truth and life to them, but he never attempts coercion or cajoling. The Carrot and the Stick of religion, promise of reward and threat of punishment, never come into his hand. He presents the truth in a no-nonsense, sober manner and leaves the rest to them. A true teacher is never shallow or offhand in his teaching; he takes every question put to him as worthy of his best answer. Believing in the spiritual dignity of his hearers he matches it in his teaching of them. He is reliable, but refuses to be relied upon, pointing his students back to their own capabilities and the need for self-reliance. He never hesitates to point out to them the consequences of negative thought and deed, however painful that may be to both him and them. He does not flatter anyone, nor does he accept flattery. He does not seek to please others, not does he wish others to please him. Gravity in this sense is also a characteristic of worthy teachings and worthy students. (For a perfect example of a true spiritual teacher, see *Light of Soham*, the life and teachings of Sri Gajanana Maharaj of Nashik.)

Authority. Authority in this Gospel passage has nothing to do with authoritarianism, domination, bullying, coercion, oppression, pretension, contemptuousness, or bluff, all of which are tools of the false teacher's trade, even if underhanded and not obvious (sometimes even seeming to be the opposite).

The trustworthy teacher is never condescending, nor does he wish to "master" those he teaches. Rather, he exhorts them to recover their own self-mastery that is innate in them. He cannot give it to them, nor does he pretend to or go along with their insistence that he do so, an insistence that is a marked trait of students of Eastern philosophy, and is a dominant trait in the East itself. Instead the teacher possesses an inner strength and assurance that he hopes to see developed in his students.

He has a clear idea of his purpose and his own capacity, including his lacks or weaknesses, which he never conceals from himself or his students. This is because he has positive confidence. One of the sterling traits of a teacher is the willingness to say "I do not know," or "I cannot." Worthy students recognize and respect that. However, he is definitely capable, and even adept in his field. Consequently he is eminently credible in the eyes of the discerning. And all this can be said of his teaching and his students.

Saint John's formality, gravity, and authority was that "which must be listened to and obeyed." This is not meant in the sense of an unchallengeable authoritarianism, but rather that it has the merit and value that morally demands our attention and our adoption. A worthy teacher may say: "You must do this" when he means that if someone is serious about something, certain things are mandatory. He is not issuing commands.

In *The Gnosis of the Ten Commandments* I have written that all of the commandments presuppose the prefacing words: "If you will gain eternal life…." If you do not want eternal life, then you need not bother with them. Here Saint John, being a worthy teacher, assumes he is speaking to qualified aspirants who are adult enough to know that everything has a price, that to attain the highest good they must pay the highest price, and will do so gladly even if it is difficult. Only those people "must" listen to and obey the principles learned from a good teacher.

Let us stop a moment and consider something that is very relevant to all the foregoing. Those without a clear understanding of Jesus' nature, mission or message like to insist that believing in or accepting Jesus as our Savior is necessary for salvation. To support this they quote: "Believe on the Lord Jesus Christ, and thou shalt be saved" (Acts 16:31). This seems to be following the teaching of Jesus, who said such things as: "He that believeth on me hath everlasting life" (John 6:47). "Whosoever believeth on me shall not abide in darkness" (John 12:46). "Whosoever liveth and believeth in me shall never die" (John 11:26). "This is the work of God, that ye believe on him whom he hath sent" (John 6:29). But we should look into that further.

The Greek word for "in," is *en*, but in each instance I have just quoted, Jesus uses the word *eis*, which means "into." (Saint John, writing in Greek, was very careful to use only *eis*, so Jesus' inner meaning would be conveyed, though Jesus, of course, spoke in Aramaic.) Therefore Jesus is not saying "believe *in* me," but "believe *into* me." He is urging us to merge our consciousness into his consciousness, which is not the limited consciousness of an individual, but the boundless Christ Consciousness.

First we unite our consciousness with Christ, the Divine Consciousness immanent in all creation, and then through That we shall be enabled to unite our consciousness with the transcendent Consciousness of God the Absolute, God the Father. The Christ Consciousness acts as the bridge by which we pass into God Consciousness. And this is what is really meant by the intercession and mediatorship of Christ: something far beyond the scope of exoteric, limited Christianity. "It is Christ who maketh intercession for us" (Romans 8:34). "Wherefore he is able also to save them to the uttermost that come unto God by him, seeing he ever liveth to make intercession for them" (Hebrews 7:25). "For there is one God, and one mediator between God and men" (I Timothy 2:5). To really understand all such declarations of the Gospels we must study and assimilate the vast wisdom to be found in Levi Dowling's *Aquarian Gospel of Jesus the Christ*. That remarkable book is like a pair of corrective glasses that makes what beforehand was blurred and chaotic into clear and precise vision. The same is true of Paramhansa Yogananda's commentary on the Gospels, *The Second Coming of Christ*.

We must become one with Jesus in Christ Consciousness; then we shall inherit the kingdom of God: the boundless Consciousness that is God himself. "Wherefore thou art no more a servant, but a son; and if a son, then an heir of God through Christ" (Galatians 4:7). "And if children, then heirs; heirs of God, and joint-heirs with Christ" (Romans 8:17).

Eis also has the connotation of moving toward that into which we shall eventually enter. So we must begin believing *toward* God right now by orienting our consciousness, will and aspiration toward the Supreme. It also means a *continual* movement toward the goal. And lastly, it means that which is actually inside or within something. So our faith must be manifesting within the Being of God. Just sitting outside God saying we believe in him means nothing. We must be inside that Light for our faith to be of any effect.

Jesus is exhorting us to meditate, for it is only through meditation that we enter into the Consciousness we seek. Then we shall no longer believe, but *know*.

The Gospel is presenting to us the picture of a successful aspirant, one who baptizes his whole life in spiritual consciousness. Let us not forget how many, very many, people Saint John baptized before Christ came to be baptized by him. The symbolization here is that we must baptize a multitude of our human faculties and traits before our inner Christ stands before us. Saint John baptized for years before baptizing Jesus. It takes time; we must make no mistake about it. Our Christhood cannot be revealed until we have baptized all that is at hand, until we have prepared the Way of the Lord by our own efforts.

People wonder why after a short time of spiritual practice they do not get enlightenment. The answer is that divine experience is not possible until all of our humanity–all the elements that comprise our human nature–has been baptized and cleansed through meditation and disciplinary purification. By meditation we baptize everything in the inner consciousness. We must all be Saint John before we can become Christ.

The coming of Christ occurs in stages like the steps in a stair or the rungs of a ladder. That is why Jesus in his first teachings would say: "the time is fulfilled, and the kingdom of God is at hand" (Mark 1:15). Saint Paul spoke of the advent of Christ "when the fulness of the time was come" (Galatians 4:4). A lot has to happen within and without us when we seek God, "that in the dispensation of the fulness of times he might gather together in one all things in Christ, both which are in heaven, and which are on earth; even in him" (Ephesians 1:10). It is this state of perfect unity that makes our Christhood possible.

Human life unfolds in stages, and so does the Christ Life. After physical conception, much takes place in those nine months before birth. And then after birth, many changes and much time must elapse before attaining adulthood. Adulthood is not instantaneous, and neither is Christhood. Like the light of day, it comes steadily and gradually.

> **And there went out unto him all the land of Judaea, and they of Jerusalem, and were all baptized of him in the river of Jordan, confessing their sins. And John was clothed with camel's hair, and with a girdle of a skin about his loins; and he did eat locusts and wild honey (Mark 1:5-6).**

And there went out unto him all the land of Judaea, and they of Jerusalem. Jerusalem and Judaea represent the higher reaches of our consciousness which respond to the inner call to prepare for Christhood. In one way of looking at it, they are the only ones who can respond.

Already through John some change is taking place; an awakening is occurring even before Jesus appears to bring the great change in the spiritual destiny of the people. Though they were not aware of it consciously, the people were preparing themselves for the advent of Jesus. And that preparation was in the form of purification.

In Hebrew the word Jordan means "a descender," one who has come down. This is exactly the meaning of the Sanskrit word *avatar*. In this case it means the spiritual current that ever descends from the Highest into the depths our being, evolving and awakening us in time, leading us upward to the conscious unfoldment of our own divine nature. This spiritual current is most powerfully revealed and assimilated in the meditations of the adept yogi.

Baptizo means total immersion in water. The ultimate Jordan is Divine Consciousness: God. So the ultimate baptism is immersion in God. "For as many of you as have been baptized into Christ have put on Christ" (Galatians 3:27). The supreme mystic of the Eastern Church, Saint Simeon the New Theologian, says that unless we know Christ intimately through union with Christ we have not really been baptized in Christ, but only made wet by water. Those who hope to be acknowledged by Jesus merely for having been baptized with water will be disappointed. "Many will say to me in that day, Lord, Lord, have we not prophesied in thy name? and in thy name have cast out devils? and in thy name done many wonderful works? And then will I profess unto them, I never knew you: depart from me, ye that work iniquity" (Matthew 7:22-23). The external rite opens the way to the real *conscious* baptism in Spirit which occurs in meditation. Actually, our whole life should be a continuous baptism of consciousness. "But we all, with open face beholding as in a glass [mirror] the glory of the Lord, are changed [transformed] into the same image [likeness] from glory to glory, even as by the Spirit of the Lord" (II Corinthians 3:18). This is the process of evolution from humanity to divinity. It is both a change and a revelation. Our humanity evolves from level to level until our divinity is revealed and manifested.

The confession of sins means an honest acknowledgment and evaluation of them, the word *exomologeo* which is used in this place having a connotation of profession and promise. It entails both an establishment in living faith and a promising to seek God. "When thou saidst, Seek ye my face; my heart said unto thee, Thy face, Lord, will I seek" (Psalms

27:8). The washing in the water symbolizes our intention to cleanse and thoroughly purify ourselves in order to attain the Divine vision. "Blessed are the pure in heart: for they shall see God" (Matthew 5:8).

In meditation our "confessing" of sins occurs when they float up to the surface of our consciousness and are beheld by us and dissolved in the light invoked by meditation. The Revelation of Saint John refers to this symbolically when it says: "And the sea gave up the dead which were in it; and death and hell delivered up the dead which were in them: and they were judged every man according to their works" (Revelation 20:13). The confessing of sins at the baptism of Saint John also represents our letting go of them. For when we are addicted to negativity in any form we hold on to it and refuse to admit its true nature. In India they use the simile of the camel who keeps on chewing nettles even though they pierce its mouth and make it bleed. So the inner baptism is also the letting go of sin.

Because of the egoic discomfort confession usually entails, there is a salutary aspect to confession that is often overlooked, and that is the ability to clearly see and evaluate the sins that are brought out. This is indicated by the verse just before the one cited: "And I saw the dead, small and great, stand before God; and the books were opened: and another book was opened, which is the book of life: and the dead were judged out of those things which were written in the books, according to their works" (Revelation 20:12). This insight (in Buddhist tradition, *vipassana*, clear sight) and ability to judge our inner impulses is of inestimable value in our spiritual endeavors.

It is only natural that human beings do not much like facing all the truth about their ego and external life, even though that is not really themselves at all. But right meditation gives both the strength of mind and the detachment from ego that enables us to face up to and face down all the negativity with which we have mistakenly identified.

Spiritual life is the coming forth into "the true Light, which lighteth every man that cometh into the world" (John 1:9) on all levels of our existence, but most especially in the mind through meditation. That light reveals all that heretofore has been hidden, both the debris that covers the inner light and the inner light itself. "In thy light shall we see light" (Psalms 36:9).

And John was clothed with camel's hair, and with a girdle of a skin about his loins. Being the master of the Essenes, Saint John lived in extreme simplicity, not because there is an innate virtue in being poor, but because the less we have, the less there will be to identify with as "mine" and the simpler and more undistracted our life will be. "Stuff" is the bane of those who live in "developed" countries, and everyone would be a lot happier if they gave it away or hauled a great deal of it to the dump. This is because "things" produce two great illusions in us: 1) the more we possess, the "bigger" or more important we are, and 2) happiness and satisfaction can be gotten by getting things. Regarding this second illusion I remember a couple of my friends telling me about two of their best friends who were tormented for years struggling to get enough money to make the payments on their auto. The day they paid it off, they celebrated by driving it out to a cliff by the ocean and pushing it over. Their bitter struggle had made them come to detest it so much that they did not even want to just sell it and get some of their money back–they only wanted to be rid of it.

It is wisdom to wear simple and humble clothes, because the body itself is simple and humble. Yet, Saint John's clothing was very practical, keeping him warm in winter and cool(er) in summer. That is why the Western monks for many centuries wore only wool clothing. Also it was the longest-wearing material. Spiritual life should always be practical and sensible (by the standards of the truly wise, of course).

And he did eat locusts and wild honey. Saint John's diet was very simple: carob pods and honey. "Locusts" (*akris*) does not mean insects, but the pods of the carob plant that are also called "Saint John's Bread," since that was his only solid food. The word *akris*, translated "locusts" also means the tips or extremities of things, and may also mean that he ate the tender tips or the roots of plants. For three years Saint Seraphim of Sarov lived on a kind of weed called sneet. The very same plant grows in the wilderness where Saint John lived, and some of the Eastern Orthodox monastics of Palestine boil it and eat it. However it may be, Saint John was a pure vegetarian as were all Essenes, including Saint Joseph, the Virgin Mary and Jesus.

Honey is very beneficial and supplies many vitamins. I well remember a time during my first trip to India where I felt myself to be literally starving. I could no longer endure the ashram food, and had gone for several days without eating a thing. Naturally I felt weak and awful. From somewhere deep in my mind there arose the idea to obtain some natural Himalayan honey. I did so and sat by the Ganges literally drinking it. It completely turned things around for me as it had done for Jonathan nearly three thousand years before (I Samuel 14:27), and I could again eat and digest the ashram food until I could escape to the plains and find something decent to eat. (By the way, Indian devotees who visited that ashram had the same problem.)

The message in all this is that simplicity, like cleanliness, is very near unto godliness. It is also an indication that the vegetarian diet is best for the spiritual seeker, if he intends to be a finder.

John Denounces the Religious Hypocrites

> But when he saw many of the Pharisees and Sadducees come to his baptism, he said unto them, O generation of vipers, who hath warned you to flee from the wrath to come? Bring forth therefore fruits meet for repentance: and think not to say within yourselves, We have Abraham to our father: for I say unto you, that God is able of these stones to raise up children unto Abraham (Matthew 3:7-9).

In Israel at the time of Jesus there were basically three religious sects: Pharisees, Sadducees and Essenes. (It is intriguing that the four Gospels make no mention of the Essenes at all.) The Pharisees were very conservative and extremely involved in ritualistic observances, including ritual purity, which is why they felt no compunction in engineering the death of Jesus, but refused to enter the precincts of Pilate's judgment hall "lest they should be defiled" and not able to celebrate Passover (John 18:28). They also believed quite strongly in the supernatural, including the existence and interaction of angels with human beings. They were, in short, painfully religious, usually causing others the pain instead of themselves. The Sadducees were at the other end of the spectrum, skeptical of all things religious and inclined to be thoroughly humanistic in their attitudes. John was the Master of the Essenes, and his baptism would have been either a preparation for entering the Essene Order or actually a form of admission.

Ordinarily both Pharisees and Sadducees despised and mocked the Essenes, so why was there this sudden turnover in attitude? Considering what Saint John says to them about "the wrath to come," something must have occurred to instill fear in them about the future. Saint Matthew does not tell us about it. However it was, there they were, believers and unbelievers alike, afraid for their safety on some level.

It cannot be denied that religion has been employed for ages by the egocentric for their private empire-building, their main tools being promise of power or pleasure for the obedient and observant and the instilling of fear of suffering and punishment for the disobedient and rule-breakers. Greed and fear are the twin pillars of ego-oriented behavior, including religion.

But Saint John had another perspective. Since he did not have an artificial religious identity to offer, but administered a baptism that imparted a very real spiritual effect, he knew three things: 1) Not everyone was capable of receiving and using that baptismal grace. 2) It was wrong to fool the incapable by baptizing them. 3) It was a transgression to impart his baptism to the spiritually incompetent. His cousin, Jesus, would put it another, and stronger, way: "Give not that which is holy unto the dogs, neither cast ye your pearls before swine, lest they trample them under their feet, and turn again and rend you" (Matthew 7:6). "It is not meet to take the children's bread, and to cast it to dogs" (Matthew 15:26). When Jesus speaks of dogs and swine he is speaking symbolically of violent, greedy, undisciplined and materially obsessed people. (At the time of Jesus "dogs" meant hyenas, jackals, and wild dogs, not what we mean today.) The idea is that we should not give spiritual things to those who cannot even understand them, much less evaluate them correctly. Moreover, some people need a bit of shocking to awaken them. So Saint John called them vipers–poisonous snakes.

We should pause and back up a bit before we investigate the meaning of such sharp words. Saint John saw the Pharisees and Sadducees coming to his baptism, but they did not become baptized. On the outer level, this was simply because he refused to baptize them, but as a symbol it means something else. It indicates that there are people who can outwardly undergo something but inwardly in the real levels of their being completely miss it. Judas missed Jesus, as did most of the people who met him. The same has been true through the ages of the people who met other great messengers of God. Physical proximity is not spiritual nearness. I met people in India who thought Swami Sivananda and Anandamayi Ma were fools.

"He answered and said unto them, Well hath Esaias prophesied of you hypocrites, as it is written, This people honoureth me with their lips, but their heart is far from me" (Mark 7:6). We often hear that seeing is believing, but the fact is, "seeing" is often *not* seeing at all. It is the same with anything holy. Since the spiritual power did not enter into their inner levels, but remained external to them for all practical reasons, it was as though they never encountered it. Of such people Jesus says: "I never knew you" (Matthew 7:23).

We may be shocked at Saint John's calling those people snakes, but the fact is: they were. *Ekhidna* means a very poisonous snake. In other words, the "vipers" are spiritually infectious people, capable of degrading anything, no matter how holy, just by their touch, while at the same time remaining themselves untouched by the sacred. This goes on a lot.

But if that is so, why would they be coming to baptism? The answer is simple but sad. Those who are middling negative usually avoid contact or remembrance of positive things, especially authentic spiritual matters. Those who are truly evil are made unsettled by the presence of the holy, and can even be pained by it. But if their evil ripens through many lives, a change takes place. They hate the holy even more than they did before, but now they are attracted to it in the hope of either destroying or defiling it. This is why morally foul men are so often attracted to really pure women. Once they defile them they cast them away in contempt. This is why some immoral women play the innocent to attract those very men.

Moths are attracted to a candle flame, but by flying into it they extinguish it. In the same way, spiritual vipers seek out, plunder, defile, and destroy holy things. And they are very cunning at it. Accordingly: "Believe not every spirit, but try the spirits whether they are of God" (I John 4:1).

"Who hath warned you…?" demanded Saint John of the "vipers." We often speak of "slipping the word" to someone. However, the real Word does not come from any external source, but from deep within where the Divine Call ever sounds. For this very reason that Word is personal and private, between us and Infinity Itself. There is never any such thing as a public Word for the masses, it is always on an individual basis. This is why such great beings like Krishna, Buddha, and Jesus may teach a great number of people, but very few attain enlightenment in comparison to the number taught. This is not a failure on the masters' part, it is just how the evolutionary scheme works. They do leave their wisdom behind, however, and millions can benefit, some even awakening. But that awakening always comes from within, never from without. The teachings of the great Way-Showers help people prepare themselves to hear that inner call. And meditation is needed to develop the "ears to hear" that inner message.

It is not only personal, it is confidential. That is, we cannot impart it to another, and we should not try. Spiritual life is totally between us and God. Anyone who tries to push in between us and God, claiming they are an appointed go-between is a liar and a destroyer of souls. The purpose of religion is to supply *individuals* with the means to purify and activate their spirit-awareness, not to command and demand of them. Certainly, it is the duty of religion to warn us about what will harm us as well as to recommend what will help us, but religion has no business trying to coerce us. It will not work. Each person has a unique path to God, even though it is travelled within the larger framework of a religion, and no one should interfere with it.

Of course mistakes will be made, but if we do not have the freedom to go wrong we will not have the freedom to go right. This is very evident in India. India abounds with charlatans, fake avatars, crooked yogis and just plain lunatics in the spiritual carnival. *And they are left alone.* For if there is no freedom to be a fool there will be no freedom to be wise. Because of karma that needs to be worked through, as well as inner characteristics (samskaras) that need erasing, it is possible for a spiritual person in some situations to engage in what seems completely useless, silly or even crazy and wrong behavior. Here is an example.

A woman was visiting her guru's ashram. One day he called for her and told her that her father had just died. Overcome with grief she ran out of the ashram and began hysterically weeping. In about fifteen minutes someone came and told her the guru needed to speak with her. When she entered the ashram her guru told her that he had not told the truth–her father was alive. She was shocked, but felt that her guru must have had a reason for what he did. A short time later she was again at the ashram, and word came that her father had really died. But she felt no grief at all. That fifteen minutes of intense sorrow months before had somehow produced this calmness. Then she understood her guru's action.

Since we cannot always judge the actions of saints, we must give everyone the latitude to act as he wishes. Freedom is the watchword. Of course, many will take advantage, and foolish people will excuse wrongdoing and scoundrels for their very wrong behavior. But still it is right to give that freedom. God gives it to us, however much we abuse it.

No one can tell you the will of God for your life. God is capable of doing that himself. It is totally foolish to adulate and run after someone else because he is supposedly close to God or enlightened. If someone can tell you the way to gain the same enlightenment he has, then learn it and try it out on your own. But once you know the way, what need will you have of him? This is extremely important, because people throw away their lives dancing around worthless gurus and teachers, never attaining anything themselves.

My dear friend Swami Sivananda of Rishikesh used to give a person instruction and after two or three months tell him to go away and gain something on his own without a dependence that could lead nowhere. And it worked, as I have witnessed myself. Those who travelled constantly with Anandamayi Ma rarely attained to anything spiritually, but those who practiced on their own, only coming to see her when they needed practical advice regarding their meditation, reached perceptible spiritual heights. Sri Ramakrishna only drew his disciples to himself in the last three years of his life, then left them on their own, and they all attained tremendous spiritual stature. His greatest disciple, Swami Vivekananda, once remarked: "A teacher does great harm to his disciples by remaining with them a long time." It is common for an aspirant to live his entire life in an ashram with his guru, but he does it for the sake of practice, not as a "groupie."

Many saints have met their teachers only once or twice, but they applied what they learned. Yogananda's greatest disciple was Sister Gyanamata, who attained total liberation. Except for public functions, some disciples figured out that she had only been in Yogananda's presence about eight hours over a span of nearly twenty years. Her secret? She practiced what he preached.

And finally, that inner word is not thunder and lighting, or a trumpet blast. It is still, quiet, as it was with Elijah. "And he came thither unto a cave, and lodged there; and, behold, the word of the Lord came to him, and he said unto him,… Go forth, and stand upon the mount before the Lord. And, behold, the Lord passed by, and a great and strong wind rent the mountains, and brake in pieces the rocks before the Lord; but the Lord was not in the wind: and after the wind an earthquake; but the Lord was not in the earthquake: and after the earthquake a fire; but the Lord was not in the fire: and after the fire a still [silent] small [subtle] voice" (I Kings 19:9, 11-12).

God does not speak to us in mighty winds, earthquakes, or fire, but in the subtle, direct communication that is The Voice of the Silence. Also, God will not tell us over and over. We must catch the message right away. It is still true that "a word to the wise is sufficient." We should ever be alert with our "ears to hear" (Matthew 11:15; 13:9; 13:43) open and attuned to the inner world, for "they that hear shall live" (John 5:25).

"Who hath warned you to flee from the wrath to come?" asked Saint John. "What are you running away from?" is a tired cliché that is fired at anyone who is trying to escape the bondage of rebirth. I have heard it tossed at people who simply wanted to learn meditation, and of course I heard it from those who learned I planned to lead the monastic life. Sometimes it got varied with the more accusatory form, "You are just running away." And my answer was always: "Yes, I am!" and without apology. Only a fool does not run away from a burning house or a sinking ship, and the world of "man" is both. To castigate a person for trying to get out of this prison is like blaming a man for trying to get out of quicksand or a sea full of sharks. Twice Jesus said of his disciples: "They are not of the world, even as I am not of the world" (John 17:14, 16).

Now, Jesus was in the world, and so were they, but Jesus was here to get us out of the world and they were here to get themselves out and pass on to others the means to escape, too. In the world but not of the world. "But what if everybody felt that way?" ask the ignorant. And the answer is: Then the world would be turned into heaven, but we would still need to get out and evolve upward.

We should not be afraid (Luke 12:32; John 14:27), but we should flee.

And what do we flee? "The wrath to come." We are reasonably disgusted with the pseudo-Christian cant about "the wrath of God," but we need to seriously look at this expression used by Saint John, for he does not say it is God's wrath. What is it, then? The Greek word used is *orge*, the same word from which we get "orgy." It literally means a violent passion, a profound desire or agitation of the mind that reaches forth to its object with mindless (heedless) intensity. The idea of anger or wrath is only by implication, and is not the root meaning. *Orge* is derived from *oregomai*, that means an intense stretching forth or reaching out, covetousness or desire.

Only God can number how many lives we have led, and in each one, from the time we were a single-celled organism right up to now, we have been motivated by one force: desire. Sometimes the desire was for attaining something, and sometimes it was for avoiding something, but it was always desire. Within us are profound subconscious yearnings that have compounded through life after life, all of them delusive and, in the fulfilling, destructive. Pain is their sole and inevitable product. First we are in pain because they are not fulfilled, and then we are in pain when they are–at first, pain that the fulfillment may not last, and later on pain that it will last. And all along there is the inherent pain of the thing desired. Buddha was right: *all* is suffering. It takes time for that to be made clear to us, and for countless lives we refuse to see that truth, so we suffer even more.

Countless desires are locked up in our inner minds: desires evil and hateful, desires foolish in the extreme, desires impossible of fulfillment by their very nature, desires for things that would destroy us and others, and desires that can only beget a chain of more desires. And they are powerful, strong with the accumulation of ages. Just as Dracula became increasingly cunning and strong through the centuries, so also have these desires that are as destructive and ego-centered as Dracula himself, and harder to kill. A simple stake through the heart will not do the needful here. Only a total purification and transmutation will work–actually our total deification (*theosis*). Otherwise they are going to break out of their tombs and ravage the countryside of our lives, strewing death and destruction throughout. This is the inescapable law: as long as we are embodied, so long are we endangered by the monsters roaming blindly in the abyss of our subconscious, seeking a way out into our lives. Even very holy people are in this danger, sometimes even more so as a result of their profound empowerment which reaches both up to the heaven of their spirit and down to the hell of their subconscious. All are in danger from these volcanic forces that really are capable of breaking out at any moment. Sadhana and a purified life are the only safeguard and safety.

But running is not enough, for Saint John continues: "Bring forth therefore fruits meet [worthy] for repentance." That could not be expressed any better, and we need a good look at it.

What is the "worthy fruit" Saint John is talking about? It is that which leads to and produces union with God or facilitates union with God. This is a very simple principle, indeed. In the same vein, whatsoever hinders or impedes this union with God must be eliminated from our life. We should continually apply this test to the elements of our life and thought.

Jesus often likens us to plants, especially trees and grapevines. The ultimate manifestation of both, and the proof of their nature, is the fruit they bear. "Ye shall know them by their fruits. Do men gather grapes of thorns, or figs of thistles? Even so every good tree bringeth forth good fruit; but a corrupt tree bringeth forth evil fruit. A good tree cannot bring forth evil fruit, neither can a corrupt tree bring forth good fruit. Wherefore by their fruits ye shall know them" (Matthew 7:16-18, 20). The fruit Saint John is speaking of is the fruit of the spirit, of which Saint Paul tells us: "the fruit of the spirit is love, joy, peace, longsuffering, gentleness, goodness, faith, meekness, temperance" (Galatians 5:22-23). And: "The fruit of the spirit is in all goodness and righteousness and truth" (Ephesians 5:9).

The idea of Saint John's statement is that we must neutralize all our negativity by producing within ourselves an equal force of positive spiritual enlightenment. Perhaps the best symbol of this process was shown to me when I was in the primary grades and attended a vacation Bible school. The minister showed us a glass bowl filled with water and explained that the water represented our souls. He then put in a drop of black ink. No change was perceptible, and he explained that in the same way at the beginning of wrong thought or activity the individual does not think he is being affected, much less harmed, in any way. But he kept on dropping in more ink, and after a while the water was murky black. What could be done to correct that? None of us had any idea, so he took some bleach and began putting it in, drop by drop. Gradually the dark water began clearing up, and at the end was as clear as it had been before.

This is exactly how it works with our consciousness. Though its nature is pure and clear, we cloud it with negativity; but we can dispel the clouds with an equal amount of positive energy. Vice is wiped out by virtue. And we must generate as much good as we have produced evil in the past. This is what Jesus was referring to when, speaking of our spiritual imprisonment, he stated: "Verily I say unto thee, Thou shalt by no means come out thence, till thou hast paid the uttermost farthing" (Matthew 5:26) as equal payment of the debt incurred by negative thought, word and deed.

A flutter and flurry of fake emotional penitence will not do the needful. All the bewailing and self-castigation will avail nothing, for that is just more negativity and egocentrism, cheap and easy. Nor will it do any good to beseech God for forgiveness and "grace." We put the bricks in the prison we built for ourselves one by one, and we must take them down in the same way. However, since positivity is of more effect than negativity, we can do so in much less time than it took to build the prison. But the total turnaround of life and thought is the only acceptable remedy.

We all know that when people find themselves mired in the quicksand of negativity their favorite ploy is just to deny it and pretend they are footloose and free. In the same way, really befouled people like to suddenly get "positive" and "affirmative" about themselves, warbling on about how we are all divine and part of God's Perfection, ever-free, etc., etc., etc. That does happen to be true, but trotting it out to deny the need for very real change and turnabout is spiritually poisonous. Anticipating this egoic ploy, Saint John continues: "And think not to say within yourselves, We have Abraham to our father: for I say unto you, that God is able of these stones to raise up children unto Abraham." Citing our eternal genealogy has no meaning when we are entangled in the delusive net of temporality. In truth, God is our Father, and we are his divine children, but children that like the Prodigal Son have wasted our divine heritage and turned ourselves into slaves and beggars (on the functional level). And like the Prodigal we have to awaken to our predicament, stir up the resolve, and make the journey back home to the Father, where we belong.

An apple tree that bears no apples is not one, practically speaking, and in the same way a child of God that does not manifest divinity is not one, either. And God is very practical: it is what we are actually manifesting that determines the whole matter. Still, we need not be discouraged or fearful as to whether we can make the return, for the same power by which God can raise up stones to be children of Abraham is innate in us; for we are all in his image and likeness (Genesis 1:26-27).

Peripherally Saint John is implying the truth that God does indeed raise up children from stones, for in the spirit's evolutionary journey through the entire range of relative existence, it spends part of its time manifesting in mineral form.

When a person is lost in a vast open expanse of land he may wander aimlessly, but usually he manages to go in one direction. Those lost in a forest, however, suffer a much different fate. For a reason that has never been discovered, they keep going around in a circle, coming back over and over to the same place. Interestingly enough, maps of the forty-year wandering of the Hebrews in the desert after escaping from Egypt show that at one point they, too, went around in a vast circle. What more perfect symbol could there be for those of us who are bound to the cycle of birth and death? No matter how far we roam in one life we invariably find ourselves right back on the earth plane in the next birth. This is also the experience of those in false religion (or in misapplication of true religion): however much they experience and think they are developing and progressing, eventually they find themselves right back in the same spot they started from, and in many instances they find themselves worse off than before they began.

Because of this, Jesus and the masters of all religions have stated that liberation from the snares of illusion is incredibly hard to attain, not so much because it takes great effort, but because human beings do not know the right ways to accomplish it. Consider Buddha. For years he perfected himself in the practice of strenuous yogas that produced astonishing psychic and physical experiences. Each of his teachers declared him to be a perfect yogi, a liberated soul. Yet, not being deluded as they and their other disciples were, he knew that he had attained nothing. The hawkers in the religious and yoga medicine-shows want us to believe that we need them and their "product"–that without them we are hopelessly lost and doomed to wander in confusion–when in reality it is our following of them and their system that confuses us and dooms us to wander.

It is our *nature* to become enlightened; that is why enlightenment is inevitable for every single human being without exception. No matter how long it takes, one day all shall reach the goal. "For this corruptible must put on incorruption, and this mortal must put on immortality. So when this corruptible shall have put on incorruption, and this mortal shall have put on immortality, then shall be brought to pass the saying that is written, Death is swallowed up in victory" (I Corinthians 15:53-54) .

And now also the axe is laid unto the root of the trees: therefore every tree which bringeth not forth good fruit is hewn down, and cast into the fire (Matthew 3:10).

This inevitability of spiritual perfection is based on two things: 1) our nature as eternal sons of God in the spirit and 2) the innate ability to manifest that divine sonship. It is in to reference this second point that Saint John the Baptist continues in his speech to those at the Jordan: "And now also the axe is laid unto the root of the trees: therefore every tree which bringeth not forth good fruit is hewn down, and cast into the fire."

Much as we would like to, we cannot just slip out of the forest or wilderness of delusion and speed onward toward the goal. Instead, we must cut down every tree (notice that he says "trees" not "tree") at the root and end the possibility of our ever returning to earthly bondage. It is not easy, but what is? Even this mess we are in took a lot of hard work on our part to get into. Fortunately the axe is waiting there for us to wield.

What is that axe? It is the *consciousness* of spirit, of our own essential being. We do not need some external tool, but that which has ever been at hand from eternity. To use the axe we must go to the root of our being, to the total awareness at our own center. And it is the entering into and experiencing of that awareness that is the plying of the axe. We need only go within through right meditation. (Once more, see *Soham Yoga: The Yoga of the Self*, for Soham itself, through japa and meditation, is the axe that sets us free.)

The usual self-satisfied or point-the-finger-so-you-won't-look-at-me interpretation is that these words refer to Israel. It is true that Saint John meant that hypocrisy and corruption were going to be exposed and their hold over the people would be cut away–at least from those that would heed the message of Jesus. But as in all reading of scriptures, we need to think how it applies universally to those who are seeking the revelation of their innate divinity.

Saint John represents the spiritual will that responds to the call to higher life and consciousness. Here he is speaking of the necessary analysis at the beginning of conscious spiritual life when we must differentiate between that which should be affirmed and strengthened in our life, both mental and physical, and that which should be rejected and eliminated. And we have the power to do it; the axe is even now at the root. And we have been given the means and the ability to cut off *from within* that which is detrimental to our spiritual growth. That means is meditation, and the ability comes from our own divine spirit-Self within us. The axe is already at the root, and the cutting off of the root is our work, although it is done through spirit consciousness. "Not by might, nor by power, but by my spirit, saith the Lord of hosts" (Zechariah 4:6). It is very much like the detergent commercials on television where the detergent is shown loosening the dirt which is then washed away. The effects of meditation loosen the muck and grime of ages and we wash it away through continuing meditation and the right ordering of our life.

Saint John's simile also points out the truth that we cannot deal with negativity in our life on a superficial level, on the level of the leaves, branches, or even the trunk of the trees of ignorance and evil. For however much we may hack away at them, they will just grow back and infest our lives as they have done for ages beyond calculation.

The work of divinization is reflected in all aspects of the seeker's life, but that work takes place solely in one place: the root, the very basis of our existence—our spirit. Once again we see that the interior life is the only spiritual life, and that the transmutation of human consciousness into divine consciousness takes place only in the depths of our spirit, which are also the depths of God. Truly, "deep calleth unto Deep" (Psalms 42:7). Meditation alone provides the opportunity to wield the axe and purify the life. Spiritual life cannot be gauged or timed by the minutes or hours spent in good deeds, study of good books, prayer or worship. Meditation alone is the "clock" of spirit. And without meditation all good thoughts, words or deeds have no lasting spiritual substance. Those good things (and they *are* good) create a positive force, a positive karma, but meditation produces a profound change of consciousness.

"How do I know I am progressing spiritually?" "What should be happening to me in meditation?" These are reasonable questions that deserve a reasonable answer, and Saint John gives it when he says: "Therefore every tree which bringeth not forth good fruit is hewn down, and cast into the fire." That is how we know there is progress: when the many trees of the forest of ignorance which bear the fruits of wrong thought, speech, and action are being cut off and burned to ash in the fire of spirit consciousness. It is not a matter of visions, intuitions, or amazing experiences (which may be illusions), but the cessation of suffering through the elimination of the pain-bearing trees of the forest. Right meditation burns up delusion, including delusive ideas about ourselves and about the spiritual path which are seen to be mostly egocentric nonsense. It is a shock to begin "seeing true," but it is the only way to be free.

Buddha explained carefully that "views" in the form of beliefs and intellectual formulations can be obstacles to our search when they proceed from the deluded mind and are therefore themselves delusions. Some centuries after Buddha the great philosopher Shankara was asked: "What is truth?" He replied: "There is no 'truth;' there is only The True." Or: "There is no 'reality;' there is only The Real." For the word *Sat* means both True and Real. "God alone is real; everything else is unreal." This is the fundamental wisdom of the Indian sages, and is the fundamental wisdom of the wise of all viable spiritual traditions. God as Spirit is inexpressible by words because He (It) is beyond the reach of the mind. As Paramhansa Yogananda said, God cannot be known intellectually, but he can be *realized* directly by our spirit. As he said in one of his prayers: "spirit to Spirit goes." The finite merges in the Infinite, the river flows into the ocean of Being. And thus it finds itself: its Self.

As in the symbolism of the Goddess Kali wearing a garland of severed heads, the sword of consciousness (prajna) cuts off the heads of delusions. So let us begin using it. The trees of delusion/illusion that we have fostered and nurtured through countless lives, and to which we have become so attached, even addicted, must now go into the fire of divinity. "For our God is a consuming fire" (Hebrews 12:29).

The forest of ignorance has to go under the axe and into the fire–there is no other way to freedom. "Therefore every tree which bringeth not forth good fruit is hewn down, and cast into the fire." As is usual, the message is about the cultivation of interior life, the true kingdom of God. And, in fact, it is God that is being spoken about: "For our God is a consuming fire." The idea is simple: by immersing our little consciousness in the greater consciousness of God, all that is within us goes into the deifying fire. That which is good and true within us is made even more good and true, stronger and more effective. That which is negative and false is consumed. It takes a lot of meditational "baptism by fire" to do so, but eventually all the evil and folly is turned to ash, "consumed by Fire." Then, like the phoenix, we ascend in the flames. "Burnt clean in the blaze of My Being, in Me many find Home" (Bhagavad Gita 4:10).

The yogis of India use the word *tapas*, the production of heat, as a descriptive synonym for meditation. Its root word, *tap*, means "to burn." Tapas is a burning inquiry and aspiration. It is a spiritual force of concentrated energy generated by the spiritual aspirant through the practice of sadhana. So we kindle ourselves with the fire of the Self through meditation and burn up all that is not God within us. Included in the fuel are all the "seeds" of the force known as karma. "The blazing fire turns wood to ashes: the fire of knowledge [of God] turns all karmas to ashes" (Bhagavad Gita 4:37).

"Sins" are the accumulations of negative karmas. They cannot be dealt with realistically by the emotion of ego-based repentance, nor can they be expunged by begging forgiveness of God or engaging in expiatory acts or prayers. This is because of the very nature of sins, to which all these things simply have no relation, and consequently are of no effect. Sins are errors produced by darkened or distorted consciousness. When the consciousness that produced them is purified in the fires of God-experience, the karmas are dissolved along with the ignorance that produced them. It is a matter of spiritual law.

John Foretells the Advent of Jesus

> I indeed baptize you with water unto repentance: but he that cometh after me is mightier than I, whose shoes I am not worthy to bear: he shall baptize you with the Holy Ghost, and with fire (Matthew 3:11).

It is this spiritual baptism "with fire" that is the beginning of our Christing, "For as many of you as have been baptized into Christ have put on Christ" (Galatians 3:27). That is why Jesus further said: "I am come that they might have life, and that they might have it more abundantly." For: "God giveth not the Spirit by measure" (John 3:34), but as the boundless ocean of Infinite Life.

So there are two baptisms, outer and inner, and two baptizers–our own awakened and empowered will and the Holy Spirit. Without the action of the first, the action of the second is impossible. Both are essential to each other, which is why Saint Paul says we are workers together with God (I Corinthians 3:9; 6:1). This is so important to know, because deluded human beings swing back and forth between the two errors of thinking that God does it all and that we do it all, when the truth is that it is a divine synergy which raises us from humanity to divinity.

The "baptism of water" is when through our own efforts profound cleansing and correction take place in the deepest levels of our subtle bodies and our consciousness. The baptism of the Holy Spirit is effected when the first baptism is fully completed and its effects established in our consciousness and all the rest of our being. That second, inner baptism infuses divine consciousness within us in potential form. From that moment on the passage from human to divine consciousness becomes possible. This is wonderful to an inconceivable degree, but it is not enough: we must realize that potential by our own continued enlightened endeavor.

The outer baptism of purification and discipline renders us capable of realizing the fullness of our human potential. The inner spiritual baptism renders us capable of realizing the fullness of our divine potential. The two must work together for the revelation of our inner Christ. We are already in the human world, but inhibited in our function therein. Consequently we need the first baptism through our applied will. When that is perfected, the baptism of the Holy Spirit opens the entire realm of superhuman life to us, that "highway of holiness" (Isaiah 35:8) reaching from earth to the highest heaven of Infinite Being.

Both baptisms put us into another dimension of being. It is just that simple and just that wonderful, but we must never lose sight of the fact that it is merely a matter of potential until we get busy and actualize it. The divine fire of the Holy Spirit and the human fire of our own tapasya merge to effect the alchemy of the spirit.

I indeed baptize you with water unto repentance. Repentance is *metanoia*, the complete turning around that we have already spoken about at length. It is introduced here to indicate the purpose of baptism.

Baptism is immersion. The first baptism is immersion in purification through various disciplines, including strict moral observances such as those which Patanjali lists as yama and niyama in the Yoga Sutras. This is not a superficial matter, but the elimination of negative physical, astral and causal energies, a deep purification of the inner and outer levels of the person, freeing him from any spiritual barnacles impeding his growth and progress. This is a wonderful and beneficial thing, and eliminates negative karmas, especially by the "axe" of higher consciousness produced by meditation. Axing the trees of ignorance is very much an active procedure that must be done by the aspirant.

The primal, unalterable law is: "Be not deceived; God is not mocked: for whatsoever a man soweth, that shall he also reap." We "reap" in two ways: by undergoing the consequences of negativity or by cutting it off with the axe of higher consciousness. This being so, we must not be deceived by exoteric Christianity and think we can mock God by engaging in evil and then through some kind of "repentance" get cleared of the karmic debt. No. We did it, and we must undo it–all of it.

When we decide to cleanse ourselves of inner darkness, we must realize that the cleansing must be done by ourselves, but what about "God's grace"? It is the grace of God that we realize we must be purified and and learn the way to purify ourselves. And the doing so is our "grace" to ourselves. Back in the "golden days" of television I saw a lot of commercials that showed women simply dipping their dirty dishes in water to which the famous Brand X had been added. Just a couple of dips and they were clean! But in real life we all had to actually wash our dirty dishes, not just give a dip or two. I remember a couple of my cousins teasing their mother by only dipping the dishes in the water and putting them in the rack to dry. "But they do it on TV!" they assured her. And then they washed them like any sensible person knew would have to be done. It is all in our hands.

He shall baptize you with the Holy Ghost, and with fire. The meaning is that the Christ within will lift us into the sphere of Divine Life and the Cosmic Fire and immerse us therein in a permanent immersion-pervasion of that Life and Fire. (See *A Treatise on Cosmic Fire* by Alice Bailey.)

Right now we pretty much live in the realm of Cosmic Death; otherwise why has this urge arisen within us to escape it and enter into Cosmic Life? The amazing truth is that the two are really one. Paramhansa Yogananda used the simile of an ocean during a storm. The surface is lashed and torn apart by the gale, but the depths of the ocean are completely still. If we are on the surface of life we are in turmoil, but if we are in the depths of Life we are at peace. We are already living in the Holy Spirit, for it is She Herself that is the dynamic power and light which manifests as creation. She is the Great Commotion and She is the Great Peace, it all depends on where we are within her infinite sphere.

We may think of Her manifestation as a cosmic wheel that is spinning around terrifically, making us all dizzy, confused, and nauseous. Those that are out on the rim of the wheel are the most dizzy, confused, and nauseous. But those that are further in are less so, since they are whirling less. Those that are very near the center are not whirling nearly so much, and those at the very center are not whirling at all. The very thing that tosses those outside its center brings rest to those who enter there. Because of this, ancient writings of the Christian Gnostics call the Mother both Prostitute and Virgin, both Death-bearer and Life-giver. It is all according to where we are in relation to her. Right now we are riding her roller coaster aspect, but if we become baptized, immersed, in her we shall find rest, the real Eternal Rest that is given not to the physically dead, but to the spiritually alive.

How is it that Saint John says "the Holy Ghost, and with fire"? He is referring to these two aspects. Spirit is both consciousness and dynamism, the creative fire of relative existence and evolution. She is still and She is unmoving. And since we are in this world, the baptism in the Holy Spirit enables us to simultaneously live in the unmoving Spirit and the ever-moving Fire. But everyone has to work toward it, and not for only a short while or continually starting and stopping. Those who align themselves with their inner Christ through meditation and correctness of life will find that continuing purification will be the order of the day for years to come. Dark elements from this life and from previous lives will arise to be eliminated by them, especially through the practice of meditation.

Whose fan is in his hand, and he will throughly purge his floor, and gather his wheat into the garner; but he will burn up the chaff with unquenchable fire. The word poorly translated "fan" is *ptuon*, a winnowing fork. A winnowing fork was a device with which wheat was beaten to separate the inedible husk (chaff) from the wheat kernel. The wheat would be spread out on a hard surface and beaten with the winnowing fork. The action would toss the wheat and husks into the air; if there was a breeze it would blow the husks off to the side as the heavier wheat kernels fell back to the threshing floor. This was used by Saint John as a symbol of the purification which all must voluntarily undergo. His words have absolutely nothing to do with separating "good" from "bad" people and burning up the bad in everlasting hellfire. (It is amazing how easily ignorant and negative people can turn the light of scriptures away from themselves and their spiritual obligations and try to turn it on those they would like to coerce and frighten.) This inner threshing is a very intense interior activity. So also is the follow-up action of burning the chaff with the unquenchable fire of the Holy Spirit's presence.

Saint Ignatius of Antioch, a disciple of Saint John the Apostle, referred to himself as "the wheat of Christ." When we think of it that way we can see another meaning. Our "husk" is externalized consciousness and externalized involvement, whereas our "wheat nature" is our divine spirit. Our husk is temporal, and our "kernel" is eternal. As serious and dedicated yogis it is our duty to thresh ourselves and separate the pernicious illusion and effects of externality from our awareness and see that only the wheat of spiritual consciousness remains.

Through meditation and right living that is the awakened spiritual life, we keep gathering our spiritual wheat consciousness into the granary of our inmost being, and at the same time consume our chaff consciousness in the fire of meditation. So we, too, need to take up the winnowing fork and begin the process of separation and harvesting. This symbolism also indicates that we must continually be internalizing our spiritual life, continually orienting our outer awareness and actions toward the inner realities and thereby establishing ourselves permanently in that inmost spirit.

The fire of the Holy Spirit is called unquenchable to indicate that nothing can prevent its action. Also, it indicates that the action of the Holy Spirit is not partial; it does not burn out part-way through the process and have to rekindled. It is invincible and inevitable, "because greater is he that is in you, than he that is in the world" (I John 4:4).

The Baptism of Jesus by John

Then cometh Jesus from Galilee to Jordan unto John, to be baptized of him. But John forbad him, saying, I have need to be baptized of thee, and comest thou to me? And Jesus answering said unto him, Suffer it to be so now: for thus it becometh us to fulfill all righteousness. Then he suffered him. And Jesus, when he was baptized, went up straightway out of the water: and, lo, the heavens were opened unto him, and he saw the Spirit of God descending like a dove, and lighting upon him. And lo a voice from heaven, saying, This is my beloved Son, in whom I am well pleased (Matthew 3:13-17).

And Jesus himself began to be about thirty years of age (Luke 3:23).

Then cometh Jesus from Galilee to Jordan unto John, to be baptized of him. Eighteen years before, when Jesus was twelve, he proved that the elders of the Essenes had nothing to teach him, that he already knew more than they. Having demonstrated this, he made arrangements to depart for India where he learned from the Wise Men, who had visited him years before, that wisdom which he then brought back to Israel, and for the teaching of which he was martyred. (For more regarding this, see *The Christ of India*.).

Yet, when he returned he went to Jordan to be baptized by John, the Master of the Essenes. Why did he do this, since he had overreached anything the Essenes could impart? The reason will be made clear to us.

But John forbad him, saying, I have need to be baptized of thee, and comest thou to me? What a great lesson there is for us in these words. Here John stood, surrounded by a multitude of disciples and seekers, the Master of the Essenes, whom many believed would be revealed as the Messiah. And in the hearing of all he declares that he needs the baptism of Jesus, not the other way around. How assiduously we guard our egos, never exposing them to disregard by either ourselves or others. Even in India it is common for religious figures to refuse to visit other leaders lest it seem that they are recognizing that person's superiority. I have met them myself and been astounded at their open admission. But here we see Saint John readily expressing before others that Jesus was his spiritual superior. Yes, he was being humble, but he was also being clear-sighted and honest.

It is important for us to realize that Jesus had nothing to receive from Saint John–just the opposite. So, why was he there, petitioning for baptism, which was the first step for aspirants to membership in the Essene order?

And Jesus answering said unto him, Suffer it to be so now: for thus it becometh us to fulfill all righteousness. Then he suffered him. Jesus began his ministry with a lesson in spiritual humility. Although his baptism was going to be the first public revelation of his Messiahship, he came to Saint John, his cousin, and appeared to recognize him as his spiritual superior. He was also presenting a symbolic, esoteric teaching as well. Symbolically, Jesus represents the inner light, and Saint John is the initiate's will. The light only emerges at the action of our will, and remains subservient to our intelligent will. We must always be in charge and using our intelligence. This is fulfilling all righteousness.

And Jesus, when he was baptized, went up straightway out of the water: and, lo, the heavens were opened unto him, and he saw the Spirit of God descending like a dove, and lighting upon him. Saint Matthew (3:6) has told us that the people were coming to Saint John "and were baptized of him in Jordan, confessing their sins." So they would spend some time in the water confessing their sins to Saint John, but Jesus "went up straightway out of the water," attesting that he had no sins to confess.

And, lo, the heavens were opened unto him. This is the core purpose of spiritual life: to open the heavens of infinite consciousness to us; for it is the consciousness symbolized by the boundless sky that is the Kingdom of Heaven, the Kingdom of God. This opening occurs when we become immersed in the purifying waters of spiritual consciousness.

The heavens of divine consciousness could not be opened to us if the capacity for such consciousness was not actually innate in us as our very nature. Spiritual life is the path of realizing the truth of ourselves, the affirmation that: "Beloved, *now* are we the sons of God" (I John 3:2). Because of this Jesus did not rant about sin, damnation and hell-fire, but instead his preaching was: "He that loveth me shall be loved of my Father, and I will love him, and will manifest myself to him:… and my Father will love him, and we will come unto him, and make our abode with him" (John 14:21, 23). Regarding the Holy Spirit, in whom he planned to baptize, Jesus said: "Ye know him; for he dwelleth with you, and shall be in you" (John 14:17). Jesus was also being our example when he said: "I and my Father are one" (John 10:30). So those who follow Jesus are united to God and are one with him. Jesus is not a mediator with God in the sense of a go-between, but rather as one who unites us with God, making us as much one with God as is Jesus himself. This is the function of a true sadguru: he shows the aspirant way to the Sat, the Real, and his work is done. Such is the tradition of the Nath Yogis which was followed by Jesus, himself a Nath Yogi. (Again, see *The Christ of India*.)

Were Jesus' promises of divine union and identity something new for the people of Israel–at least those who knew their scriptures? Not at all, for: "God said, Let us make man in our image, after our likeness.… So God created man in his own image, in the image of God created he him; male and female created he them" (Genesis 1:26-27). This possibility was destined for humanity from the very beginning, even before human beings were created. David said: "Lord, thou hast been our dwelling place in all generations" (Psalm 90:1). Obviously we have always been united to and living in God, but our consciousness has been separated from awareness of that eternal union. Reunion of our consciousness with the Consciousness of God is the only "mediatorship" of a true spiritual teacher. "For thus saith the high and lofty One that inhabiteth eternity, whose name is Holy; I dwell in the high and holy place, *with him also* that is of a contrite and humble spirit" (Isaiah 57:15).

Here are some more scriptural citations that present the true spiritual perspective.

"Ye are not in the flesh, but in the Spirit" (Romans 8:9).

"Know ye not that your body is the temple of the Holy Ghost which is in you,... therefore glorify God in your body, and in your spirit, which are God's" (I Corinthians 6:19,20).

"Ye also shall continue in the Son, and in the Father" (I John 2:24).

"Ye are of God, little children" (I John 4:4).

"We have known and believed the love that God hath to us. God is love; and he that dwelleth in love dwelleth in God, and God in him" (I John 4:16).

"Behold, I stand at the door, and knock: if any man hear my voice, and open the door, I will come in to him, and will sup with him, and he with me" (Revelation 3:20).

"To him that overcometh will I grant to sit with me in my throne, even as I also overcame, and am set down with my Father in his throne" (Revelation 3:21).

This is the teaching of Jesus Christ and his apostles about the essential nature and destiny of humanity.

"My sheep hear my voice, and I know them, and they follow me: and I give unto them eternal life; and they shall never perish, neither shall any man pluck them out of my hand. My Father, which gave them me, is greater than all; and no man is able to pluck them out of my Father's hand. I and my Father are one. Then the Jews [Judeans] took up stones again to stone him. Jesus answered them, Many good works have I shewed you from my Father; for which of those works do ye stone me? The Jews [Judeans] answered him, saying, For a good work we stone thee not; but for blasphemy; and because that thou, being a man, makest thyself God. Jesus answered them, Is it not written in your law, I said, Ye are gods? If he called them gods, unto whom the word of God came, and the scripture cannot be broken; say ye of him, whom the Father hath sanctified, and sent into the world, Thou blasphemest; because I said, I am the son of God?" (John 10:27-36). Jesus was referring to Psalms 82:6: "I have said, Ye are gods; and all of you are children of the most High."

Jesus saw the Holy Spirit descending in the form of a dove, a form of radiant light that had two rays coming out from it like wings. In early Christian writings the Holy Spirit is called "the Dove of Light." All creation-manifestation is the embodiment of the Holy Spirit, but for anything to be manifest there has to be a duality, a dual polarity, and this is represented by the two wings of the Dove. We have spoken a goodly bit about the right-and-left-hand paths; these, too, are the wings of the Dove. In yogic science the "third eye" of intuition, the center between the eyebrows, is a reflection of the ajna chakra that corresponds to the medulla oblongata. It is said that this chakra has two "petals" or rays; so the descent of the Holy Spirit is also the opening of the "third eye" of spirit.

Saint Gabriel had told Jesus' mother: "The Holy Ghost shall come upon thee, and the power of the Highest shall overshadow thee: therefore also that holy thing which shall be born of thee shall be called the son of God" (Luke 1:35). By the overshadowing of the Holy Spirit Christ Consciousness becomes manifest in us.

And lo a voice from heaven, saying, This is my beloved Son, in whom I am well pleased. God speaks out of heaven, out of the higher regions of our being. In the past five centuries Catholic mystics were usually misunderstood and even persecuted unless they had a Jesuit as their spiritual director. This is because one of the most important discoveries of the Jesuit order in their dealings with many mystics was that visions are sometimes symbolic projections of the mystic's superconscious mind to convey a spiritual truth or symbolize a spiritual change that has taken place in them. A vision therefore, unless obviously literal, should be interpreted symbolically. It is not uncommon for mystics to be given something to eat or drink in vision. This symbolizes many things. For example, in a vision one saint was given a dish of shining, white substance by Jesus. He tasted it, and it was sweeter and more delicious than anything he had eaten, so he asked for more. Then he was given a dish of something black which tasted more horrible than anything he had ever tasted. Jesus then told him that without the black he could not get the white, meaning that the bitter is what gains for us the sweet. So a vision may not be literally *real*, but it can be *true*.

One mystic saw Jesus reach into his chest and draw forth his heart, then take her heart out of her chest and put his in its place. To think that this actually took place, that Jesus did a heart transplant on her, is absurd. But as an indication that from that moment on she had attained to "the mind of Christ" (I Corinthians 2:16) is absolutely true.

"This is my beloved Son, in whom I am well pleased." This is a statement of eternal truth: *now* are we the sons of God. Divine sonship is not something to attain or become, but something to manifest, to realize in our own consciousness. "And now, O Father, glorify thou me with thine own self with the glory which I had with thee before the world was" (John 17:5). God's Self is *our* Self.

And we are not just sons of God, we are *beloved* sons. Because however much the divine likeness may have been hidden or distorted in us, "it doth not yet appear what we shall be: but we know that, when he shall appear, we shall be like him; for we shall see him as he is." What an amazing truth: *When we see God we see our Self.* For we and God are one. "For we are made partakers of Christ, if we hold the beginning of our confidence stedfast unto the end" (Hebrews 3:14). God-realization and Self-realization are the same thing.

As already stated, the descent of the Holy Spirit on Jesus did not make him God's Son, as has been erroneously supposed by some theologians, but rather it revealed that he was already the Son of God. This revelation or uncovering of our divine sonship is the work of the Holy Spirit. We are not clods of dirt that get turned into lumps of gold, we are gold hidden by the coverings of earth and ignorance. We already are children of God, and have been so eternally with God. Though eternally free, we have been seized by the illusion of bondage and live accordingly. The indwelling of the Holy Spirit eventually reveals to us that we are the immortal sons of God. The faithful aspirant to Christhood says: "My Father worketh hitherto, and I work" (John 5:17).

"And Jesus himself began to be about thirty years of age" (Luke 3:23). At the age of thirteen Jesus left Israel for India, arriving there when he was fourteen. The next fourteen or fifteen years he spent in India, arriving back in Israel when he was almost thirty. After being in Israel for three years, he returned to India and lived in the western Himalayas for thirty years or so.

The Temptation of Jesus

Then was Jesus [full of the Holy Spirit (Luke 4:1)] led up of the Spirit into the wilderness to be tempted of the devil. And when he had fasted forty days and forty nights, he was afterward an hungered.

And when the tempter came to him, he said, If thou be the son of God, command that these stones be made bread. But he answered and said, It is written, Man shall not live by bread alone, but by every word that proceedeth out of the mouth of God.

Then the devil taketh him up into the holy city, and setteth him on a pinnacle of the temple, and saith unto him, If thou be the son of God, cast thyself down: for it is written, he shall give his angels charge concerning thee: and in their hands they shall bear thee up, lest at any time thou dash thy foot against a stone. Jesus said unto him, It is written again, Thou shalt not tempt the Lord thy God.

Again, the devil taketh him up into an exceeding high mountain, and sheweth him all the kingdoms of the world, and the glory of them; and saith unto him, All these things will I give thee, if thou wilt fall down and worship me. Then saith Jesus unto him, Get thee hence, Satan: for it is written, Thou shalt worship the Lord thy God, and him only shalt thou serve.

Then the devil leaveth him, and, behold, angels came and ministered unto him (Matthew 4:1-11).

One of the most important lessons of Saint Matthew's Gospel may be missed, because it is not verbal. It is the juxtapositioning of the baptism of Jesus and the Divine Voice declaring his Divine Sonship, and his immediately being led into the wilderness for temptation by "the devil," Satan, the force of Cosmic Delusion. The teaching is simply this: "Unto whomsoever much is given, of him shall be much required" (Luke 12:48). This is a principle of spiritual life. As soon as we move up a notch we are put to work and must meet increased demands on us. So to seek spiritual blessings, advantages and development just because we want the goodies is missing the point completely. For if we do not put what we gain to use, it is all truly useless, and we incur the negative karma of wasting our spiritual advancement. This is no small thing, a risk no one should take. But to not seek spiritual growth is an even greater risk.

Spiritual empowerment is wasted if it is not put to use; and the major work must be in the wilderness of our spirits where no outer things reside, but we can be alone with God. We must get to the root of "things," the ignorance which must be vanquished from our minds and hearts. So although we may go into the wilderness to be with God, first we are going to have to get the devil out of the way.

The word translated "devil" is *diabolos* in Greek, which literally means someone who accuses, slanders or attempts to debase someone in their own eyes. The root word, *ballo*, means to throw or push down. The Hebrew equivalent, *Satan*, means an inimical opponent, an adversary that withstands our attempts–in this case, the attempt to ascend to higher consciousness. Thus, the devil is anything that degrades us, both externally and internally and opposes our ascent in consciousness. The ego and its enticements as well as the deeds it impels us to are all the devil and the works (deeds) of the devil.

Karma determines the qualities of each life, and we can say that karma brings us back to incarnation, but in the truest sense it is the satanic ego and its affinity for ignorance and illusion that brings us back again and again. "For this purpose the son of God was manifested, that he might destroy the works of the devil" (I John 3:8). We are accessing our inner son of God through the disciplines and practices of spiritual life (especially meditation) for that exact purpose.

Doing evil means a lot more than engaging in negative acts; it also means accepting a future of negative actions, even desiring such a future, fondling the memories or the effects of past evil deeds, and refusing to cut off and dissolve that root of all evil-doing: the ego and its desires.

The word translated "tempt" is *peiradzo*, which means to test or prove, as well as to entice. It also has the context of an examination, even an experiment. It also means to move something over to another side. In the case of Jesus, the test was meant on his side to demonstrate his spiritual awakening, that he was indeed a Son of God. On the side of the force of cosmic delusion—which really exists, but only as a force, not as an individual being (though it can take form and seem to be an intelligent entity, as in the testings of Jesus and Buddha)—it was an attempt to throw down Jesus from his attainment and repolarize him back to the bondage of ego and evil. So on one side it was very good, and even necessary, despite the malevolent intent on the other side.

Jesus had long before, in previous lives in this and higher worlds, passed the stage where he could be tempted to do any wrong action, so the tests are really going to be lessons for us who in our present state would find them subtle, and therefore insidious, for as Genesis tells us: "The serpent was more subtil than any beast of the field" (Genesis 3:1).

For forty days Jesus had been absorbed in spiritual realities, in the state where the things of earth, including the body, are seen as insubstantial shadows that have no effect on the consciousness whatsoever. In such a condition all the gears of the lower existence have been disengaged from the higher levels so the awareness can soar unimpeded into the sky of Spirit.

According to the yogis of India, if a person remains more than forty days in this state his body will simply drop away. Consequently, Jesus had to descend from that state to maintain his embodiment so his work could be accomplished. When he did so, he became aware of the body and its condition. Not having received food or drink for forty days, the body was clamoring for sustenance. While Jesus was absorbed in the highest levels of consciousness, the body was kept perfectly alive and unharmed. But when that current of supreme awareness was switched off, the body demanded food, as it should. Therefore he was hungry.

In English we tend to have relatively simple words for things, mutations of either Latin or Greek words that express their nature. In some languages, though, they string together several words to get the idea across. In *The Expanded New Testament* Wuest has done this, naming Satan "He-Who-Puts-To-The-Test-By-His-Solicitation-To-Do-Evil." Lengthy, but accurate. Human beings have many depictions and ideas about the nature of "the Devil," but here we have its essential nature. Satan is the magnetic force that pulls toward the path of evil. And evil need not be the obvious things such as lying, theft and murder, but those things which conduce to evil or weaken us, making us susceptible to the pull of negativity. Often a thing is evil because of what it leads to, though not evil in itself. So the Satanic force draws us toward that as a step toward evil. From this we can see that virtually everything that exists has the possibility of being "satanic." For this reason Saint Peter wrote: "Be sober, be vigilant; because your adversary the devil, as a roaring lion, walketh about, seeking whom he may devour" (I Peter 5:8). And he has many "mouths" which which to devour.

What is the purpose of Satan, this great conglomerate of cosmic delusive force that seems to function with such devastating intelligence? In one of his talks, Yogananda told about the trials of Saint Anthony the Great when he was living in a tomb in the Egyptian desert. After describing the saint's tremendous struggle in a face-to-face encounter with Satan, the Master simply comments: "Satan is nothing but a test of God." Sufi saints have gone further and said that Satan is one of God's greatest servants, meaning that it is through satanic assaults that we become strong. Just as strong wind causes trees to put their roots deeper into the ground, in the same way our resistance to Satan makes us stronger and more able to withstand its onslaughts. With this perspective we understand that Saint Paul was stating the truth when he wrote: "We know that all things work together for good to them that love God" (Romans 8:28).

The words "and when the tempter came to him" are important. We are used to the idea that Satan sneaks up on us from behind and attacks us when we are unaware. But that is because we are facing in the wrong direction. When our consciousness is oriented Godward, we have no blind spots and always see things directly from the front and understand them directly without error. It is common to say that Satan takes advantage of our weakness, but that could not be if we were not creating and indulging that weakness. In a sense the devil always fights fair; we are just heedless and unprepared. That is the truth.

To face evil and see it clearly is to be assured of eventual victory over it, for evil is illusory and deceptive, and when confronted and clearly perceived it become disarmed to a great degree. This is why evil political movements like Nazism and Communism are terrified of even a single person who sees them for what they are and speaks it out. And this is also why morally degenerate people hate those who unmask the evil in which they indulge and reveal its destructive character, and why morally degenerate people decry the "negativity" of clear sight and clear speech. When you name it, it is already on the way out. Knowledge is indeed power.

Those who aspire to Christhood must rigorously train themselves in seeing, thinking and speaking clearly and truthfully (accurately). This does not mean going around "being frank" and insulting and condemning and inciting others to anger and hatred against evil and evildoers, but it does mean calmly stating the facts and not turning away from the truth of people, things or situations. Mostly we must be truthful to ourselves about ourselves; but we must also be honest with ourselves about all that lies outside us, as well.

The temptation by Satan was not at all persuasive for Jesus since he had the wisdom eye and wisdom ears open and the Christ Mind operative. He only underwent them for our instruction. Part of the test was to see if Jesus could recognize Satan, for that would be the root of his conquering of Satan. Jesus saw Satan and knew it for what it was. That is why Satan could not move him with its tests. Those who like him are established in higher consciousness cannot be moved or swept away by that which completely engulfs those who have not the eye or ear of spirit open. Jesus had to face Satan, just as Buddha had to face Mara. They passed the test because they were prepared by the practice of meditation. We must be the same.

There is nothing outside of God, the Absolute Reality and therefore the Absolute Truth. We speak of lies and illusions and delusions, but they are only distortions of truth. In essence, all things are real and true, so once we unbend the bent and make the crooked straight the truth is perceived. Actually, Satan is going to say some very profound and truthful things–even if for an evil purpose–and we can learn from its words.

If thou be the son of God, command that these stones be made bread. We know from Genesis that the fall of humanity proceeded from the act of eating (though of course the real transgression was in the putting forth of the will in a negative manner). "When the woman saw that the tree was good for food, and that it was pleasant to the eyes, and a tree to be desired to make one wise, she took of the fruit thereof, and did eat, and gave also unto her husband with her; and he did eat" (Genesis 3:6). After untold ages "the woman," Eve, was born on the earth as Mary, and Adam as her son, Jesus (see *Robe of Light*). Lucifer, the servant of Satan, had enticed them to this folly himself. Remembering the past of Jesus quite well, Satan presented another form of the same temptation to him–both as test and as mockery. This time the temptation seemed legitimate, for it is necessary that human beings sustain their lives through eating.

Jesus had gained great power through his spiritual ascension, a power that was intended for the liberation of the race which he had brought into slavery through his eating in Paradise. Furthermore, he could do nothing except at the command of God. Lucifer's temptation, then, covered several aspects, present and past. The temptation involved:

1) identification with the body through hunger;
2) identification of life with physical existence;
3) the use of spiritual power for material purpose;
4) the use of spiritual power for personal advantage;
5) the use of spiritual power for personal desire;
6) defense of ego against mockery and denial of one's power.

If Jesus had been the Second Person of the Trinity, the Eternal God in human form, as exoteric Christian theology says, Satan would never have tempted him, for he would have known that such a temptation was idle: God cannot be tempted in any way. Moreover, it is not likely that Satan could have endured the face-to-face Presence of the Creator God. But Jesus was not Infinite God by nature; he was *participating* in the Divine Essence through his conscious union with God, but he was not himself God. Hence the temptation of Jesus demonstrates his nature and his *attainment* as well as his power.

Satan really did not know what Jesus had become. That is, it had no idea whether those who had attained such a high level of evolution could be turned back and plunged into ignorance or not. Others such as Buddha had successfully resisted it, but that did not necessarily mean that a fall was impossible for such exalted spirits. Satan was experimenting with Jesus when it came to tempt him. The question was: Can a son of God fall from that condition and again become a son of matter? Can one who attains total union with God fall away from that union? We do not know whether Satan ever figured it out, but Saint John tells us: "Whosoever is born of God doth not commit sin; for his seed remaineth in him: and he cannot sin, because he is born of God" (I John 3:9).

One thing Satan did know about, and that was the divine creative power of Word (Logos); that although human beings may have leached this power out of themselves by continual and pointless chatter, those who preserve their inner resources through silence or cultivate them through silent meditation possess the power to create change by speaking with the full force of their will. "And God said, Let us make man in our image, after our likeness" (Genesis 1:26). Those who preserve and cultivate their divine likeness are able by the simple act of speaking to make things happen.

This power is written about in Yogananda's autobiography. In that book a great deal is told about the great Master Lahiri Mahasaya. One of Lahiri Mahasaya's relatives told me that as a child his grandfather (not Lahiri Mahasaya) had once become angry and said to another boy: "You should die," and the boy immediately became deathly ill. When his parents learned of this they begged him to tell their son to live. He did, and the boy was instantly well. Jesus, too, demonstrated this ability when a child. He once brought about the death of a boy by unguarded speech, but revived him by healing speech. He even made clay images live by telling them to live. (See *The Unknown Lives of Jesus and Mary*.)

The power of Logos resides in all human beings as images of him who merely said "Let there be light: and there was light" (Genesis 1:3).

Knowing that Jesus had attained superhuman status, Satan had no doubt of his ability to turn stone into bread by a word. If it had not been possible for him, it would have been no temptation at all. Perfect union made him omnipotent, since all that exists is a manifestation of that Divinity which lies at their core. Living in that Consciousness, Jesus could control all things, for It *is* all things. The real test of Satan was not whether Jesus *could* turn stone into bread, but whether he *would* do so.

Things are not true because they are written in sacred books; rather, things are written in sacred books because they are true. (I have said this before.) This is why the lives of saints and masters prove the validity of scriptures, not the other way around. Jesus was referring to this by the words: "It is written...." Spiritual truth is eternal; it is not something that goes in and out of vogue or validity. Truths are not just written, they are recorded in the ether by the demonstrations of the saints and masters who are living scriptures. For the sacred principles are embodied in the universe itself and in the evolving lives of those within the universe. It is ultimately a matter of Eternity.

Man shall not live by bread alone, but by every word that proceedeth out of the mouth of God. This means that we live by every creative impulse that issues forth from God, that we must remain in constant and full attunement with those impulses, "for in him we live, and move, and have our being" (Acts 17:28). Meditation makes this possible.

When Jesus said, "Be ye therefore perfect, even as your Father which is in heaven is perfect" (Matthew 5:48), the word translated "perfect" is *teleios*, which does not mean without fault, but rather without any lack, that is, *complete*. Just as the Consciousness and Being of God embraces all levels of existence, so should ours, even if only in a finite way.

Then the devil taketh him up into the holy city, and setteth him on a pinnacle of the temple, and saith unto him, If thou be the son of God, cast thyself down: for it is written, he shall give his angels charge concerning thee: and in their hands they shall bear thee up, lest at any time thou dash thy foot against a stone. How Bible-believing Satan has become! Just like a lot of its children. Religion is often a tool of Satan. "God Wills It" and "For The Glory of God" are two slogans beneath which some of the greatest atrocities of recorded history have taken place. Since this test is to take place under the veneer of trust in God, of a "show of faith," Satan is providing the holiest possible environment for it. I cannot count the number of times I have heard people urged to careless and foolish actions under the banner of "take it on faith." Tennessee snake handlers and poison drinkers are proof that some people are foolish enough to follow such advice.

Accordingly, Satan challenged Jesus to jump off the temple, since the book of Psalms (91:12) said that the angels of God will lift up the believer so he will not even hit his foot against a stone. It was in the Bible! Satan is a very capable theologian and philosopher when it suits it. Of course the meaning was spiritual, not material, even though God does protect us, often from ourselves. But Satan's implication was that to not jump would be for Jesus to admit doubt in God's loving providence, or in his divine sonship—at least that is how Satan wanted him to view it. But Jesus knew (as should we) that such things do not depend on the acts and thoughts of either ourselves or others, especially Satan. It is all in the hands of God.

Jesus said unto him, It is written again, Thou shalt not tempt the Lord thy God. That is, you should not foolishly think that you can put God on the spot by some if-you-don't-help-me-the-disaster-will-be-your-fault-and-prove-you-don't-care ploy. Attempting to force God's hand betrays a complete lack of understanding of God's ways or his nature. It is to deny God, not to express faith in him. But it is the madness of the human ego to wish to command God rather than serve him. There are also many instances in which people will do negative things to see if they have been established in a spiritual state which such actions cannot injure. Many times spiritual aspirants give into this temptation by thinking they will be protected if they do something doubtful or associate with corrupt people.

Nearly every spiritual person I have seen fall into spiritual death did so by small, seemingly insignificant acts that yet had great import. It was not the act but their state of mind that ruined them. Many have fallen because they felt they could help others and so put themselves in perilous situations. How many unfortunates decide that they have gone beyond the need for spiritual practice and safeguards and subsequently plunge to their deaths. "I used to be a monk [or nun]." "I used to be a vegetarian." "I used to meditate." "I used to be religious." "I used to think I couldn't do a lot of things." These are their epitaphs.

How could Satan just pick Jesus up and take him to Jerusalem and set him atop the temple? How could he take Jesus to the top of a great mountain? Normally evil spirits could not bear the mere presence of Jesus (Matthew 8:29; Mark 1:24; 5:7; Luke 4:34; 8:28), so how did the force of Cosmic Evil move Jesus around like a doll tossed about by a child? Because it was his karma. Having succumbed to Lucifer's temptation in Paradise (the astral world), he was karmically linked to Satan. And he broke the link by resisting the three temptations of Satan. We, then, should be very wary, for it may be our karma, too, to undergo such tests. If someone like Jesus can be carried around by Satan, then what do we think might happen to us? Self-doubt is not a good thing, but caution and an awareness of our possible susceptibility to evil *is* good.

Just as Jesus was in Jerusalem and standing on the temple, so also in the depths (heights) of meditation temptations and distractions may be encountered from various sources, usually our own mind and ego. The most common test, which we encounter almost every day, is the temptation to fix our attention on the things presented to our mind or the unusual experiences that can take place when we plumb the depths of the mind and enter into astral and causal awareness. If we train ourselves to ignore these distractions, then all will be well.

People mistake "being high" for being in a high state of consciousness. They are not the same. Most people are astral drunks when they think they are being enlightened. Often meditators have remarkable, exalted experiences, experiences that would seem from natural reasoning to indicate the attainment of a very high level of spiritual development. But it may not be so at all, and will only engender in them the false belief that they have attained perfect self-realization. Meditators need to be especially aware of this very real danger.

Remember: Jesus did not tread the path for us; rather, he underwent everything we are going to experience in order to show us how to deal with them ourselves. He has even shown us how to survive crucifixion and burial. Most of the things he demonstrated in his outer life symbolize what may occur to us in our inner life. And Satan in the form of our ego is with us right up to the end, which is perfect liberation, the dissolution of the ego.

Again, the devil taketh him up into an exceeding high mountain, and sheweth him all the kingdoms of the world, and the glory of them; and saith unto him, All these things will I give thee, if thou wilt fall down and worship me. There is a profound error in Christianity: the idea that this world belongs to the devil, who is "the Lord of the world" (they think). This is ignorant blasphemy. God alone owns all things, however much we may use and abuse them for a short time (only). By this we see that corrupted Christianity operates on the same erroneous premises as Satan–and therefore is itself Satanic. There is a basis for this misunderstanding, though. Three times in the Gospel of John, Jesus refers to "the prince of this world" (John 12:31; 14:30; 16:11). He does not mean Satan in the sense of Cosmic Evil, but the archangel who was put in charge of the world, just as every sun and planet has a guardian angel who supervises the development and evolution of the sun or planet and all that live therein. This archangel fell at the time of the insurrection of Lucifer. Although Archangel Michael was put in charge of the earth after breaking the hold of Lucifer and the other rebels against God, they are still around making trouble, permitted to do so by the cosmic plan.

"And there was war in heaven: Michael and his angels fought against the dragon; and the dragon fought and his angels, and prevailed not; neither was their place found any more in heaven. And the great dragon was cast out, that old serpent, called the Devil, and Satan, which deceiveth the whole world: he was cast out into the earth, and his angels were cast out with him.… Woe to the inhabiters of the earth and of the sea! for the devil is come down unto you, having great wrath, because he knoweth that he hath but a short time" (Revelation 12:7-9, 12). However, Satan only has power when it is ceded to it by foolish and negative human beings. So it was lying when it pretended that it owned the world and could give it away. Satan has power, but it is not its own; it usually proceeds from those it dupes, who give up their very life energy, thinking that Satan is *giving* it to them in return for their allegiance.

How does a person become a dupe of Satan? Easily. 1) By not standing upright in his integrity and consciousness. 2) By not cultivating his potential as an image of God. 3) By living beneath his present and possible level of evolution and consciousness. 4) By immersion in material, egocentric consciousness. This how a person falls downward, degrades himself and devotes himself to (worships) Cosmic Ignorance. He will be rewarded by Satan accordingly with further descent into the darkness of ignorance. But all the time he will boast about how high he is rising, how clever and competent he is becoming. At last, sunk head-down in the muck, he will boast that he has ascended to the heights of heaven.

Of such a one it can also be said: "How art thou fallen from heaven,… how art thou cut down to the ground,…! For thou hast said in thine heart, I will ascend into heaven, I will exalt my throne above the stars of God: I will sit also upon the mount of the congregation, in the sides of the north: I will ascend above the heights of the clouds; I will be like the most High. Yet thou shalt be brought down to hell, to the sides of the pit" (Isaiah 14:12-15). The word translated "pit" is *bowr*, which has the connotation of being pit used as a prison. This world is the prison of us all who wander in samsara. That is why when someone asked Yogananda if he believed in hell, he replied, smiling: "Where do you think you are?" This condition of imprisonment is spoken of in the Yoga Sutras of Patanjali as being *prakritilaya*, merged in materiality. "Upon thy belly shalt thou go, and dust shalt thou eat all the days of thy life" (Genesis 3:14).

Then saith Jesus unto him, Get thee hence, Satan: for it is written, Thou shalt worship the Lord thy God, and him only shalt thou serve). Perseverance, maintaining the momentum of spiritual life, is perhaps the number one problem the aspirant faces. Inertia is a law of existence, and those who wish to pierce beyond the veil of illusion have to overcome and reverse it in themselves. The spiritual history of the world consists mostly of individuals and movements that started out well and then either slowed to a halt, began going in reverse or dissolved. Failure is the usual scenario. Why? Spiritual life consists of two parts: (1) the continual invocation of higher consciousness and life, and (2) the continual expulsion of lower consciousness and its accoutrements. The problem is that seekers do not maintain these two flows–positive inward and negative outward–consistently and steadily. Many think that only one will do the necessary, so they ignore the other side of the process. They also keep the movements going in fits and starts and fluctuations in intensity. Almost always the result is defeat.

The most commonly neglected thing is the process of eliminating the foolish and the negative from our inner and outer life. It must never stop, for the dust of illusion keeps settling on the mirror of our mind. To teach us this, Jesus told Satan: "Get thee hence." I cannot count the number of people I have personally known who started the process of purification, but did not keep it up. They all fell away, and many became much worse than they were when they began. "When the unclean spirit is gone out of a man, he walketh through dry places, seeking rest, and findeth none. Then he saith, I will return into my house from whence I came out; and when he is come, he findeth it empty, swept, and garnished. Then goeth he, and taketh with himself seven other spirits more wicked than himself, and they enter in and dwell there: and the last state of that man is worse than the first" (Matthew 12:43-45).

The closing words of Jesus: "Thou shalt worship the Lord thy God, and him only shalt thou serve," mean that God must be made the exclusive focus of our lives, that ever-increasing higher consciousness must constantly be the main function of our minds and hearts. As Jesus himself defined it: "Thou shalt love the Lord thy God with all thy heart, and with all thy soul, and with all thy mind, and with all thy strength" (Mark 12:30).

Then the devil leaveth him, and, behold, angels came and ministered unto him. Once the demons are gone, then the angels can come to us. In the lives of the saints we find many instances in which they struggled painfully against evil spirits or Satan itself almost to the point of breakdown. But then their opponents dissolved away and Christ himself came to be their consolation. On quite a few occasions they demanded of Jesus where he had been during their tribulation. Each time he told them that he had been invisibly present, actually in their heart, waiting to see if their love would persevere; for only love enables us to pass through the purgation fires of deification (*theosis*).

I have to relay this, one of my favorite stories of a saint. Saint Teresa of Avila was sick and exhausted, yet never stopped her spiritual work. One time in the winter she was crossing a river in a rickety cart which dumped her out and up to her neck in freezing water. "Oh, Lord!" she expostulated, "Why did you do this to me?" God answered, "I always treat my friends this way." "Then no wonder you have so few!" was her comment. But she remained His friend. And so must we.

Do not think of angels as wispy phantoms or little fat babies with tiny wings–or worse, little baby heads with no bodies, but wings where their necks should be. Angels are those that have evolved beyond the human plane and attained levels completely beyond our comprehension. Yet, though they have progressed so much, they do not reign, but serve. This is, in fact, a measure of evolution: the more evolved a being, the more he serves God and his fellow beings. And the higher he is, the more he cares for the lowly. God is the Supreme Servant whose care extends even unto the lowest and smallest atom in creation.

Angelos means a messenger, but in the sense of one who fosters and looks after. It comes from the word *ago*, which means to lead, bring, urge, move forward, bring forth, carry and open up. All these things the angels, among which the saints are numbered, do for those who turn away from Satan, who lift their heads from the earth, stand up, and begin their ascent–the same ascent the angels and the saints made so long ago. After Jesus' ordeal, the angels did indeed bear him up. When we study the life of Jesus, the pattern our lives must follow, we see what it takes to really communicate with angels.

The scene at the Jordan when Jesus was baptized was glorious: the voice of God proclaimed him a son of God. But the necessary follow-up was this formidable testing. It came right at the beginning of his earthly ministry. So we must right away face the same. It will be much less intense, since we are not great like him, but for where we are at the moment it will be intense enough. And it will not be the last testing, as it was not the last for him. "And when the devil had ended all the temptation, he departed from him *for a season*" (Luke 4:13). Many more tests awaited him, and finally Gethsemane and Golgotha.

John the Baptist Witnesses to Jesus

These things were done in Bethabara beyond Jordan, where John was baptizing.

The next day John seeth Jesus coming unto him, and saith, Behold the Lamb of God, which taketh away the sin of the world. This is he of whom I said, After me cometh a man which is preferred before me: for he was before me. And I knew him not: but that he should be made manifest to Israel, therefore am I come baptizing with water.

And John bare record, saying, I saw the Spirit descending from heaven like a dove, and it abode upon him. And I knew him not: but he that sent me to baptize with water, the same said unto me, Upon whom thou shalt see the Spirit descending, and remaining on him, the same is he which baptizeth with the Holy Ghost. And I saw, and bare record that this is the Son of God (John 1:29-34).

The next day John seeth Jesus coming unto him, and saith, Behold the Lamb of God, which taketh away the sin of the world. Unfortunately, because of the contemporary obsession with blood sacrifice it was assumed that Saint John called Jesus "the Lamb of God" because he was to be sacrificed to expiate the sins of humanity. When stated that plainly it is obvious how silly that idea is, but if such attitudes have prevailed in a religion it is equally obvious how its adherents can erroneously view Jesus in that way.

A lamb is considered the embodiment of innocence, meekness and harmlessness. Isaiah had prophesied: "He was oppressed, and he was afflicted, yet he opened not his mouth: he is brought as a lamb to the slaughter, and as a sheep before her shearers is dumb, so he openeth not his mouth" (Isaiah 53:7). As we will see much later, Jesus will not defend himself when he is brought to trial for his life. As Isaiah (42:3) also prophesied: "A bruised reed shall he not break, and the smoking flax shall he not quench." For he was perfected in the virtue of ahimsa, of non-violence and non-injury in relation to others. By his example Jesus shows us the need for humility, gentleness and meekness. Yet he was also our example of justice, courage and defense of the truth.

Saint John said that Jesus "taketh away the sin of the world." This is another example of the divine work in us of the inner Christ. The word translated "taketh away" is *airo*, which means to lift up and take away, to dispel something as though it were a mirage–which sin really is. The idea is that when Christ consciousness is established in us all ignorance and sin are dispelled like the darkness and dream they are. "Sin" is the translation of *amartia*, which comes from the root word *amartano*, which means to miss the mark, to fail. It has nothing to do with breaking rules and displeasing God. It means to fall short of attaining and manifesting our Christhood. That why the word "shortcoming," now so seldom used, gives the right idea about "sin."

And what is the world, the *kosmos*? It is the dream of relative, ego-centered existence. Interestingly, *kosmos* means something put on like a mask or costume, an assumed illusion. Its root word *komidzo* means to carry off something, and the *kosmos* truly does carry us away and immerse us in its dreamworld. The idea is that the Christ in us the hope of glory will take away from us the illusion which takes us away from and blinds us to our real nature as gods within God.

This is he of whom I said, After me cometh a man which is preferred before me: for he was before me. Saint John and Jesus were cousins, and it was Saint John who was Jesus' example and teacher in leading the contemplative life. But John now says that Jesus "is preferred before me," which is a very poor translation. *Ginomai* means to cause or be made to become something other, to be completed or fulfilled in the sense of growth (evolution). *Emprosthen* means to become in front of or ahead of something or someone, and its root word *protos* means to be the best. So Jesus has gone far beyond and transcended the evolutionary path and is a siddha-purusha, an avatar, truly Immanuel: God With Us.

And I knew him not: but that he should be made manifest to Israel, therefore am I come baptizing with water. The English is strange here, but the idea is that at first Saint John literally did not recognize Jesus when he came to the Jordan because of the alteration in him that had come about from his years in India when all veils were dissolved and his siddha nature became revealed. However, Saint John knew upon seeing him that he was the Messiah and his destiny was to be a part in revealing him.

And John bare record, saying, I saw the Spirit descending from heaven like a dove, and it abode upon him. And I knew him not: but he that sent me to baptize with water, the same said unto me, Upon whom thou shalt see the Spirit descending, and remaining on him, the same is he which baptizeth with the Holy Ghost. And I saw, and bare record that this is the Son of God. That is certainly clear!

JESUS MEETS AND CALLS HIS FIRST DISCIPLES

Again the next day after John stood, and two of his disciples; and looking upon Jesus as he walked, he saith, Behold the Lamb of God! And the two disciples heard him speak, and they followed Jesus.

Then Jesus turned, and saw them following, and saith unto them, What seek ye? They said unto him, Rabbi, (which is to say, being interpreted, Master,) where dwellest thou? He saith unto them, Come and see. They came and saw where he dwelt, and abode with him that day: for it was about the tenth hour.

One of the two which heard John speak, and followed him, was Andrew, Simon Peter's brother (John 1:35-40).

Again the next day after John stood, and two of his disciples; and looking upon Jesus as he walked, he saith, Behold the Lamb of God! And the two disciples heard him speak, and they followed Jesus. Now this is the way things work when they are going to be successful. No shillying and shallying and wondering "what shall I do" and "what about…" or "what if…," but direct, straightforward action. The two men considering themselves disciples of Saint John heard his declaration about Jesus and they immediately went to follow him.

Swami Vivekananda had a very devoted disciple who went with him everywhere. The man had been the superintendent of a major railroad station. One day he saw Vivekanandaji waiting for a train. When the train came and Swamiji got in, the superintendent got in also and sat down.

"Wherever you are going, I am going," he told the Swami. Just think, he abandoned that important position of authority and trust and could have gotten in terrible trouble for just walking off. One day Swamiji asked him: "If you meet someone you think is a better teacher than I am, will you leave me and follow him?" Without a moment's hesitation the man replied: "Yes!" Vivekanandaji hugged him and said: "Now I know you really are my disciple."

Different was an occasion when I was in a taxi in New Delhi with my friend the yoga siddha Sri Dattabal and a man who aspired to be his disciple. The man had his arm hanging out the window in very heavy and close traffic. Dattabalji said to the man, "Pull in your arm." Why?" asked the man. "Do it first and then I will tell you why," answered Dattabal. I had a pretty good idea that this man would never become a disciple of Dattabal.

"And it came to pass after these things, that God did tempt [test] Abraham, and said unto him, Abraham: and he said, Behold, here I am" (Genesis 22:1). Instant response. We are told in the book of First Samuel (3:10) that when the prophet was just a little child and God spoke to him he replied: "Speak; for thy servant heareth." That is how it is done. It is not a matter of being impractical or being slavishly obedient, but the readiness to go after God in a moment. When I was little we often heard the expression "Johnny on the spot," meaning a rapid and ready person when there was something to be done. This is a necessity in spiritual life, as well.

Then Jesus turned, and saw them following, and saith unto them, What seek ye? They said unto him, Rabbi, (which is to say, being interpreted, Master,) where dwellest thou? This is a marvelous parable-symbol of the true seekers finding a true teacher. They do not ask about philosophy or religion or any ego-centered desires they want fulfilled. Rather, they want to know how to attain the same state of consciousness as the teacher.

He saith unto them, Come and see. A true teacher does not boast of his attainments and make great claims about himself, but tells people that he will show them the way they can themselves attain to Self-realization: "knowledge of God which is nearer than knowing, open vision direct and instant" (Bhagavad Gita 9:1; Prabhavananda translation.)

They came and saw where he dwelt, and abode with him. They learned and applied and lived in the same state of realization as the teacher.

One of the two which heard John speak, and followed him, was Andrew, Simon Peter's brother.

More Disciples Come to Jesus

He [Andrew] first findeth his own brother Simon, and saith unto him, We have found the Messias, which is, being interpreted, the Christ. And he brought him to Jesus. And when Jesus beheld him, he said, Thou art Simon the son of Jona: thou shalt be called Cephas, which is by interpretation, A stone.

The day following Jesus would go forth into Galilee, and findeth Philip, and saith unto him, Follow me. Now Philip was of Bethsaida, the city of Andrew and Peter.

Philip findeth Nathanael, and saith unto him, We have found him, of whom Moses in the law, and the prophets, did write, Jesus of Nazareth, the son of Joseph. And Nathanael said unto him, Can there any good thing come out of Nazareth? Philip saith unto him, Come and see.

Jesus saw Nathanael coming to him, and saith of him, Behold an Israelite indeed, in whom is no guile! Nathanael saith unto him, Whence knowest thou me? Jesus answered and said unto him, Before that Philip called thee, when thou wast under the fig tree, I saw thee. Nathanael answered and saith unto him, Rabbi, thou art the Son of God; thou art the King of Israel.

Jesus answered and said unto him, Because I said unto thee, I saw thee under the fig tree, believest thou? thou shalt see greater things than these. And he saith unto him, Verily, verily, I say unto you, Hereafter ye shall see heaven open,

and the angels of God ascending and descending upon the
Son of man. (John 1:35-51).

He first findeth his own brother Simon, and saith unto him, We have found the Messias, which is, being interpreted, the Christ. And he brought him to Jesus. And when Jesus beheld him, he said, Thou art Simon the son of Jona:... We see from this that in his omniscience Jesus knew Saint Peter, and knew all about him.

This reminds me of an evening in Kanpur (India). Anandamayi Ma was sitting on a cot at the front of a crowded satsang hall. Sitting in front of Ma on the floor was a friend of mine who had a few weeks earlier met Ma for the first time. Within the hour she would have to go to take a train to Delhi and fly back to America. Naturally she was feeling sad at the prospect of leaving Ma, who leaned forward and said, smiling: "You are not new to me. I know you very well."

When Brother (Swami) Bimalananda met Yogananda for the first time, he was standing in a line after the Sunday service at the Hollywood SRF center waiting to pranam to the Master. Yoganandaji looked away from the person in front of him and looked over at Bimalananda and began to laugh heartily. Later he told Bimalanandaji that he laughed because he remembered the funny antics he used to perform in a previous life as a kind of clown in India when Yogananda knew him in that life.

...thou shalt be called Cephas,... which is by interpretation, A stone. The word *Kephas* means a rock. Later the symbolism of this will be revealed in a conversation between Peter and Jesus.

The day following Jesus would go forth into Galilee, and findeth Philip, and saith unto him, Follow me. Now Philip was of Bethsaida, the city of Andrew and Peter. It is said that during his morning meditation Buddha would actually see clairvoyantly those people who were nearby and ready to accept his message of enlightenment. After his meditation he would then go and find them and speak with them. Here we see Jesus doing the same. What is striking about this account is that Jesus simply said "Follow Me." No introductions or preambles. Just: Come. Such meetings and such responses indicate profound affinities between teacher and student, often with roots in previous lives together.

Philip findeth Nathanael, and saith unto him, We have found him, of whom Moses in the law, and the prophets, did write, Jesus of Nazareth, the son of Joseph. And Nathanael said unto him, Can there any good thing come out of Nazareth? Philip saith unto him, Come and see. Here we find the kind of regional prejudice that is found throughout the world. I remember how shocked I was when a woman told me that my beloved friend the Russian Orthodox bishop of Chicago, Archbishop Seraphim, was greatly disliked by the Russians in San Francisco. "That is because they are from a different place in Russia than the people here in Chicago," she explained. Some years later a friend of mine told me that in a Lebanese (Syrian) Orthodox church he belonged to in Tulsa the members would not speak to those from a different part of Lebanon than theirs, and would even refuse to exchange greetings with them at Christmas and Easter. Once I took a Pakistani friend to lunch in an Indian restaurant. Our waiter was also a Pakistani, and the two spoke briefly together. When the waiter walked away my friend said to me: "People from his part of Pakistan and those from my part never trust each other and never associate with one another."

Galilee was despised by most non-Galileans, the Galileans being considered backward and of no consequence. Later we will encounter the expression "Galilee of the Gentiles" (Matthew 4:15). Galilaia (Galiloea) means "the heathen circle," and Gentile also means heathen–non Jewish. Apparently various nationalities lived there and intermarried, so the racial "purity" of those from Galilee were suspect to those from other regions. It is known that the Romans stationed quite a number of European soldiers there and of course there was illegitimate intermixture.

Jesus saw Nathanael coming to him, and saith of him, Behold an Israelite indeed, in whom is no guile! Nathanael saith unto him, Whence knowest thou me? Jesus answered and said unto him, Before that Philip called thee, when thou wast under the fig tree, I saw thee. This brings to mind an incident recorded in Chapter Forty Two of *The Gospel of Sri Ramakrishna*. The author, Mahendranath Gupta, called "Master Mahasaya the Blissful Devotee" in Chapter Nine of *Autobiography of a Yogi*, was speaking with

Sri Ramakrishna who suddenly asked him: "Do you remember the great storm of the month of Aswin?" He replied: "Yes, sir. I was very young at that time–nine or ten years old. I was alone in a room while the storm was raging, and I prayed to God." Master Mahasaya was surprised and said to himself: "Why did the Master suddenly ask me about the great storm of Aswin? Does he know that I was alone at that time earnestly praying to God with tears in my eyes? Does he know all this? Has he been protecting me as my guru since my very birth?" Such things are not uncommon in the lives of great masters, especially in their encounters with those who were disciples in previous lives.

Nathanael answered and saith unto him, Rabbi, thou art the Son of God; thou art the King of Israel. Jesus answered and said unto him, Because I said unto thee, I saw thee under the fig tree, believest thou? thou shalt see greater things than these. And he saith unto him, Verily, verily, I say unto you, Hereafter ye shall see heaven open, and the angels of God ascending and descending upon the Son of man. In Genesis we find this incident: "Jacob went out from Beersheba, and went toward Haran. And he lighted upon a certain place, and tarried there all night, because the sun was set; and he took of the stones of that place, and put them for his pillows, and lay down in that place to sleep. And he dreamed, and behold a ladder set up on the earth, and the top of it reached to heaven: and behold the angels of God ascending and descending on it" (Genesis 28:10-12). In that instance it was the holiness of the place that drew the angels, but in this one it was Jesus who was the purpose of the angels' ascent and descent. We have no record of the fulfillment of Jesus' prophecy but it surely did take place. Sri Ramakrishna told Mahendranath Gupta that he (Mahendranath) had been a disciple of Jesus. Perhaps he was Nathanael. The path to God is long and has many turnings but everything eventually comes into the unwaning light and all loose ends become perfectly joined.

Jesus Performs His First Public Miracle

And the third day there was a marriage in Cana of Galilee; and the mother of Jesus was there: And both Jesus was called, and his disciples, to the marriage. And when they wanted wine, the mother of Jesus saith unto him, They have no wine. Jesus saith unto her, Woman, what have I to do with thee? mine hour is not yet come. His mother saith unto the servants, Whatsoever he saith unto you, do it. And there were set there six waterpots of stone, after the manner of the purifying of the Jews [Judeans], containing two or three firkins apiece. Jesus saith unto them, Fill the waterpots with water. And they filled them up to the brim. And he saith unto them, Draw out now, and bear unto the governor of the feast. And they bare it. When the ruler of the feast had tasted the water that was made wine, and knew not whence it was: (but the servants which drew the water knew;) the governor of the feast called the bridegroom, and saith unto him, Every man at the beginning doth set forth good wine; and when men have well drunk, then that which is worse: but thou hast kept the good wine until now. This beginning of miracles did Jesus in Cana of Galilee, and manifested forth his glory; and his disciples believed on him (John 2:1-11).

Jesus Performs His First Public Miracle

And the third day there was a marriage in Cana of Galilee; and the mother of Jesus was there: And both Jesus was called, and his disciples, to the marriage. Saint John tells us that the Virgin Mary was there because she is going to be a key figure in the event to be described.

Catherine Emmerich saw in her supernatural visions that the only reason Jesus agreed to come to wedding was because the bride and groom, both his Essene friends, told him they would be observing lifelong celibacy–a common practice among the Essenes.

And when they wanted wine, the mother of Jesus saith unto him, They have no wine. Jesus saith unto her, Woman, what have I to do with thee? mine hour is not yet come. For Jesus to address the Virgin Mary as "woman" may seem a rebuff or outright rudeness, but it just the opposite. It was not considered respectful to address someone in public by their name or a familiar term or relationship such as "mother." "Woman" was actually a term of respectful formality in a public situation.

However, we see that Jesus says that the time had not come for him to begin revealing himself by miracles. Yet he will work a miracle before the time because his mother wants him to. This shows the regard he had for her, which is natural since she was his equal in evolution and destiny. So Jesus' ministry begins at the intercession of the Holy Virgin.

His mother saith unto the servants, Whatsoever he saith unto you, do it. This has tremendous significance, for it shows the absolute assurance of the Virgin Mother that Jesus would do as she asked. She had no doubt whatsoever of her intercessory status with him in the divine order. Also, this simple sentence is in a sense the only spiritual instruction the Virgin gives in the Gospels. Whatever Jesus says to do, we should do it, and that includes following his perfect example.

The subsequent conversation of the governor of the feast with the bridegroom reveals that the wine miraculously produced by Jesus was vastly superior to what had been served before. There is a tradition that the wine actually made everyone who drank it sober and clear-headed. However that may be (and I believe it), "this beginning of miracles did Jesus in Cana of Galilee, and manifested forth his glory; and his disciples believed on him."

The First Cleansing of the Temple at Passover

The Jews' [Judeans'] passover was at hand, and Jesus went up to Jerusalem, and found in the temple those that sold oxen and sheep and doves, and the changers of money sitting. And when he had made a scourge of small cords, he drove them all out of the temple, and the sheep, and the oxen; and poured out the changers' money, and overthrew the tables; and said unto them that sold doves, Take these things hence; make not my Father's house an house of merchandise.

And his disciples remembered that it was written, The zeal of thine house hath eaten me up (John 2:13-17).

The Jews' [Judeans'] passover was at hand. This an important expression. The Jews [Judeans] and the Galileans dated Passover differently. For example, according to John's Gospel, at the end of Jesus' life Jesus and the apostles had observed Passover on Thursday, whereas the Jews [Judeans] were observing it on Saturday. This was a major conflict between the Jews [Judeans] and Galileans, just as later on controversy raged (not too strong a word) for centuries between Christians over the dating of Easter.

Uppermost in Jesus' mind in this account is the spiritual defilement of the temple by the commerce going on right in the place where only prayer and worship was to be offered. Actually, shameless racketeering was going on daily in the temple. Nothing would be offered by the priests that was not bought in the temple with temple money. So first the worshipper had to change his ordinary money into temple money, and this was done at a tremendously unfair rate–so much so that wealthy people coming from outside Israel with a great deal of money to purchase offerings ended up being able to buy very little. "Fleecing" is a perfect word for what went on daily for everyone who came to make offerings. Adding even more insult to injury, when the worshipper wanted to change any leftover temple money back into ordinary money the exchange rate was again outrageously to their disadvantage. It was not unknown for some pilgrims to return home virtually a pauper.

The scourge Jesus made and used to drive out the racketeers was only made of small cords. So how was he able to drive them all away? By the power of his will which was that of divinity, not mere humanity. As Jesus said to Saint Peter who tried to defend him from arrest by drawing his sword, "Thinkest thou that I cannot now pray to my Father, and he shall presently give me more than twelve legions of angels?" (Matthew 26:53).

The disciples were reminded of Psalms 69:9: "For the zeal of thine house hath eaten me up," though "consumed me" is a better translation.

There is also an important symbolism and principle in this incident. Our body is a temple of God. "Know ye not that ye are the temple of God, and that the Spirit of God dwelleth in you?" (I Corinthians 3:16). "Know ye not that your body is the temple of the Holy Ghost which is in you?" (I Corinthians 6:19). "For ye are the temple of the living God" (II Corinthians 6:16). This body temple has one fundamental purpose: the realization of God, just as the external temple was meant for the ritual worship of God. Every one of us is an incarnation of God, for our spirit-Self is an eternal part of God, and all our body-vehicles–physical, astral and causal–comprise that living temple complex. Therefore our entire life must be dedicated to this realization and manifestation. To that end, all that is "us" must be preserved in a state of the highest purity. This is the purpose of the yogic observances known as yama and niyama.

Yama means self-restraint in the sense of self-mastery, or abstention, and consists of five elements. Niyama means observances, of which there are also five. Here is the complete list as given in Yoga Sutras 2:30, 32:

    1) Ahimsa: non-violence, non-injury, harmlessness
    2) Satya: truthfulness, honesty

3) Asteya: non-stealing, honesty, non-misappropriativeness

4) Brahmacharya: sexual continence in thought, word and deed as well as control of all the senses

5) Aparigraha: non-possessiveness, non-greed, non-selfishness, non-acquisitiveness

6) Shaucha: purity, cleanliness

7) Santosha: contentment, peacefulness

8) Tapas: austerity, practical (i.e., result-producing) spiritual discipline

9) Swadhyaya: introspective self-study, spiritual study

10) Ishwarapranidhana: offering of one's life to God

(For a complete analysis of each one of these, see Chapter Six: The Foundations of Yoga, in *Soham Yoga: The Yoga of the Self*.)

> **Then answered the Jews [Judeans] and said unto him, What sign shewest thou unto us, seeing that thou doest these things? Jesus answered and said unto them, Destroy this temple, and in three days I will raise it up. Then said the Jews [Judeans], Forty and six years was this temple in building, and wilt thou rear it up in three days? But he spake of the temple of his body. When therefore he was risen from the dead, his disciples remembered that he had said this unto them; and they believed the scripture, and the word which Jesus had said (John 2:18-22).**

The Jews. It is singularly important for us to realize that in the Gospels the expression "Jews" does not always mean the Hebrews, all the descendants of Abraham, but can also be translated "Judeans" when the text is referring only to the residents of Judea, many of whom collaborated with the Romans in their occupation of Israel. The high priest, the major figure in the religion, was a Judean toady appointed by the Roman governor. Just as in the twentieth century there were officials of the Russian Orthodox Church that cooperated with the Communists (Bolsheviks) and subordinated the Church to the control of the Communist government, engaged in propaganda for the Communists, claiming that there was complete religious freedom in the Soviet Union and even having any "dissidents" who disagreed with their betrayal of the Church put into prisons and concentration camps and often executed. For this reason the refugee Russian Orthodox always referred to these people as "the Soviet Church," and not at all spiritually legitimate. This should be kept in mind when reading the Gospels.

Throughout the Mediterranean world the Hebrews considered the Judeans as betrayers and collaborators with their enemies. Those who became Christians considered Judas a perfect symbol of the Judeans and their betrayal. Since most Christians were Hebrews in the beginning, even in ancient texts we find denunciations of the Judeans with very disparaging terms. "O, you perfidious Judeans," was a common one. Unfortunately the non-Hebrew Christians came to consider that such expressions were to be applied to Hebrews in general, just as today Americans are often called "Yankees" by Europeans, even though that expression refers only to those from New England. Since the collaboration of the Judeans with the Romans ended nearly two thousand years ago along with the Roman empire, it is incredible that these expressions and attitudes should have continued until now.

The Insight of Jesus

> Now when he was in Jerusalem at the passover, in the feast day, many believed in his name, when they saw the miracles which he did. But Jesus did not commit himself unto them, because he knew all men, and needed not that any should testify of man: for he knew what was in man (John 2:23-25).

This last sentence is a sad truth: human beings are filled with ego, greed and selfishness–hardly foundations on which a genuine spiritual life can be built. The inner Christ will only "commit himself" to those who have driven out of themselves all the qualities of a Judas–the betrayers of spirit that subject it to its enemies that are the opposites of the principles of yama and niyama.

I once got an email from a man who asked me how he could *make* God answer his prayers. This is the attitude of many: how to persuade or force God to pay attention to their desires. Of course these people never think that God might have some input in this. Certainly we do not need to please or placate God to get his "favor," for God is not an egotist or a being that can be influenced by anyone or anything else. The real situation is one of alignment. God has an essential divine nature, and so do we. The less we cultivate and manifest that nature, the "farther" we are from God and the more he is "deaf" he is to us and we are "deaf" to him. The more we purify ourselves by yama and niyama, the more our inner, divine nature is revealed and begins to function in a practical matter. This is what I mean by "alignment" with God.

Saint James wrote: "Draw nigh to God, and he will draw nigh to you. Cleanse your hands, ye sinners; and purify your hearts, ye double minded"

(James 4:8). Here, too, we see it is a matter of purification. Of course, God is always with us, seated in our heart, one with our total being. But we are out of phase with that divine presence. People need to cleanse their will and minds. They are double-minded in relation to God. They want God to be completely in conformity with their will and wishes, but consider that the idea of their being completely in conformity with the will and ways of God to be impossible, unnecessary or fanaticism—"cracked on religion," "overboard" and "extremist." God is to come to them, they are not to go to God. So every time something they do not like happens either to them or in their environment they demand why God "allows" or does not "do" something about it. It never crosses their mind that the "doing" might have to be on their part.

When I was a child three sisters in our church formed a trio and sang very beautifully on Sundays. One of their best songs began: "What shall I give Thee, Master?" and concluded: "Not just a part, or half of my heart. I will give all to Thee." And the congregation responded: "Amen. Praise the Lord." But no one actually gave any of their heart or their life. In *Almost An Angel* the main character dreams he meets God. At one point he says to God (Charlton Heston), "You're God. I can't lie to You." And God replies: "You can try." A lot of people try; but you cannot fool God.

Nicodemus Speaks With Jesus

There was a man of the Pharisees, named Nicodemus, a ruler of the Jews [Judeans]. The same came to Jesus by night, and said unto him, Rabbi, we know that thou art a teacher come from God: for no man can do these miracles that thou doest, except God be with him.

Jesus answered and said unto him, Verily, verily, I say unto thee, Except a man be born again, he cannot see the kingdom of God.

Nicodemus saith unto him, How can a man be born when he is old? can he enter the second time into his mother's womb, and be born?

Jesus answered, Verily, verily, I say unto thee, Except a man be born of water and of the Spirit, he cannot enter into the kingdom of God. That which is born of the flesh is flesh; and that which is born of the Spirit is spirit. Marvel not that I said unto thee, Ye must be born again. The wind bloweth where it listeth, and thou hearest the sound thereof, but canst not tell whence it cometh, and whither it goeth: so is every one that is born of the Spirit.

Nicodemus answered and said unto him, How can these things be?

Jesus answered and said unto him, Art thou a master of Israel, and knowest not these things? Verily, verily, I say unto thee, We speak that we do know, and testify that we have seen; and ye receive not our witness. If I have told you earthly things, and ye believe not, how shall ye believe, if I tell you of heavenly things?

And no man hath ascended up to heaven, but he that came down from heaven, even the Son of man which is in heaven. And as Moses lifted up the serpent in the wilderness, even so must the Son of man be lifted up, that whosoever believeth in him should not perish, but have eternal life. For God so loved the world, that he gave his only begotten Son, that whosoever believeth in him should not perish, but have everlasting life. For God sent not his Son into the world to condemn the world; but that the world through him might be saved. He that believeth on him is not condemned: but he that believeth not is condemned already, because he hath not believed in the name of the only begotten Son of God.

And this is the condemnation, that light is come into the world, and men loved darkness rather than light, because their deeds were evil. For every one that doeth evil hateth the light, neither cometh to the light, lest his deeds should be reproved. But he that doeth truth cometh to the light, that his deeds may be made manifest, that they are wrought in God (John 3:1-21).

There was a man of the Pharisees, named Nicodemus, a ruler of the Jews [Judeans]. Saint Nicodemus was a member of the Sanhedrin and did his best to prevent the condemnation of Jesus. He also helped Saint Joseph of Arimathea prepare the body of Jesus for burial. In *The Unknown Lives of Jesus and Mary* I have included a text called *The Gospel of Nicodemus* that gives very interesting information about the crucifixion and resurrection of Jesus.

The same came to Jesus by night, and said unto him, Rabbi, we know that thou art a teacher come from God: for no man can do these miracles that thou doest, except God be with him. Miracles are a very poor basis on which to decide the spiritual status of anyone. Many miracle-workers have come to a very bad end. I myself witnessed a man working incredible miracles, which he continued for many years, but he ended up claiming to be Elijah returned to earth to announce the soon-to-be second coming of Jesus. Another miraculous healer I saw on television ended up a hopeless alcoholic and a moral and mental wreck. The famous evangelist Amy McPherson worked astonishing miracles and had great psychic powers, but she was an embezzler, a drug and sex addict that committed suicide.

Jesus answered and said unto him, Verily, verily, I say unto thee, Except a man be born again, he cannot see the kingdom of God. Here is the truth of the matter. It is a rebirth, a permanent entering into the pure consciousness of the divine Spirit, that indicates when someone is "of God." Jesus is not the Son of God because of what he did or taught, but because of what he WAS.

We must be "born" into spirit consciousness and live in that perpetually and irrevocably. Perhaps the most influential spiritual magazine in India is the *Kalyan Kalpataru*, which was begun in 1926 and continues today. They have a policy of never publishing photos of, or articles about, any living spiritual figure, because they have seen through nearly one hundred years that those who begin well, even as spiritual teachers, can end in total spiritual ruin.

Without a spiritual rebirth in consciousness we cannot even "see" the Kingdom of God, the Infinite Being of God (Brahman). To enter into and evolve within the Kingdom of God is what yoga is all about, and without which it is impossible.

Nicodemus saith unto him, How can a man be born when he is old? can he enter the second time into his mother's womb, and be born? Here we can assume that Nicodemus is asking whether time can be reversed and a man find himself again in his mother's womb, to perhaps manage better in subsequent years the second time around than on the first time. Jesus has a different perspective as we will see.

Jesus answered, Verily, verily, I say unto thee, Except a man be born of water and of the Spirit, he cannot enter into the kingdom of God. It takes a rebirth of consciousness to just see the kingdom, and a further much more far-reaching rebirth/transformation of consciousness to actually enter the kingdom. Then to really grow and evolve within the kingdom to attain the status of god within God on all levels of his being, the yogi has to live consciously and increasingly within the cosmic Self and his own individual, divine Self, the two being essentially one.

In both Genesis and the cosmology of India water is a symbol of the primal, causal, undifferentiated energies from which all relative existence is manifested. First the atman-self enters into those causal waters and begins evolving throughout many creation cycles in countless forms, slowly ascending the evolutionary ladder until it become capable of extending itself beyond the evolving energies into the consciousness of pure spirit, into the spirit-being of the Absolute Itself. The center of its awareness moves from the most refined subtle energies into consciousness and begins expanding in its scope until it can encompass the fulness of Spirit Itself. This evolution of consciousness is not moving from point to point as in the prior energy-based development. There is no change in the vehicles of the spirit, but in the "width" and "depth" of that Consciousness—in which those concepts really have no place. Yet we have to speak in that way to give our presently finite and conditioned minds a chance to grasp at least dimly the meaning of this rebirth which ends all further birth. As Yogananda said, it cannot be comprehended intellectually, but it can be experienced as "knowledge of God which is nearer than knowing, open vision direct and instant," as I cited earlier.

That which is born of the flesh is flesh; and that which is born of the Spirit is spirit. Marvel not that I said unto thee, Ye must be born again. The wind bloweth where it listeth, and thou hearest the sound thereof, but canst not tell whence it cometh, and whither it goeth: so is every one that is born of the Spirit. This second rebirth effects a very real distinction between flesh and spirit. Flesh gives birth to flesh, but the Holy Spirit Mother gives birth to spirit. This is completely incomprehensible to those who have not experienced it, as are those who are embodying it. Once some university students came to see Swami Akhandananda, the head of Ramakrishna Mission. They told him that they were studying diligently the words of Sri Ramakrishna found in the *Kathamrita*, the *Gospel of Sri Ramakrishna*, so they could understand Sri Ramakrishna better. Swamiji smiled and said:

"You may try to understand him if you wish. But we lived with him and never even tried to understand him." Wise are those who know what they can and cannot know. When a disciple of Swami Sriyukteswarji remarked to Yogananda that he could not understand the master, Yogananda told him that only a master can understand a master. It truly does take one to know one. And as Yogananda used to sing: "He who knows, knows. None else knows."

Nicodemus answered and said unto him, How can these things be? Jesus answered and said unto him, Art thou a master of Israel, and knowest not these things? Now this is very significant. Jesus assumes that a true teacher of Israel will know all about everything he has been speaking to Nicodemus. He proved when he was twelve that the Essene teachers could not comprehend what he knew as second nature, no doubt from past life recall as well as from his experience in the desert with John the Baptist. But he apparently expected that the non-Essene teachers would know at least some more than the Essene teachers had. But it was not so.

There is another aspect to this. Jesus had lived over half his life up to this time in India and must have learned much, including the fact that the Yadava clan to which Krishna belonged–and which had completely vanished from India shortly after Krishna's death–were his ancestors. The Yadavas had carefully guarded their blood line, only marrying among themselves, as is the custom among the gotras (clans) in India today. Abraham, Isaac and Jacob were descendants of the ancient Yadavas. The Shiva lingas worshipped by Abraham and Moses were proof of their Shaivaite spiritual heritage. (See *The Christ of India*.) It is not improbable that the Indian sages who came to Israel seeking the child Jesus were themselves Yadavas conversant with ancient oral traditions of their clan, perhaps even that one of their own in Israel would be the Messiah destined to return to India. It is all tied up together, like the roots of plants growing near one another become intertwined and inseparable. One thing is sure: India was Jesus' ancestral home and Sanatana Dharma was his ancestral religion. Back in the yoga boom days of the 'sixties and early 'seventies it was noticed that an unusually large percentage of those who had adopted yoga and Sanatana Dharma were Jewish. There were even jokes about gurus in India that turned out to be American Jews. But like Jesus, they were only coming home after long disassociation from their true roots.

Verily, verily, I say unto thee, We speak that we do know, and testify that we have seen; and ye receive not our witness. Who does Jesus mean when he says "we" to Nicodemus? The Essenes? The yogis of India? Perhaps it includes all who have direct spiritual experience and perceive higher spiritual realities. It is certain that "we" have true knowledge and speak about it freely. And it is not intellectual, theoretical knowledge, but the result of genuine spiritual insight. But of course those who are not on the vibrational level or wavelength of such seers (rishis) or knowers (gnostics) do not and cannot accept what "we" have to say because of their natural limitations. And really that is no fault of theirs, for why should they believe them if they have no background or frame of reference into which their words can be integrated? Really it becomes like the joke about a man who stood for a long time in front of a rhinoceros in a zoo. Finally he said: "There ain't any such animal!"

Certainly those with purified minds are intuitive and can intuit the vibration of truth behind someone's words. It is a matter of being sensitive to subtle vibrations. Yogis are not meant to be "true believers" with a cult mentality. Rather, they are to know through their own inner integrity. And that is developed through the thorough adoption of yama and niyama and the diligent practice of meditation.

If I have told you earthly things, and ye believe not, how shall ye believe, if I tell you heavenly things? Although the things Jesus has just said to Nicodemus are spiritual/metaphysical, Jesus says they still are just "earthly" and not at all high spiritual truths. Many people think they are flying high in the spiritual sky if they believe in reincarnation and karma, the existence of many worlds and the progression of the soul from life to life. But in Jesus' view these truths are really earthly and not of any high level at all, because their meanings are confined to earth or existence in subtler worlds and not at all in the realm of the pure spirit. They are real phenomena, but not ultimate realities. Only the yogi can rise above the realm of the merely intellectual or psychic and enter into the realities and knowledge of spirit.

And no man hath ascended up to heaven, but he that came down from heaven, even the Son of man which is in heaven. What is the heaven Jesus is speaking about? The word *ouranos*, translated "heaven," means the boundless sky and comes from the root word *oros*, which means to rise up. So heaven is the infinite supreme consciousness that is the very Being of God. We have all come down from that highest realm into relative existence and must return there.

We tend to think that ordinary people are really at the beginning, when they actually have countless ages of development already behind them. For all relative beings have begun in the transcendent realm of the Divine Absolute and then moved out and began a long descent through all the worlds from the most subtle to the most gross material world in which we are now. Passing through each world or level, they took on an energy vehicle proper to that world, like putting on many layers of clothing. Finally they entered this material universe as an atom of hydrogen, and began the incredibly long and complex journey upward through gaseous, mineral, plant and animal forms, incarnating in a form many times before passing on to the next higher form. When the human form is reached, it takes innumerable incarnations as a human being to reach the level where we know higher knowledge exists, what to say of seeking or learning it. Believe me, it takes an old, old, old soul to even know there is something to learn on a higher level. A "beginner" is really one who has come very far and taken creation cycles to do so. Therefore we should respect them greatly, even though they may be metaphysical crawlers or toddlers, for they alone can become walkers on the path to the Infinite. And they will fall, fail or regress many times. But still they are on the right path, however poorly they may be navigating it. Just the fact that you are holding this book and reading it indicates that you have already come a very long way.

Only those can ascend into the realms of higher consciousness who have ages ago passed down through those levels in a descent to material existence. Only those who have first come down the ladder can go back up. And the amazing truth is this: at all times we are still in the highest world of the transcendental Reality. Our descent and our future ascent are really exercises in consciousness and have no (or very little) objective reality. "You dream you are the doer, you dream that action is done, you dream that action bears fruit. It is the world's delusion that gives you these dreams. The Atman is the light: the light is covered by darkness: this darkness is delusion: that is why we dream" (Bhagavad Gita 5:14-15). As I say, it is an exercise in consciousness, in a complex and far-reaching form of Creative Visualization.

And as Moses lifted up the serpent in the wilderness, even so must the Son of man be lifted up, that whosoever believeth in him should not perish, but have eternal life. In the twenty-first chapter of Numbers there is an account of many poisonous serpents killing a great number of people. Moses made a brass serpent and put it on a high pole. Whenever someone was bitten by a serpent, if he turned and looked at the brass serpent he did not die. This was considered a symbolic prophecy of the crucifixion of Jesus, as were the words of this verse spoken by him, the idea being that the crucifixion was necessary for the fulfillment of his mission. Yogis, however, have an additional view: that the spiritual aspirant must "lift up" his human nature and transcend it to gain the eternal life of his eternal spirit.

But there is more implied.

For God so loved the world, that he gave his only begotten Son, that whosoever believeth in him should not perish, but have everlasting life. As pointed out before, in Greek there are two words translated "in." *En* means in, as "in the house." But in this verse the word is *eis*, which means "into." It is not enough to believe in God, we must believe *into* God by merging our consciousness with his, by uniting ourselves totally and irrevocably with him. It is not enough to believe in Jesus who was *a* Christ; we must become one with *the* Christ, with Ishwara, just as did he. God is Everlasting Life Itself, and those who believe into–become one with Him–do not just possess life, they *are* life, transcending time itself.

The word translated "everlasting" is *aionios*, which means "lasting throughout all ages." It is derived from *aion*, which means "age" in the sense of embracing an infinite series of time spans. In ancient Greek writings, including those of the early Christians, we find the expression "the ages of ages," meaning that which encompasses all time and within which time exists. It is transcendental "time" and transcendental, eternal life.

For God sent not his Son into the world to condemn the world; but that the world through him might be saved. This is going to take a bit of analyzing. It was understood from the beginning of Christianity that the Son, the Second Person of the Trinity, is not a separate being, but an emanation of the Father. This was especially notable in the writing of Terullian (155-220 AD). In the Bhagavad Gita (14:3-4) we find: "For me great Brahma is the womb, and in that do I place the seed. The origination of all beings comes from that. Whatever be the forms produced within all wombs, the great Brahma is their womb, and I the seed-casting Father."

Ishwara, the personal aspect of God, the "Son" of God, emanates from the Transcendent, the Father, and enters into the field of divine creative energy that is the Holy Spirit in manifestation as the Cosmos. The Cosmos is the Mother, the Womb, and Ishwara is the Divine Seed, the matrix around which all manifestation takes place.

Although Ishwara and the Cosmos are both divine in essence, there is a kind of opposition to one another inherent in them. We see this in the Biblical expositions of the flesh "warring" against the spirit. This duality, the opposition of polarity, is essential to the manifestation and evolution of the world. Unity is functioning as duality. And it is true that one can overcome or overshadow the other. Spiritual consciousness can be dimmed or even erased by material consciousness, and material consciousness can be dimmed or erased by spiritual consciousness. This conflict is essential to the manifestation of relative existence. Yet unity always prevails, for both are consciousness, though of opposing polarities. Due to the limitation of our present evolution as human beings we cannot really figure out how all this can be. But it is nonetheless true and important for us to at least assent to intellectually.

In India there is the symbol of Kali standing on the chest of Shiva, who appears to be unconscious beneath her feet. The idea is that the individual atman-spirit for the purpose of its evolution is subordinated temporarily to matter or energy. Actually the depictions carry a very significant flaw: the contact of Shiva with Shakti. For it said: "The moment the feet of Kali touch Shiva She disappears" because of this primal antithesis. A correct depiction would show Kali suspended above the body of Shiva to indicate that matter/energy never really touches the jivatman, and when spirit encounters matter "face to face" matter disappears, is seen to be a dream, only an illusion: Maya. Yet it is a divine illusion for a divine purpose.

"For God sent not his Son into the world to condemn the world." That is, Ishwara did not enter into creation to be its canceller or destroyer/dissolver, "but that the world through him might be saved"–that he might bring about the evolution of the world to absolute perfection so it would be revealed for what it was all along: divine spirit. The word translated "saved" is *sozo*, which means to deliver, heal and make complete. And this is not done just for the cosmos, but for each individual spirit-Self evolving within it. This is liberation (moksha) in every sense of the term. Both the world and all the inhabitants of the world are eventually perfected and assumed into spirit-consciousness.

He that believeth on him is not condemned: but he that believeth not is condemned already, because he hath not believed in the name of the only begotten Son of God. Whether people hold the ignorant idea that if they "do wrong" God will hit them with a stick, or believe in karma and think that when they make a misstep some kind of "bad person" destiny mark goes on their record to eventually hit them with the same kind of stick that the non-karma people believe in, the idea is wrong. It is an affirmation of the principle that virtue is its own reward because it is itself a positive energy which produces positive effects. Consequently vice is its own reward/retribution in the form of negative energy that produces negative effects. The law really is that for every action there is a reaction in kind.

Negative thought, word or deed is its own condemnation. The word *krino* translated "condemn" implies a reaction. The character of the reaction will be determined by the character of the action. It also has a secondary meaning to invoke or put into operation the law, even to sentence one's self. All the responsibility belongs to the one doing the thought or deed.

The word translated "belief" or "faith" is *pistis* which means to believe or trust, to have the conviction that something is true or so. Saint Paul tells us: "Faith is the substance of things hoped for, the evidence of things not seen" (Hebrews 11:1). There is an implication that it may be based on perception. So it is confidence or belief based on actual perception, including intuition. It is in some instances its own evidence or proof.

And what is believed in? The "name" of God (Ishwara). The Greek word translated "name" is *onoma*, which means a name that designates a person, but it also includes the life and character and even the energy being of a person. It also means something by which an object or person is known–is revealed. It also means awareness, knowledge, perception or comprehension (understanding) of an object or person. In the East a person and his name are considered intimately connected with one another.

"In the beginning was the Word, and the Word was with God, and the Word was God" (John 1:1). Many descriptive or symbolic titles have been given to God throughout history. According to the yogis, however, the primary (primal, original) name of God was spoken by him in the beginning. According to the Brihadaranyaka Upanishad: "In the beginning this (world) was only the Supreme Self [Paramatman], in the shape of a person. Looking around he saw nothing else than the Self. He first said, 'I am Soham' [*Soham asmi*]" (1:4:1). Soham is the "first speaking" of the Absolute Itself: the expression of the knowledge and knowing of the Self of all, the Self of our Self. We, too, are Soham. (See *Soham Yoga: The Yoga of the Self*.) Soham itself is our Liberator.

And this is the condemnation, that light is come into the world,.... Phos is the word translated "light." It means both to shine and to reveal, for true, spiritual life gives knowledge and wisdom, not just a passive experience. It also means illumination–enlightenment. Therefore Saint John speaks of walking (living) in the light (I John 1:7). This is the state for which we should be seeking and embodying as much as we can according to the level of spiritual development we have presently attained. *Phos* also means abstract or intellectual, conceptual "light" that is purely in our mind–an "illuminating thought." If we lack that, we are self-condemned.

Phos also means fire, for the true light (John 1:9; I John 2:8) is the power of purification. This is an essential for us, since "Blessed are the pure in heart: for they shall see God" (Matthew 5:8). The word *katharos* means both pure and clear, for when we are truly purified our consciousness will become absolutely clear without taint or shadow. "And every man that hath this hope in him purifieth himself, even as he [God/Christ] is pure" (I John 3:3). Jesus said: "I am come to send fire on the earth; and what will I, if it be already kindled?" (Luke 12:49).

Erchomai, translated "come," has several meanings. Its root word, *eltho*, has a few interesting meanings or implications. 1) It is inherent in the world. When the world came into manifestation the light was revealed as present in the world, which brought the light along with it. This indicates that the saving and purifying light is part of the world, inseparable from it. In other words, that light is the divine life itself. Yet it has been made visible, as well. The teachings of the illumined masters is the light itself. They are light-bearers to the world. *Eltho* also implies that the light is a growth, an expansion. It is a living thing, for "God is light" (I John 1:5). So those who live in the light live in God.

...and men loved darkness rather than light,.... The word translated "darkness" has some very important aspects. *Skotos* means darkness, shadiness and obscurity, and comes from *skia*, which means "shadow." Many times in the Bible we encounter the expression "shadow of death." It is a darkness that brings death and a darkness that indicates the presence of death to come. Those under its influence may see the truth, but they see it unclearly, in obscurity, and thus are in a sense partially blind. They are those who congratulate themselves that they may not be "too good," but they are not "too bad" either. This is a deadly delusion. To think that light can be mixed with shadow and not eventually bring us into the total darkness that is death is terrible folly. When I was still in grade school the hiss of the serpent in the form of the insistence that "there is no such thing as black and white–there are only shades of gray," began to be propagated in school, in the media and even at church. The first time I heard it I knew I was hearing the voice of The Shadow of Death. I kept quiet, but I rejected and resisted it with all my heart. And now today it pervades and poisons nearly everywhere.

...because their deeds were evil. Ergon means any kind of action, physical or mental. This includes the faculties or capacities for such action, and the very energies of which the persons' bodies (physical, astral and causal) are comprised. The vibrations of an evil person's bodies are evil. To be near

them or even touched by them is to be defiled. "Out of the abundance of the heart the mouth speaketh" (Matthew 12:34). Consequently the vibrations of their voices are also evil and defiling. Many times in my life just hearing the voice of an unclean person has made me feel repulsion.

What, then, is the meaning of "evil"? The word translated "evil" in this verse is *poneros*, which basically means harmful or destructive. It is nothing as superficial as breaking rules or laws, but a fundamentally poisonous nature. "The wages of sin is death" (Romans 6:23) because evil action has the vibration of death and destruction. "Old and seasoned in evil" is an accurate description of many people, including those who have compounded their evil from life to life.

Poneros is not just a static condition, but is a very active and effective influence. This is why Yogananda often said: "Company is greater than will power." Many times I have seen very decent people transformed into monsters because they fell into evil company whose negativity was so intense and powerful they were overwhelmed and swept along to disintegration and destruction. Of course they were weak in their own personalities, and therefore were susceptible to evil influence.

Poneros does not remain a superficial thing, but becomes the deep-seated condition of a person. I have known several people who made an effort to lead a spiritual life but were overcome by evil, and when I saw them after some time I absolutely did not know who they were. Their entire personality and appearance were so altered they did not at all look like they had earlier, nor were their voices the same. ("For out of the abundance of the heart the mouth speaketh" Matthew 12:34.) It was a terrible thing to experience.

There is a legend that when Leonardo da Vinci painted his famous Last Supper he first painted a young man who looked the very incarnation of purity and radiant goodness to portray Jesus. Then through a long expanse of time he searched out and found exactly the right faces for the twelve apostles, except for Judas. To complete the picture, he needed a truly evil face for Judas. He sought for a very long time in the worst and most dangerous places of the city, and one day saw exactly what he was seeking–a face that was the incarnation of depravity and willful evil. With real apprehension he approached the man, who upon seeing him greeted da Vinci by name. Seeing da Vinci's blank look of non-recognition, the man asked, "Don't you remember me? You were painting the Last Supper, and I posed for your painting of Jesus!" I have had the same experience as da Vinci.

Poneros is also a degenerating and corrupting power. Its touch is deadly. It also has the connotation of being diseased and ravaged by the disease. Interestingly, it is a derivative of the word *ponos*, which means pain and suffering! It also means to putrefy and decay. *Poneros* truly is the shadow of death; and becomes death in time.

There is no way to adequately convey the absolute necessity to purify ourselves, our deeds, our environment and our associations. We must take seriously the words: "Wherefore come out from among them, and be ye separate, saith the Lord, and touch not the unclean thing; and I will receive you" (II Corinthians 6:17)

For every one that doeth evil... The word translated "doeth" is *prasso*, which means to repeatedly or habitually do something. It is a way of life.

...hateth the light, neither cometh to the light, lest his deeds should be reproved. Such a person hates the truth and insight into the truth. *Miseo*, translated "hate," does not mean just intense dislike but a hatred which impels a person to actively oppose the truth and those who follow it, even persecuting them if it is possible. The motive is protection of the corrupted ego, for the word *elegcho*, translated "reproved," means to be revealed, shown and proven to be evil in intent, word and deed.

But he that doeth truth cometh to the light, that his deeds may be made manifest, that they are wrought in God. The righteous person hides nothing, even his failings and faults. In fact, he wants the truth about him to be known so his ego cannot put up a shield of falsehood or false appearance around itself. Only if there is truth can there be the possibility of good conduct and true reformation of life. It has been seen over and over that the first step to correction is admission of a fault. This is why in Alcoholics Anonymous the participants say freely and openly: "I am an alcoholic."

An honest and truthful person will certainly in time be openly living and acting "in God."

John the Baptist Speaks to His Disciples About Jesus

> After these things came Jesus and his disciples into the land of Judaea; and there he tarried with them, and baptized. And John also was baptizing in Aenon near to Salim, because there was much water there: and they came, and were baptized. For John was not yet cast into prison. Then there arose a question between some of John's disciples and the Jews [Judeans] about purifying (John 3:22-25).

So now we have the ego-struggle between different kinds of spiritual groupies. I do not use the word disciples, for such people do not deserve to be called such.

We may ask the question, how did an argument between the followers of John and the Pharisees (the Sadducees were not interested in such things) about ritual purity turn into a questioning about Jesus? It did not. It was used as an excuse to meet with Saint John so they could somehow get him to say that he–and therefore they–were superior to Jesus and his disciples. Then they could go back and taunt Jesus' disciples with Saint John's words and remind them that Jesus had been baptized by John, not John by Jesus. This is known as a cult mentality. Rivalry prevails between cultists, and like the white supremists today they hate most those groups that are most like themselves because there are no strong differences to wage a war over or prove them inferior since they are both too much alike.

> **And they came unto John, and said unto him, Rabbi, he that was with thee beyond Jordan, to whom thou barest witness, behold, the same baptizeth, and all men come to him (John 3:26).**

This is not just an exaggeration, it is a lie. Because we have just read that people were flocking to be baptized by John. This is also a cult mentality classic. Ego being the sole master and motive, cultists lie to their leader all the time and manipulate him as much as they can. Like the members of little neighborhood gangs between the ages of six and twelve, cultists joins themselves to a teacher or group to make themselves the biggest in the spiritual neighborhood. The teacher and his teachings mean nothing to them unless they can use them to prove themselves superior to others. Even the leader is disposable if it moves them above and forward. Often a dead guru makes more money and more members to be gained by the cultists and their leader. Once a sadhu in India told me that in certain areas it was considered the norm in extremely wealthy ashrams for a senior disciple to murder his guru (poison was the preferred way) so he could take over and run the kingdom.

Anyhow, this verse is an insult to Saint John by his worthless groupies. But his greatness put him above such foolishness. And he speaks only wisdom to them.

> **John answered and said, A man can receive nothing, except it be given him from heaven (John 3:27).**

It is obvious that Saint John is telling them that the notoriety and influence of Jesus was according to divine law. But I would like to stay on this subject for a bit, since no matter how much people use the word "karma" they have very little practical grasp of its nature.

Yogananda's most advanced disciple, Sister Gyanamata, once wrote in a note to another nun: "Your own will always come to you. Indeed, you can have nothing but your own." This is absolutely correct. Everything that happens to us is "our own." We created it by actions in this or a previous birth. The law is best expressed by Saint Paul: "Whatsoever a man soweth, that shall he also reap" (Galatians 6:7). That is, whatever we have done previously to others will be done to us. If we have lied about someone, we will be lied about; if we have stolen we will be stolen from. It is exact: For every action there is an opposite and equal reaction. It is both the physics and the metaphysics of the universe. Conversely, what we have not sown we will not reap. So if we want good to come to us we must first do good ourselves. We create our future by what we do in the present.

Actually, our karma is not just "ours" it is *us*. Our karma reveals our true inner nature. Buddha was very insistent on the fact that karma is purely a matter of mind alone–that a genuine change in the mind is a change in our karmas. Both the Christian idea of getting forgiven or the Hindu idea of "roasting" or wiping out our karmas by various means are ignorant superstitions. As Sri Ramakrishna said: "The mind is everything." Only when the mind is completely changed will our karmas melt away. Authentic yoga sadhana alone produces this necessary change, not happy thoughts or good deeds.

> **Ye yourselves bear me witness, that I said, I am not the Christ, but that I am sent before him. He that hath the bride is the bridegroom: but the friend of the bridegroom, which standeth and heareth him, rejoiceth greatly because of the bridegroom's voice: this my joy therefore is fulfilled (John 3:28-29).**

Saint John knew his destiny as the forerunner of Jesus the Christ. Happy are those that know their destiny and recognize what is not their destiny. The same is true of our abilities. Only the foolish ego tries to overreach itself and be or gain what is beyond its capabilities.

I knew a very competent corporate attorney. Once I was present when he was discussing a future case with a businessman. He told the man that he would not be presenting a case that concerned the man's business, that his strong point was preparation of the material needed for the case, and he would have someone else do the presentation in court. The intense look of contempt on the businessman's face because the attorney knew his limitation and admitted it was a shock to me. To despise a person because he was not blinded by egotism but acknowledged what he could not do well was incredible to me. But so the world runs.

He must increase, but I must decrease (John 3:30).

This is a primary principle in spiritual life: the spirit in us must continually increase in manifestation, and our ego, ignorance and delusion must steadily decrease. There is no truce between wisdom and folly. One will eventually eliminate the other, and we must be on the side of wisdom and truth. But only through cultivation of spiritual awareness will we be able to manage this. When I was quite young I came to truly value a song that was sometimes sung in church and which concluded:

> Let me lose myself and find it, Lord, in Thee.
> May all else be slain, till naught remains but Thee.
> Though it cost me grief and pain, I will find my life again.
> If I lose myself I'll find it, Lord, in Thee.

"Self" in this case means the selfishness and pride of the ego. And when I became a yogi I realized even more how necessary this increase and decrease really is.

Spiritual Wisdom of John the Baptist

> **He that cometh from above is above all: he that is of the earth is earthly, and speaketh of the earth: he that cometh from heaven is above all (John 3:31).**

We all have a dual nature: a higher Self and a lower self. The higher Self is our eternal spirit, our Atman. The lower self is our ego and ego-oriented mind, as well as our lower bodies or levels of manifestation. We must be sure that only that which "cometh down from the Father of lights" (James 1:17), from our true, divine Self and the Divine Itself, the Self of our Self, prevails in our heart and life. "Heaven" must be continually invoked in our life if we would be transformed by the renewing of our mind (Romans 12:2) from glory to glory (II Corinthians 3:18).

> **And what he hath seen and heard, that he testifieth; and no man receiveth his testimony (John 3:32).**

When the consciousness of spirit begins to dominate in us, our entire outlook on life and our approach to it and the way we live it, become drastically changed. For spiritual and not material values begin to prevail. And it is not based on fantasy or spiritual romanticizing, but on the knowing of our awakening divine Self. But that in us which is material and of the earth earthly will consider it alien, utter nonsense and even harmful. Thus we can become enemies of our own Self. And we alone must decide which will remain and which will melt away. Besides that, many people will consider that we are foolish–fools of the first order. It is valueless to try to explain our outlook to them in hope that they will come to see things as we do. It will not happen. And if the naysayers and objectors refuse to at least respect our views or be silent about them, we should consider ending our association with them.

He that hath received his testimony hath set to his seal [attested] that God is true (John 3:33).

Many people claim to believe in God, but according to this only those who are in touch with their higher Self and conform to that which is shown to them from above truly believe in God. The rest only believe in their ideas about God which are not based on any reality whatsoever. Religion does not even come into this, for religion has never opened anyone's consciousness and revealed the life of the spirit. Only yoga sadhana can open our consciousness and reveal the life and the truth of the spirit. There is no true religion but yoga. The rest is theory, speculation, guesswork and superstition that is often the deepest ignorance.

For he whom God hath sent speaketh the words of God: for God giveth not the Spirit by measure unto him (John 3:34).

Our higher Self is sent to us to "speak" the realities of the divine life to us. And there is no limit to the scope of the awakening and understanding that is made possible to those who listen to the insights of the Self. "And the Spirit and the bride say, Come. And let him that heareth say, Come. And let him that is athirst come. And whosoever will, let him take the water of life freely" (Revelation 22:17). The invitation is for those who hear, thirst, come and take freely. Not just a sip or so, but a deep drinking of the water of life.

This reminds me so much of my beloved friend Annie McKinney who once said in a public church meeting: "It isn't hard to live holy. Just live it!" She was a real powerhouse spiritually and inspired many people, including me. All we need is perseverance. As Saint James, the Son of

Thunder (Mark 3:17), wrote: "Resist the devil, and he will flee from you" (James 7:7). *Anthistemi* means to stand up against and oppose something. That is all it takes, for: "Greater is he that is in you, than he that is in the world" (I John 4:4). That is, the spirit-Self that is in the depths of our being is greater and stronger than the mind that is immersed in the world.

The Father loveth the Son, and hath given all things into his hand (John 3:35).

Saint John assures us: "Beloved, now are we the sons of God, and it doth not yet appear what we shall be: but we know that, when he shall appear, we shall be like him; for we shall see him as he is" (I John 3:2). He who knows his Self knows God and knows himself as a son of God.

He that believeth on the Son hath everlasting life: and he that believeth not the Son shall not see life; but the wrath of God abideth on him (John 3:36).

Here again the word translated "on" is also *eis*. He who believes into the Son, who unites himself with the Son in the totality of his being, has everlasting life because God is everlasting, eternal life, and he who unites with God reveals his own divine sonship. But those who remain "outside" God in their consciousness will neither comprehend nor experience life, but will be "dead" to real life, to God. To such a one God will remain unseen and unrevealed. And that will be their own free choice.

In exoteric Judaism, Christianity and Islam, "the wrath of God" has a curious fascination and attraction, perhaps because it reveals their own inner vengeful and wrathful ego in relation to all that displease it. And since exoteric religion makes God in the image of man, including the worst of man, egoistic anger and vengeful retaliation is assumed to be a divine–even though really a demonic–attribute.

However, it is very different here if we carefully analyze the Greek words used. *Orgay*, translated "wrath," really means an agitation, a shaking up, of something. It is a reactive force, *oregomai*, caused by some situation, object or action. The character of this force is according to its source. If someone is electrocuted deliberately by another person it is murder or legal execution, but if someone is electrocuted by accident it is not. Karma, for example, is a divine law. Its purpose is the ultimate benefit and evolution of the individual human being. It is never reward or punishment: simply reaction.

A misunderstood incident in the Bible is the following. "When they came to Nachon's threshingfloor, Uzzah put forth his hand to the ark of God, and took hold of it; for the oxen shook it. And the anger of the Lord was kindled against Uzzah; and God smote him there for his error; and there he died by the ark of God" (II Samuel 6:6). The ark was an object of great power, so much so that no one ever touched it. It had rings on its side, and when it needed to be carried, poles were put through the rings and only the Levites, the priests, could carry it. So great was the power around the ark that it was like a whirlwind or a powerful river or ocean swell. The Hebrew word translated "anger" is *'aph*, which means nose or nostril and is derived from *'anaph*, which means intense breathing. When we realize that the word *ruach* means spirit or breath and that the power of God, the Holy Spirit, is called the *Agia Pneuma*, the Holy Breath, we understand that the entire cosmos is the manifestation of the Holy Spirit, that it is Primal Power which like a whirlwind or a powerful river or ocean swell can destroy something (or someone) opposing it, but can also be the irresistible cooperating force if the opposition turns into cooperation with it. This Power is the power of both life and death. We ourselves determine which it will be for us.

So the power that is amrita, the nectar of heavenly immortality, to some is to others the very fires of hell. The determining factor is their own fundamental state of consciousness. Sri Ramakrishna sometimes would touch a very pure person and they were enter exalted states of consciousness or even samadhi. Seeing this, a very corrupt priest of the Dakshineshwar Kali temple demanded that Sri Ramakrishna touch him. Sri Ramakrishna refused, but the priest persisted, so Ramakrishna just touched him with a fingertip. Instantly the priest fell down and rolled on the ground screaming, "I am burning up! I am burning up!" Ramakrishna touched him again, smiling and saying: "Perhaps in a future life." The priest got up and ran out of the room. "For our God is a consuming fire" (Hebrews 12:29).

Saint Paul (at that time called Saul) was originally a hate-filled persecutor of Christians. "And Saul, yet breathing out threatenings and slaughter against the disciples of the Lord, went unto the high priest, and desired of him letters to Damascus to the synagogues, that if he found any of this way, whether they were men or women, he might bring them bound unto Jerusalem. And as he journeyed, he came near Damascus: and suddenly there shined round about him a light from heaven: and he fell to the earth, and heard a voice saying unto him, Saul, Saul, why persecutest thou me? And he said, Who art thou, Lord? And the Lord said, I am Jesus whom thou persecutest: it is hard for thee to kick against the pricks. And he trembling and astonished said, Lord, what wilt thou have me to do? And the Lord said unto him, Arise, and go into the city, and it shall be told thee what thou must do. And the men which journeyed with him stood speechless, hearing a voice, but seeing no man. And Saul arose from the earth; and when his eyes were opened, he saw no man: but they led him by the hand, and brought him into Damascus. And he was three days without sight, and neither did eat nor drink. And there was a certain disciple at Damascus, named Ananias; and to him said the Lord in a vision, Ananias. And he said, Behold, I am here, Lord. And the Lord said unto him, Arise, and go into the street which is called Straight, and enquire in the house of Judas for one called Saul, of Tarsus: for, behold, he prayeth, and hath seen in a vision a man named Ananias coming in, and putting his hand on him, that he might receive his sight. Then Ananias answered, Lord, I have heard by many of this man, how much evil he hath done to thy saints at Jerusalem: and here he hath authority from the chief priests to bind all that call on thy name. But the Lord said unto him, Go thy way: for he is a chosen vessel unto me, to bear my name before the Gentiles, and kings, and the children of Israel: For I will shew him how great things he must suffer for my name's sake. And Ananias went his way, and entered into the house; and putting his hands on him said, Brother Saul, the Lord, even Jesus, that appeared unto thee in the way as thou camest, hath sent me, that thou mightest receive thy sight, and be filled with the Holy Ghost.

And immediately there fell from his eyes as it had been scales: and he received sight forthwith, and arose, and was baptized. And when he had received food, he was strengthened. Then was Saul certain days with the disciples which were at Damascus. And straightway he preached Christ in the synagogues, that he is the Son of God" (Acts 9:1-20). Something happened! And it can happen to us.

What is interesting and relevant to us in this account is that when the heavenly voice said: "It is hard for thee to kick against the pricks," the word translated "pricks" is *kentron*, which literally means "the point" or "the center." Paul had been resisting and even warring against the center of his own being: God. The pain experienced by striking against a sharp point is the result of our own action. The point itself is neutral. So the love of God and the wrath of God is the same thing. The difference, the determining factor, is us.

"How think ye? if a man have an hundred sheep, and one of them be gone astray, doth he not leave the ninety and nine, and goeth into the mountains, and seeketh that which is gone astray? And if so be that he find it, verily I say unto you, he rejoiceth more of that sheep, than of the ninety and nine which went not astray" (Matthew 18:12-13). Later we will consider the spiritual meaning of this parable. But there is an immediate meaning we should have in mind right now.

Jesus in Samaria Meets a Former Disciple

And he must needs go through Samaria. Then cometh he to a city of Samaria, which is called Sychar, near to the parcel of ground that Jacob gave to his son Joseph. Now Jacob's well was there. Jesus therefore, being wearied with his journey, sat thus on the well: and it was about the sixth hour. There cometh a woman of Samaria to draw water: Jesus saith unto her, Give me to drink. (For his disciples were gone away unto the city to buy food.) Then saith the woman of Samaria unto him, How is it that thou, being a Judean, askest drink of me, which am a woman of Samaria? for the Jews [Judeans] have no dealings with the Samaritans (John 4:4-9).

Yogananda said that the future Saint Photini, usually known as "the Samaritan woman," was a disciple of Jesus in a previous life, yet had fallen away from her spiritual ideals and in her subsequent life was immersed in the ignorance and bondage of the world. But Jesus has not forgotten her, and now makes his way into Samaria specifically to meet with her and bring her back to the upward way.

We have already seen regional prejudice, and here is another. Years ago I read the account of an American who visited Israel, then called Palestine. While staying in Jerusalem, one morning he spent some time walking around the open air markets. When he returned to the house where he was renting a room, the owner demanded that he immediately take a bath. He asked why, and was told that perhaps in his wanderings that morning he had been touched by the shadow of a Samaritan and thereby made unclean!

So the lapse of Jesus' disciple had resulted in her being born among people with whom most Hebrews/Israelites would have no contact whatsoever. Yet the Good Shepherd had come for his sheep.

> **Jesus answered and said unto her, If thou knewest the gift of God, and who it is that saith to thee, Give me to drink; thou wouldest have asked of him, and he would have given thee living water (John 4:10).**

There is so much background to the conversation that is now to follow. In the poetic version of the life of Sri Ramachandra, the avatar, written by the great poet-saint Tulsidas, there is an account of how some of Rama's friends wanted to arrange an "accidental" meeting between him and the princess Sita whom he would eventually marry. So they secretly made a plan for some of Sita's girl friends to bring her to a park where they would bring Rama so the two would meet. And Tulsidas remarks: "They did not know that theirs was an ancient love" with roots far in the past. Here in this Gospel account we are witnessing a meeting based on previous lives. But this is a serious meeting, for the woman must be awakened and tested as to whether the previous spiritual connection can be renewed. Now Jesus begins to speak with her about the fundamentals of spiritual life.

If thou knewest the gift of God.... Saint Paul simply says: "The gift of God is eternal life" (Ephesians 2:8). By "eternal life," he does not mean living forever, because as immortal beings we can do nothing else. Rather he means ever living in and sharing in the Consciousness of God that is Eternal Life. He wrote to his disciple, Saint Timothy: "Wherefore I put thee in remembrance that thou stir up the gift of God, which is in thee" (II Timothy 1:6). Though buried deep in forgetfulness, the spiritual connection with Jesus and the seeds of life planted in her in the past are still there, hopefully to be reawakened by Jesus.

The meaning of word *dorea*, translated "gift," is spiritually profound. It is not just something given, but a *doron*, a sacrifice. For both the giver and the receiver make a sacrifice. The giver has sacrificed to gain the gift, and often has made some kind of sacrifice to hand it on to the receiver. Jesus has been revealed by John the Baptist and the descent of the Holy Spirit accompanied by the voice of God. He has called his first disciples and begun his ministry. But he suddenly turns from it all and goes into a land where the people will scorn and hate him. For he seeks a lost sheep whose welfare he places above all those he might be teaching and awakening. The prospective receiver, for whose sake he will break rabbinical tradition by even speaking to her, must also make a sacrifice as we shall see.

...and who it is that saith to thee, Give me to drink.... Those who are fortunate to live where men and women of enlightenment can be met may also be so unfortunate as not to recognize the spiritual status of those they meet, especially if they meet someone who could show them the way to eternal life.

One time at Howrah Station in Calcutta I was standing with a small group of people who had come to see Anandamayi Ma leave by train. For over a week Ma had been mobbed by thousands at the Agarpara Anandamayi Ashram. Day and night she had been with those who sought her help and blessing. Now having had hardly a moment of peace, when she came to the train car reserved for her and those traveling with her, she went inside and lay down on a berth by the window. Yet in no more than a few minutes she quickly got up and came to stand in the door where we all could see her. Heavenly moments passed as we stood there in contented silence. Other trains had come into the station, and passengers were hastening by to make connections or leave the station for their destinations in town. Occasionally one of them would glimpse Ma, slow down and join us, quietly asking who this "mahatma" was. Then they stood there at peace, looking at her until the train left. They walked along with us to the entrance, seeking to learn more about Ma.

Some months later in the New Delhi train station it was different. Ma came in the deep of night, and when we who had come to meet her followed her out of the station we passed through an immense hall where hundreds of people were asleep on the floor, awaiting their connections on the next day. Ma carefully picked her way through them to get to the door.

We were all in complete silence, but some of the sleepers would suddenly awake and sit up and look at Ma, somehow sensing of her presence. But after just a minute or so they would lie back down and go to sleep. They did not follow after her with us. It is the same in spiritual life. Who will arise and follow? Who will even know or consider the possibility?

So the straying disciple has no idea what a great spiritual destiny might become open to her, and how easily she might miss it.

...thou wouldest have asked of him, and he would have given thee living water. Our bodies are mostly water, but earthly water. Jesus has something quite different in mind. The word used in this account is *huetos*, which specifically means rain–water coming "down from above from the Father of lights" (James 1:17). This spiritual water has a heavenly source and is not of the earth, but of the spirit. Jesus has come all that way that she might live in the spirit. But she does not know such a thing exists, and so could not ask. But Jesus has now told her of this living water.

> **The woman saith unto him, Sir, thou hast nothing to draw with, and the well is deep: from whence then hast thou that living water? Art thou greater than our father Jacob, which gave us the well, and drank thereof himself, and his children, and his cattle? (John 4:11-12).**

She is going to find out! The water Jesus has to give comes not from earth but from the heaven of spirit, the realm of limitless consciousness.

> **Jesus answered and said unto her, Whosoever drinketh of this water shall thirst again: but whosoever drinketh of the water that I shall give him shall never thirst; but the water that I shall give him shall be in him a well of water springing up into everlasting life (John 4:13-14).**

Water is a symbol of both the cosmos and the consciousness that is the source of the cosmos. Jesus is speaking of the "water" that is consciousness, the essential nature of the Self (Atman) and God, the Self of the Self.

Once we are established in that consciousness, we have no more desires, because we will possess Infinity Itself. For it will be a *pege*, an artesian well flowing from the Self. It will be both cause and effect, both infinite and finite. It is not drawn up in a container or parceled out. Rather, it shoots up like a geyser by the force of its own eternal Being. And it "waters" all that surrounds it. For it is divinity itself. It is both gift and Giver.

The woman saith unto him, Sir, give me this water, that I thirst not, neither come hither to draw (John 4:15).

This woman had been a disciple of Jesus in a previous life. Therefore she had to be of a significant degree of evolution. To even see someone like Jesus is a profound spiritual experience. To form a spiritual bond with them is a rare thing indeed. But until you are there, you are not there. So like nearly all of us she is a mixture of wisdom and ignorance. Many people think that if they learn a bit about spiritual life they are "spiritual." But they are not. They are like a cloudy day: a mixture, alternating in light, shadow and darkness. This is normal.

The woman sensed the spiritual greatness of Jesus, therefore she did not call him "Sir" as the King James Version text has it. She called him "Rabbi" which means both Master and Lord, as does the word *kurios* in the Greek text. Her higher mind remembered their former spiritual bond.

Yet, being also enmeshed in materiality, like the members of all exoteric religions, she took his spiritual words in a completely material manner. So she asked that Jesus give her the water he spoke of so she would never be thirsty again or have to come to the well for water.

However, his disciples were not much ahead of her. For example, once when they had embarked in a ship, "the disciples had forgotten to take bread, neither had they in the ship with them more than one loaf. And he charged them, saying, Take heed, beware of the leaven of the Pharisees, and of the leaven of Herod. And they reasoned among themselves, saying, It is because we have no bread. And when Jesus knew it, he saith unto them, Why reason ye, because ye have no bread? perceive ye not yet, neither understand? have ye your heart yet hardened? Having eyes, see ye not?

and having ears, hear ye not? and do ye not remember?" (Mark 8:14-18). After all the times they had heard Jesus speaking of the kingdom of God, and the fact that he had even said to Pilate: "My kingdom is not of this world" (John 18:36), just before his ascension "they asked of him, saying, Lord, wilt thou at this time restore again the kingdom to Israel?" (Acts 1:6). No wonder he had said earlier: "Have I been so long time with you, and yet hast thou not known me?" (John 14:9).

Despite all the talk about being "spiritual but not religious," hardly anyone is spiritual. Because "where your treasure is, there will your heart be also" (Matt. 6:21; Luke 12:34), nearly everyone views even the highest teachings in the context of materiality. This is rampant in every religion, though those that promise physical immortality to their adherents are surely dealing from the bottom of the deck.

Yoga does not escape this mentality. Health and flexibility are the order of the day. One time a very devout Catholic nun told me: "The Poor Clares of X are urging us to all take up yoga because not one of them ever has a cold since they took up yoga." By "yoga" she meant Hatha Yoga, not yoga meditation. When two of my meditation students told an acquaintance that they were learning yoga she brightened up and asked: "Oh! Has he got you on your heads, yet?" They had to ask me later what she meant by that, and found it very funny and sad simultaneously. So did I. Much "yoga" is nothing but a mishmash of Hatha Yoga and Tantra seasoned with emotion ("bhakti")–not yoga at all.

Jesus saith unto her, Go, call thy husband, and come hither (John 4:16).

Yogananda said that this was the crucial moment. Would she bring the man she was living with and pretend they were married? Would she lie to Jesus? If she would, then all would be lost and Jesus could not help her.

The woman answered and said, I have no husband. Jesus said unto her, Thou hast well said, I have no husband: for

> thou hast had five husbands; and he whom thou now hast is not thy husband: in that saidst thou truly (John 4:17-18).

Well, there we have it! Sri Ramakrishna said that truthfulness scrupulously observed could lead to Self-realization. And she was truthful.

But it is uncomfortable to her ego, so she tries a distraction to turn away attention from her personal situation that needs drastic correction. Religion is at hand, and age-old religious controversy at that, which would guarantee that any discussion would go around and around to no conclusion. And hopefully the subject of adultery would be forgotten in the go-around. They could "agree to disagree" and go their separate ways. At least this was her intention and hope. So she tries.

First she flatters.

> The woman saith unto him, Sir, I perceive that thou art a prophet (John 4:19).

Then she brings in the safely unresolvable controversy.

> Our fathers worshipped in this mountain; and ye say, that in Jerusalem is the place where men ought to worship (John 4:20).

The Samaritans were in Israel when the Hebrews returned from Egypt. They did not attempt to officially convert to Judaism, but they adopted some of the ways of the Torah and built a temple on Mount Gerasim and worshipped there somewhat in conformity with the Hebrew customs. Human nature being what it is, there was intense animosity between the two groups. And the old theological merry-go-round of Which Of Us Is Right, beloved by all exoteric religionists, was set in motion and continued for centuries. So to silence Jesus regarding her irregular personal life, the woman puts up this smokescreen to distract from the truth about herself.

> Jesus saith unto her, Woman, believe me, the hour cometh, when ye shall neither in this mountain, nor yet at Jerusalem, worship the Father (John 4:21).

As in Jesus' calling his mother "woman" in Cana (John 2:3-4), this was a respectful way to address a woman in public.

Jesus has come to open an entirely new era in the spiritual history of the world in general. For such a thing to take place, much has to be removed or replaced and much has to be introduced into the world. Therefore he tells her that in the future the true worship of God will not be offered in either temple; that they will be superseded. For nearly two thousand years there has not even been a temple in either Samaria or Jerusalem.

> Ye worship ye know not what: we know what we worship: for salvation is of the Jews [Judeans] (John 4:22).

Eido means to have full (complete) understanding and knowledge. *Soteria* means deliverance, in this case the knowledge of the delivering *soter*, the savior, the Messiah, who was to come from Israel. Jesus does not mean that everyone but the Hebrews are "damned," but that the Christ is the deliverer promised to the Hebrews and shall be a World Savior.

This verse also shows that when plain speaking is needed, even if not very pleasant, the true teacher of righteousness does not hesitate to speak so.

> But the hour cometh, and now is, when the true worshippers shall worship the Father in spirit and in truth: for the Father seeketh such to worship him. God is a Spirit: and they that worship him must worship him in spirit and in truth (John 4:23-24).

True worshippers of God do so in their spirit, in the truth of their being–for they are essentially spirit alone. Meditation, then, is the true worship of God. And we are told that God "seeks such to worship him."

Zeteo, translated "seek," means to desire and seek after. This entire relative creation is a living call, a seeking for us to return to our Source. And that return, although supported by external discipline, is a fundamentally interior return.

> **The woman saith unto him, I know that Messias cometh, which is called Christ: when he is come, he will tell us all things. Jesus saith unto her, I that speak unto thee am he (John 4:25-26).**

"Messiah" and "Christ" are Hebrew and Greek words that literally mean "the anointed one" in the sense of a consecrated and appointed messenger of God. In Jewish mysticism there is an exalted spiritual realm that itself is called "Messiah." This is the highest spiritual world that in India is called Siddhaloka because only absolutely perfected (divinized) beings (siddha purushas) can ascend to that level. Therefore anyone who attains that status is a Messiah, a Christ. In original Christian teaching, such as is found in *The Aquarian Gospel of Jesus the Christ*, Ishwara, the personal aspect of God, is *the* Christ, and any totally perfected being is *a* Christ. The two must never be confused with one another. This mistaking of Jesus for Ishwara is the fundamental error of Christianity that destroys any possibility of understanding the truth about God, Jesus or ourselves. Nothing good can come of it, as the history of corrupted Christianity abundantly proves.

> **And upon this came his disciples, and marvelled that he talked with the woman: yet no man said, What seekest thou? or, Why talkest thou with her? (John 4:27).**

Rabbis never spoke with women in private, so the disciples were very surprised and asked nothing of either her or Jesus.

> **The woman then left her waterpot, and went her way into the city, and saith to the men, Come, see a man, which told me all things that ever I did: is not this the Christ?**

Then they went out of the city, and came unto him (John 4:28-30).

The symbolism of this verse is the real message, but there are two external points to notice.

First: The woman told the men about Jesus, not the women. We can assume this is because women would not speak to her since she was living with a man without being married. In today's atmosphere this may seem strange or extreme, but it really was the norm for thousands of years, as it certainly was in my home town. I vividly remember my aunt Eva being shocked to the depths when she saw the daughter of a very respected family speaking to the daughter of a woman whose mother had not been married.

Second: As with Nathanael, such a simple demonstration of clairvoyance makes people think Jesus is the Messiah. This is because of their very limited and uncomprehending idea of who/what the Messiah would be, and what his effect in their lives would be. Today people accept someone as their guru if they just "feel something" when that person comes in the room, or if the guru shows a bit of intuition about them in conversation. Sometimes just reading a book by a groupie convinces them. And of course there are the devotees of the "Mayi Ma's" that arose after Anandamayi Ma left the body, who think that a hug and a "I love you" cliché spoken to them means they have found their guru. Who really wants to become "a well of water springing up into everlasting life" as Jesus told the woman at the beginning of their meeting, and not a "Goo-Goo Da-Da" type of disciple?

Jesus sitting outside the city by the well has a symbolic message for all seekers. To find inner spiritual truth we have to leave mundane life and its cheap values behind and go beyond them to where our own inner Christ sits by the source of Life Itself. Genuine meditation is the only way to do this. Going beyond our mind and its antics and thoughts we sit at the Source and fill ourselves with the Living Water that is our Self within the Infinite Self that is God.

In the mean while his disciples prayed him, saying, Master, eat. But he said unto them, I have food to eat that ye

> know not of. Therefore said the disciples one to another, Hath any man brought him ought to eat? Jesus saith unto them, My food is to do the will of him that sent me, and to finish his work (John 4:31-34).

The true life is the life in the spirit, and that which feeds or maintains the spirit is the true food.

Thelema, the word translated "will," also means a purpose. There is a purpose behind the entire cosmos: evolution into the liberation of the spirit. Those who act to achieve that end truly do the will of God, who sent all of us into this world, into relative existence, that we might realize that we are the sons of God. One of the root words of *thelema* is *etheleo*, which means a subjective impulse rising from deep within the person. The eternal Will is implanted in our essential being. As Saint Ignatius of Antioch wrote: "There is in me a living spring calling, 'Come to the Father.'"

The word translated "finish" is *teleioo*, which means to complete and make perfect. We ourselves are the work of God, and our self-perfection is our completion of that work.

> Say not ye, There are yet four months, and then cometh harvest? behold, I say unto you, Lift up your eyes, and look on the fields; for they are white already to harvest (John 4:35).

Our spiritual destiny is not in the future, but right now we must be working toward it, because "now is the accepted time; behold, now is the day of salvation" (II Corinthians 6:2). Liberation is both our goal and the means to that goal, since in our true being we are ever free. It will not be many lives in the future, for when the future comes it is today. So only those who "seize the day" will attain. Saying, "I am not ready" really is saying, "I do not want to do it." It truly is Now Or Never because only Now exists for us. The fact that we have come to know about liberation (moksha) is itself the proof that we are ready and able to begin attaining it.

> And he that reapeth receiveth wages, and gathereth fruit unto life eternal: that both he that soweth and he that reapeth may rejoice together. And herein is that saying true, One soweth, and another reapeth. I sent you to reap that whereon ye bestowed no labour: other men laboured, and ye are entered into their labours (John 4:36-38).

This has two meanings. One is that great liberated beings have left us a spiritual heritage to show us the way to our own liberation. The other is that our present progress is based on our endeavors in previous lives. We are ourselves our past, present and future. There is no one else to rely on. If we had not all engaged in spiritual practice in many previous lives we would not be where we are now: learning to go further on to the Goal. There are no accidents. To just hear about liberation indicates that we have a great deal of positive spiritual karma from previous lifetimes. Those who get busy and start building on–and expanding–that foundation will reach the Goal. It is only Maya and our own egoic delusion that says it will take many lives to get there. As the yogis of India have said for centuries: "Doing, doing, done!" And the Buddhist masters have said: "Going, going, gone!"

> And many of the Samaritans of that city believed on him for the saying of the woman, which testified, He told me all that ever I did. So when the Samaritans were come unto him, they besought him that he would tarry with them: and he abode there two days. And many more believed because of his own word; and said unto the woman, Now we believe, not because of thy saying: for we have heard him ourselves, and know that this is indeed the Christ, the Saviour of the world (John 39-42).

This is the secret of spiritual success: knowing for ourselves because we have experienced spiritual realities ourselves. We may in the beginning believe the words of those who have progressed before us, but we must hasten on to the day when we can say on our own: I Know.

Jesus Returns to Galilee and Heals

Now after two days he departed thence, and went into Galilee. For Jesus himself testified, that a prophet hath no honour in his own country. Then when he was come into Galilee, the Galilaeans received him, having seen all the things that he did at Jerusalem at the feast: for they also went unto the feast.

So Jesus came again into Cana of Galilee, where he made the water wine. And there was a certain nobleman, whose son was sick at Capernaum. When he heard that Jesus was come out of Judaea into Galilee, he went unto him, and besought him that he would come down, and heal his son: for he was at the point of death.

Then said Jesus unto him, Except ye see signs and wonders, ye will not believe. The nobleman saith unto him, Sir, come down ere my child die. Jesus saith unto him, Go thy way; thy son liveth. And the man believed the word that Jesus had spoken unto him, and he went his way.

And as he was now going down, his servants met him, and told him, saying, Thy son liveth. Then enquired he of them the hour when he began to amend. And they said unto him, Yesterday at the seventh hour the fever left him. So the father knew that it was at the same hour, in the which Jesus said unto him, Thy son liveth: and himself believed, and his whole house (John 4:43-53).

Jesus himself testified, that a prophet hath no honour in his own country. This seems to be a constant in human behavior. There were people that knew Sri Gajanana Maharaj (see *Soham Yoga: The Yoga of the Self* and *Light of Soham*) as a child and young man and refused to believe that he could ever become a master yogi. Not because he was of bad character when young, but only because "we knew him when." Which is completely silly.

I knew a renowned yogi from northern India who left home and began to practice tapasya in a distant place. There he was shown great respect and he felt that he might become egotistical. So he decided to return to his home place and live there outside the town in solitude and beg for his food. No one there would give him anything to eat and only sneered at him and told him to go home and finish his education and quit embarrassing his family. As a result he barely survived on what little he got to eat, but he was content knowing that he would never be respected or treated with great deference.

Except ye see signs and wonders, ye will not believe. I had read this verse before in the Bible, but I began to grasp its deeper meaning when I read it on the title page of *Autobiography of a Yogi*. Later, when I was living next door to the Self-Realization Fellowship center in Hollywood, I met several people who either complained about or scorned the *Autobiography* for containing "too much phenomena." One woman said to me: "So much phenomena! I just had to stop reading it!" Another said to me: "If I want science fiction I can always read *Autobiography of a Yogi*." This amazed me, for that book was really a great teaching instrument that gave me insights I had never even come near to gaining before I read it. Every "phenomenon" described by Yogananda was a demonstration of a principle vital to spiritual life. None were just Amazing Stories. They embodied truths that opened up vistas undreamed of by me. The word *semaino* (sign) means a mark, a signification of something. Yes, the incidents were "wonders" (*teras*), but proofs of greater, spiritual wonders that had meaning for all who seek higher consciousness. The *Autobiography of a Yogi* is a masterful textbook of both truths and the way to know those truths for oneself. The miracles of Jesus were demonstrations of truth. His healings demonstrated the reality of health and the illusion of sickness. His raising of the dead proved the reality of immortality; for the same spirit that had left the body returned to it at his word. Truly, as we shall later find Saint Peter saying, Jesus had "the words of eternal life" (John 6:68).

Yesterday at the seventh hour the fever left him. Jesus' healing of the man's son from a distance was a demonstration that for the perfect space is an illusion. His perfect consciousness was everywhere and unlimited in its power. I have seen things like this happen in India, but also in America as well. The world people usually live in is not just small, it is miniscule. And as a result they are miniscule, as well.

> And leaving Nazareth, he came and dwelt in Capernaum, which is upon the sea coast, in the borders of Zabulon and Nephthalim: that it might be fulfilled which was spoken by Esaias the prophet, saying, The land of Zabulon, and the land of Nephthalim, by the way of the sea, beyond Jordan, Galilee of the Gentiles; the people which sat in darkness saw great light; and to them which sat in the region and shadow of death light is sprung up. From that time Jesus began to preach, and to say, Repent: for the kingdom of heaven is at hand (Matthew 4:13-17).
>
> And Jesus returned in the power of the Spirit into Galilee: and there went out a fame of him through all the region round about. And he taught in their synagogues, being glorified of [honored by] all (Luke 4:14-15).

In the power of the Spirit. This is the secret of successful spiritual life: we must become established in the power, the strength, of our own spirit-Self. Saint Paul was not boasting when he wrote: "I can do all things in Christ which strengtheneth me" (Philippians 4:13). If we come to dwell in our own Christhood, then it will empower, strengthen and enable (*endunamoo*) us to accomplish all that we need do.

More Disciples Are Called

And Jesus, walking by the sea of Galilee, saw two brethren, Simon called Peter, and Andrew his brother, casting a net into the sea: for they were fishers (Matthew 4:18).

And it came to pass, that, as the people pressed upon him to hear the word of God, he stood by the lake of Gennesaret, and saw two ships standing by the lake: but the fishermen were gone out of them, and were washing their nets. And he entered into one of the ships, which was Simon's, and prayed him that he would thrust out a little from the land. And he sat down, and taught the people out of the ship (Luke 5:1-3).

There was a very practical aspect to Jesus teaching from the boat: that way he would not get mobbed or pushed back from the land into the water. But there is a spiritual lesson also. We are on the land of material life and consciousness. Jesus speaks to us from the realm of spirit. So only those oriented to the spirit can really comprehend the message of the saints and masters.

Now when he had left speaking, he said unto Simon, Launch out into the deep, and let down your nets for a draught. And Simon answering said unto him, Master, we have toiled all the night, and have taken nothing: nevertheless at thy word I will let down the net. And when they had this done, they inclosed a great multitude of fishes: and

> their net brake. And they beckoned unto their partners, which were in the other ship, that they should come and help them. And they came, and filled both the ships, so that they began to sink (Luke 5:4-7).

If we wish to catch higher consciousness in the net of our awareness, we have to launch out into the depths, not just paddle around in the shallows. And our "net" must be immersed in the subtle levels of our being. Those who will not move out and go deep can never attain anything significant in the spiritual realm.

"Then said he unto them, Therefore every scribe which is instructed unto the kingdom of heaven is like unto a man that is an householder, which bringeth forth out of his treasure things new and old" (Matthew 13:52). Those who are wise in the inner things of the spirit bring into their consciousness from the depths of their own Self wisdom that they have known before and wisdom that is new to them. That is why God promised: "All thy children shall be taught of the Lord" (Isaiah 54:13).

Furthermore, it is not our limited earth-oriented will that can ensure success. Simon and his assistants had labored the whole night and caught nothing, but now the inner day has come and at the word from on high we can succeed. And what we will gain will burst the boundaries of our present limited scope of understanding and lead us into vaster consciousness than we could imagine would be possible for us.

The timid and the cautious never manage it. Only the daring and courageous attain to higher being, because the opening of their consciousness will "sink" their former states of mind. Then all those around them will begin fussing about how they "just aren't the same any more," and "something's going on with them that I can't figure out." But they know that they want to stop it and reverse it and bring them back to "normal." That is why Jesus said: "A man's foes shall be they of his own household" (Matthew 10:36).

Those who do not strengthen and defend themselves against this enmity are in very real danger of giving in and leaving spiritual life. The answer often is to get out of your present life situation which endangers your own perseverance in spiritual life. In the beginning of my true life I met many yogis who had done that very thing, as I had myself. It was a matter of spiritual survival for all of us. And those who are not willing to do so if it is required will not get very far on the journey.

Later we will be examining these words of Jesus: "The kingdom of heaven is like unto treasure hid in a field; the which when a man hath found, he hideth, and for joy thereof goeth and selleth all that he hath, and buyeth that field. Again, the kingdom of heaven is like unto a merchant man, seeking goodly pearls: who, when he had found one pearl of great price, went and sold all that he had, and bought it" (Matthew 13:44-46). In both examples the men paid all that they had to gain the spiritual kingdom. The sixteenth century poet-saint Mirabai wrote: "I have sold everything in the market-place of this world and bought my Khanaia [Krishna]. Some laugh at me and say the price was too high, and others say it was too little; but all I know is that it was all I had." So it always is. Those who are not willing to give all will receive nothing.

> When Simon Peter saw it, he fell down at Jesus' knees, saying, Depart from me; for I am a sinful man, O Lord. For he was astonished, and all that were with him, at the draught of the fishes which they had taken: And so was also James, and John, the sons of Zebedee, which were partners with Simon. And Jesus said unto Simon, Fear not; from henceforth thou shalt catch men. And when they had brought their ships to land, they forsook all, and followed him (Luke 5:8-11).

Depart from me; for I am a sinful man, O Lord. For some reason people often get it wrong at the beginning of spiritual life. This can take many forms, but here it is Peter's own negativity wanting to get rid of Jesus. So he says "I am a sinner; I should not even come near you." How falsely humble and self-deprecatingly noble! "I am not worthy.... It will be many lives before someone like me can take up spiritual life.... I know I need to do it, but right now I am just not ready.... I am not evolved like you.... I would do it in a moment, except I already have all these other obligations." And so it goes–and "goes" is the significant word. I knew a man who neglected his spiritual life, using his family as an excuse, and neglected his family, using his spiritual life as an excuse.

Fear not; from henceforth thou shalt catch men. Leaving a little boat in a little lake to travel the Mediterranean world enlightening more people than could be counted: this was the real destiny of Saint Peter. He could never have imagined such a thing to be possible, much less to happen to him. It is always like this when the real awakening comes and the aspirant arises and enters the kingdom of boundless life. Even his outer life is transformed and his life becomes a continual movement forward "from glory to glory, even as by the Spirit of the Lord" (II Corinthians 3:18).

When fish are brought out of their natural element, water, they die; but when human beings are lifted up from their habitual condition of limited humanity they become gods. This was to be the mission of Saints Peter and Andrew: to draw men upwards into higher consciousness and the transcendence of the compulsion of earthly rebirth. The Prodigal Son, though born in wealth, eventually hired himself out to a pig farmer; and even worse, he wanted to eat the husks the pigs were eating. But when he awoke to his situation he said: "I will arise and go" back to his home (Luke 15:18). Jesus called his disciples to help those that had awakened to effectively arise and return to God. He turned them from the sea of materiality to the world of Infinite Light.

And when they had brought their ships to land, they forsook all. When the flux and change of being "at sea" spiritually ends and we awaken to our real nature, we leave behind all that has bound and deluded us, all that we called "me" and "mine," and enter into life unbound and undeluded. This is itself proof that we have heard and answered the call from above. I once saw a cartoon showing a drunk lying in a gutter and saying to a woman dressed in a Salvation Army uniform: "Can you save me here, or do I have to go somewhere?" The answer is obvious. Only those who like the prodigal Son arise and go, leaving the dead world behind, will enter the kingdom of Spirit and live in Life.

The newly-called apostles left everything behind. The old focus of our consciousness has to be left behind–not just gradually, but immediately, if we would be true disciples. Sometimes the externals of our life have to be abandoned either completely or to a great degree. Sometimes there is nothing wrong with the way our life is set up, just our attitudes and interests need changing. But this thing is sure: to be a disciple of higher consciousness there must be permanent change, whether inner or outer. We must join ourselves unto our inner Christ. This must be done, not just with words, but with the disciple's life.

Even though they were getting their nets ready for use, they dropped them instantly and followed Jesus. They did not reason that since they had spent all that time getting them ready, they should go on and use them for one last time. This is a common foible. "Well, since we have this meat we may as well eat it up and then go vegetarian." "Let's drink it up and then quit alcohol." "As soon as this carton of cigarettes is finished I am quitting smoking." "We've got the tickets, so let's go." "We made the promise: we have to keep it." "But I made the commitment before…." "Just one last fling…." "After all, we have come this far…." "Next week…." "Tomorrow…." And note that even though the father of James and John depended on them for his livelihood ("After all, doesn't family count for something…?"), they walked away at the call of Jesus without hesitation. Those who do not get out of the boat and leave the nets will go nowhere.

And followed him. Thus they became his disciples. Actually, the word "disciple" will not occur until later, but it should be examined now. *Mathetes*, disciple, comes from the root *mathano*, which means to learn in the sense of coming to understand. To "believe in" or "confess" Christ means absolutely nothing–often worse than nothing if it becomes a delusive substitute for taking up the yoke of Christ and learning of him the Way of Christhood. ("Take my yoke upon you, and learn of me" Matthew 11:29.).

There is no other way to join with God. Great numbers came to Jesus and also went. Only the disciples remained. Only the disciples sought to live with him. It is real disciples who entreat God: "Abide with us" (Luke 24:29). They speak from deep intuition, for Jesus told them: "If a man love me,… my Father will love him, and we will come unto him, and make our abode with him" (John 14:2). To those who give themselves to God, God gives himself. It is a contractual union.

In the Synagogue at Capernaum

And they went into Capernaum; and straightway on the sabbath day he entered into the synagogue, and taught. And they were astonished at his doctrine: for he taught them as one that had authority, and not as the scribes.

And there was in their synagogue a man with an unclean spirit; and he cried out, saying, Let us alone; what have we to do with thee, thou Jesus of Nazareth? art thou come to destroy us? I know thee who thou art, the Holy One of God. And Jesus rebuked him, saying, Hold thy peace, and come out of him. And when the unclean spirit had torn him, and cried with a loud voice, he came out of him. And they were all amazed, insomuch that they questioned among themselves, saying, What thing is this? what new doctrine is this? for with authority commandeth he even the unclean spirits, and they do obey him. And immediately his fame spread abroad throughout all the region round about Galilee. And forthwith, when they were come out of the synagogue, they entered into the house of Simon and Andrew, with James and John. But Simon's wife's mother lay sick of a fever, and anon they tell him of her. And he came and took her by the hand, and lifted her up; and immediately the fever left her, and she ministered unto them (Mark 1:21-31).

And they went into Capernaum; and straightway on the sabbath day he entered into the synagogue, and taught. And they were astonished at his doctrine:

for he taught them as one that had authority, and not as the scribes. I think that the most obvious trait of exoteric Christianity is its complete lack of legitimate authority. It has no historical continuity with the origins of Christianity, and even more it is easy to intuit that its teachers have no authority at all. This is because although they claim to teach truth, they actually only dispense theory bolstered by ignorance.

Personal experience brings authority with it. This is why Paramhansa Yogananda said that the practice of yoga itself produces perseverance in yoga. The proof of the pudding truly is in the eating. Jesus spoke from his perfected consciousness and the very vibrations of his words opened the hearts of his hearers and produced in them the conviction that "never man spake like this man" (John 7:46).

The word *exousia*, translated "authority," means power, strength, authority and freedom. A person possessing such authority will radiate the power of truth, will freely speak that truth against all opposition and will prevail over all enemies and nay-sayers. History has demonstrated this over and over. That is why evil people fear a single person speaking the truth. And this is especially true of evil religion and its leaders. Truth Alone Prevails (*Satyam Eva Jayate*).

And there was in their synagogue a man with an unclean spirit. The demon (*daimonion*) is described as "unclean." The word used is *akathartos*, impure, but it carries with it the connotation of morally foul or lewd. There are all kinds of spirits swarming in the atmosphere of the earth, attaching themselves to human beings in hope of influencing (obsessing) or even controlling (possessing) them. Spirits who become earthbound wanderers because of their immoral consciousness and acts try to obsess or possess human beings and get them to entertain them by committing indecent acts. Earthbound alcoholics try to get people to drink themselves into a stupor so they can get a kind of secondary high. Extreme nicotine addicts do the same, and violent spirits try to make people commit violent acts. A great deal of human behavior is not human at all, but demonic.

And he cried out, saying, Let us alone; what have we to do with thee, thou Jesus of Nazareth? The words "us" and "we" reveal that there were several obsessing and possessing spirits there in the synagogue.

Art thou come to destroy us? Apollumi, the word translated "destroy," means both punish and annihilate. Of course Jesus intended to do no such things, but evil people always accuse others of evil deeds and purposes. Of course to very evil people the idea of being delivered from their vile state is worse even than death.

I know thee who thou art; the Holy One of God. I think that we can conclude from this that "confessing" Jesus as Christ does not "save" a person. For we are told in the Gospels that many possessing spirits declared the Messiahship and divine holiness of Jesus.

And Jesus rebuked him, saying, Hold thy peace, and come out of him. Epitimao (rebuked) means to command or forbid. "Hold thy peace" is a very genteel translation of *phimoo,* while literally means "muzzle it!" *Exerchomai* means to go far away. To exactly where we are not told, but obviously Jesus did not intend for the spirit to just go down the street and possess someone else. So there must have been a place of banishment from whence the spirit could not escape to again possess a person.

And when the unclean spirit had torn him, and cried with a loud voice, he came out of him. Apparently the spirit tossed the man off as we would a coat. But as he left he harmed (tore) him in some way. I remember a man telling about an exorcism he had witnessed in which the spirit kept threatening to tear out the possessed man's stomach. But he did not. However, one time on Mount Athos some monks were attempting to exorcise another monk. The possessing spirit kept saying: "I will kill him! I will kill him!" They did not believe it and persisted and the man died. Such was his karma. And perhaps the incompetence of the would-be exorcists.

And they were all amazed, insomuch that they questioned among themselves, saying, What thing is this? what new doctrine is this? for with authority commandeth he even the unclean spirits, and they do obey him. And immediately his fame spread abroad throughout all the region round about Galilee. It is no surprise that "his fame spread abroad throughout all the region round about Galilee," again underlining the fact that all Israel knew of Jesus and his invincible spiritual power.

And forthwith, when they were come out of the synagogue, they entered into the house of Simon and Andrew, with James and John. But Simon's wife's mother lay sick of a fever, and anon they tell him of her. And he came and took her by the hand, and lifted her up; and immediately the fever left her, and she ministered unto them. In the account of the same event by Saint Luke (4:38-39), it is said that Jesus "rebuked the fever; and it left her." Sometimes illness comes from negative spirits, and illnesses themselves have a kind of thought form which psychically sensitive people can see. When Anandamayi Ma cured someone of a disease she usually spoke to it and said: "You have done enough. Now leave."

In her own life there was an incident that shows either that evil spirits cause a disease or the disease has an actual form that can be seen.

Once in the holy city of Hardwar (Haridwara), Ma was staying in a dharmashala on the east bank of the Ganges. She became very ill, and a doctor who was staying almost opposite on the west bank of the Ganges came to see her. He was horrified to find that Ma had advanced cancer of the liver, and demanded that she undergo treatment immediately. Ma refused, but he went daily and saw her getting worse every day until he was positive that she would die within a day; and he told her so. Ma asked him to wait just one more day. Early the next morning as he was getting ready to go see Ma he looked out his window and saw a hideous black ape come out of the window of Ma's room. Even though the window had bars on it, the creature just passed right through them and jumped into the Ganges and disappeared. The doctor rushed over and found Ma in perfect health. Of course he "just could not understand it," but I do, and I hope you do, too.

Jesus Heals the Sick

> Now when the sun was setting, all they that had any sick with divers[e] diseases brought them unto him; and he laid his hands on every one of them, and healed them. And devils also came out of many, crying out, and saying, Thou art Christ the Son of God. And he rebuking them suffered them not to speak: for they knew that he was Christ (Luke 4:40-41).

Astheneo, translated "sick," includes those with diseases, paralysis and wasting diseases. Any kind of infirmity is implied.

He laid his hands on every one of them, and healed them. Later in this Gospel we will be told: "there went virtue out of him, and healed them all" (Luke 6:19). The human body is a pulsing entity of life force, and this force can be used to heal. (See my book *Magnetic Therapy: Healing in Your Hands*.) Jesus was in a human body, but that body was formed of omnipotent divine consciousness, so his touch and even his mere presence could heal. Since exoteric religion is based on material consciousness and "sin," when Mary Baker Eddy wrote that sin and disease were unreal, all its adherents went into a tailspin of hysterical denial of her words. But it is true. Remission of sins proves that sin is not real. Healing proves that disease is not real. Otherwise sin and disease could not be dispelled. They are states of mind, just as Mrs. Eddy also said.

And devils also came out of many, crying out, and saying, Thou art Christ the Son of God. And he rebuking them suffered them not to speak: for they knew that he was Christ. Once again we see that believing in Jesus and confessing his divine status in no way makes anyone closer to Christ or God. Only when we are in touch with our true, inner Christ nature do our words and actions matter.

Jesus' Ministry in Galilee Continues

> And in the morning, rising up a great while before day, he went out, and departed into a solitary place, and there prayed. And Simon and they that were with him followed after him. And when they had found him, they said unto him, All men seek for thee. And he said unto them, Let us go into the next towns, that I may preach there also: for therefore came I forth (Mark 1:35-38).

It was Jesus' regular routine to get up some hours before dawn and go to a quiet solitary place to meditate. It is a good practice for the yogi do the same according his ability, hopefully having a meditation room or corner where he goes to meditate.

> And the people sought him, and came unto him, and stayed him, that he should not depart from them (Luke 4:42).
>
> And Jesus went about all Galilee, teaching in their synagogues, and preaching the gospel of the kingdom, and healing all manner of sickness and all manner of disease among the people (Matthew 4:23).

The fact that the synagogues of Galilee were open to Jesus to teach shows that right away in his public ministry he was recognized as legitimate and even welcomed.

Jesus proclaimed the good news of the inner kingdom before he healed. When I was in my beginning teens I became very unsettled one Sunday morning when our Sunday School teacher said that before the Gospel could be preached to people in economically stressed countries we needed to first take care of their material needs. This was contrary to Jesus' counsel: "Seek ye first the kingdom of God, and his righteousness" (Matthew 6:3), and betrayed a mind certainly contrary to "the mind of Christ" (I Corinthians 2:1). Rare are those who live the motto: The Kingdom First.

This verse speaks of "sickness" and "disease." "Sickness" is the translation of *nosos*, which means an actual disease or an infirmity such as being crippled or having a limiting deformity. "Disease," on the other hand, comes from *malakia*, which means a lack of strength, a debility of some kind, rather than an actual diagnosable ailment. This is very significant, for people are afflicted with both conditions: a condition of inner negativity and a condition of spiritual weakness, a lack of spiritual initiative or perception.

Spiritual health is the forerunner of physical health. Often disease may be a prerequisite of spiritual healing since it is the most common way of dissolving negative karmas. Although Jesus healed bodily disease, he also healed the sickness of the soul, sicknesses which also are chronic and serious. The idea is that he healed *all* disease, not just one type. And we, too, must seek healing for all our interior ills, not just the worse or dangerous ones. It is common among followers of all religions to eliminate the worst moral disorders but keep (and often foster) the "little" ones that "don't do any real harm." But this is impossible for those who aspire to Christhood, for Jesus tells us: "He that is faithful in that which is least is faithful also in much: and he that is unjust in the least is unjust also in much" (Luke 16:10). This is a principle we must always keep in mind. In the pursuit of spiritual perfection there are no little or harmless things.

I have mentioned it before, but I want to repeat that I have never seen a person deflected from the spiritual path by doing something big that was negative. Always the turning away from the light was begun by doing or tolerating something negative that was very small. But the descent to the big things occurred very swiftly afterward like the unravelling of a cloth. This principle is frighteningly illustrated in the Gospel of John. When Jesus told the apostles that one of them would betray him, and Saint John asked him who it was, "Jesus answered, he it is, to whom I shall give a sop, when I have dipped it. And when he had dipped the sop, he gave it to Judas Iscariot, the son of Simon. And after the sop Satan entered into him" (John 13:26,27). Although the King James translators used "sop"--a word that only means something that has been dipped in a liquid to make it easier or more flavorful to eat--the word used by Saint John in the original text was *psomion*, which means a tiny piece of something, just a crumb or little bit. "And after the sop Satan entered into" Judas. Just a little thing, but see the effect.

Jesus is teaching us a profound lesson that there is indeed no "little" thing in the perspective of spiritual life. Think of the size of the human body as compared to bacteria or viruses. Yet those infinitesimally tiny things can kill the body. One of the largest giant redwoods in northern California suddenly died. Upon examination it was found that an insect the size of a gnat had burrowed into the heart of the tree and caused its death. So to argue that something is harmless because it is small is very foolish. We must be as wary of the little things as the big things—sometimes even more so, because the little things fool us into disregarding them. Hence Solomon said in spiritual allegory: "Take us the foxes, the little foxes, that spoil the vines: for our vines have tender grapes" (Song of Solomon 2:15). "And what I say unto you I say unto all, Watch" (Mark 13:37). Beware and be wary.

And his fame went throughout all Syria. At the time of Jesus "Syria" was the name of the area that today includes Syria, Iraq, Lebanon, Jordan, and Israel. His notoriety, then, was very great, extending far beyond the boundaries of modern Israel, causing huge numbers of people to seek him out for healing.

And he healed them. So Jesus cured *all* diseases. He did not only cure the obviously serious ones, he healed the slightest disease as well, for all disease is a result of violation of the law of God. The higher meaning is that all ignorance must healed, and healing is elimination, not amelioration or reduction.

The word translated "diseases" is *nosos*, that we have already considered. *Basanos*, the word translated "torments," means pains, for people often have terrible pains but no cause can be found, or they are not a result of actual disease but may come from structural problems.

"Possessed with devils" is the translation of the word *daimonizomai*, which means to be controlled or strongly influenced by a *daimon*, a spirit. *Daimon* does not mean demon in the usual English sense, that of a fallen angel, but means any discarnate entity. This can include consciously evil spirits of various sorts, including malevolent spirits, but can also mean ignorant or uncomprehending spirits such as nature spirits and earthbound human spirits. On occasion the "demon" is a semi-intelligent energy form or force that was intentionally or unconsciously created by the will or thought of one or more persons. These thought-forms can take on an artificial life of their own and work great harm. People can be either possessed or obsessed by these beings, and we should know the difference between possession and obsession.

Possession is when an entity enters into and occupies the entire body and brain, becoming its "soul" for all practical purposes. Obsession occurs when an entity enters into a part of the body and controls it, or when the entity invades the auric (biomagnetic) field and influences the mental or bodily functions of the person. Possession is not as common as we might think, because the body is formed around the person's spirit as its matrix, and for an alien astral body to enter into and fully control it is extraordinarily difficult. Usually possession produces malfunctions or non-functions in the body and mind. So may obsession, but not always. In possession, an entity becomes actually incarnate in the body, but in obsession there is just partial influence or control. Both are terrible. And obsession is *very* common, often coming and going in cycles. Obsession usually occurs from the auric invasion of discarnate human beings, resulting in aberrations in both behavior and thinking. Addictions and criminal behavior are to a great extent the result of obsession, as are many psychological aberrations.

It is a grave truth that many people are possessed or obsessed, either permanently or temporarily. Both conditions are ultimately destructive of both physical and mental health.

"Lunatick" is the translation of the word *seleniazomai*, which means "moonstruck." The moon has a great influence on the earth and its living beings. Since the moon causes the tides in the ocean, we can assume that its influence greatly affects the fluids in our bodies also. And since they are mostly water, the influence would have to produce an effect, even in the mind. The phases of the moon affect the growth of plants, and our mental states. A friend of mine was supervisor of the psychopathic ward at the state mental hospital in Austin, Texas. He told me that the atmosphere in that ward–which numbered almost four hundred patients–at the full moon was indescribably negative.

Seleniazomai actually covers all mental illness or disorientation that is produced by purely physical imbalances or conditions.

Paralytikos means to be feeble, afflicted with muscular tremors, or completely immobilized: paralyzed in our English sense.

Palsy is the continual shaking of one or more limbs of the body. But the word so translated is *paralutikos*, which really means paralytic–paralyzed.

A Leper is Healed

And there came a leper to him, beseeching him, and kneeling down to him, and saying unto him, If thou wilt, thou canst make me clean. And Jesus, moved with compassion, put forth his hand, and touched him, and saith unto him, I will; be thou clean. And as soon as he had spoken, immediately the leprosy departed from him, and he was cleansed. And he straitly charged him, and forthwith sent him away; and saith unto him, See thou say nothing to any man: but go thy way, shew thyself to the priest, and offer for thy cleansing those things which Moses commanded, for a testimony unto them. But he went out, and began to publish it much, and to blaze abroad the matter, insomuch that Jesus could no more openly enter into the city, but was without in desert places: and they came to him from every quarter (Mark 1:40-45).

And there came a leper to him, beseeching him, and kneeling down to him, and saying unto him,.... Leprosy is a terrible disease in which the body literally disintegrates. It has only become curable in my lifetime. I saw a great deal of it in India in the middle of the last century, though I have not seen a leper in India for a long time. The nose, fingers and toes are the first to disintegrate, and there are lesions on the body that often bleed. It is truly a living death.

If thou wilt, thou canst make me clean. "With men this is impossible; but with God all things are possible" (Matthew 19:26). We can assume that the man believed that Jesus could heal him because, as Nicodemus said, God was "with him" (John 3:2). But the real reason he could heal was the fact that he was perfectly one with God and able to truthfully say: "I and my Father are one" (John 10:30). And: "He that hath seen me hath seen the Father" (John 14:9). Yet they are two, as the Greek word *heis* implies. For it not only means one in the sense of number, but it also means "one another." That is why Isaiah (7:14) had foretold that the Messiah would be Immanuel: God With Us. We simply cannot conceive the status of a perfected being, a siddha-purusha. The truth is, because our minds are so limited a siddha-purusha is far beyond our concept of God. All avatars are much greater than our idea of God.

Being one with God and inseparable from God in his consciousness, Jesus could heal the leper by his divine will. Because of the decaying effect of the disease, its cure was spoken of as being made "clean."

But there is a lesson here for us. If we truly will it, we can purify, make clean and heal ourselves of the terrible disease of ignorance and bondage to the wheel of birth and death.

And Jesus, moved with compassion, put forth his hand, and touched him, and saith unto him, I will; be thou clean. It was the loving mercy and care of Jesus that motivated his healing, just as it motivated his incarnation. And we, too, should put forth our "hand" to ourselves through profound meditation and become pure and healed.

And as soon as he had spoken, immediately the leprosy departed from him, and he was cleansed. As the centurion had said to Jesus, "Speak the word only, and my servant shall be healed" (Matthew 8:8).

I met a man who developed some kind of skin problem that got so bad he could not go out in public. In desperation he went to the medical school of a nearby university and was examined. The doctor was amazed, and told him that he not only had leprosy, he had "white leprosy" which was the type of leprosy spoken of in the Bible, and which was assumed to be extinct. The man went home, assuming he might die. But the church to which he belonged believed very strongly in healing through prayer—in fact they never took medicine. They often sang a song that said:

> Oh, that precious, loving Jesus!
> His compassion still the same,

Toward poor sinful, suff'ring mortals
> Who seek refuge in His name.

Heed the present invitation,
> Oh, you need not stay away!

Just receive His healing favor,
> For He's just the same today.

Yes, He healed in Galilee,
> Set the suff'ring captives free,

And He's just the same today.

So the next time there was a gathering of ministers he went to them and told about his plight. They prayed for him and within a week every trace of the leprosy was gone. He went back to the medical school and in equal amazement they declared him perfectly free of the disease.

> **And he straitly [strictly] charged him, and forthwith sent him away; and saith unto him, See thou say nothing to any man: but go thy way, shew thyself to the priest, and offer for thy cleansing those things which Moses commanded, for a testimony unto them (Mark 1:43-44).**

Jesus never wanted people to make a great fuss about his miracles, but rather to quietly live according to his teachings which worked a much greater miracle in the consciousness of those who followed him. However, here we see that he wanted the priests to know of the healing, because this was required in the Mosaic Law.

> **But he went out, and began to publish [proclaim] it much, and to blaze abroad the matter, insomuch that Jesus could no more openly enter into the city, but was without in desert[ed] places: and they came to him from every quarter (Mark 1:45).**

> **But so much the more went there a fame abroad of him: and great multitudes came together to hear, and to be healed by him of their infirmities. And he withdrew himself into the wilderness, and prayed (Luke 5:15-16).**

This is the response Jesus received from a man whose life he had saved: total opposition to his instructions. So people were coming from all four directions to pester him and demand healing.

As your friend I am asking you to never do any healing, unless you can do it at a distance and never tell anyone about it. Otherwise you will be besieged by people wanting you to cure them—even of things an aspirin would take care of. And some get very vicious if they do not get healed by you. Please do not put yourself in that situation! I speak from my own experience. Once a very dear friend of mine was seriously ill. I prayed for her and she was instantly healed. So she began telling people to come to me for healing. I was only fourteen or fifteen, and you can imagine my parents' reaction when the phone began ringing with healing requests!

What I have said applies to anything out of the ordinary, including psychic matters. Once I foolishly explained to another friend what it was in her past lives that had brought about her present situation. She told about it and I began to get demands for past life readings, some from rich people who offered me a lot of money. And all got miffed when I said No. Learn to be ignored and thought a nobody. Ego is always there, both on your side and that of others. Like Jesus, withdraw and meditate.

Return to Capernaum

And again he entered into Capernaum after some days; and it was noised that he was in the house. And straightway many were gathered together, insomuch that there was no room to receive them, no, not so much as about the door: and he preached the word unto them (Mark 2:1-2).

No matter what the motive might be of the people who came to Jesus, they were sure to hear the message of the divine kingdom and the way to it. Even if they ignored his words, they still went into their subconscious and were seeds of future awakening.

And it came to pass on a certain day, as he was teaching, that there were Pharisees and doctors of the law sitting by, which were come out of every town of Galilee, and Judaea, and Jerusalem: and the power of the Lord was present to heal them. And, behold, men brought in a bed a man which was taken with a palsy: and they sought means to bring him in, and to lay him before him. And when they could not find by what way they might bring him in because of the multitude, they went upon the housetop, and let him down through the tiling with his couch into the midst before Jesus (Luke 5:17-19).

And, behold, they brought to him a man sick of the palsy, lying on a bed: and Jesus seeing their faith said unto the sick of the palsy; Son, be of good cheer; thy sins be y were all amazed, and they glorified God, and were filled with fear, saying, We have seen strange things to day (Luke 5:25-26).

Son,.... The word in Greek is *teknon*, which really means "child," but is translated son or daughter according to the gender of the person addressed. Why did Jesus call the man "son"? Certainly because he was a child (son) of God, and Jesus honored and respected him as such–an example that is good to follow. We must also remember that Jesus did not look upon him with the eyes of ignorance, but with the true sight which he had opened in India with the Nath Yogis.

It is a mistake to think of Jesus as even part of, much less a product of, Judaism. When Jesus met the king of Kashmir after his return to India, as recorded in the *Bhavishya Maha Purana*, he told the king, "O King, I hail from a land far away, where there is no truth, and evil knows no limits. I appeared in the country of the mlecchas [barbarians] as Isha Masiha [Jesus Messiah/Christ] and I suffered at their hands." As a pure Sanatana Dharmi, a follower of the Eternal Dharma, he viewed every sentient being as a divine Self (Atman), and therefore as a child of God, a part of God. And he addressed the man accordingly.

Thy sins be forgiven thee. The important part of this is the fact that illness and physical defects come from negative karmas called "sins" in the English translation of the Gospels. In our consideration of the words of the angel to Saint Joseph at the beginning of our study, we looked at the meaning and nature of sin. But a little review is not amiss here.

I have mentioned earlier that *amartia*, the word translated "sin," does not mean to break a rule or anger or displease God. Rather it means literally "to miss the mark" or "to fall short [of the mark]." Fundamentally it means to fail, and can mean incurring a harmful or negative result. "Shortcoming" is a very good translation of *amartia*. The word "sin" has been imposed on *amartia*. It literally means to lack something, to be deficient. It also means "to miss the mark," to not be what we should be, but to be less than what God intends. It also includes losing our way or wandering from the path. *Amartia* also means to make a mistake in judgment, to not understand correctly. Here the need for true spiritual knowledge (jnana) is expressed. Notice that none of these meanings have anything to do with wrongdoing, whereas exoteric Christianity gives it no other meaning. Certainly wrongdoing is to be avoided, but "sinful actions" are symptoms of *amartia*, not *amartia* itself.

Amartia is an inner disposition that will certainly result in suffering and confusion for those afflicted with it, and certainly is not to be taken lightly. But it is a condition of mind, a state of consciousness, and until it is expunged from our minds and hearts we will wander in ignorance and delusion. It does not need to be forgiven, it needs to be eliminated. And that is done only by our efforts, by purification through the cultivation of higher consciousness through meditation and spiritual discipline.

Jesus tells the man his sins are forgiven. The word used by Saint Mark is *aphiemi*, which means to leave (abandon) something, to turn from it completely. It even has the connotation of refusing to touch something. It is an active word, a verb, and has nothing to do with God forgiving us. Rather, it is something *we* do, not something that is done *to* us. How different this, too, is from Christianity's corrupted and false interpretation. *Aphiemi* also means to send something away or demand it to depart. So it is a word implying uncompromising and vigilant separation from *amartia*. It also means to ignore or disregard something, to no longer retain it. It even means to leave and go somewhere else–to change one's consciousness and life. A minor meaning is to "die" to something–to *amarti*a. As Saint Paul wrote: "The world is crucified unto me, and I unto the world" (Galatians 6:14).

When Jesus spoke of "sins" being "forgiven" he meant something vastly beyond the conception of exoteric Christianity, especially Fundamentalist Protestantism. He meant that because the sick man came to him desiring healing, his faith was a psychic and spiritual channel between him and Jesus so he could receive the purifying and healing light and power that always emanated from Jesus.

Here again, Jesus is speaking as a Sanatana Dharmi–as he always acted and spoke throughout his public ministry after returning from India.

Saint Catherine of Genoa was a spiritually heedless young girl. Her older sister once went on a long retreat to a convent. Catharine visited her there, and her sister insisted that before she left Catharine should go to the convent priest and get his blessing. Catherine did not want to, being utterly alien to religion, but to please her sister she did so. She knelt before the priest, who blessed her, and then she suddenly jumped up and shouted,

"No more sin! No more world!" And proceeded to become a saint. She was as surprised as anyone else. This is the true forgiveness of sins.

And the scribes and the Pharisees began to reason, saying, Who is this which speaketh blasphemies? Who can forgive sins, but God alone? A *grammateus* [scribe] was a secretary, sometimes a town clerk, who obviously had a religious function as a record keeper. They were *dialogizomai*–talking inwardly to themselves. It also means to be arguing, rejecting and even despising. In other words they were disagreeing with and detesting what they heard.

And Jesus knowing their thoughts said, Wherefore think ye evil in your hearts? This is an important point. Jesus knew "in his spirit" what they were thinking.

There are two kinds of clairvoyance: psychic and spiritual. Psychic clairvoyance occurs in the astral bodies and is an almost material perception. It has nothing to do with the evolution of a person. In fact, many animals are quite clairvoyant and perceive what is not externally manifest. Dogs and cats especially can come to read the minds of those they live with. So such clairvoyance does not indicate a spiritual person. Many evil people are quite clairvoyant. It is a mistake to think that a psychic clairvoyant is spiritual, or to ask them questions concerning spiritual matters. Yogis abound in India that are considered liberated masters and gurus when they are merely psychics, often of a very low grade.

As Patanjali said (see *Yoga: Science of the Absolute*), psychic abilities can come from the ingestion of herbs or drugs. Some people become clairvoyant when drunk. A friend of mine was given a mine claim by someone. He was not interested, but an acquaintance said he would like to go live there and try to find the gold. My friend had no objection, so the man went and stayed there some years. Whenever the man saw he was about to run out of money he would go into town and buy a large amount of liquor. When he got back to the claim he would drink until he passed out. In that state he could see a small, strange spirit that was eager to communicate with anyone. He would ask the spirit the names of the horses that were going to win at several racetracks in the next season. The spirit would obligingly tell him, and when he became conscious he would write down the names. Then when the tracks opened he would go and bet as much as he could on the horses whose names he had been given. They always won, and he got enough money to live on for a year or more, and then he would repeat the process. He apparently never found the gold. This is an example of psychic clairvoyance of a low and chancey order. Manly Palmer Hall used to say that dogs and cats can see the spirits of the dead, and those human beings who "develop mediumship" are merely regressing themselves to the level of cats and dogs.

Spiritual clairvoyance manifests in people of a pure and spiritually evolved nature, and is a result of their spiritual illumination. They do not exercise their abilities at their will or whim as do psychic clairvoyants, but look to God alone to reveal things to them. They may ask something of God, but usually the spiritual communication comes to them at God's will and not by request. I have known and lived with holy people who had spiritual clairvoyance. My maternal grandmother was a spiritual clairvoyant and I observed her abilities from my early childhood. Of course I did not understand these things, but I saw her work great miracles of healing in secret. Those she healed never knew she had done so, and most of those she healed never heard of her–she learned of their need from others. She also was guided by spiritual clairvoyance in her personal life and had many visions. She spoke with God as a child to a loving parent. After her death I found records of her visions and divine conversations.

It is difficult for us to distinguish between these types of clairvoyance unless we know the person very well. But it is safer to assume that any manifestation of clairvoyance is psychic, and not put too high a value on it. After all, God and the holy ones will not be offended.

When the religionists thought (they did not speak aloud) that Jesus was blaspheming because their misunderstanding of the nature of sin and freedom from sin made it seem so, Jesus decided to challenge their defective views.

One of America's great spiritual treasures was Metropolitan Anastassy (Gribanovsky), a great leader in the Eastern Christian Church and a known miracle-worker. Whenever during a meeting of the bishops of the Russian Orthodox Church Outside Russia (of which he was the head) anyone would be sitting in silence while inwardly disagreeing with something being said, Metropolitan Anastassy would turn to them and say: "Speak out! Don't just think it: say it." And so they would. I never had the privilege of seeing or meeting him, but was one of the first allowed into his room to venerate his body and pray on the evening of his passing away (May 22, 1965). The next day I attended his eight-hour funeral and traveled to Holy Trinity Monastery near Jordanville, New York for his burial. It was an awesome experience.

So Jesus, like the Metropolitan in our own time, knew the thoughts of complainers and nay-sayers and spoke of it openly.

It is very interesting that the word translated "evil" is *poneros*, which means something that causes great mental pain, stress, annoyances, and hardships (irreconcilability). It causes great distress and may even be considered as mental harassment. Outwardly it may also cause great troubles, dangers and even harm. The problem is not the thoughts, but the thinkers of the thoughts–their negative (and therefore egocentric) state of mind.

Purification from sins is invisible, and it can be doubted or denied, so Jesus goes further and heals the man instantly, telling him to stand up, carry his pallet and go home. There was no way to deny that when the man was seen to be perfectly healed and walking. The healing of the man was proof of Jesus' ability to release human beings from the bonds of disease-causing karma. I have seen this for myself in both East and West when being with saints and masters.

For whether is easier, to say, Thy sins be forgiven thee; or to say, Arise, and walk? But that ye may know that the Son of man hath power on earth to forgive sins, (then saith he to the sick of the palsy,) Arise, take up thy bed, and go unto thine house. Jesus spoke of himself as both "Son of God" and "Son of man." In his spirit he was an illumined Son of God, a god within God, a perfect siddha-purusha who had evolved beyond all relativity and entered into the depths of the Eternal Absolute. Although established in that divine state of Son of God, he had willed to descend through all the worlds into this lowest material plane and appear on earth as a human being, a son of man. The word translated "man" is *anthropos*, which means a human being, but also has the meaning "man-faced," meaning he entered into a human body and had the full experience of the human condition. But he was at all times fully dwelling and functioning in Infinite Consciousness. As I have said, our limited and dim concepts of God are far beneath what Jesus the Avatar really was–and is.

And immediately he rose up before them, and took up that whereon he lay, and departed to his own house, glorifying God. And they were all amazed, and they glorified God, and were filled with fear, saying, We have seen strange things today. To react with fear (*phobos*, intense fear or terror) when encountering something, someone or situation that is holy is often (usually) a sign of intense negativity. All the time godless and God-hating people react with fear when something positive is done through spiritual power. The idea that God both can and will intervene in human life horrifies them, for they want God to be a childish abstraction or superstition. When the reality of the unseen impinges on them they feel threatened to the depth of their being because they are fundamentally evil–demonic–as Krishna explains at length in the sixteenth chapter of the Bhagavad Gita.

The Calling of Levi

> **And after these things he went forth, and saw a publican, named Levi, sitting at the receipt of custom: and he said unto him, Follow me. And he left all, rose up, and followed him (Luke 5:27-28).**

As I have said before: this is the way it is done. Jesus spoke only two words. The call is heard and acted upon, or it is unperceived or ignored. There is no wheedling, promising, explaining or urging on the part of the one making the call. That is the way of samsara, the realm of ignorance and constant flux and change. When God calls you, you either arise and follow or you do not. There is no in between. Those who have to think it over, reason it out, figure if they are really able to do it, decide the right time and get ready for it, never take a step on the journey to the Light. They remain full of temporary resolves and aspirations, fall back asleep and sleep the sleep of spiritual death. As a *Pogo* character once said: "Cut the philosophy and run!" Levi (Matthew) was a representative of the Roman Imperial government, but "he left all" and followed Jesus. To do such a thing–leaving the money and all records behind and walk away–would result in execution. But he did so, anyway, considering his life as nothing when he heard the call.

An interesting aspect of the word *akoloutheo*, "follow," is that one meaning is to reach someone–to come to them or accompany them. This is certainly part of the call of Christ, for we are called to be with Christ–to become a Christ and become united to the infinite, Cosmic Christ.

> **And it came to pass, that, as Jesus sat at food in his house, many publicans and sinners sat also together with Jesus and**

his disciples: for there were many, and they followed him. And when the scribes and Pharisees saw him eat with publicans and sinners, they said unto his disciples, How is it that he eateth and drinketh with publicans and sinners? When Jesus heard it, he saith unto them, They that are whole have no need of the physician, but they that are sick: I came not to call the righteous, but sinners to repentance (Mark 2:15-17).

And it came to pass, that, as Jesus sat at food in his [Levi's] house, many publicans [tax collectors] and sinners sat also together with Jesus and his disciples: for there were many, and they followed him. It is essential for aspirants to higher life and consciousness (yogis, especially), to be very careful about the kind of people they associate with, for as Yogananda said, "Company is greater than will power." Saint Paul said, "Be not deceived: evil communications corrupt good manners [behavior]" (I Corinthians 15:33). The word *homilia* translated "communications" means both companionship and association. Please do not let your ego fool you by telling you that by association with people you can "help" them. Eventually they will infect you with their negativity. I have seen people's lives destroyed by the kind of people they associated with. One man I knew was an example of positive thinking and living. Then he went to a foreign country and fell into evil company. When I next saw him he was addicted to alcohol and drugs and completely corrupt and coarse in his mind and life. But Jesus was not an ordinary man. He was a god, a savior, whose company could purify and enlighten. As the old Roman adage says: *Quod licet Iovi non est licet bovi*: "What is permitted [allowed to] Jove [the king of the gods] is not permitted the cattle." It may sound snobbish, but it is absolutely true.

And when the scribes and Pharisees saw him eat with publicans and sinners, they said unto his disciples, How is it that he eateth and drinketh with publicans and sinners? Jesus was associating with those people as though they were friends and equals. And he most certainly was their Friend.

When Jesus heard it, he saith unto them, They that are whole have no need of the physician, but they that are sick: I came not to call the righteous, but sinners to repentance. If Jesus treated those people as though they were evil and worthy of condemnation he would have been no better than the scribes and Pharisees. But because he had the spiritual power to encompass them with his love and elevate and purify them, he was in very truth their friend. Here are three interesting stories about Anandamayi Ma. All three happened in the holy city of Varanasi, the City of Shiva, he who accepts all, even the snakes and the scorpions.

Once when Ma was in the Anandamayi Ashram in Varanasi, a man came and began to complain about some of the people who lived there, even describing their faults. Ma listened to his list and then calmly said: "Baba, this ashram is a 'hospital.' If you are not 'sick,' then you do not need to come here."

A man came to live in the ashram that eventually displeased and alienated everyone else living there. They waited till Ma came there and right in public before the devotees who had come for Ma's darshan each one made a detailed complaint about him and demanded that he be put out of the ashram. When they were finished Ma called the man to come before her. When he knelt there, Ma leaned forward and embraced him (something Ma almost never did) and said: "If no one else wants you, how could I send you away?"

A brahmin cannot even touch alcohol, much less drink it. A brahmin devotee of Ma was, naturally, shocked and horrified when she secretly called him and asked him to buy some whiskey and take it to another devotee who was an alcoholic. He objected at first, but then did what Ma told him. Now in the meantime the alcoholic devotee was struggling to break his habit and was yearning for a drink. When the brahmin came, bringing him the whiskey as a present from Ma, he was overcome by her loving mercy and the kindness of the brahmin. He shed many tears, and was instantly cured of his alcoholism.

These incidents demonstrate exactly what Jesus meant when he said to those who did not like his association with "bad" people: "Go ye and learn what that meaneth, I will have mercy, and not sacrifice: for I am not come to call the righteous, but sinners to repentance" (Matthew 9:13).

Fasting

And the disciples of John and of the Pharisees used to fast: and they come and say unto him, Why do the disciples of John and of the Pharisees fast, but thy disciples fast not? And Jesus said unto them, Can the children of the bridechamber fast, while the bridegroom is with them? As long as they have the bridegroom with them, they cannot fast. But the days will come, when the bridegroom shall be taken away from them, and then shall they fast in those days (Mark 2:18-20).

In our present time there is an obsession with fasting which began in the yoga boom by former hippies, who were in the majority of the aspiring yogis. Obviously they traded their obsession with that they put in their mouths–the drugs that were supposed to make them "high"–to obsession with not putting anything in their mouths, so the resulting light-headedness and feelings would be a "spiritual" high and somehow be a purification.

The fasting in the Gospel was the observance of certain holy days or seasons in which food was either fully abstained from or markedly reduced in quantity or in which certain foods were not eaten. It was meant to keep the faster in remembrance of the holy time and its spiritual meaning. It was supposed to be voluntary, but the self-virtuous sorry-but-I-am-not-eating-today-because-I-am-fasting crowd was shocked at the hedonism of Jesus and his disciples.

During fasting times the Eastern Orthodox Christians abstain absolutely from meat, fish, eggs, dairy products and oil–this latter to make sure they will not eat anything with lard or animal-derived fats. It is great wisdom to *always* abstain from meat, fish, eggs, dairy products and animal-derived fats. That is not asceticism, but just good sense, especially for the yogi.

So Jesus explained that those who are the family of the bridegroom do not fast when with him during the festivities. But when the bridegroom is gone, then they will fast. And so it was. When Jesus returned to India his disciples were as "strangers and pilgrims on the earth" (Hebrews 11:13).

Wisdom in the Spirit

And he spake also a parable unto them; No man putteth a piece of a new garment upon an old; if otherwise, then both the new maketh a rent, and the piece that was taken out of the new agreeth not with the old. And no man putteth new wine into old bottles; else the new wine will burst the bottles, and be spilled, and the bottles shall perish. But new wine must be put into new bottles; and both are preserved. No man also having drunk old wine straightway desireth new: for he saith, The old is better (Luke 5:36-39).

For about ten years in this country a little after the middle of the twentieth century there was what I call the Yoga Boom, with gurus streaming in from India and establishing centers and ashrams and spiritual communities populated with eager disciples disillusioned with the current state of things here and in the world. A new age was here! But it was not. Today we just have a few dwindling organizations left, a few small "families" around an unknown teacher of sorts, and a number of huggees who flock to the "Mayi Mas" as they make their continuous world tours to make a profit. And that is all.

Why? Because no real foundation was (or today is) laid for it in the life and minds of the the disciples. Just the opposite. The gurus assured them that they did not need to "become Hindus" and be out of step with the times, or even to follow any disciplines. Just fill out the form to get a mantra and they were on their way. To nowhere, as it eventually became obvious.

There is a deadly delusion that a spiritual aspirant can ascribe to in all innocence: that all that is needed is to just add some meditation to our life as though adding salt or some flavoring to food. Just add and stir and everything will be fine—no need to go overboard and not lead a normal life, no need for disciplines and forcing of yourself. You don't want to become weird or antisocial and separate yourself from others.

We live in a culture that is completely averse to commitment and sacrifice, but avid after self-gratification without any sense of personal responsibility or obligation. But there is no way to have a viable spiritual life if in the very beginning there is not a complete inventory taken of all areas of our life in order to see what needs to be changed or eliminated or added to make sure of our success in the pursuit of higher consciousness and ultimate liberation. The passage from humanity to divinity is not like taking a bus to the other side of town. It is a matter of transcending the universe and entering into Infinite Being. There must be a complete turn-about in all aspects of the yogi. And it is begun right at the first. Otherwise nothing will come of it but wasted time.

This is the purpose of Jesus' simile of the old and new cloth and wine. The idea is very simple. New cloth cannot be sewn into or made a patch in old cloth, otherwise under any tension they will rip apart for they are not compatible. The symbolism here is also quite simple. The old cloth is the old way of life and thought. The attempt to put a new way of life and thought into the old way and assume they will work together is a mistake. Both will be ruined, for there will be conflict. The word for tear or rend is *schizo*, the root word of schizophrenic. Trying to unite and make the two as one is to create a kind of spiritual schizophrenia—a very real spiritual disorder that can only end in very real harm, the usual harm being that the aspirant gives up under the conflict and discards the new awakening and puts himself back to sleep in his old ways—for this and who knows how many future lives.

The same with the example of old and new wine. The word translated "bottle" is *askos*, which really means a leathern bag in which wine is stored. "New" wine is freshly pressed juice and not fermented. As it sits in the bag (or any container) it begins to ferment and produce gas, which puts intense pressure on the bag. If the bag is new there is no problem, but if it is old the pressure will rip apart the bag and both the bag and its contents will be destroyed. Profound changes are produced in a person that seriously practices yoga meditation, changes that may conflict with his way of life or thinking or with other factors in his life, not the least being personal relations with family, friends and associates.

In summation, yoga practice can only succeed in a yoga-oriented life and mind. A house is not just put up with the walls sitting on the ground. First the area is cleared and made level and some kind of foundation is made on which the house can stand securely. In the same way, no matter how sincere and interested a person may be in meditation, he must realize that more than just "doing meditation" is absolutely necessary. His entire life must be scrutinized by him and brought into total conformity with the endeavor to pass from humanity to divinity in this life. The foundation must be laid, and laid well.

"Whosoever cometh to me, and heareth my sayings, and doeth them, I will shew you to whom he is like: He is like a man which built an house, and digged deep, and laid the foundation on a rock: and when the flood arose, the stream beat vehemently upon that house, and could not shake it: for it was founded upon a rock. But he that heareth, and doeth not, is like a man that without a foundation built an house upon the earth; against which the stream did beat vehemently, and immediately it fell; and the ruin of that house was great" (Luke 6:47-49). The aspirant must right at the beginning "dig deep" and lay his spiritual foundation on the rock of intelligent understanding and application of the requisite observances and disciplines: the following of the principles of yama and niyama. (See Chapter Six: The Foundations of Yoga, in *Soham Yoga: The Yoga of the Self*.)

The basic idea is this bedrock fact: "If any man be in Christ, he is a new creature: old things are passed away; behold, all things are become new. And all things are of God" to him (II Corinthians 5:17-18). When we just begin entering into the life of our inner Christ-Self we become in all ways new. Now the degree of newness grows–just the opposite to earthly things that begin growing old the moment they come into being. And the more we begin growing new, the more the old things just fade away in our mind and heart, and in our life. Then in time we see "all things are of God." This is glorious! It is worth it to jettison the old life of comparatively little value and lay hold on the inner kingdom that is of infinite value. Then we really begin to live.

There is a song that I first heard in my teens and which I have valued ever since. Naturally I now see it with a yogi's perspective.

> So straight is the gate and so narrow
> The way to eternal day,
> And few are the pilgrims who find it,
> Too great is the price they must pay.
>
> Salvation is free, yet to gain it
> The soul must leave all things behind;
> Deny self [ego] and follow the Savior,
> The way straight and narrow to find.
>
> How rugged the path, yet God's glory
> Attendeth each soul on that way;
> And brighter and brighter it shineth,
> Revealing a glad, perfect day.
>
> But it's worth all it costs to be holy,
> It is worth all it costs to be true;
> God's blessing and honor shall crown thee
> With power thy life to endue.

But there is a catch in all this. Everything I have said about how much better the new life is than the old is true, but Jesus warns us: "No man also having drunk old wine straightway desireth new: for he saith, The old is better" (Luke 5:39). We are used to our old life and ways. They "fit" us, for they are a habit. We are at ease in them and may even prefer them. So Jesus tells us that immediately we will not lose all liking for the old life, but will maybe even have a preference for the old life. The word translated "better" is *chrestos*, which also means easy and accommodating. "Comfortable like an old shoe," goes the adage. But life is something more than a shoe, and so is our eternal Self.

Great wisdom is found in these two verses from the Katha Upanishad: "Different is the good, and different, indeed, is the pleasant. These two, with different purposes, bind a man. Of these two, it is well for him who takes hold of the good; but he who chooses the pleasant, fails of his aim. Both the good and the pleasant approach a man. The wise man, pondering over them, discriminates. The wise chooses the good in preference to the pleasant. The simple-minded, for the sake of worldly well-being, prefers the pleasant" (Katha Upanishad 1.2.1-2). So even though the new life is glorious and the old life drab by comparison, still our will must be exercised in taking up the new life. We must choose it.

Healing Waters

After this there was a feast of the Jews [Judeans]; and Jesus went up to Jerusalem. Now there is at Jerusalem by the sheep market a pool, which is called in the Hebrew tongue Bethesda, having five porches. In these lay a great multitude of impotent folk, of blind, halt, withered, waiting for the moving of the water. For an angel went down at a certain season into the pool, and troubled the water: whosoever then first after the troubling of the water stepped in was made whole of whatsoever disease he had.

And a certain man was there, which had an infirmity thirty and eight years. When Jesus saw him lie, and knew that he had been now a long time in that case, he saith unto him, Wilt thou be made whole? The impotent man answered him, Sir, I have no man, when the water is troubled, to put me into the pool: but while I am coming, another steppeth down before me. Jesus saith unto him, Rise, take up thy bed, and walk. And immediately the man was made whole, and took up his bed, and walked: and on the same day was the sabbath (John 5:1-9).

After this there was a feast of the Jews [Judeans]; and Jesus went up to Jerusalem. It is speculated that the feast was Passover, which the Jews [Judeans] dated differently from the Galileans, and therefore this distinction is made.

Now there is at Jerusalem by the sheep market a pool, which is called in the Hebrew tongue Bethesda, having five porches [porticos: entrances]. Bethesda means House of Kindness, and it was no doubt built for the ill.

In these lay a great multitude of impotent folk, of blind, halt, withered, waiting for the moving [stirring] of the water. For an angel went down at a certain season into the pool, and troubled [stirred] the water: whosoever then first after the troubling of the water stepped in was made whole of whatsoever disease he had. This is told us simply as fact, with no background history of the phenomenon. We are told that only the first person to step into the water was cured. This indicates that a certain energy or vibration was imparted to the water and whoever touched it first absorbed all of that power and was healed.

Water is the most psychically receptive substance in our world. This is why every religious tradition with roots in authentic spiritual experience and knowledge has some form of holy water. In sacramental Christianity the water of baptism is highly magnetized, and when it touches the body of the one being baptized (which itself is mostly water), that intense energy enters into him and affects his causal, astral and physical bodies. In traditional Eastern Christianity holy water is sprinkled in certain rituals, but it is also drunk so its effects will pervade the body. Many Eastern Christians drink every morning some holy water and eat a small piece of antidoron, the bread blessed and given to the worshippers at the end of the Divine Liturgy, before eating or drinking anything else.

This incident also is symbolic. The building Bethesda represents the human body with its five senses and five basic energy levels. The pool itself is the inmost being and consciousness, the *hridaya guha*, the "cave of the heart." When a messenger (for that is what "angel" means) from God stirs up our awareness and perception and we enter into it and absorb the powers of awakening, then inner healing takes place. But like the people at the pool we have to be alert to detect that stirring and quick to immerse ourselves (our minds) within. The way to ensure this is to practice meditation daily.

And a certain man was there, which had an infirmity thirty and eight years. When Jesus saw him lie, and knew that he had been now a long time in that case,... This is an example of the omniscience of Jesus through spiritual clairvoyance.

He saith unto him, Wilt thou be made whole? You often cannot apply the principles of logic to metaphysical and spiritual matters. For example, a lot of "positive thinking" is not just bunkum, it is actually negative in its effect. For example, denial that a problem or a negative situation exists is foolish. You must face it and then set about to change it–with a positive attitude and perspective. Also: who does prosperity affirmations? Who does health affirmations? Only those who do not have money or health. So to simply do such affirmations is to keep saying by action that we are poor or sick. This is the negative power of "positive thinking."

It is not enough to wish or want: we must *will* (*thelo*). The will resides in the anandamaya kosha, the etheric body, which borders on the spirit. So it is a major power in our makeup, and very much a spiritual one. The word *thelo* means to have a subjective impulse towards something, to be intent on gaining what we will to possess, whether material or immaterial. When we really want something we are willing to put forth the effort or pay the price to gain what we will to have. This is paramount in spiritual life. We must understand what is needed and put forth our will to attain it. Oftentimes the first step is producing in ourselves the needed insight and capacity to gain either within or without the desired thing–which need not be material, but mental or spiritual. Sensible people do not wish upon a star: they get busy and produce the conditions needed to get what they want.

"Whole" is not a very satisfactory translation for healthy, as the English word has changed over the four centuries since the King James Version was published. The word *hugies* also means sound in the sense of stable and having strength. This is necessary for the questing spirit to find its goal. It is interesting that it comes from a root word *auzano*, which means to grow, enlarge or increase. When understood as a matter of evolution and expansion in consciousness we can grasp the nature of real, inner spiritual healing. What the true Christ is asking us is simple: do we aspire to Christhood? For we have no other real destiny.

The impotent man answered him, Sir, I have no man, when the water is troubled, to put me into the pool: but while I am coming, another steppeth down before me. Now we are coming to a very interesting and vitally important lesson. The paralyzed man has no help to enter the water after the healing energies have been infused into it by an angel, so while he would be trying to move himself into the pool, another would enter. This is emblematic of the negative passivity and disempowerment of the individual that we find in ordinary religion. God is supposed to do everything for us, or it is to be done for us by angels or saints or good people, the implication being that we are incapable of helping ourselves. We are told that we are sinners and spiritually sick and helpless, that we must "trust and obey" and "surrender to the will of God." But Jesus had a different approach.

Jesus saith unto him, Rise,... Stand up on your own two feet! Homely advice that I have heard almost from infancy. All the resources we need are within us. We need only awaken to that fact, access those powers and use them. That is what being a yogi is all about.

The word *egeiro* translated "rise" has various meanings and implications. First of all it basically means "awaken," just as we say to a sleeping person, "Rise and shine!" So the first requisite in conscious spiritual life is to truly awake and become alive on all the levels of our existence and being. It also literally means to rise up in the sense of orienting our consciousness to higher things. It also means to stand, to be fixed and steady, a quality always needed in spiritual endeavors. And finally it means to actually lift up, to bring our consciousness to higher levels than it has been functioning on before.

This is a great deal to be asked to do, but we have the ability to do all this on our own. For just as the plant or tree is potentially in the seed waiting for the right conditions for germination and growth, so all potential is in our subtle (astral and causal) bodies, potential that the ordinary person cannot even conceive is really within him. So he feels helpless and thinks God or some messenger from God is supposed to do the needful for him. But he is wrong. And if he never awakes and arises then all the religion and religious observances in the world will have only a superficial effect that will eventually dissipate and come to nothing.

A peripheral meaning comes from the root word *agora*, which means to gather yourself together, to unite your scattered faculties and powers and by this unity make them effective and able to be directed and brought to bear whenever and wherever there is need for them to effect a required change. "Wherefore he saith, Awake thou that sleepest, and arise from the dead, and Christ shall give thee light" (Ephesians 5:14).

...take up thy bed,... We are all sleeping or languishing in our various bodies, gross and subtle, and once we awaken we need to take control of them through yoga sadhana and put them to their intended use in our spiritual development (evolution). A true spiritual master is not someone who tells or makes others do that is wise and good, but who himself knows and does what is true and good by his own personal power. "He that ruleth his spirit [is better than] than he that taketh a city" (Proverbs 16:32). But "he that hath no rule over his own spirit is like a city that is broken down, and without walls" (Proverbs 25:28).

...and walk. Peripateo means to walk without restraint and also simply to go somewhere. In authentic spiritual life we are always moving forward.

Peripateo also comes from a root word *peran*, which literally means to pierce through something and go beyond where we have been up to now. It also means "the farther side," just as Buddha spoke of "the farther shore." Our walking must bring us to the far goal of perfected consciousness–for that is what Nirvana is; not a place, but a level of consciousness which is boundless and eternal, the true kingdom of heaven. Jesus commanded the man to follow the path of of profound and continual change until he reached The Changeless that was his own true Self.

And immediately the man was made whole, and took up his bed, and walked. He heard the word and acted on it immediately and left that place in perfect health and strength. In effective spiritual life there can be no hesitation, no "getting ready," no hemming and hawing and shuffling of feet. Arise and Go is the message. Our inner Christ heals, empowers and enables us for the journey.

And on the same day was the sabbath. In esoteric life there are many divisions, but the most common is that of the number seven, which is the number of completion, the end of a cycle. And so it was with this man symbolically. The time of his darkness and paralysis was ended. When that happened he was healed by the light of his own Christhood.

> **The Jews [Judeans] therefore said unto him that was cured, It is the sabbath day: it is not lawful for thee to carry thy bed. He answered them, He that made me whole, the**

same said unto me, Take up thy bed, and walk. Then asked they him, What man is that which said unto thee, Take up thy bed, and walk? And he that was healed wist not who it was: for Jesus had conveyed himself away, a multitude being in that place (John 5:10-13).

The Jews [Judeans] therefore said unto him that was cured, It is the sabbath day: it is not lawful for thee to carry thy bed. Here we see the indefensible ignorance and destructive negativity of externalized religion that goes "by the book," no matter what. This man was miraculously healed, but when "the righteous" saw he was carrying his own pallet they stopped him and objected to that which he was doing only by the divine power Itself.

Most religion is enmity with God, however it is packaged. As a bishop once said to me: "The problem with nearly all religion is the way it tries to tell God what he can and cannot do." Most religion is Luciferic in origin and effect: arrogant and unbounded egotism.

He answered them, He that made me whole, the same said unto me, Take up thy bed, and walk. The man's reasoning is correct. He that could heal him could certainly tell him to do what he was doing, whatever the rules might be. For as Jesus himself said: "The Son of man is Lord even of the sabbath day" (Matthew 12:8; Mark 2:28; Luke 6:5).

Then asked they him, What man is that which said unto thee, Take up thy bed, and walk? And he that was healed wist not who it was: for Jesus had conveyed himself away, a multitude being in that place. This is a significant situation. Often we find that faith on the part of the afflicted person is a necessity before they can receiveing the healing power of Jesus. But here there is no question of faith, or even of knowing who Jesus was. This indicates that in some instances certain things are required of the person needing help–either faith or actions on their part. As a result there can be no absolute rule in these matters. In the same way, when we need divine or spiritual assistance we need to see if we ourselves are blocking the needed help, if something is required of us either inwardly or outwardly. A little later, in the Gospel of Matthew (13:58), we will be told about Jesus' own home territory, that "he did not many mighty works there because of their unbelief."

> Afterward Jesus findeth him in the temple, and said unto him, Behold, thou art made whole: sin no more, lest a worse thing come unto thee (John 5:14).

Obviously the man's affliction was a result of his negative karma, and Jesus could tell that he might incur physical problems in the future because he was capable of negative deeds that would result in an even worse condition. Just as inner, physical toxins manifest as outer symptoms in our bodies, so those symptoms are also a manifestation of negative karmas. It is an absolute: "Whatsoever a man soweth, that shall he also reap" (Galatians 6:7).

> The man departed, and told the Jews [Judeans] that it was Jesus, which had made him whole. And therefore did the Jews [Judeans] persecute Jesus, and sought to slay him, because he had done these things on the sabbath day (John 5:15-16).

Business as usual. No need for comment. Just remember that "the Jews" means the Judeans, who had a special dislike of Galileans.

The Way Things Are

> But Jesus answered them, My Father worketh hitherto, and I work. Therefore the Jews [Judeans] sought the more to kill him, because he not only had broken the sabbath, but said also that God was his Father, making himself equal with God (John 5:17-18).

My Father worketh hitherto, and I work. This is an affirmation of the perfect unity between Jesus and God. Whatever God does, Jesus does; and whenever Jesus does anything we can know that the power doing it and the doing itself is the act, the work, of God–the manifestation of God. And it should be the same with the yogi.

Therefore the Jews [Judeans] sought the more to kill him. The word *zeteo*, translated "sought" means not only to want something, but to actively seek the means to accomplish one's aim–to ascertain the means and plot the way to bring it about. It also implies seeking permission. The enemies of Jesus were "by the book" people, as I have pointed out. This early in his ministry there are those who are determined to bring about his death. But it will not be an act of virtue as they wish to present it. It will be murder, however much it may be cloaked in false righteousness and zeal for God. Such persons wish to make God their accomplice in evil.

Because he not only had broken the sabbath.... External observances comprised the only "righteousness" Jesus' enemies had. If those observances were to be seen as unnecessary and without value and were discontinued, they would loose their entire religious identity and reputation–and control over others. Jesus was a threat to all they were–or pretended to be.

But said also that God was his Father, making himself equal with God. At this point in time we are so used to the idea of God as Father and

Mother that we do not realize how outrageous and even blasphemous such a concept seemed to the people in Israel. To call God "Father" was to imply that a person was himself God–not godlike but the actual Divinity. For *isos* means both like and equal to something–in this instance, God.

> **Then answered Jesus and said unto them, Verily, verily, I say unto you, The Son can do nothing of himself, but what he seeth the Father do: for what things soever he doeth, these also doeth the Son likewise. For the Father loveth the Son, and sheweth him all things that himself doeth: and he will shew him greater works than these, that ye may marvel (John 5:19-20).**

Verily, verily, I say unto you. The actual words were "Amen, amen," which were the usual preface to a solemn declaration or oath. It was a kind of calling God to witness that what was going to be spoken was absolutely true.

Oudeis means absolutely nothing–no exception. Jesus did nothing but what he "saw" God doing–or intending to do. Jesus and God were absolutely ONE without any separation whatsoever. This is the innermost state of each sentient being at the present, but it is the destiny of all to eventually manifest and live in that state on a totally conscious level. "Beloved, now are we the sons of God, and it doth not yet appear what we shall be: but we know that, when he shall appear, we shall be like him; for we shall see him as he is" (I John 3:2). This is the essence of the Gospel of Christ. Where that is not taught openly there is neither God nor Christ.

> **For as the Father raiseth up the dead, and quickeneth them; even so the Son quickeneth whom he will (John 5:21).**

Of course we are all alive because we exist, but Jesus is speaking of the condition of consciousness. And nearly every human being is "dead" in the sense of having neither awareness nor understanding of themselves and

God. When that consciousness is possessed by anyone fully, then alone are they truly alive. To know God is to be god.

I have mentioned the Trinity several times in this commentary, but I have not considered the whole subject; and it is time to do so.

God as absolutely ONE. That can never change. Yet God is triune, or threefold: Father, Son and Holy Spirit. These are not three "Persons" as exoteric Christianity postulates, but symbolic titles that express the three fundamental modes in which God exists and functions. Not that there can be any divisions or differences in God. But when we who are immersed in relative existence ponder the nature of God we have to temporarily speak of God as though such things were real, although when we truly see God we will perceive that only Unity is the real state of Divinity.

The Father is God as Transcendental Being beyond all relativity and is totally impersonal. The Son is God as Immanent Being within all relativity or creation, and is totally personal as the guiding Intelligence within creation. The Holy Spirit is God as Divine Power manifesting as the entire range of evolving creation, of relative existence in which all relative beings are immersed and individually evolving beyond relativity into the Absolute. This Threefold Being was known to the ancient rishis of India as Brahman, Ishwara and Mahashakti or Prakriti. It is also known as Sat-Tat-Om or Satchidananda.

We cannot reduce God to a formula, but we can express the Divine Nature well enough to give us a partial, working comprehension of It. And from that partial comprehension we can progress onward through yoga to direct experience of the Divine Nature and therefore experience of our own eternal nature, the divine Self.

In this passage of the Gospel, "Son" means the Only-begotten of the Father and whoever has become one with the Son, with Ishwara. But of course it also includes Jesus since he is one with the Son–and therefore with the Father. This is why when Jesus went to India he was given the spiritual name Isha, meaning Ishwara, the Lord. (See *The Christ of India*.)

The practical application of this is the fact that as God gives life, so also an avatar such as Jesus can also open up the way to life and unfettered consciousness to those capable of receiving it. For to "as many as received him, to them gave he power to become the sons of God" (John 1:12), and also avatars of Ishwara.

> **For the Father judgeth no man, but hath committed all judgment unto the Son: (John 5:22).**

Being impersonal and transcendental, there is no difficulty in realizing that Brahman (the Father) has no relationship with any relative being other than being its Essence. Brahman never reacts with anything or anyone, as that is antithetical to Its nature. But the Father has emanated himself as the Son–not as an action, for that is impossible, but as an ideational thought-image. (This is much too rarefied to be put into words and conceived of. I can speak of it only in symbolic approximations.) All beings in relative manifestation relate directly with Ishwara. And Jesus, being in perfect union with Ishwara, reveals the interaction of Ishwara with all relative beings. The laws which govern the cosmos are the will of Ishwara and therefore the will and action of Jesus as an avatara of Ishwara.

The words *krino*, "judge," and *krisis*, "judgement," means to distinguish something, such as the nature, quality or character of something or someone. This is basically a mental action, and can be either positive or negative, so it can mean either approval or disapproval. A human being judges something by what it seems to be, but someone like Jesus knows exactly the character of something and declares it. A human classifies something according to what he thinks it is, but Ishwara and those in union with him speak the truth of its essential being.

> **That all men should honour the Son, even as they honour the Father. He that honoureth not the Son honoureth not the Father which hath sent him (John 5:23).**

The word *timao* means to honor and value–even revere.

These words of Jesus have profound metaphysical implications. There are two approaches in the definition of–and relationship to–Divinity. In

India particularly we find those called "impersonalists" and those known as "personalists."

The impersonalists accept the view of Reality as absolutely transcendent and impersonal, without any qualities or possibility of verbal description or definition. There can be no interaction between the individual human being and the Absolute in a personal way. There can be a union of the individual with the Absolute, but only on the level of the eternal identity of the individual with the Absolute. Such a state is utterly beyond words or even concepts. Direct knowledge, vijnana, alone results in the practical union of the two. Total, non-dual union, advaita, is the only true and possible experience in this union.

The personalists consider the Divine as a Person whose image is inherent in all individual persons. The Cosmic Being and the individual are alike and can relate to one another in a deeply personal manner. Love and devotion are considered the necessary means to their union with one another. The union between the Divine and the individual is one of servant to master or devotee to the beloved.

The impersonalist and personalist views are both correct, but each is only partial. And the very real problem with both of them is their insistence that their view is the only possible one, that the opposite view is false.

However, there is a third viewpoint: that Reality is far beyond the impersonalist and personalist views—that they are themselves a kind of duality that prevents real unity. As long as language of any kind is used, as long as there is any type of concept, Reality cannot be really comprehended or approached. This is the way of the yogis. The only way to the realization of this third approach is to approach Reality as embracing yet beyond both impersonal and personal.

To get some comprehension of this incomprehensible way of seeing things, we should look at our own experience. We have three states of awareness: waking, dreaming sleep and dreamless sleep. Although we commonly speak of our experiencing dreamless sleep as "awareness of nothing" it cannot be so, otherwise we would not have an experience of it to remember. This indicates that there is a fourth state of awareness: the awareness of awareness itself. This is known as turiya, the state of pure consciousness. *A Ramakrishna-Vedanta Wordbook* defines it as: "The superconscious; lit., 'the Fourth,' in relation to the three ordinary states of consciousness–waking, dreaming, and dreamless sleep–which it transcends." The yogis speak of the Turiya-Turiya, "the consciousness of Consciousness," the Absolute Consciousness of God, the Consciousness behind our individualized consciousness (turiya).

This seems like a real ring-around-the-rosey, but it is very necessary for a practical, yogic understanding of all I have written above. So let me try to encapsulate all the foregoing. And the first thing is to repeat Jesus' words: "All men should honour the Son, even as they honour the Father. He that honoureth not the Son honoureth not the Father which hath sent him."

Basically this means that we must keep in mind that the transcendent and the immanent must both be "honored" by the intelligent ordering of our minds and lives to include action and thought which enable us to foster in ourselves both the transcendent and immanent aspects of our being and produce the maximum degree of personal evolution. We must cultivate both our inner and outer living accordingly. And this cannot be meaningfully done in a whimsical and hit-or-miss manner. The only way to do this is by following the wisdom of the yogi-sages of India.

Truth: The Call to Life

Verily, verily, I say unto you, He that heareth my word, and believeth on him that sent me, hath everlasting life, and shall not come into condemnation; but is passed from death unto life (John 5:24).

Ishwara has sent into this world enlightened men and women who were really gods: those who had ascended the ladder of evolution, evolving though all the worlds until they transcended all relativity and entered into the depths of Infinite Being and Consciousness. Returning to this world, they were incarnations of divinity, avatars and deliverers from darkness and bondage through their teachings. Those who honor them as they do the Absolute and who follow their teachings without reservation with full dedication and purpose shall truly attain everlasting life, having ultimately themselves passed through all the worlds where there is death and rebirth and entered into Life Itself: Brahman the Absolute. The avatars Krishna, Buddha and Jesus were Showers of the Way, divine messengers that themselves embodied the Living Truth they taught. An excellent summary and presentation of their teachings is found in the books *Sanatana Dharma: The Eternal Religion* and *Hinduism: The Universal Religion*. Both should be read to get a complete picture.

The word translated "condemnation" is *krisis*, the word previously translated "judgment" in verse twenty-two. Judgment and condemnation are not arbitrary acts or declarations by an "offended" God, but the condition of one who has violated his own true nature by thinking and acting contrary to the principles of evolution and enlightenment. Negative and foolish actions are not "offences" against God as ignorant religion teaches, but transgressions against our own divine Self, the "wages" of which truly are spiritual death (Romans 6:23).

The word *metabaino*, translated "passed," means to move onward and leave behind even the possibility of spiritual death and enter permanently into Life, into Spirit.

> **Verily, verily, I say unto you, The hour is coming, and now is, when the dead shall hear the voice of the Son of God: and they that hear shall live. For as the Father hath life in himself; so hath he given to the Son to have life in himself; and hath given him authority to execute judgment also, because he is the Son of man (John 5:25-27).**

The spiritual power of an avatar is such that his very words can awaken the spiritual consciousness of those who are ready to hear and live. It is a matter of magnetism, literally. Just as a magnet only attracts certain substances, in the same way the vibrations of an avatar's words only bring life to those whose mental energies are purified and responsive enough to "hear" them and act on them. The inherent power of an avatar's teachings is itself the authority (*exousia*) that determines the reaction of his hearers. Those who are negative will react negatively, even with violence in some instances. Those who are positive will "receive the word with joy" (Luke 18:13) and act on it with equal joy–not as a dose of medicine but as the opening of greater life to them.

The Two Resurrections

> Marvel not at this: for the hour is coming, in the which all that are in the graves shall hear his voice, and shall come forth; they that have done good, unto the resurrection of life; and they that have done evil, unto the resurrection of damnation (John 5:28-29).

Just now as I read the first of these two verses I vividly recalled the conversation I had with a beloved aunt who had been my first spiritual teacher when I was a child. I had just completed what was my final visit to my family after many years. My family was very large, and I had met with most of them who had all been very close to me. All my cousins (a lot) had married and had families themselves, and I could tell my aunt was thinking I might be feeling that perhaps I should have done the same. So I said to her: "If you are wondering what I am thinking about my cousins and the rest of our family, it is this: they are all just sitting in their graves waiting to eventually be buried when their bodies die. But they are dead already." Outwardly all human beings are alive, but inwardly most are dead–unconscious of, and therefore unresponsive to, spiritual realities. Truly, "that which is born of the flesh is flesh; and that which is born of the Spirit is spirit" (John 3:6).

Eventually all hear the voice of God calling them to life, and momentarily they wake up. Those who have accumulated good (positive) karma and have a positive consciousness, rise up and follow the way that leads to life eternal. But those who have only negative karma and a negative consciousness–which includes a lack of spiritual awareness within themselves–will either go back to sleep or willfully choose the path of evil. Those who have awakened to some degree and have made the choice for continuing in evil or spiritual deadness, will be fully responsible for the evil they do (and the good they do not do) after their awakening, and so will be condemned for consciously choosing and doing evil. "Damnation" is a completely inaccurate translation of the word *krisis*, that really means accusation or condemnation, but the result of their evil choice will be bad enough.

THE RIGHT SELF-PERSPECTIVE

I can of mine own self do nothing: as I hear, I judge: and my judgment is just; because I seek not mine own will, but the will of the Father which hath sent me (John 5:30).

I can of mine own self do nothing. There are two meanings to this statement. One is regarding Jesus. Being totally in union with the Absolute there was no possibility that any of his actions would not be an act of God, literally. For, as he said to the Apostle Philip, "He that hath seen me hath seen the Father" (John 14:9). The second meaning relates to us. Since we draw our very existence from God and cannot even exist without him, we also draw from him the power to do any action. So we, too, can do nothing on our own.

There is, however, a vast difference between us and Jesus. Jesus acts only in and with the divine will, but we can use the power allotted to us to commit, foolish, useless and negative acts that are not in harmony with the divine will. That is the "price" we pay for having free will. All my life I have heard negative, ignorant people demand, "Why does God allow…?" and then name something that is the inevitable result of the exercise of free will. They do not want God to suspend our free will, but they complain about the consequences of free will. If we wish to be sensible in our living we will take responsibility for everything that happens to us, because it is our karma which is a result of our wrong actions of which we are capable because we possess free will. Action and reaction or result is the universal law.

As I hear, I judge. Akouo means hear in the sense of heed: to understand. *Krino* means to have judgement regarding something, to decide or determine the merit or demerit of something. We are not just given free will, we are also given intelligence–though not wisdom. Wisdom comes through intelligent observation. And from that we can judge something. If we did not have the capacity to do that then free will would be a very dangerous thing indeed. And it is, for a lot of people.

And my judgment is just. Dikaios means correct in the sense of being in harmony with reality–not denying or trying to bend reality to suit our shortsighted desires and goals. We must not only speak truth, we must know, think and live truth.

I seek not mine own will. Zeteo means to seek after the attainment or accomplishment of something. Jesus sought to act and realize the good and the true in harmony with his own divinity. And we, too, should seek not the desires of our childish ego, but that which is in accord with the Supreme Will with which we should wisely harmonize and unite our will and efforts.

But the will of the Father which hath sent me. We, too, have come into the world by both our own will and the will of God together. Originally we were in the depths of the Absolute, but with the potential to transcend that passive state and attain total mastery through entering relative existence and evolving into total, conscious union with God. When we say with Jesus, "Not my will, but thine, be done" (Luke 22:42), it is not a surrender or passivity, but an act of will, a turning from our finite egoic will (which gets us into trouble all the time and hinders our inner growth) and uniting with our higher, spiritual will which is a perfect reflection of the divine will. We are actually affirming our essential unity with God. This is the way to freedom.

If I bear witness of myself, my witness is not true (John 5:31).

Martureo means testimony. If our definition of ourself is based on our limited experience and the viewpoint of our truly limited (and limiting) ego, it cannot be otherwise than partial and therefore erroneous. And wrong vision results in wrong action which results in negative karma which produces trouble and misery.

> There is another that beareth witness of me; and I know that the witness which he witnesseth of me is true (John 5:32).

God himself is that other (*allos*) witness whose witness regarding us is true. And that witness tells us that we are not merely human, limited and finite, but divine, unlimited and potentially infinite. As David said, "I will declare the decree: the Lord hath said unto me, Thou art my Son; this day have I begotten thee" (Psalms 2:7).

> And the Father himself, which hath sent me, hath borne witness of me. Ye have neither heard his voice at any time, nor seen his shape. And ye have not his word abiding in you: for whom he hath sent, him ye believe not (John 5:37-38).

Ye have neither heard his voice at any time, nor seen his shape. The word translated "heard" is *akouo*, which does not just mean to hear, but to actually listen attentively. It also implies to both hear and understand. Very few people indeed have "heard" the voice of God, though a lot of deluded people think they have.

There are many definitions of what "hearing God" means. For example, a yogi friend of mine grew up in a fundamentalist Protestant church in which people had impressions or feelings which they considered the voice of God. When he was called up to the draft board he had become one of the first beatniks of North Beach, California. Seeing his beard, longish hair and unusual clothes, he was turned over to the draft board's psychiatrist who questioned him to determine his mental state. At one point the psychiatrist asked him, "Do you usually do things on your initiative?" "Yes," Dave said, "but believe me, when God talks to me I listen." "God talks to you?" asked the examiner. "Yes. Doesn't he talk to you?" was Dave's answer. So he was immediately deferred as mentally unfit–from a matter of semantics!

But to hear the voice of God is a matter of profound insight–indeed of spiritual revelation. The word *phone* means to learn something through hearing. Not many people have this experience, because they are not capable of it, they do not believe in it or they do not want God interfering in their life.

The word *eidos* means the seeing of an actual visual impression, either literal or symbolic, either clear or cloudy (dim). But it is a seeing.

And ye have not his word abiding in you. Right in the beginning we looked at the meaning of *logos* which is translated "word." Another look will be appropriate here, because Jesus is saying that one aspect of being what Guru Nanak called a "godward" is having the divine word living in us. Not just present in us as a potential or something passive, but actually functioning and producing results as an essential part of our spiritual life.

Logos can mean:
spoken words
the faulty of speech
mental speaking–thinking
an object of mental concentration or awareness
reasoning–rational thought
intention, purpose or motive–impulse to action, including will
reason in order to come to a decision
the Divine Word
revelation or expression of the Divine Being
a cause of something
communication
a discourse on a subject
teaching or doctrine
a command

All of these can be either an active or passive event, entity or condition. They all are either results or producers of enlightenment, insight or understanding. It is summed up in the words of Saint Paul: "We have the mind of Christ" (I Corinthians 2:16). The Divine Mind, the Divine Word, is present in each one of us as the Divine Self. If we carefully read through this list with that in mind we can understand the profound and far-reaching meaning of Jesus.

And all these things must not be temporary, coming and going, but abiding in us. The word *meno* means to be permanently present and by implication actually part of our own Self. This is one aspect of "Christ in you, the hope of glory" (Colossians 1:27).

For whom he hath sent, him ye believe not. Pistueo is believing because of a profound conviction coming from the very core of our being. It is a form of revelation, actually of self-revelation. If we possess this conviction, then it follows as a matter of course that The Word will abide in us in a dynamic, transforming manner indicated by Jesus when he said, "I am come that they might have life, and that they might have it more abundantly" (John 10:10).

The Wrong Way To Go About It

> Search the scriptures; for in them ye think [dokeo: suppose] ye have eternal life: and they are they which testify of me (John 5:39).

Back in my fervent fundamentalist days I fatuously bought some stickers with Bible verses that I put on the envelopes of my letters to somehow spread the Word. One of them was this verse, apparently to inspire people to read the Bible, but even I could see that this was a rebuke of Pharisaical ignorance and not an exhortation to get eternal life by reading the Bible. As I have said before, the Pharisees were By The Book religionists, so Jesus tells them to look at the prophetic books that prophesied of him quite clearly and in detail. Saint Matthew's Gospel was written with this in mind. Of course it did no good at all, because most religionists are cultists that worship their religious egos. They are not really looking for truth but for affirmation of themselves as God's elite. So, as Jesus said, "They have their reward" (Matthew 6:2, 5, 16), which is themselves.

> And ye will not come to me, that ye might have life (John 5:40).

Erchomai means to go to something, but its root word *eltho* implies accompanying someone, walking the same path that they walk. Jesus is not just our example to wonder at and be revered, but he is to be our companion as we walk the very way which he went and reach the same goal of divine union which he attained. "Christian" actually means "another Christ." The way of Christ is the way to Christhood.

"The universal Love of which the sages speak is Christ. The greatest mystery of all times lies in the way that Christ lives in the heart. Christ cannot live in clammy dens of carnal things. The seven battles must be fought, the seven victories won before the carnal things, like fear, and self, emotions and desire, are put away. When this is done the Christ will take possession of the soul; the work is done, and man and God are one" (Aquarian Gospel 59:9-12).

"Men call me Christ, and God has recognized the name; but Christ is not a man. The Christ is universal love, and Love is king. This Jesus is but man who has been fitted by temptations overcome, by trials multiform, to be the temple through which Christ can manifest to men. Then hear, you men of Israel, hear! Look not upon the flesh; it is not king. Look to the Christ within, who shall be formed in every one of you, as he is formed in me. When you have purified your hearts by faith, the king will enter in, and you will see his face" (Aquarian Gospel 68:11-14) .

"And Jesus said, I cannot show the king, unless you see with eyes of soul, because the kingdom of the king is in the soul. And every soul a kingdom is. There is a king for every man. This king is love, and when this love becomes the greatest power in life, it is the Christ; so Christ is king. And every one may have this Christ dwell in his soul, as Christ dwells in my soul. The body is the temple of the king, and men may call a holy man a king. He who will cleanse his mortal form and make it pure, so pure that love and righteousness may dwell unsullied side by side within its walls, is king.... The man of God is pure in heart; he sees the king; he sees with eyes of soul: and when he rises to the plane of Christine consciousness, he knows that he himself is king, is love, is Christ, and so is son of God" (Aquarian Gospel 71:4-9).

We are called to Christhood. Believing in the Christhood of Jesus means very little if we not are daily walking the way to our own Christhood.

I receive not honour from men (John 5:41).

Doxa means glory, honor, praise and worship. God is the true source of these things, and a wise person pays no attention to what other human beings offer him. The life of Jesus demonstrates the wisdom of this. On Palm Sunday the crowd shouted, "Hosanna in the highest, blessed is he that comes in the Name of the Lord." And on Friday they shouted: "Away with him! Crucify him!"

Many years ago I had a recording of a talk given by a very famous Indian yogi. A translator was speaking over his words, and at one time he said, "When I give you what you want, you love me. When I do not give you what you want, you hate me." That he was speaking the truth I observed a few years later when an American who taught philosophy at a major American university told me that he had visited the yogi and was very impressed and even wrote an article for a magazine praising him. "But when I went back later," he told me, "there was such a crowd that I could not get a private interview like before, and I began to have doubts about him."

But I know you, that ye have not the love of God in you (John 5:42).

Ginosko, the word translated "know," also means to be aware of someone and understand them. Earlier in Saint John's Gospel it says: "Now when he was in Jerusalem at the passover, in the feast day, many believed in his name, when they saw the miracles which he did. But Jesus did not commit himself unto them, because he knew all men, and needed not that any should testify of man: for he knew what was in man" (John 2:23-25). The word translated "commit" is *pisteuo*, which means to trust in or believe in someone. Jesus was not being cynical, he was being realistic. This should also be the insight of all those who seek spiritual growth. Everything comes from within, and no external factor should be considered reliable. After all, God Himself is within us as the very core of our being. The Indian yogis have a saying: "He who looks outward is drowned, but he who looks inward is saved." Outside is the ocean of samsara in which we drown, but inside is the Spirit in which we live.

Saint John himself wrote, "He that loveth not knoweth not God; for God is love.... and he that dwelleth in love dwelleth in God, and God in him" (I John 4:8, 16). The word translated "love" is *agapao*, which comes from *agape*, which means spiritual love, not mere affection or even profound liking. True love for God is love for his very being, and only those who are in touch with their own spiritual being are capable of loving God or anyone else. Those to whom Jesus was speaking believed, grovelled, praised and repented and followed the rules, but they did not love God. They were incapable of such love.

THE EFFECTS OF IGNORANCE AND EGO

> I am come in my Father's name, and ye receive me not: if another shall come in his own name, him ye will receive (John 5:43).

I am come in my Father's name, and ye receive me not. Lambano, translated "receive," also means to take hold of in the sense of full personal acceptance–to make something one's own–and even identification with something. To receive Christ is also to recognize our own already-existing relationship with him. This is especially true in relation to the cosmic Christ, the Christ Principle, Ishwara. It has nothing to do with the usual Christian belief regarding Christ Jesus. Perhaps the most valuable element in *The Aquarian Gospel of Jesus the Christ* is the distinction made between Jesus, who was *a* Christ, and Ishwara who is *the* Christ–that whoever enters into union with Ishwara the Cosmic Christ becomes himself a Christ. To receive Christ is to become ourselves Christs.

If another shall come in his own name, him ye will receive. It is a sad fact that many people will believe in a fake and not believe in something genuine. Just look at the history of religions and religions today. Fakery is the dominant characteristic. This is because a deluded person feels a natural affinity for delusion. A fake seeker follows a fake teacher because they are literally on the same wavelength. In my early teens I saw a movie called *Lady From Lisbon*. It was made during the Second World War and was about the theft of the Mona Lisa from the Louvre. It was brought to Lisbon, where people could still get a plane for the Americas, and offered for sale. At the same time criminals had fakes made and did a continual business in selling them. But no would would buy the real Mona Lisa. The reason? It looked fake to them! So no one ever bought the real one and fakes were sold readily and bought eagerly.

Those who are ego-oriented are attracted to other egotists, including in spiritual leadership. Usually the motive is to in time become a successful fake themselves. They are fakes in training, just as many seeming victims are really victimizers in training.

The ego-oriented will scorn a genuine spiritual teacher. That is the way of the world. Saint Paul speaks of this situation when he says: "Scarcely for a righteous man will one die: yet peradventure for a good man some would even dare to die" (Romans 5:7). The word translated "righteous" is *dikaios*, which means innocent, just, deserving and even holy. *Agathos*, translated "good," means something from which a person can be benefitted or from which they can gain something themselves. Basically the idea is that for a righteous and holy person no one will sacrifice anything, but for "a nice guy" or "a really great guy" quite a number will gladly sacrifice and deny or inconvenience themselves.

> **How can ye believe, which receive honour one of another, and seek not the honour that cometh from God only? (John 5:44).**

Elsewhere Jesus put it very simply: "Ye cannot serve God and mammon" (Matthew 6:24; Luke 16:13). *Mammonas* is that which pertains to man in his most selfish and greedy aspects. "Gimme" is its summation. The operative word of course is "me." The more there is of "me" the less there is of "He." The ego is satan in all of us and it will not share the throne with its only rightful owner and occupant: God.

> **Do not think that I will accuse you to the Father: there is one that accuseth you, even Moses, in whom ye trust. For had ye believed Moses, ye would have believed me: for he wrote of me. But if ye believe not his writings, how shall ye believe my words? (John 5:45-47).**

It is a common practice for religionists to loudly trumpet their faith in some teacher or scripture while at the same time either completely ignoring or violating the teacher's teachings. Therefore we should be cautious in assuming that someone is sincere simply because they keep saying they believe in someone or some holy book. As Jesus shall shortly point out: "Why call ye me, Lord, Lord, and do not the things which I say?" (Luke 6:46).

Testing the Testers

> And it came to pass also on another sabbath, that he entered into the synagogue and taught: and there was a man whose right hand was withered. And the scribes and Pharisees watched him, whether he would heal on the sabbath day; that they might find an accusation against him. [And they asked him, saying, Is it lawful to heal on the sabbath days? (Matthew 12:10).] But he knew their thoughts, and said to the man which had the withered hand, Rise up, and stand forth in the midst. And he arose and stood forth. Then said Jesus unto them, I will ask you one thing; Is it lawful on the sabbath days to do good, or to do evil? to save life, or to destroy it? (Luke 6:6-9).
>
> And he said unto them, What man shall there be among you, that shall have one sheep, and if it fall into a pit on the sabbath day, will he not lay hold on it, and lift it out? How much then is a man better than a sheep? Wherefore it is lawful to do well on the sabbath days (Matthew 12:11-12).

This is the kind of thing the By The Bookers both fear and hate. They fear that good sense might prevail, and they hate the idea of not subjecting others to harsh and absurd conditions and actions in the pretense that God wills it. Such people are really more demon than human.

> And he entered again into the synagogue; and there was a man there which had a withered hand. And they watched him, whether he would heal him on the sabbath day; that they might accuse him. And he saith unto the man which

> had the withered hand, Stand forth. And he saith unto them, Is it lawful to do good on the sabbath days, or to do evil? to save life, or to kill? But they held their peace. And when he had looked round about on them, being grieved [saddened] for the hardness of their hearts, he saith unto the man, Stretch forth thine hand. And he stretched it out: and his hand was restored whole as the other (Mark 3:1-5).

Often it is necessary that we align our will with the divine will in order to obtain what we need. So we should consider at such times if there is something we must do to produce the favorable situation to receive what we require. It is common that saints sometimes direct that certain things should be done or certain objects gotten before the desired result occurs. Here are three examples known to me personally.

1) A man with severe gastro-intestinal illness appealed to an Indian saint for help. The saint's advice was that he eat in large quantities those items which his physician had told him would be fatal for him. He did so unhesitatingly, and was immediately and permanently cured.

2) An acquaintance of mine lived in Warsaw, Poland. Being very poor, he and a friend frequently slipped into the estate of a wealthy man and caught fish. They knew that this was a most risky thing to do, because anyone caught would be given the severest sentence by the judges because of the rich man's political influence. The verdict of guilty and a severe penalty was assured for anyone caught poaching. The two boys were caught, indicted, and a court date was set, though they were allowed to go free until then. Sure that they would be given a heavy jail sentence, especially because they were Jews, they appealed to a renowned Hasidic rabbi, who told them to search through Warsaw and find the smallest padlock available, and one of them should have the padlock in his pocket when they went into the courtroom. They followed this seemingly nonsensical directive and for two weeks spent their days and nights searching for the smallest padlock they could find. They did as the rabbi said, and the judge, a longstanding friend of the rich man who had often severely punished people to please him, threw the case

out of court and severely rebuked the wealthy man for treating the young men so harshly.

3) A monastic novice woke up one morning in terrible pain, hardly able to move. By forcing himself to move, he managed to get to the abbot's room, though once there he could not describe to him what he felt, because his teeth were literally chattering from the pain. Instead of showing sympathy, the abbot complained at him for wasting his time, and then in a disgusted and offhanded way commented that perhaps he just needed a drink of water! Although it was a tremendous struggle, the novice managed to get down the stairs and into the kitchen, where he drank a glass of water. As the water went down his throat, the pain drained completely away.

Jesus' Ministry Continues

But Jesus withdrew himself with his disciples to the sea: and a great multitude from Galilee followed him, and from Judaea, and from Jerusalem, and from Idumaea, and from beyond Jordan; and they about Tyre and Sidon, a great multitude, when they had heard what great things he did, came unto him. And he spake to his disciples, that a small ship should wait on him because of the multitude, lest they should throng him. For he had healed many; insomuch that they pressed upon him for to touch him, as many as had plagues.

And unclean spirits, when they saw him, fell down before him, and cried, saying, Thou art the Son of God. And he straitly charged them that they should not make him known (Mark 3:7-12).

And unclean spirits, when they saw him, fell down before him, and cried, saying, Thou art the Son of God. And he straitly charged them that they should not make him known. Although malevolent and preying on those they possessed, these spirits were far ahead of Jesus' persecutors because they knew his divine status. However, their "confessing" of Jesus had no bearing on their spiritual condition. Those who say that we need only believe and confess Christ to be "saved" are certainly not in agreement with Jesus. Simply acknowledging the holy does not make the unholy any better. Words cannot change anyone. Action is needed.

There is another aspect of this that is sad but needs to be examined. When the evil spirits merely saw Jesus they recognized his divine status and were tormented. This is true of negative people as well. They recognize truth and spiritual atmosphere but hate them. This reaction is often subconscious, but their inner mind knows what is true and holy though on a conscious level they really do consider the positive to be negative and even threatening to them personally. Certainly it can indicate obsession or possession by one or more evil spirits and we must not ignore that, but most of the time it is their own evil nature which causes the reaction. For just as when we enter the presence of a holy person or place we feel peace and upliftment–even inner healing–they feel great discomfort and even pain. So they either leave as soon as possible or sit there and just hate the source of their misery. Often they speak out in a challenging manner or behave very rudely and try to discomfit the person or to disrupt his teaching. Sometimes they physically attack them. So a yogi should carefully note the behavior of such people and be aware of the reality of the situation.

The Ordaining of the Twelve

And it came to pass in those days, that he went out into a mountain to pray, and continued all night in prayer to God. And when it was day, he called unto him his disciples: (Luke 6:12-13).

And they came unto him, and he ordained twelve, that they should be with him, and that he might send them forth to preach (Mark 3:13-14).

Now the names of the twelve apostles are these; The first, Simon, who is called Peter, and Andrew his brother; James the son of Zebedee, and John his brother; Philip, and Bartholomew; Thomas, and Matthew the publican; James the son of Alphaeus, and Lebbaeus, whose surname was Thaddaeus; Simon the Canaanite, and Judas Iscariot, who also betrayed him (Matthew 10:2-4).

The word translated "disciple" is *mathetes*, which means a learner, a student. *Apostolos* (apostle) means a representative or official messenger, "he that is sent." One is a student and the other is himself a teacher. The fact that Judas was appointed an apostle shows that he was very special, as were the other eleven. Later we will see that he, too, had the power to heal the sick and exorcise evil spirits. He had a negative history when as a child he knew Jesus (see *The Unknown Lives of Jesus and Mary*), but that was not considered an impediment by Jesus. Certainly Jesus knew the future of Judas, because he was omniscient as well as omnipotent, as his miracles demonstrated. Trying to second-guess Jesus and God in a "why did" and "how come" question session has no profit at all. What was done, was done.

But we can ourselves draw a lesson from Judas: no matter how high we may rise, until we are permanently established in that state we are capable of falling from it, even into self-destruction. I have seen this myself throughout my life. I have witnessed seeming angels turn into demons– and stay that way for this incarnation. But in each instance it was because all their virtue was external and they did not cultivate the inner life and truly change themselves into what they should be. The tragedy of falling was completely their choice and will. We are all the authors of our story, no one else.

Healing

And he came down with them, and stood in the plain, and the company of his disciples, and a great multitude of people out of all Judaea and Jerusalem, and from the sea coast of Tyre and Sidon, which came to hear him, and to be healed of their diseases; and they that were vexed with unclean spirits: and they were healed. And the whole multitude sought to touch him: for there went virtue out of him, and healed them all. And he lifted up his eyes on his disciples, and said (Luke 17-20):

And the whole multitude sought to touch him: for there went virtue out of him, and healed them all. Relative existence, from lowest to highest, is formed of vibrating energies which react upon one another. There are vibrations that darken and impair and others that enlighten and heal. Jesus embodied the Supreme Life and therefore his very touch could heal anything, outer or inner. The wise seek out places, things and persons which emanate the divine healing power. We must also realize that some places, things and people emanate destructive and even death-bearing power, and train ourselves to seek the healing power and avoid the harmful and deadly power.

The highest benefit is to "touch" Divine Consciousness itself and fill ourselves with its healing and perfecting powers. There are various ways to do this, but the surest and most effective is meditation. And I mean right meditation. (See *Soham Yoga: The Yoga of the Self.*) We must touch and link our awareness with our own divine Self which is one with the Supreme Self, God. Then we will be in touch with the Divine and draw into ourselves the same healing power that flowed perpetually from Jesus.

Jesus did not always heal everyone. Catherine Emmerich saw in her visions that on occasion Jesus healed everyone and at other times passed through the sick and healed only those he chose. At one time in her early life Anandamayi Ma cured every sick person who came to her. Then she stopped healing altogether. When asked why, she simply replied: "I used to do it and now I do not." As I said, second-guessing gets us nowhere.

The Wisdom That Heals

And he opened his mouth, and taught them, saying,
Blessed are the poor in spirit: for theirs is the kingdom of heaven.
Blessed are they that mourn: for they shall be comforted.
Blessed are the meek: for they shall inherit the earth.
Blessed are they which do hunger and thirst after righteousness: for they shall be filled.
Blessed are the merciful: for they shall obtain mercy.
Blessed are the pure in heart: for they shall see God.
Blessed are the peacemakers: for they shall be called the children of God.
Blessed are they which are persecuted for righteousness' sake: for theirs is the kingdom of heaven.
Blessed are ye, when men shall revile you, and persecute you, and shall say all manner of evil against you falsely, for my sake.
Rejoice, and be exceeding glad: for great is your reward in heaven: for so persecuted they the prophets which were before you (Matthew 5:2-12).

Blessed are the poor in spirit: for theirs is the kingdom of heaven. The word translated "blessed" is *makarios*, which can mean both blessed and happy, but both expressions are too weak. *Makarios* means *supremely* blessed or happy in the sense that it is the ultimate degree of blessedness or happiness. And it also means to be fortunate in the literal sense of possessing a fortune and being well off: prosperous. The idea is that of spiritual abundance, even superabundance. "God is able to make all grace abound toward you; that ye, always having all sufficiency in all things, may abound to every good work" (II Corinthians 9:8). The fullness of spiritual capacity and manifestation is implied here.

Modern Christianity is so materialistic that virtually every time they speak of being blessed they mean gaining money. This is especially true of the televangelists and their forerunners, the "New Thought" churches. But Jesus' words should be understood spiritually, otherwise the Sermon on the Mount will just be another "God's Prosperity Plan."

The word translated as "poor" is *ptochos*. This has several meanings, some on the surface and others more subtle, especially in the implications of the root words from which it is derived. They are:

1) To see oneself as a total pauper, destitute of all things, not in the sense of self-pity or self-denigration, but from the knowledge that God being All, all is to be found in Him, that nothing is of ourselves. "Not that we are sufficient of ourselves to think any thing as of ourselves; but our sufficiency is of God" (II Corinthians 3:5). We possess absolutely nothing. Everything that we have comes from God. Consequently we see all things as being in the realm of God and rejoice accordingly in Him. We do not feel fearful or lacking in anything because God is our sustainer. In exhorting the Christians of Corinth to be confident and fearless, Saint Paul reminded them: "Ye are Christ's; and Christ is God's" (I Corinthians 3:23). That is, we have nothing, but God has everything, and we belong to Him, so in the belonging we possess Him and possess all.

2) To be totally dependent on God. This is only good sense, since we can neither do or be anything apart from Him. Even the most arrogant atheist is thoroughly dependent on God, he just does not realize it. The essence of this aspect, though, is the continual turning of our awareness Godward. That is, we should be looking to God for everything we need until we come to the realization that it is God Himself we need, that He is ours for the seeking.

3) Those who do realize their dependency on God will then be spiritually prosperous because God will abundantly bestow on them all the riches of the spirit. Only empty hands can be filled. That is why an Indian

poet sang: "A beggar at Thy door, Lord, pleading I stand. O grant to me an alms, Lord: love from Thy loving hand." The love he is asking for is love *of* God, not love *from* God. In this realm it is truly "more blessed to give than to receive" (Acts 20:35).

4) To be "destitute" of the ego, that which is ever grasping after things and claiming to be so much, is to be rich in the spirit. All the things of this relative life (death) lie only in the realm of the ego. Those who divest themselves of those things will then live in the spirit and be blessed.

5) A beggar has no home, but roams about seeking sustenance. Truly "the Son of man hath not where to lay his head" (Matthew 8:20). So the spiritually prosperous are those who realize that they are "strangers and pilgrims" (Hebrews 11:13; I Peter 2:11) and do not frustrate themselves by trying to be at home or rest or live anywhere in either the physical, astral, or causal worlds, but who seek God alone. "For our hearts are ever restless till they find themselves in Thee," said Saint Augustine.

6) It may not sound so pleasant, but *ptochos* also means to be distressed. In this instance, though, it means to be "divinely discontent," to refuse to be satisfied with anything less than the highest spiritual attainment, to never be satisfied with anything less than infinity.

7) *Ptochos* comes from *pipto*, which means to rely–literally to "fall"– utterly on something or someone. Those who trust fully in God and place themselves unreservedly in His hands will not be disappointed. "My hope is in God" is the motto of the spiritually wise. But there is more. *Pipto* is related to *petomai*, which means "to fly," the imagery of *ptochos* being that of a flying bird or butterfly that lands and comes to rest. In *Whispers From Eternity* Yogananda wrote: "Endowed with a spark of immortality, I have flown from life to life.... I shall alight at last, O Lord, upon Thine outstretched hand." Those who are coming in for a landing in the Infinite are the spiritually prosperous.

8) No simile is perfect, and neither is that of a beggar. A beggar ideally is one who has nothing through no choice or fault of his own. However, another word from which *ptochos* is derived is *peno*, which means "to toil for daily subsistence." So a *ptochos* is a beggar who works. That is, although we are completely dependent on God and look to Him alone, at the same

time we labor in the inner vineyard of God-realization for our spiritual daily bread. As with all reality, it is contradictory, but it is consistent with truth. This is an important point because there are a lot of spiritual layabouts in all religions who excuse their indolence by saying that it is a manifestation of their faith in God and their awareness of their own helplessness. The words are noble, but the motive is ignoble and hypocritical. There is a lot about work and labor in the Bible. Just use a good concordance and see.

9) A minor root word for beggar (*ptochos*) is *ptoeo*, when means to be apprehensive, The spiritually prosperous are always aware of their own capacity for failure and act accordingly. They strive to make God their strength and their safety.

In these matters of the spirit, destitution and helplessness are voluntary. That is, we intentionally divest ourselves of the illusions of possession and power, remembering the words of Jesus: "Thou sayest, I am rich, and increased with goods, and have need of nothing; and knowest not that thou art wretched, and miserable, and poor, and blind, and naked" (Revelation 3:17). Patanjali's *Yoga Sutras* state that those who are perfectly detached, divested of all things, find themselves inundated with "all kinds of precious things." So those who are in perfect spiritual poverty become incalculably wealthy in the spirit.

Why are the destitute and helpless in the realm of the spirit spiritually prosperous? "For theirs is the kingdom of heaven." "Kingdom of heaven" is the translation of the words *basileia ton ouranon*. A *basileus* is a kingdom in the sense that it is a place where a king has established himself in power and reigns. The root word *basis* (just like the word in English) implies a point of establishment, or abidance.

Firstly we should note the symbolism. In a kingdom there is a king, a sole absolute power. There is only one king. So the kingdom of heaven is that state of consciousness in which God alone reigns, and reigns effectively, in the life of the individual. The kingdom of heaven is an absolute monarchy. And a worthy soul recognizes the sole authority and power of God. But in this kingdom there is perfect freedom. Each citizen freely chooses to be ruled by the king. God becomes our king by invitation only. It must be our choice. The moment some outside agency is (seemingly) pushing us into the kingdom or keeping us there, we are no longer in the kingdom. Freedom is essential in spiritual life. But freedom "under God." The kingdom of heaven is not a place, but a state of mind and being.

The word translated "heaven" is *ouranos*, and is a very interesting word indeed. *Ouranos* means the boundless sky, the idea being that the kingdom of heaven is Infinite Consciousness. The sky is vast space, nothing more. In a sense it is not even an object at all. So the consciousness that is "heavenly" is both without boundaries or conditioning qualities, and not an object of perception to the limited and conditioned mind. It is Pure Consciousness Itself (in Sanskrit: *Chidakasha*, the Space of Consciousness). It, too, is freedom beyond conception.

Interestingly, *ouranos* is from the root word *oros*, which means "to have been lifted up." Our English word "heaven" means that which was heaved upward. The idea behind both words is expansion, in this case the limitless expansion of consciousness. The kingdom of heaven is gained by the expansion of our consciousness, something we must do for ourselves. It is innate in us, but we must bring it to fruition. *Oros* also means mountain, a high place, and that implies the same thing: we must ascend from finite to Infinite. That is why climbing up a sacred mountain is such a common symbol in world religions. The ascent is not done with the feet but with the spirit. The Bible often uses eagles as symbols of spiritual aspirants, and the Greek word for bird, *ornis*, also is derived from the same root. The Hebrew word for heaven means the same as *ouranos*. And that word is… NASA.

Blessed are they that mourn: for they shall be comforted. Pentheo means to grieve, to mourn, to wail, to sorrow. It includes both the inner feeling and the overt act. It encompasses inner and outer grieving, and is not at all appealing. But if we understand the root of this mourning then we will see that it really is blessed.

What we should be mourning is our separation from God, our confinement in the prison world of constant birth and death and the narrow consciousness which is both the cause and the result of that confinement. We should both feel it deeply and act fervently to end it. If we do so, then Jesus assures us that we "shall be comforted."

In the King James Version the word "comforted" is used to translate the Greek word *parakaleo*, which means to call someone near and comfort them. So this is not an impersonal matter of somehow becoming contented inwardly, but of being called to God, received into His arms of love, and lifted up beyond all capacity for pain or sorrow. *Parakaleo* also has the idea of someone being called for in an intensely personal and feeling way. Immediately there comes to mind the depictions of the Sacred Heart of Jesus in which his heart is shown aflame with love for all mankind. Further, his heart is encircled and pierced by the thorns of the suffering of humanity which he also experiences. The intensely personal character of the comfort we seek is made clear by this. The roots of *parakaleo* give support to this and confirm the idea of the fervent nature of God's calling for us, of God's yearning for our union with Him.

Anyone who is making effort in spiritual life runs into the matter of discouragement and a feeling of weakness or outright incapability. The consolation of God reverses all this and makes us confident, courageous and strong.

Blessed are the meek: for they shall inherit the earth. This has either been used to persuade people to shut up, lie down and be run over, or it has been a point of rebellion by those who consider passivity unintelligent and harmful. But if we look at the Greek text we will see the actual idea in Jesus' mind. *Praus* means mild and gentle. This does not mean insipid, banal, bland, vapid, feeble and timid–all "virtues" of the ineffectual and those who would render others ineffectual. Jesus does not want us to become squeaking mice.

Mildness and gentleness are symptoms of the truly peaceful, those who are at rest in God and confident. Simplicity is implied here as well. Those who are truly strong are the mild and the gentle. Mildness is not characterlessness, either. It is really difficult to explain what is meant by this beatitude, but if you have ever met a truly enlightened person you know what is meant. The saints I have met were varied in their personalities and style, yet they were all mild and gentle people. This is partially because all saints are perfect in *ahimsa*, non-injury. They are incapable of harming another, not because they cannot in a mechanical sense, but because they are above such a thing. Saints can speak plainly, and often do, but never with an edge to them. As I am writing this I am seeing in my mind the radiant and merciful faces of saints that I have met in my life. They were firm and true, yet they were amazingly mild, gentle, and kind. They would not lie or dissemble, but they were always firm and rational, devoid of any sting or bitterness.

"We should blunt our sharp points," says the Tao Teh King; and if we do, we "shall inherit the earth." *Kleronomeo* means to be an heir or to inherit. This implies that we are being freely given something through our merit: our meekness. *Kleronome* comes from *kleronomos*, which means to share in something, to actually possess it. So this is not a figurative matter, but something very literal. And what do the meek inherit? *Ge*, the earth. Not the world of human society and social constructs, but the very earth itself, the world of God's making as opposed to the world of man's fevered construction. The land itself will accrue to the meek. How many tyrants and empires have ground the meek into the earth only to vanish and become either forgotten or empty names in historical accounts. But the meek continue and abide upon the earth. The patient and the endurant eventually possess the land.

This is an external truth, and also a spiritual one. Those who remain sober, calm, and clear-sighted in their spiritual endeavors, without overblown ideas about their spiritual greatness or what glory they shall obtain, are those that shall attain everything. They shall master both the earth and the heaven parts of themselves. They shall themselves be kingdoms, reflections of the heavenly kingdom to which they are called. Meekness (mildness and gentleness), then, is the way rather than a martial, brash attitude. Many people turn spiritual life into another craze or passion and burn themselves out in the process. Again, we see the value of the tortoise and the hare story. "In your patience possess ye your souls" (Luke 21:19), counseled Jesus.

Blessed are they which do hunger and thirst after righteousness: for they shall be filled. Because we are so enslaved by our desire for pleasure and our aversion for pain, we try to avoid even discomfort or inconvenience, considering wanting something we cannot have to be a form of suffering.

We may say "no pain, no gain" to others, but we do not want that to apply to ourselves. This beatitude, however, commends discontent to a great degree: the hunger and thirst for righteousness.

Peinao means to be famished, to crave desperately, not just to be simply hungry. Without food we will die, so those suffering from intense hunger are desperate to be fed. In the same way we must see that God-contact is not a wonderful option but an urgent necessity without which we inwardly die. David said: "As the hart panteth after the water brooks, so panteth my soul after thee, O God. My soul thirsteth for God, for the living God" (Psalms 42:1-2). It was believed at the time of David that deer were avowed enemies of poisonous serpents. Consequently, they would search out the holes of snakes and literally suck them up and swallow them. In their stomachs the snakes would release their venom. This would cause an intense burning sensation, and if the deer could not get to a source of water and drink a great deal to dilute the poison, it would die. So it was a matter of life and death to the deer, and is the same to the aspiring soul, as well. Our yearning for God must be intense, otherwise we will not do the needful for the attainment of God-vision. We will foolishly feel that the price is too high. *Peinao* carries with it the connotation of keenly knowing our lack, and this knowledge spurs us on to spiritual fulfillment.

Peino has another meaning that is significant: both it and its root word *penes* mean to labor intensively, to strive for subsistence. Here the idea of strong spiritual desire is supplemented with the concept of intense spiritual practice, also a necessity for blessedness. Since thirst (*dipsao, dipsos*) can be even worse than hunger, it, too, is being used by Jesus to symbolize the urge toward union with God.

The word *dikaiosune* does not mean righteousness in the sense of social goodness or approval, or even the approbation of God. Rather it means correctness or rightness of the person's character, inner and outer. It means to be straight, square and true in our mind, our personality and their expression in our daily life. Rectitude might even be a better word than righteousness. It is not an external matter, but an internal disposition of spiritual health that of course does manifest outwardly, as is indicated by one of the root words of *dikaiosun*: *deiknuo*, which literally means "to show."

There are two other significant root words: *dikaios* and *dike*. *Dikaios* means to be just and fitting in deed and thought to such a degree that a person is innocent of all wrong, the idea being that the individual has been purified from all fault by becoming righteous. So righteousness is an effective, positive thing, not just a passive characteristic. *Dike* is very interesting, for it literally means the judgment and punishment of wrong. In the context of this beatitude it means that a righteous person clear-sightedly detects his defects and eliminates them consciously through self-discipline and mastery.

For they shall be filled. The Bible frequently uses eating as a spiritual symbol, so much so that spiritual life is likened to a banquet or feast. The Greek word employed by Saint Luke in his translating of Jesus' words is *chortazo*, which means to eat beyond the point of satiety to that of outright incapacity to eat a bite more. "Gorge" is a synonym given by Strong. In other words, we shall be filled to total capacity with the righteousness of God if we hunger and thirst sufficiently. Abundance is the key thought here, and *chortazo* also means to completely satisfy all desire. "Seek ye first the kingdom of God, and his righteousness; and all these things shall be added unto you" (Matthew 6:33). There is more. The root word *chortos* means edible herbage or vegetation, but its literal meaning is "garden," the idea being that the righteous are restored in spirit to Paradise, the Garden of Eden, and fed from the Tree of Life and thereby made immortal. Can it be without significance that Saint Luke chose a word that explicitly implied *vegetarian* fare?

Blessed are the merciful: for they shall obtain mercy. "With the merciful thou wilt shew thyself merciful; with an upright man thou wilt shew thyself upright" (Psalms 18:25), sang David, and Solomon his son wrote: "The merciful man doeth good to his own soul" (Proverbs 11:17).

Mercy which includes compassion is singled out in this beatitude to represent all other virtues in relation to other people, because whatever the positive behavior may be there is always at least a touch of mercy there. Furthermore, mercy carries within it lack of ego as well as kindness, good will, and love.

This beatitude also sets forth the law of karma, of sowing and reaping, assuring us that all right actions come back to us in the form of blessings.

"Then shall the King say unto them on his right hand, Come, ye blessed of my Father, inherit the kingdom prepared for you from the foundation of the world: for I was an hungered, and ye gave me food: I was thirsty, and ye gave me drink: I was a stranger, and ye took me in: naked, and ye clothed me: I was sick, and ye visited me: I was in prison, and ye came unto me. Then shall the righteous answer him, saying, Lord, when saw we thee an hungered, and fed thee? or thirsty, and gave thee drink? When saw we thee a stranger, and took thee in? or naked, and clothed thee? Or when saw we thee sick, or in prison, and came unto thee? And the King shall answer and say unto them, Verily I say unto you, Inasmuch as ye have done it unto one of the least of these my brethren, ye have done it unto me" (Matthew 25:34-40). "For he that loveth not his brother whom he hath seen, how can he love God whom he hath not seen?" (I John 4:20).

Blessed are the pure in heart: for they shall see God. In our relative experience, seeing something is not much in the way of comprehension, partly because there is so much more to an object than outward appearance, and also because of the limitation and conditionings of our faculty of seeing. Also, the ordinary seeing of an object has no lasting effect on us since the seeing brings about no touching or linking of us with the thing seen. But God essentially is not an object but a subject, just as are we in our true nature. Therefore the seeing of God is the joining of the two subjects in a union of consciousness. This is a profound condition, the goal of all yoga, for if meditation is persisted in, the merging of the two becomes inevitable. So a promise of the vision of God is a promise of union with God. Knowing what is requisite for that vision is then of prime concern to the intelligent seeker: purity in the sphere of the heart.

Kardia means not just the physical organ that circulates the blood, but embraces the ideas of thoughts, feelings and mind. It means the core, the center of our being, our spirit, and thus the source of life itself. Jesus is speaking of the essence of our being as well as its adjuncts of body and mind and their activities internal and external.

The Greek word *katharos* (from which we get catharsis) is very rich in meaning, and therefore very instructive for us. It appears twenty-eight times in the New Testament, and has these meanings:

1) *Clean* in the sense of having been made free from all impurities and implies a vigorous and thorough expulsion of all impurity.

2) *Purged*—as above.

3) *Clear* in the sense of having nothing obscuring it.

4) *Transparent*—as above.

5) *Unmixed* with any other thing whatsoever, absolute singleness of constitution as in chemical purity. This is an ideal symbol for perfect unity of consciousness.

6) *Without defect*—both without any flaw and also without any lack, complete in all ways.

7) *Spotless*, without any alien marking, and without any marking at all, as that would disrupt its purity in the sense of perfect unity.

By using this word Saint Luke is conveying the idea that we must be clean, clear, undivided, and complete in our consciousness from all conditionings or limitations whatsoever. (The Hebrew/Aramaic word *tahowr*, which was no doubt used by Jesus, conveys the identical meanings.) This is no small thing. And it cannot be accomplished without meditation as a major component of our life.

When this is accomplished we shall see (know) both ourselves and God. The Greek term *optanamai* means to see with wide-open eyes without obscurity, impediment or interruption. Interestingly, it also means *to be seen*, anticipating the words of Saint Paul: "For now we see through a glass, darkly; but then face to face: now I know in part; but then shall I know even as also I am known" (I Corinthians 13:12). It also means to experience that which is seen. So the vision of God is the experience of divinity Itself and of assimilation to That.

A final meaning in this beatitude is conveyed by the word *autos*, which Wuest accurately renders *themselves*, the idea being that the pure in heart see God directly without any intermediary, and certainly see God for themselves, there being no need for another person to do it for them. This is most important, for it strips away the fraudulent mask of most religion. Despite the lip-service to the nature of the Self (Atman) and the capacity of human beings for enlightenment, even in India we hear nonsense about gods or avatars or gurus doing the needful for us either altogether or in some degree.

What a clever evasion for the ego clinging to its idols and toys of ignorance. "I need do nothing (or little) for it has been done for me by the mercy and grace of N." This is degrading foolishness. *If we do not do it ourselves it will not be done.* Knowing this is the real grace and mercy of God and the saints.

Blessed are the peacemakers: for they shall be called the children of God. This beatitude has nothing to do with people who plead for peace, demonstrate for peace, protest for peace or in some other way bully or blackmail for peace. It is about *making* peace, actually creating peace rather than making a cause out of it. This requires a level of spiritual development that must first be obtained by each individual. So the first step in peacemaking is personal spiritual development.

The Greek word is *eirenopoios*, which is made up of two words: *eirene* and *poieo*. *Poieo* means both making and doing, and also means to abide. Peacemakers, then, create, act out and live in peace. A peacemaker commits peace just as others commit war. Peace can be actively practiced. *Poieo* not only means to cause something, it means to perpetuate (preserve) it. Only in the spiritual realm can there be real peacekeepers. So peacemaking is a continual process. It also means to provide something, implying that peacemakers know how to share peace. In my experience this is an essential mark of a saint. *Eirene*, the word translated "peace," means peace, quietness (tranquility), and rest. It occurs ninety-two times in the New Testament, so it is an important subject indeed. It comes from the root word *eiro*, "to join," and so has the same connotations as *yoga*. It also means oneness, unity, and the restoration of unity.

From all this it has to be evident that peacemaking is an exclusively spiritual matter, even though it naturally will have external manifestations in the world around us. I had a bit of experience of this when I returned from my first trip to India. For quite some time I lived in a small room in a slightly rundown part of Los Angeles. This was no problem for me as a monk, but what was not so positive was the nature of the people in the house my room faced. Although a minister's family, throughout the day two of the daughters argued with one another and yelled at their little brother whose constant running around could somehow be heard in my house as though he was romping in there. On occasion they engaged in what they thought was singing, usually pop songs of the most annoying type. Late one afternoon after some hours of meditation, I was sitting by the open window looking at a small statue of the Virgin Mary in my room. The dynamic duo were washing dishes across the way and burst into raucous strains of something awful. Ignoring the din, I mentally began reciting the Hail Mary. Instantly the caterwauling stopped and the two began sweetly singing *Ave Maria*. That was no coincidence, I was sure. This was confirmed by the fact that after I had been meditating there a little less than a month the arguing and yelling stopped completely. Whenever I heard the little boy spoken to it was always with kindness, and he stopped bouncing off the walls. At least five people in that house were sharers in my peace. Later I had the same kind of experience when working with nearly a hundred of the nastiest, most hostile people I ever dealt with. It only took a few weeks before peace reigned and the people were quiet and gentle to one another in place of the shouting, cursing and name-calling that had prevailed when I first came there.

Peace is born in silence, born in the hearts of those who enter and abide in the peace of meditation. They, too, are reborn and "shall be called the children of God." The word *kaleo* does not mean "called" in the sense of being declared or named something. Rather, it means to be bidden, to hear themselves being called for. "As many as received him, to them gave he power to become the sons of God" (John 1:12). So the peacemakers shall be called to become the sons of God. *Kaleo* also means to be called in the sense of being urged on or incited to something. Peacemakers do not sit around feeling tranquil; they are stirred to move ever onward toward the divine Goal. It also means to hail someone with their name or title. So the peacemakers shall, like Jesus, hear the words: "This is my beloved Son, in whom I am well pleased." Sons are of the same species as their father and mother. Even more, physically they are of the very substance of their parents. To be sons of God is to be essentially the same as God our Father, to have that status revealed to us and manifested by us to the world.

Blessed are they which are persecuted for righteousness' sake: for theirs is the kingdom of heaven. Those who embody this beatitude get the same reward as those who manifest the first beatitude.

The nature of righteousness has already been considered, so we need only look at what is meant by persecution. The Greek word is *dioko*, which means to pursue, to hound someone, to put pressure on them. From its root word *deilos*, it means to attempt instilling fear in someone in order to make them timid. Oddly, it is itself the root word of *diakonos*, minister or deacon. Persecution, then, is inverted service: oppression.

The blessedness lies not in being maltreated but in the purpose for the maltreatment: the pursuit of righteousness. It is also important to realize that the persecution does not ultimately come from any individuals but from the forces of ignorance in the cosmos *and in us*. If we deal with the latter, the former will be defused. Jesus continues this subject, saying:

Blessed are ye, when men shall revile you, and persecute you, and shall say all manner of evil against you falsely, for my sake. Those who hate the teacher hate the students as well. I know this by personal experience. Often hypocrites pretend to respect the teacher while being openly contemptuous of the disciples. This was very much the case in an ashram I often visited in India. Over and over I heard, especially from Westerners, that they revered the guru but had no use for and even disliked the disciples, whom they blamed for anything they did not like about the ashram.

Anyhow, what is in store for those who would become righteous?

1) *Oneidizo*–being slandered, railed at, chided, taunted, reproached, reviled, and upbraided. All this and more, you can be sure. Mockery and defamation are hard gifts to accept but they are showered on those that seek the kingdom. "Oh! I've heard of you…," "I know your kind…," and the recitation begins.

2) *Dioko*–already covered, but no less bitter in the receiving.

3) *Eiposi pan poniron rema kath' umon*–all manner of evil-speaking directed against you. The sky–and hell–is the limit.

How should we react? With sweet but wan acquiescence and pardon? Not a bit of it.

Rejoice, and be exceeding glad: for great is your reward in heaven. There it is, as plain as need be. Ignore the braying, the barking and the howling, and rejoice in your spirit. Saint Luke uses the words *chairo* and *agalliao*. *Chairo* means to be cheerful in the sense of being calmly happy and content.

It implies a kind of impersonal satisfaction. It does mean to rejoice and be happy, but in a very peaceful way. *Agalliao*, on the other hand, means to jump for joy and exult, to rejoice greatly. We should rejoice both outwardly and in the peace of our inner being.

That in us which usually produces resentment, anger, or pain in evil people who encounter us should be the cause of our great rejoicing. Why? "For great is your reward in heaven"—not a mythological heaven little better than earth, but the true heaven, the boundless expanse of the Spirit. When we have our sights set on infinity, why would we do anything but rejoice, whatever comes?

Furthermore, there are people we should not want to be our friends or friendly to us. Evil naturally hates good, and if evil people do not dislike us there is something wrong. We should note that our reward is because of *righteousness*, not because of the maltreatment and slander of the wicked and the foolish.

For so persecuted they the prophets which were before you. Jesus really honors us by putting us in the company of the prophets, and the persecutors likewise honor us by their contempt and enmity. You can judge a person by both his friends and his enemies.

Do we know of a single holy person that was not persecuted, slandered—and worse? Many have been tortured and killed for the sake of righteousness. But: "Fear not them which kill the body, but are not able to kill the soul" (Matthew 10:2).

All those who go against the current of the world are reacted to in a negative, even a hateful and destructive way, and this is one of the signs that they are going in the right direction.

Let us be going.

Spiritual Salt

> Ye are the salt of the earth: but if the salt have lost his savour, wherewith shall it be salted? it is thenceforth good for nothing, but to be cast out, and to be trodden under foot of men (Matthew 5:13).

To the people of the Mediterranean world at the time of Jesus salt was very precious. The Roman Empire paid its soldiers not with money but with salt. That is why we have the word "*salary*"–salt–for a worker's wages. And we speak of people being worth their salt. In ancient China, because of its importance the government monopolized and controlled the production of salt, and so have many others since then.

Salt is essential for the maintenance of life, as anyone who has lived in a tropical climate knows. Salt is necessary for proper brain functioning, and for the electromagnetic functions of the body. Intense heat causes salt depletion through perspiration which results in complete loss of physical and mental vigor. One summer in Benares I became so confused in mind and weak in body that I was seriously thinking of cutting my trip short, returning to the States and checking into a hospital. I was sitting in the office of a publisher of religious texts located in the attic of a building. As I sat in the cluttered oven I felt my life was in danger. As we left, I told my companions that it seemed I really ought to arrange to fly back to the States as soon as possible. Fortunately, as I was laboring down the roasting street I suddenly remembered being told years before that it was necessary to take salt tablets during the hot weather in India. Equally fortunately there was a pharmacy just a little way along the street. I stopped there and bought some salt tablets. That night I took nine of them and went to sleep. The next morning I woke up completely all right with a perfectly clear mind. So from then on I regularly took salt tablets when traveling in India and was just fine.

There is an old European story of a merchant who had several daughters. One day he asked them: "How much do you love me?" They all said various poetic and abstract things except for the youngest, who replied: "I love you like salt loves food." This seemingly silly and frivolous answer angered the merchant who expelled her from the house to wander as a beggar. Her family lost track of her completely. In time the young woman became married to a very wealthy and influential man. When many years had passed it happened that her father was invited to her house. Because of the passing years he did not recognize her. She directed the cook to prepare all the food without salt. As they were eating the merchant began to weep violently, saying, "I had a daughter who told me she loved me as salt loves food. Now I realize that she loved me most of all!" Anyone who has ever been on a saltless diet knows how he felt. Salt gives food flavor that makes it worth eating. "Can that which is unsavoury be eaten without salt?" asked Job (6:6). Another valuable trait of salt is its preservative quality. Until the advent of modern refrigeration salting and drying were the only ways to keep food unspoiled.

Even more precious than salt are those who live the life of the spirit. It is they who bring clarity and spiritual sanity to the world. Without the presence of the spiritual, the world is insipid and ultimately corrupt and poisonous. That the righteous preserve the world is seen in the Bible. In the eighteenth chapter of Genesis God promises Abraham that he will preserve Sodom from its deserved destruction if there are only ten righteous men living there. In the first paragraph of his autobiography, Paramhansa Yogananda speaks of "the great masters who are India's sole remaining wealth. Emerging in every generation, they have bulwarked their land against the fate of Babylon and Egypt." The insightful governments of all ages have fostered religion, knowing that this was the major hope for their continuance. With this perspective the founders of this country provided for the free exercise of religion of all kinds, being themselves, every one, men of deep faith in God.

But if the salt have lost his savour, wherewith shall it be salted [its flavor restored]? There is no substitute for salt; it is unique in taste and value. So also is spiritual "saltiness." We cannot hope to live to any degree as conscious beings if we lose the salt of spiritual awareness, and those of us who are wise will work to increase our saltiness, to develop our spiritual consciousness.

Sadly, people are frantically seeking here and there in a doomed search for that which can be found only in spiritual awakening. There are people who do not like salt, or they do not like much salt. In the same way there are those who have no taste for spiritual things. They want God to leave them alone to live their life, not knowing that God *is* their life. Others want a touch, a sprinking of spiritual ideas, usually when they are in trouble or want something. They get very huffy about people becoming extreme or "fanatical" in religion. This indicates that they have an aversion to dedication to spiritual ideals. Blind and selfish children, they want the blessings of God but not the Blesser.

Salt is indeed pungent, and so are those who live in the spirit. There are people who like bland, tasteless, saltless food. In the same way the world of whom we are the salt yearns for us to be saltless, to not have pungency, to not be so sharp or harsh. (By that they mean demanding something of them or making them feel guilty in comparison to us.) As a result there is a constant struggle. Those who are of God strive to salt the world, and the world constantly wars against them to make them lose their saltness.

It is thenceforth good for nothing, but to be cast out, and to be trodden under foot of men. "I was made for Thee alone," wrote Paramhansa Yogananda in *Whispers From Eternity*. We have one single purpose for existing: to seek and find God. There is no value to a life devoid of spiritual awareness and aspiration.

What is the destiny of those who insist on being inwardly saltless? The Greek word for loss of saltness is *moraino*, which means to become insipid. But it is also an idiomatic word that means to become a simpleton, a fool. The idea is plain: those without spiritual intelligence are completely foolish, whatever their intellectual level might be or how much they accomplish in their outer life. *Moraino* comes from the root word *moros*, which means to be dull, stupid, heedless, absurd and foolish–a moron. Does this need any exposition? Just look at modern life, political, intellectual, financial, social and (sad to say) religious. All these words certainly apply to almost the maximum degree. However, *moros* also means to be enclosed or imprisoned. This is certainly true of the materially-conscious individual, for relative existence is itself entombment in ignorance. Those who seek only the external shrink and collapse back into their egos.

"How hard to break through is this, my Maya, made of the gunas! But he who takes refuge within me only shall pass beyond Maya: he, and no other. The evil-doers turn not toward me: these are deluded, sunk low among mortals. Their judgment is lost in the maze of Maya, until the heart is human no longer: changed within to the heart of a devil" (Bhagavad Gita 7:14-15).

There is more. *Moros* comes from *muo*, which means to have the mouth forcibly closed, to become mute. In ancient Western occult writings we find the expressions: "I send a voice" and "I seek a voice." In the Greek story of Alceste the oracle says that Alceste's husband can be saved if someone "gives his voice"–that is, gives his life–for him. To be without a voice means to be without life, to dwell in death. Spiritually speaking, the salty are living, the saltless are dead.

Recently I spoke with a man who told me that many years ago he was almost killed in an auto accident. As he was thrown from the car he saw his whole life pass before him and heard himself think: "I have wasted my life." Although he recovered, he could not escape the conviction that his life, although successful materially and socially, was being wasted, that it counted for nothing. He began to search, and when he found yoga (meditation) he found the way to make his life really count for something, to be "saved" rather than thrown away.

There is an obscure Protestant hymn that describes most people as "busy, yet idle, if only they knew." As Krishna told Arjuna: "Lose [spiritual] discrimination, and you miss life's only purpose" (Bhagavad Gita 2:63). And: "Among those who are purified by their good deeds, there are four kinds of men who worship me: the world-weary, the seeker for knowledge, the seeker for happiness and the man of spiritual discrimination. The man of discrimination is the highest of these. He is continually united with me. He devotes himself to me always, and to no other. For I am very dear to that man, and he is dear to me. Certainly, all these are noble: but the man of discrimination I see as my very Self. For he alone loves me because I am myself: the last and only goal of his devoted heart. Through many a long life his discrimination ripens: he makes me his refuge, knows that Brahman is all. How rare are such great ones!" (Bhagavad Gita 7:16-19). Let us be rare.

It is thenceforth good for nothing, but to be cast out, and to be trodden under foot of men. The word translated "thrown out" is *ballo*, which means not a simple toss, but a violent, intense casting down, being struck down or pushed down ruthlessly. This casting down through their own nature is described in the Bhagavad Gita by Krishna, saying:

"Men of demonic nature know neither what they ought to do, nor what they should refrain from doing. There is no truth in them, or purity, or right conduct. They maintain that the scriptures are a lie, and that the universe is not based upon a moral law, but godless, conceived in lust and created by copulation, without any other cause. Because they believe this in the darkness of their little minds, these degraded creatures do horrible deeds, attempting to destroy the world. They are enemies of mankind.

"Their lust can never be appeased. They are arrogant, and vain, and drunk with pride. They run blindly after what is evil. The ends they work for are unclean. They are sure that life has only one purpose: gratification of the senses. And so they are plagued by innumerable cares, from which death alone can release them. Anxiety binds them with a hundred chains, delivering them over to lust and wrath. They are ceaselessly busy, piling up dishonest gains to satisfy their cravings.

"'I wanted this and today I got it. I want that: I shall get it tomorrow. All these riches are now mine: soon I shall have more. I have killed this enemy. I will kill all the rest. I am a ruler of men. I enjoy the things of this world. I am successful, strong and happy. Who is my equal? I am so wealthy and so nobly born. I will sacrifice to the gods. I will give alms. I will make merry.' That is what they say to themselves, in the blindness of their ignorance.

"They are addicts of sensual pleasure, made restless by their many desires, and caught in the net of delusion. They fall into the filthy hell of their own evil minds. Conceited, haughty, foolishly proud, and intoxicated by their wealth, they offer sacrifice to God in name only, for outward show, without following the sacred rituals. These malignant creatures are full of egoism, vanity, lust, wrath, and consciousness of power. They loathe me, and deny my presence both in themselves and in others. They are enemies of all men and of myself; cruel, despicable and vile. *I cast them back, again and again*, into the wombs of degraded parents, subjecting them to the wheel of birth and death. And so they are constantly reborn, in degradation and delusion. They do not reach me, but sink down to the lowest possible condition of the soul" (Bhagavad Gita 16:7-20).

That is the fate of the saltless in relation to God and the law of karma and rebirth. Their fate in relation to human beings has been expressed by the declaration that they shall "be trodden under foot of men." The word *katapateo* means to trample something underfoot with contempt. If they can, world-oriented people wear you down and when they have broken you, from contempt for your virtue they pass to contempt for your vice, showing their own self-contempt (for now they condemn you for being like them) and grind you into the "earth" which heretofore they touted as good, beautiful, natural, real and even "holy." They are like the immoral men who mock a virgin for her virginity and then spit on her and call her foul names when she submits to them. Jesus spoke of those who said John the Baptist was possessed because he was ascetic and that Jesus was a glutton and a drunk because he was not (Matthew 11:18-19). These people are implacable enemies of themselves and all others. "And even as they did not like to retain God in their knowledge, God gave them over to a reprobate mind, to do those things which are not convenient; being filled with all unrighteousness, fornication, wickedness, covetousness, maliciousness; full of envy, murder, debate, deceit, malignity; whisperers, backbiters, haters of God, despiteful, proud, boasters, inventors of evil things, disobedient to parents, without understanding, covenantbreakers, without natural affection, implacable, unmerciful: who knowing the judgment of God, that they which commit such things are worthy of death, not only do the same, but have pleasure in them that do them" (Romans 1:28-32).

"They think it strange that ye run not with them to the same excess of riot, speaking evil of you" (I Peter 4:4). But once you start running with them they despise you, since they secretly despise themselves. What a terrible dilemma they live in! They hate those who consider their behavior to be wrong and hate themselves for engaging in it, however much they may deny this. Having degraded themselves they accuse the virtuous of making them guilty. This terrible schizophrenia becomes well-nigh incurable in time. (There is a very positive and necessary aspect to admitting guilt and culpability. Buddha listed the capacity for feeling ashamed of wrong action as one of the signs of spiritual proficiency.)

"In the beginning I was fanatical; I wouldn't even...." Have you ever heard this from the lips of a spiritual sellout? I have, many times. "I used to be so afraid of... but then I realized: 'This won't hurt me. Come on,' I told myself, 'Be *human*.'" That is the self-justification of the spiritually desolate. How many that start out well, fervent in spirit and filled with hope, listen to the voices of the world, compromise and fall out of the race, having lost their saltness and become as insipid (and corrupt) as those who urged them to "be a good sport" and "loosen up" and "get balanced" and "quit being so uptight about everything." Well, they are not any more–they are nothing.

This is all summed up beautifully and inspiringly by the thirty-eighth Ode of Solomon, so I include it here in conclusion:

> I went up into the Light of Truth as into a chariot, and the Truth led me and caused me to come.
>
> And it carried me across hollows and gulfs, and from the cliffs and gullies it preserved me.
>
> And it became to me a Haven of Salvation, and set me on the step of deathless life.
>
> And He went with me and made me rest and suffered me not to err, because He was and is the Truth.
>
> And there was no danger for me because I walked with Him, and I made no error in anything because I obeyed Him.
>
> For Error fled away from Him, and would not meet Him.
>
> But Truth was proceeding in the right way, and whatever I did not know He made clear to me:

All the drugs of Error, and the torments of death which are considered sweetness.

And the corrupting of the Corruptor, I saw when the Bride who was corrupting was adorned, and the Bridegroom who corrupts and is corrupted.

And I asked the Truth: Who are these? and He said to me: This is the Deceiver and the Error:

And they imitate the Beloved and His Bride, and they lead astray the world and corrupt it.

And they invite many to the Banquet, and give them to drink of the wine of their intoxication.

And they make them vomit up their wisdom and intelligence, and they make them mindless.

And then they leave them, and so these go about like madmen and corrupt.

For they are without heart, and do not seek it.

And I was made wise so as not to fall into the hands of the Deceiver, and I congratulated myself that the Truth had gone with me.

And I was established and lived and was redeemed, and my foundations were laid on account of the Lord's hand, for He planted me.

For He set the root, and watered it and endowed it and blessed it, and its fruits will be for ever.

It struck deep and sprang up and spread wide, and it was full and was enlarged.

And the Lord alone was glorified, in His planting and in his cultivation;

In His care and in the blessing of His lips, in the beautiful planting of His right hand;

And in the splendor of His planting, and in the understanding of His mind. Alleluia.

The Light of the World!

Ye are the light of the world. A city that is set on an hill cannot be hid. Neither do men light a candle, and put it under a bushel, but on a candlestick; and it giveth light unto all that are in the house. Let your light so shine before men, that they may see your good works, and glorify your Father which is in heaven (Matthew 5:14-16).

Ye are the light of the world. How different is the real Jesus of the Gospels from the pseudo-Jesus of the churches. Their Jesus tells us we are sinners deserving damnation, but he will save us from justice if we only "accept" him. Still, we will remain worthless and inclined to evil by our very nature. But see what the true Jesus says to us: "You are the light of the world." We are the light, not just unto ourselves but unto the whole world. What an astounding statement of his belief in us.

We are not surprised when Jesus says that he is the light of the world (John 8:12; 9:5), but lifetimes of negative conditioning block our readiness to conceive of this truth in relation to us, much less accept it and even less to dare to act upon it. Yet, as already cited, in the first paragraph of his autobiography, Yogananda speaks of "the great masters who are India's sole remaining wealth. Emerging in every generation, they have bulwarked their land against the fate of Babylon and Egypt." The "salt of the earth," they have preserved India through the ages, and as "light of the world" the wisdom of the masters of India is shining throughout the world "as the lightning cometh out of the east, and shineth even unto the west" (Matthew 24:27). This is to be our function, too, if we cooperate with the divine plan. We are to be the presence of the Christ just as was he.

"God is light" (I John 1:5). When we link our consciousness with God, the Absolute Consciousness, through the practice of meditation, then we too are light. More, we become sources of that light as it shines from us into the world. We are aspirants, hardly world-changing masters, yet through our continual pursuit of higher consciousness we change the world for the better, making ourselves a presence of God in the world. It says later in the Bible, "Ye shine as lights in the world" (Philippians 2:15). So we see that the real benefactors of the world are those who fix their minds on God.

Swami Brahmananda explained that when you drop a rock in water, especially in a small pond, the waves go out to the side of the pond and then they come back and meet again in the middle. In the same way, he said, every thought goes out like a ripple through the entire creation, and then comes back to us and affects us according to its vibration. We speak of actions creating karma, but we forget that continual thought of God is the supreme karma, so we create God-consciousness karma for us and the world. The japa and meditation of Soham produces the highest and most effective benefit for not just the individual yogi, but for the entire range of creation. A lamp has no light of its own, but when fire is added, it becomes a source of light. Through us God's light can shine into the world through us, and yet it is our own light, as well.

A city that is set on an hill cannot be hid. We have a grave problem at this point in time. The forces of ignorance and anti-spirituality have for a long time been dinning away at spiritual people that they are not supposed to be "fanatics" or "unbalanced," meaning that they are to be unseen and therefore ineffectual. "Religion is a private matter!" they fume, while having no objection to openly foul talk or the expression of hatred toward what they do not like or approve. Free speech is apparently denied only to the religious and the spiritual. Attempting to coerce others into negative or foolish behavior and ways of thought is just fine, but to merely speak of spiritual matters is to be "extreme" and "trying to cram your ideas down other people's throats." Don't fall into the trap! Forget not the words we have just recently considered: "Ye are the salt of the earth: but if the salt have lost his savour, wherewith shall it be salted? It is thenceforth good for nothing, but to be cast out, and to be trodden under foot of men."

We are supposed to be visible and and pungent. We are supposed to be annoying to the servants of the dark, because we dissolve their whole world of darkness by being what we are. If we are not infuriating to them, then we are not of the light. That is why Jesus said: "Blessed are ye, when men shall revile you, and persecute you, and shall say all manner of evil against you falsely, for my sake. Rejoice, and be exceeding glad: for great is your reward in heaven: for so persecuted they the prophets which were before you."

A man wrote to me that after he took up the meditation and continual repetition of Soham, when he walked down the street there were people who upon seeing him began making ugly faces at him, and some even turned and ran away when they caught sight of him. The principle "as above so below" applies here absolutely. If something is going on in our higher levels it will manifest on our lower levels, including our outer life. Spiritual life manifests right here in this world. People may not be able to define or express it, but they will know something is going on with us. The positive ones will like and appreciate us even if they cannot articulate their reasons for doing so, and the negative ones will wish we would go away or die. However we may be reacted to, we will be visible. The light that we are will reveal us. If we do not lose our saltness they will never be able to trample us underfoot as they want.

Yes, we will be clearly seen by those down in the valley of confusion and ignorance, but that is because we are not in the misty flats below, but on the mountain of higher consciousness and life. To the outer eye two people may be walking along side-by-side, but the inner eye can see that they are miles, even worlds, apart. Similarly, the saints walk among all men, but never walk with them in the inner sense. Many times I have seen holy people right in front of me, but I could tell that they were dwelling in another world. They were aware of me, but they were not in this world with me. I understood that I had to pass over into their world if I would truly live. Most people spend their life trying to pull God and the holy ones down into their little world so they can get out of them what they want. Blessed are the few who seek to lift themselves into the "heavenly places" (Ephesians 2:6), to truly be with the holy.

Writing these words, my mind turns back over fifty years to Sivanandashram in Rishikesh. In the morning satsang with Swami Sivananda, he would announce: "Kirtan by Swami Sivananda-Hridayananda." Plying a little one-note sruti box, "Doctor Mother" would lead us in beautiful kirtan. Swami Sivananda would sit there in his chair with closed eyes, deeply absorbed within. The atmosphere would be so divine that I was sure the entire hall had been lifted up miles beyond the earth into a realm of divine life. (After all, the ashram was also known as The Divine Life Society.) It was a real shock to look out the open doorway and see the roofs and trees of the ordinary outside world. We were in heaven and on earth at the same time, foreshadowing the state of enlightenment in which the finite and the Infinite are lived simultaneously.

Until we reach that goal, we must do our utmost to keep our consciousness elevated in every way. Most important is the fact that the citizens of a city on the top of a mountain are not just tourists or occasional visitors. They live there. In the same way, we must dwell continually in higher consciousness, not just drop in occasionally.

A further point. Jesus refers to us as a city, not a small group of isolated individuals. Sri Ramakrishna said that devotees of God form a caste to themselves. Throughout the world those who seek higher life form a great spiritual association, even if they are not aware of one another. In I Kings 19:9-18, we find that the prophet Elijah thought he was the only one in Israel who had not forsaken the Covenant, but God told him that there were seven thousand (a great number in those days) who were true to Him.

We have already considered the remarkable incident of the spiritual power and effectiveness of devotees in the account of Gideon and the chosen few soldiers who routed the enemy without striking a blow. No wonder Jesus said to his disciples: "Fear not, little flock; for it is your Father's good pleasure to give you the kingdom" (Luke 12:32).

When evolved human beings see others living a higher life, they are attracted, and the most evolved among them see the glory of higher consciousness and begin seeking it themselves. In this way, one lamp lights another, so to say. This is our purpose: not just to shine, but to inspire others to shine as well.

Spiritualizing External Laws

> Think not that I am come to destroy the law, or the prophets: I am not come to destroy, but to fulfill. For verily I say unto you, Till heaven and earth pass, one jot or one tittle shall in no wise pass from the law, till all be fulfilled (Matthew 5:17-18).

Many times Jesus was reprimanded by the "orthodox" because he did or permitted what was considered contrary to the Mosaic Law, or at least their interpretation of it. But in this instance no such incident had taken place. Instead he had just delivered the Sermon on the Mount and told his disciples that they were the salt of the earth and the light of the world. They had never heard such words from the teachers of the Mosaic Law–just the opposite. The positive and hope-bearing words just spoken by Jesus presented a completely different perspective of spiritual life. So it would only be natural that the disciples expected him to follow this up with a denunciation of the traditional scriptures of the Hebrews and an exhortation to turn away from them. But Jesus had something much better in mind. Certainly he had a mission in relation to the law and the prophets, but it was to fulfill them, to make them living and meaningful. Unfortunately "fulfill" is not a very good translation of the word *pleroo*, which means to make something full and overflowing–abundant. It also means to supply that which is lacking, to complete, to perfect. Jesus intended to give the spiritual dimension that was lacking in what had gone before, or had been lost over the centuries. He intended to take what was material and render it spiritual.

In doing this, another thing would be achieved. For *pleroo* also means to accomplish something and finish it. Upon the completion or accomplishment of something there is no more use for it. When we pass into adulthood, childhood is left behind, not destroyed but transcended, and it does cease to be except as a memory. So Jesus certainly did intend to end the law and the prophets, just as childhood is ended, but he did so by building upon them. For, as we say: "The child is the father of the man." Thus the law and the prophets would live on in a transfigured life.

Jesus looked upon the law and prophets as pointers toward "a more excellent way" (I Corinthians 12:31), actually a prophecy "of good things to come" (Hebrews 9:11). That is why he told his detractors: "Search the scriptures; for in them ye think ye have eternal life: and they are they which testify of me" (John 5:39. See Luke 24:27, 44). And Saint Paul gave the assurance: "Now therefore ye are no more strangers and foreigners, but fellow citizens with the saints, and of the household of God; and are built upon the foundation of the apostles and prophets, Jesus Christ himself being the chief corner stone" (Ephesians 2:19-20). So our life in Christ is a transfigured continuation of the law and the prophets.

Yet there is another way these words of Jesus can be understood in a more inward or spiritual context. The Law represents the external laws of spiritual life. Since spirit is the source of all, it embraces external, material life. Spiritual life, then, includes outer observances that correspond to the Law. But it also includes mental activity, and regarding this God said through the prophet Isaiah: "I will put my law in their inward parts, and write it in their hearts" (Jeremiah 31:33). And the inner law is "the prophets"–that which works mostly through intuition, through direct insight.

So there is observance of outer and inner right conduct which, when perfected, renders life in pure spirit possible. And this is the advent of Christ, extending our awareness into divinity. As Jesus says: "I am come that they might have life, and that they might have it more abundantly" (John 10:10). There is a whole body of spiritual law, a procedure by which we must live inwardly and outwardly to discover and possess the kingdom of God. The more objective principles are represented by the Law, and the psychological, interior principles by the Prophets. In Sanskrit this body of law is known as *Ritam*, Cosmic Law or Cosmic Order. The "Law" and the "Prophets" being part of the Cosmic Order, they cannot be abrogated "till heaven and earth pass," and that only because there will no longer be a need for them. But the moment they re-emerge in the next cycle of creation, there they are, intact and operative.

Now in consideration of this we come to one of the most important points for people to realize: *Never at any time or in any way is any law abrogated.* In other words, there is no such things as legitimately setting aside the law. Since God cannot be other than perfect, all of his laws are perfect, and to abrogate or suspend them is to violate his own nature, but "he cannot deny himself" (II Timothy 2:13).

Every religion is filled with tricks and gimmicks for getting around the Law and God. This makes sense in those religions who believe that divine law is really divine caprice based on what God (or gods) like or dislike. But the Eternal Dharma is based on The Way Things Are, which is impossible to change. "God is not a man, that he should lie; neither the son of man, that he should repent: hath he said, and shall he not do it? or hath he spoken, and shall he not make it good?" (Numbers 23:19).

Therefore we need to wisely follow every smallest letter and smallest letter-marking of the inner and outer law and prophets. For Jesus also tells us: "He that is faithful [*pistos:* trustworthy] in that which is least [*elachistos:* very little or very small] is faithful also in much [*polus:* a great deal]: and he that is unjust [*adikos:* unjust, unrighteous] in the least is unjust also in much" (Luke 16:10).

We only go beyond the Law when we embody it and heaven and the earth pass away for us, and we pass into "the temple of my God, and shall go no more out" (Revelation 3:12).

Until we are totally out of the game we have to play by the rules of the game.

> **Whosoever therefore shall break one of these least commandments, and shall teach men so, he shall be called the least in the kingdom of heaven: but whosoever shall do and teach them, the same shall be called great in the kingdom of**

> heaven. For I say unto you, That except your righteousness shall exceed the righteousness of the scribes and Pharisees, ye shall in no case [never] enter into the kingdom of heaven (Matthew 5:19-20).

Why human beings who are supposedly religious get obsessed with being either the greatest or the least is an easily solved mystery: ego. They just must be seen and remarked on, so they aspire to either the front or the end of the line. This will be evident later on when "came the disciples unto Jesus, saying, who is the greatest in the kingdom of heaven?" (Matthew 18:1). Obviously they had not paid any attention to what Jesus said to them in the verse we are about to consider. And even worse, after that: "Then came to him the mother of Zebedee's children with her sons, worshipping him, and desiring a certain thing of him. And he said unto her, What wilt thou? She saith unto him, Grant that these my two sons may sit, the one on thy right hand, and the other on the left, in thy kingdom. But Jesus answered and said, Ye know not what ye ask" (Matthew 20:2-22). It was going to take Pentecost to change all this.

Our interest should be the perspective of Jesus, and here it is in the just-cited verse. For those of us who were processed through Sunday School, the word "commandment" always means one of the Ten Commandments. But Jesus is speaking here of the Beatitudes which he has just spoken to the disciples. The Ten Commandments certainly never lost their force in Jesus' perspective, but since he had come to add a far greater dimension to spiritual life than the Law could ever reach, he gave the New Commandments. (See *The Gnosis of the Ten Commandments and the Beatitudes* on our ocoy.org website.) The Old Commandments could be followed by even a materialistic person, but the Beatitudes require a real transformation of consciousness before they can be followed completely. And it was Jesus' intent to open the way for that transformation of consciousness.

For us who aspire to Christhood, the word *entole*, translated "commandment," means any precept or prescription that comes from a viable spiritual source. In *The Aquarian Gospel* we find that the Essenes, of which Jesus' family was a part, taught the wisdom of many spiritual traditions.

This was one of the reasons the other religious people in Israel shunned them. (See *The Christ of India*.) And it should be the same with us. Precepts from any sacred book should be taken seriously by us. The "law" and the "prophets" Jesus said he had come not to destroy but fulfill (5:17), included all the authentic spiritual traditions of humanity. To confine our study to the writings of only one religion is to deny ourselves greater understanding of the religion we identify with. For the divinely illumined masters speak from the same Light. A religion that contradicts this fact is a false religion, or at least a wrong understanding of that religion. Every precept given by the Masters of Wisdom is invaluable for us. And Jesus tell us that to break the least of them is to make ourselves least in the kingdom of spirit. The word *elachistos* means the absolutely least or small.

The word *luo*, translated "break," is very interesting, for it carries many connotations. It means to break, destroy/dissolve, loose, melt, or put off. We see this every day. The spiritually astray not only break the precepts of righteousness, they try to destroy, dissolve or melt them away by convincing people that they are either false, valueless or do not mean what they seem to mean. They are masters at weaseling out of the truth and trying to keep others from learning the truth. They are those to whom Jesus said: "Woe unto you, for ye shut up the kingdom of heaven against men: for ye neither go in yourselves, neither suffer [allow] ye them that are entering to go in" (Matthew 23:13). They cast away from themselves the truth and try to snatch it away from others, even those who want it. Such are the least in wisdom, honor, and honesty.

It is just the opposite with those that are great and strong (*megas*) in the realm of spirit. They follow all the precepts of wisdom, from the most important to the very least hint. The word translated "do" in relation to the commandments is *poieo*, which also has many meanings. The primary meaning is "do," but it also means to remain steadfast (literally: abide); to agree to, to carry (in the sense of fulfilling obligations), to be content (with the precept), to continue in observance, to follow without any delay (very important!), to make the precept one's own in the sense of assimilating its benefits, to observe and ordain. And, interestingly, it means to move forward, to go somewhere, which of course is the very purpose of any spiritual principle. This gives us a very good idea of the psychology of those that are great in the kingdom of heaven.

In the most important sense, "least" and "great" refer to scope of consciousness. Those who neglect even the least precept shall have the least breadth and depth of consciousness, of spiritual awareness and understanding. Those who follow all, even the least, will have the greatest expansion of consciousness, the greatest degree of awareness and insight. Infinity will be theirs. Those who neglect the ways of wisdom are the small-minded, but the great-minded follow them all.

Nearly all religion is hopelessly externalized, and Jesus now warns us against it: "Except your righteousness shall exceed the righteousness of the scribes and Pharisees, ye shall in no case [never] enter into the kingdom of heaven." Before going further, we must set in mind that Jesus is not speaking of being barred from heaven and sent to hell. He is speaking of entering into Divine Consciousness, the Being of God, of attaining total liberation into Spirit. He is not threatening anyone, just stating the facts for those who really want to know.

The scribes were those obsessed with the rule aspect of the Torah, the Talmudists of that time. Interestingly, they were also skeptics with virtually no belief in anything but Follow The Rules. They were living examples of how external consciousness can displace spiritual awareness. The Pharisees were extremely religious and virtuous (at least they thought so) and firm believers in the supernatural. At the same time they were as obsessed with external religious observance and ceremonial purity as the Scribes were obsessed with The Rules. Their religion basically replaced God, though they would not have perceived or admitted it. So "the righteousness of the scribes and Pharisees" was all in Dogma and Doing. Both hated the Essenes, among whom Jesus was numbered, for their mystical and ascetic ways, and most of all because they accepted and studied "alien scriptures" (their actual words in official decrees condemning the Essenes).

Jesus does not tell us to reject the righteousness of the Scribes and Pharisees, but that our righteousness must exceed theirs. The word translated "righteousness" is *dikaiosune*, which means both righteousness and that which "makes righteous." It also means rectitude, the state of being "right"—of conforming to the divine nature within and the divine purpose or pattern without. So Jesus is speaking both of spiritual attainment and that which produces the attainment. In other words, he is speaking of spiritual practice.

The word "exceed" is *pleion*, which means to be "more" both in quantity and quality. It comes from a root word, *polus*, which means abundant. So we need to be even more observant than the Scribes and Pharisees in outward matters (that is the quantity) and much more spiritually aware than they (that is the quality). Further, it means "the major portion," implying that our spiritual life must be the major element in our life, that it must occupy far more time in our thinking, speaking and acting than anything else. To the contemporary Scribes and Pharisees we will seem blazing fanatics, but I learned long ago that unless the insipid and lukewarm of this world call a seeker a fanatic his seeking does not amount to much. I always knew I was on the right track when they protested and argued with me. To those with diseased eyes the slightest beam of light is an agony. So it is with the unrighteous, the dwellers in darkness. Like insects living beneath a rock, they scuttle away at the advent of the light.

Pleion also means to go further, to move on out and down the road to the goal. Today's Scribes and Pharisees also fuss about those who "go too far" in their religion—another sign of being on the right course, on the way to the Kingdom of Heaven with a guarantee of entry. For the only way to enter the Kingdom is to exceed the Scribes and Pharisees in everything.

> **Ye have heard that it was said by them of old time, Thou shalt not kill; and whosoever shall kill shall be in danger of the judgment. But I say unto you, That whosoever is angry with his brother without a cause shall be in danger of the judgment: and whosoever shall say to his brother, Raca, shall be in danger of the council: but whosoever shall say, Thou fool, shall be in danger of hell fire. Therefore if thou bring thy gift to the altar, and there rememberest that thy brother hath ought against thee, leave there thy gift before**

the altar, and go thy way; first be reconciled to thy brother, and then come and offer thy gift.

Agree with thine adversary quickly, whiles thou art in the way with him; lest at any time the adversary deliver thee to the judge, and the judge deliver thee to the officer, and thou be cast into prison. Verily I say unto thee, Thou shalt by no means come out thence, till thou hast paid the uttermost farthing (Matthew 5:21-26).

Just a little way back, in verse seventeen, Jesus said that he had come to fulfill the Law. Let us look at that word. *Pleroo* means to make full and complete, to supply whatever is missing. It also means to fill up a hollow and make it level, reminding us of Isaiah's declaration that the valleys of consciousness are to be lifted up and made level (Luke 3:4). It also means to bring something to fulfillment and finish it. Another meaning is to bring something into conformity with truth or reality. It is also the means to accomplish the desired goal.

So now Jesus is going to outline to us in what the Fulfilled Law he has brought to us consists. Logically, he takes up the subjects of the Ten Commandments

Ye have heard that it was said by them of old time, Thou shalt not kill; and whosoever shall kill shall be in danger of the judgment. The word *phoneuo* means to kill, just as does the Hebrew *ratsach* used in the Torah. "In danger" is a rather poor translation of *enochos*, which actually means to be liable or subject to something, with the implication of having incurred actual guilt. "Judgment" is a translation of *krisis*, which means a decision or declaration of justice, and implies a matter of Divine Law. It means both accusation and condemnation. We who have been conditioned by exoteric Christianity must note that there is no connotation or implication here of any after-death judgment by God. Rather, it tells us that those who break the Divine Law (*Ritam*) shall be subject to the law of cause and effect: Karma. Actually, Newton did a good job of defining karma when he formulated his universal law: For every action there is an equal and opposite reaction. That is, someone who kills a human being will himself be killed by a human being. It is that simple.

In the *Daily Prayer Book*, edited by Philip Birnbaum and published by Hebrew Publishing Company in New York, in the second chapter of the section entitled *Ethics of the Fathers*, the seventh section gives an incident from the life of Hillel, perhaps the greatest Rabbi in Jewish history, and a contemporary of Jesus: "He [Hillel] saw a skull floating on the surface of the water. He said to it: Because you drowned others, others have drowned you; and those who have drowned you shall themselves be drowned." Such a law implies reincarnation as a necessity, for reincarnation was an orthodox Jewish belief at the time of Jesus. (See *May a Christian Believe in Reincarnation?* for more about this.)

But I say unto you, That whosoever is angry with his brother without a cause shall be in danger of the judgment: and whosoever shall say to his brother, Raca, shall be in danger of the council: but whosoever shall say, Thou fool, shall be in danger of hell fire. The law stated in the Torah dealt only with actual physical murder, but now Jesus fills out and perfects that law. Since this verse has a lot of specific terms, and since the Bible Bullies use it to point a finger at whoever is at hand, we need to take a very close look at it.

First of all, this statement of Jesus is not about simple conflict. It is about *orgizo*–being provoked to anger or exasperation by another person. He does not simply censure that emotion, which is really thwarted ego, but causeless anger, and does not qualify it by speaking of a "just cause." What is he talking about then? He is speaking of a spontaneous wrath that just erupts without any cause whatsoever, a reflexive anger that indicates an inner turmoil that has no connection with the present situation, the breaking forth of a poisonous evil. Such a person is literally in danger of *krisis*, the divine law of karma. In this instance it is the bursting forth of a samskara, something from the past buried in the subconscious, an instinctual reaction that circumvents all reason or intelligence. It is not a moral transgression, but a danger–and a perilous one. The reason should be obvious. Many murders result from such anger, as well as a multitude of violent acts and words. So Jesus is telling us that such mindless negativity must be dealt with. But since it is not originating on the conscious level the cure must be deeply interior. A profound healing is needed, and meditation is the best and surest remedy of all.

Next, Jesus speaks of those who say to anyone (for all are our brothers) *raka*, which means: "O empty, worthless one!" It is an Aramaic word with a Hebrew root (*ruwq*) that implies a person that is an outcast, execrable and valueless. Now this may be the truth about a lot of words and deeds, but never about a human being that is made in the image and likeness of God, however buried that may be at the moment. To look upon any human being in this way is a terrible thing, for it can lead to great evils. Whenever we decide that someone or some type of person is not really human and need not be regarded as such, we commit the worst of wrongs. This is the basis of colossal social evils, as history attests. Those who engage in this shall be "in danger of the council," the word being *sunedrion* (sanhedrin). The idea is that those who engage in such vile attitudes shall be liable to society itself, and from society shall the retribution come. History proves this, too.

Finally, Jesus speaks of those who call another *moros*, the root word of our English "moron." It means someone who is not only stupid, but virtually unconscious, they are so devoid of understanding. What is interesting is that, as already said, it is believed to come from a root word that implies a person who is mute. Perhaps in this case it would mean mentally retarded. Whichever, it follows right along with the prior meaning: declaring that a person is mindless, worthless and therefore of no value at all. The consequence is also interesting: to be subject or liable to "hell fire." This is a thoroughly dishonest translation, made to boost the hellfire-and-damnation fixation of the Protestants favored by King James. The actual words are "*Gehenna* fire."

Gehenna, the Valley of Hinnom, was the garbage dump of Jerusalem. All kinds of filth was cast there, and they attempted to get rid of it by burning. But much was not really flammable, so the result was a continual smoldering and smoking. Almost always the Gospel says "Gehenna," where "hell" appears. Hell really comes from *adis* (hades), and only means the unseen world, having no connotation of a place of torment for the wicked. Maggots lived in Gehenna, but the fire never got rid of them. So Jesus spoke of Gehenna "where the worm dies not, and the fire is not quenched" (Mark 9:44) as a symbol of samsara, the realm of constant birth, suffering, and death. The soul experiences the death of the body so many times in the process of reincarnation, but it never really does die. It is a cycle of inevitable suffering. So those who denounce a fellow human being as *moros* are buying for themselves a return ticket to Gehenna. It is not the calling that brings that about, but the negative state of mind that inspires it. To wish suffering for others is to guarantee it for ourselves.

All these things listed by Jesus are a form of moral murder, a real destruction of another person's integrity. Any form of hatred is a form of murder, and of suicide, as well.

Therefore if thou bring thy gift to the altar, and there rememberest that thy brother hath ought against thee, leave there thy gift before the altar, and go thy way; first be reconciled to thy brother, and then come and offer thy gift. This is of course a spiritual principle that can be applied to far more than formal liturgical offering or activity. The fact is that spiritual life requires a complete cleaning up and straightening out of our life and personal relations at the very start. When Jesus went to the house of Zacchaeus (Luke 19:1-10), as a first step in spiritual life he promised the Lord that he would seek out every person he had wronged and set things right. This is very important, because ill-will has a way of developing into malice and hatred, going deep into the heart and poisoning the very well-springs of life. Many people live in this spiritually toxic state so long that they do not even realize the devastation it is working in them. Even more, they have become indifferent to the welfare of those that have wronged them or been wronged by them. It is a very dangerous state to be in, especially considering the way it becomes extended into future lives. Because of this, Jesus continues:

Agree with thine adversary quickly, whiles thou art in the way with him; lest at any time the adversary deliver thee to the judge, and the judge deliver thee to the officer, and thou be cast into prison. Verily I say unto thee, Thou shalt by no means come out thence, till thou hast paid the uttermost farthing. The word translated "adversary" is *antidikos*, which means anyone who opposes us and, justly, has something against us—someone we have in some way wronged. We owe them a karmic debt according to what our offense might be. And that debt should be willingly discharged by us as soon as possible lest it turn into something worse, be compounded and follow us into a subsequent life. The "judge" is the law of karma, and the "officer" is the means by which our karma comes to us. The prison is right here–the earth itself. And there will be no freedom from that prison until we have paid even the smallest karmic debt, for a farthing was the smallest coin used in the Roman Empire.

Origen said that most people were somas, physical bodies, rather than spirits. Their religion is the same, based on purely physical do's and don'ts, rarely taking into account either mind or spirit, unless it is to coerce others into believing their doctrines. Jesus had an entirely different perspective. Whereas the Ten Commandments were purely behavioral in nature, the Beatitudes were purely psychological and spiritual. Both approaches were needed, but at that time only the physical side was taken into account. Jesus contrasts the traditional way with the more complete view, saying:

> Ye have heard that it was said by them of old time, Thou shalt not commit adultery: But I say unto you, That whosoever looketh on a woman to lust after her hath committed adultery with her already in his heart.
>
> And if thy right eye offend thee, pluck it out, and cast it from thee: for it is profitable for thee that one of thy members should perish, and not that thy whole body should be cast into hell. And if thy right hand offend thee, cut if off, and cast it from thee: for it is profitable for thee that one of thy members should perish, and not that thy whole body should be cast into hell.
>
> It hath been said, Whosoever shall put away his wife, let him give her a writing of divorcement: But I say unto you, That whosoever shall put away his wife, saving for the cause of fornication, causeth her to commit adultery: and whosoever shall marry her that is divorced committeth adultery).
>
> Again, ye have heard that it hath been said by them of old time, Thou shalt not forswear thyself, but shalt perform unto the Lord thine oaths: but I say unto you, Swear not

at all; neither by heaven; for it is God's throne: nor by the earth; for it is his footstool: neither by Jerusalem; for it is the city of the great King. Neither shalt thou swear by thy head, because thou canst not make one hair white or black.

But let your communication be, Yea, yea; Nay, nay: for whatsoever is more than these cometh of evil.

Ye have heard that it hath been said, An eye for an eye, and a tooth for a tooth: but I say unto you, That ye resist not evil: but whosoever shall smite thee on thy right cheek, turn to him the other also.

And if any man will sue thee at the law, and take away thy coat, let him have thy cloke also. And whosoever shall compel thee to go a mile, go with him twain.

Give to him that asketh thee, and from him that would borrow of thee turn not thou away (Matthew 5:27-42).

Ye have heard that it was said by them of old time, Thou shalt not commit adultery: But I say unto you, That whosoever looketh on a woman to lust after her hath committed adultery with her already in his heart. "Lust" is only a partial translation of *epithumeo*, which means to obsess upon, to long for, covet, desire, and even lust after. Obviously, it is the final meaning that is mostly being considered, but the age-old urge to acquire another person as a kind of toy or possession is an egoistic denial of both the reality and the value of another human being. No matter how much the bluster may go on about how wonderful the object of that desire may be, it is really nothing more than selfish, predatory desire, however well it may be masked. Since in most cases there will be plenty of lustful imagination and projection, it is indeed mental adultery. And since the mind is what marks out the human being from the rest of the earth's inhabitants, this is no trifling matter.

Whenever we think of something intently a psychic connection is formed and we affect it and it affects us. There is an actual union or touching on a mental level. When an object is thought of with intense desire, a powerful connection is made, and that desire-energy is conveyed to the object. So to think of a person with any negative or destructive feeling, especially if it includes vivid mental imagery, is to harm them in some way unless their auras are so strong the energy is deflected. In which case it comes back and harms us, even if only by strengthening our obsession. So desire and lust are not personal, private things, but involve their object as well. Although lust is used here as an example, any negative intention or emotion creates a similar inner-plane situation. And in the same way positive thoughts and feelings can help and even heal another.

However, mental adultery is not as grave as physical adultery. I say that because I have known people who said that since thinking about something was doing it, then they might as well do it physically. That is morally insane. I knew a man that raped a woman because he claimed she had made him lust after her, and so the deed had been done anyway. He was, as you might imagine, a very devout and staunch church member, quite involved with liturgics and theology. But not with Christian life. He later married the woman and made her life even more miserable until they divorced (something prohibited in their particular church). So twisting the scriptures to suit our desires is a perilous endeavor.

And if thy right eye offend thee, pluck it out, and cast it from thee: for it is profitable for thee that one of thy members should perish, and not that thy whole body should be cast into hell. And if thy right hand offend thee, cut if off, and cast it from thee: for it is profitable for thee that one of thy members should perish, and not that thy whole body should be cast into hell. These verses are really misunderstood, and turned into a kind of threat and condemnation, when they are really cool-headed, wise counsels for those who aspire to higher consciousness.

First of all, the "right eye" is a symbol of our powers of perception, our mental makeup. Our mind, too, is material, but of a subtler, material and causal energy. Yet it is an objective entity and can be worked with and trained just as much as the physical body. This is the basis of all spiritual methodology, including yoga. It is not a matter of personal whim or a hit-or-miss chance that is mistakenly called the will of God.

Second, the word *skandalidzo* does not at all mean "offend you," but really means to ensnare, to trip up and make to stumble, or to entice to wrong or wrongdoing. All of this is in the province of delusion, and Jesus is saying that if any aspect of our mind and thought draws us toward ignorance and negativity, or fools us into committing folly on any level, it should be immediately and ruthlessly thrust from us and our life sphere, along with anything that fosters or creates it. Whatever weakens us should be cast aside. In this way we will avoid Gehenna fire, the pain and sorrow of samsara, not the wrath of God or any such blasphemous nonsense. It is all up to us. If we want to hold on to what makes us suffer, we are completely free to do so.

"Right hand" means any power or faculty by means of which we act. Any will or deed that sinks us into ignorance and evil, that operates on us like quicksand, stifling and drowning our true nature, must be thoroughly expunged from our heart and life if we would not be burned by the fires of karma.

These verses teach us that it is not a bit, a piece of us, that will suffer if we do not cast these things from us, but the whole of our being. Just as infection or disease in a single part can kill the whole body, so harboring a single germ of delusion can in time destroy our entire consciousness. We see this all the time. From a little thing, thought or deed, people are drawn down into the quagmire of ignorance and an entire lifetime is ruined, plus the habit of ignorance is reinforced for future lives. This is a serious and sobering thing. Yet, it is all our choice. God really does not come into it. We are free to live or die.

It hath been said, Whosoever shall put away his wife, let him give her a writing of divorcement: But I say unto you, That whosoever shall put away his wife, saving for the cause of fornication, causeth her to commit adultery: and whosoever shall marry her that is divorced committeth adultery. The obvious meaning here is that marriage should never be dissolved except for immorality, but there is more to it than that. The implication is that immorality alone dissolves a marriage. It is not a matter of an offense that is so serious it justifies divorce, but rather an act that has the inner, metaphysical effect of actually breaking the marriage bond. In such a case divorce is not a reaction of anger or disgust, but a recognition that the marriage is already destroyed and rendered invalid. The lesson here is, as I say, a metaphysical one.

Now obviously a marriage should not be continued in which one of the people is insane, tortures the other, beats the children, is a drunk or an addict, a criminal, etc. But in such cases the marriage remains intact on the subtle levels of existence. That does not mean, however, that the innocent partner is obligated to keep living with the offender. But separation and divorce should only be done for serious matters, for it is the duty of both persons to take the marriage most seriously and value it. To capriciously separate or divorce is a very real crime against the other person. If the offender demands a divorce, the innocent one should grant it to be rid of them and should give thanks to God for their escape and stay away from further entanglements.

Remember, Jesus is speaking to the chosen twelve, not to everyone in general. He is explaining the law that binds the seeker for higher consciousness. Just as he said at the close of his life: "I pray for them [the disciples]: I pray not for the world, but for them which thou hast given me; for they are thine" (John 17:9), in the same way he is speaking of the law for seekers of higher consciousness. What other people do is their concern. The big problem is when we assume that what applies to seekers for God applies to everyone. It does not.

Again, ye have heard that it hath been said by them of old time, Thou shalt not forswear thyself, but shalt perform unto the Lord thine oaths: but I say unto you, Swear not at all; neither by heaven; for it is God's throne: nor by the earth; for it is his footstool: neither by Jerusalem; for it is the city of the great King. Neither shalt thou swear by thy head, because thou canst not make one hair white or black. Not only are false assertions or oaths (forswearing) to be avoided, all oaths whatsoever made in connection with something ("I swear by God." "I swear on my life." "I swear that if I am lying, may… happen to me." "I swear by all that is holy.") are not to be made by us. For example, in England they say: "I swear by almighty God." Not to be done. Here in America we do not swear by anything, but say that we solemnly swear/vow to tell the truth. It is important to make the distinction between saying "I swear" and "I swear by…." The context shows that Jesus is making this distinction. Those who say it is contrary to Jesus' teachings to say "I swear" are not reading the Gospel carefully enough. Jesus explains why in the next verse.

But let your communication be, Yea, yea; Nay, nay: for whatsoever is more than these cometh of evil. An honest person need only speak the truth, declaring that it is the truth. His integrity should be his security. Adding in all kinds of oaths or declarations to emotionally manipulate the hearers or impress them is wrong, for the speech of an evolved or evolving person carries power and must be carefully used. Theatrics are not for the honest person. Either what we say is true or it is not. It must stand on itself, needing no other basis.

Jesus is also telling us that we should be very direct and honest in our speech. Yes must never mean Maybe or an avoidance of saying No. No must never mean You Have To Plead With Me, or I Will Think It Over. We must both speak and live in a straight line. And Yes should never indicate we are in a good mood or No that we are in a bad mood, as is the case with children and childish adults. We must say what we mean and mean what we say. There must be truth in word and deed. There must be no inconsistency between our thoughts, words, and deeds.

Ye have heard that it hath been said, An eye for an eye, and a tooth for a tooth: but I say unto you, That ye resist not evil: but whosoever shall smite thee on thy right cheek, turn to him the other also. Jesus is not telling us to invite more abuse, but is dramatically conveying to us the idea that because someone wrongs us is not justification for wronging or resenting him in return. "He asked for it" is not an acceptable attitude. We must not return evil for evil. As the cliché says, two wrongs do not make a right, however much that is the common attitude.

The law of karma must be kept in the foreground of our mind when considering Jesus' words. The person who slaps us creates the karma to be slapped himself in the future. And if we slap them back, we create karma for getting another slap ourselves in the future! Where will it end? It will only end for us if we follow the policy of non-retaliation mentally, verbally and physically. Also, we must realize that they hit us because it was our karma–a past slap coming back to us. So whom should we blame? Only ourselves. This is not easy to do, but we are supposed to be striving for higher life. In the light of that ambition, it is a small requirement to so do.

It is not Jesus' intention for us to not stand up against evil. But when we have these personal misfortunes we must understand their cause and not think we can retaliate and be guiltless. If someone starts to hit us, we can step out of the way, but we do not hit them back and create a new karma.

And if any man will sue thee at the law, and take away thy coat, let him have thy cloke also. And whosoever shall compel thee to go a mile, go with him twain. This is not a negative passivity, but a compassion for the demander. It is also a freeing from all karmic obligations from the past. It was the law that a Roman soldier could compel an ordinary citizen to carry things for him to the distance of one mile, but no further. The Romans were occupying Israel, and were the oppressors, so they were not beloved by anyone Jesus was speaking to. Yet Jesus says to go another mile beyond the obligation. That is generous and noble, a gift of kindness to those that were usually unkind. But notice that he did not say to go any further because that would be foolish and lacking in self-respect. Good sense is an essential ingredient of spiritual life, not noble foolishness.

As has been said, Jesus is not advocating a spineless, timid passivity. Rather, he is advising us to realize that these situations, and many like them, are a matter of karma, and we must respond to them intelligently and positively. If we resist we will create even more negative karma.

If it is a matter of reaping bad karma, we should reap it and go on. If part of that karma involves others, then we must do good to them, no matter how negative they have been. For in this way we neutralize the karma we have created in the past by being ourselves like they are in the present. We may do more than pay the karmic debt, we may create positive karma through kindness and generosity.

Jesus is speaking about how to live life: if negativity comes, accept it and learn from it. If we are compelled to do something that is good we should not just do it minimally, but do it abundantly.

Give to him that asketh thee, and from him that would borrow of thee turn not thou away. Do you remember the tiresome little children that would visit someone's house and say: "I'm going to take this home," or: "Can I have this"? Well, they grow up and have the same selfish, irresponsible outlook. Jesus is not advising us to give them anything but the gate. Otherwise we would have nothing, and neither would they, since they would have frittered it away immediately. When a drunk asks you for money for food he means money for booze. Respond to his real request by refusing. As Sri Ramakrishna used to say: "Be a devotee, but why a fool?"

Also, you can only give what you really have. It is foolish to deprive yourself because someone asks you for what little you possess. If you do not have enough to give away, then you are justified in saying that you have nothing to give; this is simple good sense.

However, when we can really help and not just be throwing away our resources to no good, we are obligated to do so, recalling the principle: "thy neighbor as thyself." Such assistance is not the charity that the egotistical so indignantly refuse, but rather a sharing of what we have received from God. It is an investment in our neighbor and in ourself, for "it is more blessed to give than to receive" (Acts 20:35).

There is an important implication in this verse. There are two kinds of people: those that have need and cannot pay you back, and those that are in need but can pay you back in the future. We have considered the first type, now we should look at the second.

Jesus says that there are those that want to borrow from us. Now the wording here in very interesting. For centuries the Church authorities, especially in the West, said that it was wrong to loan money at interest, that it was the sin of usury. This being so, Christians would not loan money, so everybody went to borrow money from the Jews, who were then denounced as greedy and merciless when they rightly demanded repayment. Considering that Jews were not allowed to own property, but were forced to rent from Christians, and were regularly looted of all they had on the pretense that they had crucified Jesus (did the American people shoot Abraham Lincoln?), and were at any time liable to be tossed out of the country and dispossessed of everything: who were the greedy and merciless ones? The "righteous," as usual.

Anyway, the word *daneidzo* means "to borrow on interest." So it is not greedy, selfish, or unChristian to loan someone money and charge interest, providing the interest rate is just and even charitable. Loaning is also a form of sharing. The broader principle here is that we should always help the worthy, those that *can* be helped, in whatever way we are able. But if we give to those that are not truly in need or will waste what they receive, we are collaborating with their thievery and prodigality. "Turn not thou away" does not mean to give foolishly.

> **Ye have heard that it hath been said, Thou shalt love thy neighbour, and hate thine enemy. But I say unto you, Love your enemies, bless them that curse you, do good to them that hate you, and pray for them which despitefully use you, and persecute you.**
>
> **That ye may be the children of your Father which is in heaven: for he maketh his sun to rise on the evil and on the good, and sendeth rain on the just and on the unjust (Matthew 5:43-45).**

Ye have heard that it hath been said, Thou shalt love thy neighbour, and hate thine enemy. But I say unto you, Love your enemies, bless them that curse you, do good to them that hate you, and pray for them which despitefully use you, and persecute you. In the New Testament two words are translated "love": *agapao* and *phileo*. *Phileo* means to be a friend, to be fond of someone, to have real affection for them. To have such feelings for our enemies would be incredibly noble, but since in a few verses we are going to be called to the perfection of God himself, that is not enough. Instead we are told by Jesus that our feeling for our enemies must be *agapao*, the highest form of spiritual love that is based not on feeling or emotion, but on intelligent will. Those who exercise this level of love do so by choice, by enlightened understanding. They see with the eyes of God, who is love, and act accordingly.

Before this it was stated that we should love our neighbor, and the same word, *agapao*, was employed. "Neighbor" is a translation of *plesion*, which literally means anyone who is near by–in other words, any person we meet or contact. So when we put these two together we are told to love everyone–not just innocuous people who are at hand, but even those who hate us and wish us harm, even doing us harm by speech or action. God loves everyone, seeing everyone as an extension of his own Being.

That is why we are told to love "thy neighbor as thyself." This is a literal truth. But Jesus has expanded this to include our enemies, so there will be no exceptions. How can we love everyone? Only by becoming one with God. Until then we must set our will to love them and look for the day when it will be an actuality.

Bless them that curse you. This is a hard one. The word translated "bless" is actually *eulogeo*, the word from which we get "eulogy." It means to speak well of someone, to bless them in the sense of thanking them or invoking a benediction on them, and even to praise them. Not easy! And we are to bless in this way those that "curse" us. The Greek word is *kataraomai*, which means to execrate, imprecate, condemn and curse. Truly there is good in everyone, however hard it may be to perceive, and since those that curse us are being instruments of our karma and bringing about our purification (if we respond in the right way) they do merit our thanks. It is easy to pray for God to bless such people, that is just good sense (and good karma), but to completely fulfill this injunction we must become saints. So we can use those defamers and cursers as goads to push us forward on the path to God.

Do good to them that hate you. Kalos means good, but it also means means to be honest and fair, virtuous, fitting, worthy, and better than what has been received. In other words, there is no tit-for-tat here, but we must react in a much better way than we have been treated. It is a matter of seeing truly, of understanding the inner suffering that manifests in negative behavior, and of returning healing for actual or attempted injury. We must respond virtuously, otherwise we have no virtue. So these people are a valuable test for us. Those to whom we are to respond in this way are those that hate us. *Miseo* means to hate, detest, and even persecute. We must counteract the bitter with the sweet. We must not just think kindly about them; if the chance arises we must actively help and benefit them. The loving and blessing we have previously been told about are psychological, but this response is overt and practical. It is the living out of the beatitude: "Blessed are the merciful."

Pray for them which despitefully use you, and persecute you. We all know what prayer is, especially intercessory prayer for the blessing of others.

This we must offer for two kinds of people: *epireadzo* and *dioko*. The first are those that insult, slander, threaten, injure, and falsely accuse us. Their harm is usually verbal, whereas the second are those that persecute, pursue, hound, and oppress us overtly, trying to intimidate, demoralize, and fill us with fear. During Nero's persecution of the Christians the Romans often joked that if Nero got lost in the catacombs where the Christians were hiding from the soldiers sent to arrest or kill them, they would feed him, give him new clothes and lead him out of the maze. Pray, pray, and pray some more–that is what we must do. And at the same time we must use good sense and not let ourselves be run over and oppressed.

Here is some practical wisdom from Sri Ramakrishna.

"Listen to a story. Some cowherd boys used to graze cattle in a meadow where a very poisonous snake lived. Everyone moved about with great caution for fear of the snake. One day a brahmachari [monk] was going through the pathway across the meadow. The cowherd boys came running to him and said, 'Revered sir, please do not go that way. A very poisonous snake lives over there.' The brahmachari said, 'So be it, my good boys! I have no fear of that! I have a charm.' So saying, the brahmachari went that way. Out of fear the cowherd boys did not accompany him. Now the snake was moving swiftly toward him raising its hood; but no sooner did it come near the brahmachari than he recited a charm and the snake at once lay down at his feet like an earthworm. The brahmachari said, 'Hi, why do you keep injuring others? Come, I will give you a sacred formula [mantra]. If you repeat it you will acquire love of God; you will realize God and no longer have a violent nature.'

"So saying he gave the mantra to the snake. The snake bowed down to the teacher after it had received the mantra and asked, 'How shall I practice spiritual discipline?' The teacher said, 'Repeat this sacred word and do not harm anybody.' As he was leaving the brahmachari said, 'I shall come again.'

"Some days passed and the cowherd boys noticed that the snake no longer came forward to bite. Even if they threw stones it did not get angry, as if it had turned into an earthworm. One day one cowherd boy went near, took it by the tail and whirling it round and round dashed it again and again on the ground and threw it away. The snake began to bleed at the mouth and became unconscious. It did not move at all. The cowherd boys thought that the snake had died and so thinking, they all left.

"The snake regained consciousness late at night and crawled back slowly with great difficulty into its hole. Its bones were broken and it could not move. After many days when it was no more than skin and bones it would come out at night to crawl around looking for food. It did not come out during the day because of fear, and it never harmed anyone since receiving the mantra from the teacher. It lived on dirt, leaves and fruit which had dropped from the trees.

"About a year later the brahmachari came that way again and immediately made inquiries about the snake. The cowherd boys said that the snake had died. But the brahmachari did not believe it. He knew that the snake would never pass away without accomplishing the mission of the mantra. So he went searching, going in its direction and calling it by the name he had given it. Hearing the voice of the teacher it came out of the hole and made a bow with great devotion. The brahmachari asked, 'How are you?' It said, 'I am all right, sir!' The brahmachari said, 'But why then are you so thin?' The snake said, 'Sir, you commanded me not to do harm to anybody. It is perhaps because of living on leaves and fruits that I have become thin.' It had acquired the mood of sattva (serenity) and so it had no anger against anybody. It almost forgot that the cowherd boys nearly killed it. The brahmachari said, 'Such a condition is never the result of mere lack of food. There must be other reasons; just think.' The snake then remembered that the cowherd boys had dashed it against the ground. Then it said, 'Master, I remember now. One day the cowherd boys flung me against the ground. They were ignorant about the condition of my mind. How could they know that I would not bite or do harm to anyone?' The brahmachari said, 'Shame on you! You are such a fool that you do not know how to protect yourself. I told you just not to bite but never not to hiss. Why did you not scare them away by hissing?'

"One should scare wicked people away by hissing at them lest they do harm; one should not, however, inject poison into them or harm them."

The Mosaic Law was lacking, and Jesus is speaking of the Greater Law that is complete, fulfilled. But whereas the Mosaic Law was intended to produce right action, this Law has a far, far greater purpose:

That ye may be the children of your Father which is in heaven: for he maketh his sun to rise on the evil and on the good, and sendeth rain on the just and on the unjust. Mary Baker Eddy pointed out in *Science and Health* how unwise it was to assume that because our family members often have a disease or defect that we will be subject to it ourselves, and yet not realize that we are even more subject to the virtues and glories of our Heavenly Father. There are physical and spiritual genetics, and we should be intent on the spiritual ones. Just as diet and environment cause the physical genes to manifest, in the same way spiritual diet and environment will bring out our divine genes. Since it is a matter of innate nature we need not attain divinity, but manifest it. Since the divine nature has been buried beneath the debris of countless lifetimes we must labor to unearth and release it. Right thought and right action are potent tools for this deliverance. That is why Jesus has explained to us what it is to fulfill the Law, so we may be revealed as the offspring-images of God.

Who are the evil, good, just and unjust people he has mentioned? The word *poneros*, translated "evil," is very interesting. It comes from the root *ponos*, which means great travail and pain resulting from intense desire. So Jesus is not speaking of "bad" or "evil" people in the usual negative sense. He is speaking of people who are afflicted and driven by their own misguided wills, who are slaves of material consciousness and its attendant desires. They are not to be condemned but healed, and if they are not interested in healing they should be treated kindly and not pestered and missionaried. *Poneros* carries the connotation of being diseased, and even blind. This, too, is meant spiritually and not in a condemnatory way. The picture given is of the blind frantically grasping after what gives them only pain. Of course God sends blessing on them as much as on the good, for in time they will be the good. Until then they are to be regarded with sympathy.

As could be anticipated, *agathos*, the word translated "good," also has a purely spiritual meaning and has little to do with the standard "goodness" of exoteric religion of whatever tradition. *Agathos* means having a good constitution or nature—in this instance, someone who manifests his true spiritual Self. It also implies personal health and benefit to others—in a spiritual sense, of course. A good person is healthy in spirit and uplifts others, not only by words and deeds but by his natural spiritual radiation. (I have known saints whose mere presence cured physical disease and awakened spiritual consciousness.) The secondary meanings are significant, too: pleasant, agreeable, joyful, happy, distinguished and honorable. Such is the description of a true yogi.

Dikaios, the word translated "just" is another multilayered term. It means "righteous" in the very literal sense of being "right" or "true" as in building, following the divine pattern exactly and being "straight" in all things. It also means a person who is fit for living, the equivalent of *adhikari* in Sanskrit. This, too, has many connotations, one of the most important being one who in all things lives according to the divine law. And by "divine law" is not meant a body of scriptural rules regarding what God supposedly likes and dislikes, but rather the true order of things in the universe.

This is one of the major points of difference between Eastern and Western religion. In Western religion "the law" is given to others by some individual(s) making the claim to a revelation. In Eastern religion "the law" is that which not only has been the uniform experience of seekers of all ages, but which every single aspirant can come to experience for himself. For experiential knowledge, not belief or "fear of God," is the basis of his understanding of the law. In the East, something is not true because the scriptures say so, but the other way around: because something is true the scriptures state it. No one is crazy enough to think that two and two are four because a math book says so, and the spiritually sane do not think a scripture is the truth, but rather that it records the truth—a truth that all can come to know for themselves. It is all based on simple reality, not the whims of a dictatorial or testy deity.

So a just person is one who follows the divine pattern of the path to liberation, who intentionally observes the rules of the universe in order to ascend upon them, like the rungs of a ladder, to higher consciousness. Another secondary meaning is that of being correct and faultless in that ascent. In such a just person the divine image is clear and undistorted.

Finally, *dikaios* has an interesting root: *deiknuo* which means one who shows and proves something, who demonstrates or teaches by his living example. This is the real value of the saints and masters of the spiritual life. They are living expositions of Divine Reality. Naturally, Swami Sivananda comes to my mind in this matter, because he was living proof of the divine potential of humanity. As I have said before, in him I saw every possible virtue revealed to the maximum degree. He proved the truth of Sanatana Dharma; he incarnated it. He was indeed one of the "just men made perfect" (Hebrews 12:23), who pointed us to the way of similar perfection. He made us confident that we, too, could "go and do likewise" (Luke 10:37).

And who are the unjust? The *adikos*, those who are the opposite of the just, lacking their qualities and their capacities, not because goodness is not innate in them, but because they have not yet developed it. Because of this lack, they constantly think, speak and act contrary to cosmic law, to reality itself. Therefore they suffer and undergo constant birth and death, not as a punishment but as a simple consequence. When we get burned by touching fire we are not being punished. In the same way no sorrow or misfortune is a punishment from God. Rather, it is a lesson to be learned. If we learn it we will not be burnt in the future; but if we do not learn, we will keep on getting burned. It is all up to us. God has nothing to do with it.

The root word, *dike*, does carry the connotation of someone suffering the consequences of wrongdoing. It is, however, their own doing. As Isaiah said: "The wicked are like the troubled sea, when it cannot rest, whose waters cast up mire and dirt" (Isaiah 57:20). Again, it has nothing to do with "God's wrath" (an impossibility, anyhow). That is why Isaiah also said: "Woe unto the wicked! it shall be ill with him: *for the reward of his hands shall be given him.*" (Isaiah 3:11). It is all a matter of karma, the basic law of the universe. The universe is like a mirror or an echo: it reflects back to us our own doing. As Solomon said of the unjust: "They eat the bread of wickedness, and drink the wine of violence" (Proverbs 4:17). Until they lose the taste for such a diet, there will be no end to the natural and inevitable reactions. "For whatsoever a man soweth, that shall he also reap" (Galatians 6:7). It is simple metaphysical mathematics.

In conclusion, we must realize that God sends blessing on all because all are going to the Goal, all are evolving to perfection. Today's righteous were the unrighteous of yesterday, and today's unrighteous will be tomorrow's righteous. This is the happy and blessed truth of things.

The Golden Rule

And as ye would that men should do to you, do ye also to them likewise (Luke 6:31).

Here we have The Golden Rule, which Jesus would no doubt have learned in India from the Buddhist texts–for Buddha said these very words centuries before Jesus cited them.

Being Nice To Others is a good idea, but both Buddhists and Christians miss the real meaning of this: the Law of Karma. Whatever we do to others shall be done to us. "Whatsoever a man soweth, that shall he also reap" (Galatians 6:7). If this does not get the idea across to us, more words certainly will not.

For if ye love them which love you, what reward have ye? do not even the publicans the same? (Matthew 5:46).

Having told us that God is benevolent to all in equal measure, Jesus asks this pertinent question. To only love or like those who love or like us is egotism. Even further from egotism is the ability to love or like those who are not lovable or likable, at least when judged from externals or their behavior. When Jesus prayed for those who hated him and had brought about his impending death (Luke 23:34), he gave us the example to follow. Undoubtedly only Christs can rise to such heights, but if Christhood is not our aspiration, we are not worthy aspirants. It must be our endeavor at all time to see with the eyes of spirit and acknowledge all sentient beings as part of the Divine Life, inseparable from that Life and therefore inseparable from us. To do otherwise is to be as the publicans, the tax collectors that were universally hated. They were given no salary by the Roman government, but were allowed to take and keep as much money as they could get above the amount wanted by Rome. So they were civilly franchised thieves. Only the most despicable would engage in such a profession. They employed any evil means to extract money from their victims, and there was no appeal from their oppression. So when Jesus hints that those who do not follow the high level he is presenting are really no better than the publicans, he is letting us know how crucial this is for our spiritual development.

> **And if ye do good to them which do good to you, what thank [benefit; satisfaction] have ye? for sinners also do even the same. And if ye lend to them of whom ye hope to receive, what thank have ye? for sinners also lend to sinners, to receive as much again. But love ye your enemies, and do good, and lend, hoping for nothing again; and your reward shall be great [abundant], and ye shall be the children of the Highest: for he is kind unto the unthankful [ungrateful] and to the evil. Be ye therefore merciful [compassionate], as your Father also is merciful (Luke 6:33-36).**
>
> **Take heed that ye do not your alms before men, to be seen of them: otherwise ye have no reward of your Father which is in heaven. Therefore when thou doest thine alms, do not sound a trumpet before thee, as the hypocrites do in the synagogues and in the streets, that they may have glory of men. Verily I say unto you, They have their reward.**
>
> **But when thou doest alms, let not thy left hand know what thy right hand doeth: that thine alms may be in secret: and thy Father which seeth in secret himself shall reward thee openly (Matthew 6:1-4).**

Although "alms" is usually monetary assistance given to the poor, *eleemosune* (from the root *eleos*) means any kindness or help given to another human being. The important thing about this word is that it means deeds that spring from genuine mercy and kindness, from a positive, caring attitude toward those being helped. That is the real virtue being commended to us. It is not a mechanical "doing good" from any other motivation than a loving desire to help someone else. Good will is definitely implied here, as well. It is a reflection of the lovingkindness toward all that characterizes God. The merciful truly are the godly.

So Jesus is telling us that when we do a kindness we must never wish it to be known and admired by others. For if that is our motive there will be no positive karma–*misthos*, or reward–coming to us. That is because anything we give will really be for us, not others. Karma is a revelation of the truth of all our actions.

Salpidzo really means "make a trumpet sound" in the sense of making a big noise about something. A great many individuals and institutions make a very loud trumpet sound so they will get more and more money. The statement that "X percent of all money will go to X" is a classic method (the really hard cases only say: "*a percentage* will go…"), as are the countless numbers of "donate to relief for the victims of X" that appear overnight after a major natural disaster. (I am not speaking of legitimate organizations whose purpose is the relief of the unfortunate, but the opportunists that proliferate every time there is a real need.).

The word translated "hypocrite" is *upokrites*, which both means someone who is false and someone who is making a display of themselves to gain admiration and good will. False philanthropists abound, especially the type that make a point of letting people know their good deeds to offset the fact that they are foul in their morals and general lifestyle.

In Greek they have a very appropriate expression: *agia fania*–holy show. We must avoid it, and any self-display, if we would be real seekers for higher consciousness.

If our left hand does not know what the right hand is doing, then certainly no other person will know. The idea here is the need for utmost secrecy in our well-doing. For if we do good in secret, then the all-knowing God will recompense us outwardly–not by any intermediary, but directly Himself. Such is not mere karma, but divine blessing. The implication here is that mercy directly "reaches" God, whereas a lot of praying and religious behavior goes nowhere. After all, "thy neighbor as thyself" is the second part of the Great Commandment (Matthew 22:39).

Go Within!

And when thou prayest, thou shalt not be as the hypocrites are: for they love to pray standing in the synagogues and in the corners of the streets, that they may be seen of men. Verily I say unto you, They have their reward. But thou, when thou prayest, enter into thy closet, and when thou hast shut thy door, pray to thy Father which is in secret; and thy Father which seeth in secret shall reward thee openly. But when ye pray, use not vain repetitions, as the heathen do: for they think that they shall be heard for their much speaking. Be not ye therefore like unto them: for your Father knoweth what things ye have need of, before ye ask him (Matthew 6:5-8).

Because the danger of ego is always lurking, and because religion is perhaps the most fertile ground for it, Jesus advises this. He is not censuring public, corporate prayer, unless it is only for show. In all religions there are ways people can be exaggerated in their devotion, including making a spectacle of themselves by eccentric behavior and exaggerated discipline. No country and no culture is free from this kind of aberration.

In *Raja Yoga*, Swami Vivekananda wrote: "All over the world there have been dancing and jumping and howling sects, who spread like infection when they begin to sing and dance and preach; they also are a sort of hypnotists. They exercise a singular control for the time being over sensitive persons, alas! often, in the long run, to degenerate whole races. Ay, it is healthier for the individual or the race to remain wicked than be made apparently good by such morbid extraneous control. One's heart sinks to think of the amount of injury done to humanity by such irresponsible yet well-meaning religious fanatics. They little know that the minds which attain to sudden spiritual upheaval under their suggestions, with music and prayers, are simply making themselves passive, morbid, and powerless, and opening themselves to any other suggestion, be it ever so evil. Little do these ignorant, deluded persons dream that whilst they are congratulating themselves upon their miraculous power to transform human hearts, which power they think was poured upon them by some Being above the clouds, they are sowing the seeds of future decay, of crime, of lunacy, and of death. Therefore, beware of everything that takes away your freedom. Know that it is dangerous, and avoid it by all the means in your power."

But thou, when thou prayest, enter into thy closet, and when thou hast shut thy door, pray to thy Father which is in secret; and thy Father which seeth in secret shall reward thee openly. On the external level this means to find a solitary place and pray secretly, making sure that no one knows about it. I have known people who made a big show of going away to pray and staying a long time doing heaven-knows-what so others would be impressed. Some always prayed whenever they were needed to do something, so they could control others by making them wait until they returned to earth. They were, every one, sociopaths, believing in themselves rather than in God. This includes the yogis that get extremely meditative when it is time to eat. It virtually impels them into samadhi! Especially if they are the "let's all join hands" type.

What Jesus is really talking about is meditation, for he was a yogi in the Indian tradition–a yogi-monk, actually. Remember, the word translated "prayer" means "to draw near," an expression far more applicable to meditation than mere prayer.

Tameion means an inner, secret room for the storing of valuables. Every house needed one in those days when there were no banks or other pubic depositories. In some areas of India this is still the practice, and many brahmins keep their precious palm-leaf manuscripts there. The body is a house, for it harbors the eternal atman-spirit. In meditation we enter into our inmost consciousness, our Self. That is the most inner, secret "room," for it can never be entered or even known by anyone but ourselves and God. This is where yoga takes place.

Shut thy door. The "door" is manifold: the five senses, the lower, sensory mind, and the intellect. It is good to eliminate any external distractions from the place of our meditation, but the real closing of the door is the withdrawing of our awareness into our spirit-consciousness. Meditation is the best way to shut the door and keep it shut.

Meditation is not something abstract, fluffy, or daft; it is eminently practical. Just as we sleep so we can wake and engage in outer activity, it is the same with meditation. It is intended to awaken, develop, and stabilize our consciousness in order that outside meditation we will be able to "walk in the spirit" (Galatians 5:16, 25) all the time. That is why Jesus said we shall be "rewarded openly."

Apodidomi means to give what is due. Meditation creates the most effective spiritual karma, and God dispenses it to us directly, according to Jesus. The yogi does not need a chain of intermediaries in his life, but lives directly unto God.

The spiritual karma accrued in meditation will of course be a matter of inner consciousness, but since the external is a mirror of the internal, we shall also reap openly what we have sown inwardly in secret. Our yoga life will manifest in our daily conduct and in the entire ordering of our life. By meditation a yogi erases karmic bonds and impels himself toward freedom.

No one can practice authentic yoga and not change–inside and out. Yoga is not a cosmetic or a gimmick; yoga changes the life, unless the yogi foolishly abandons the practice and lapses into his former condition. Yoga also changes the yogi's environment, sometimes getting him out of it. Many yogis quit because they cannot endure the change or withstand the opposition of those around them. America's Westward Expansion and yoga are fundamentally the same: "The cowards never started, and the weak died along the way." It is not accidental that the life-giving teachings of the Gita were given on a battlefield. "Fight the good fight, lay hold on eternal life" (I Timothy 6:12).

"Can a man take fire in his bosom, and his clothes not be burned?" (Proverbs 6:27). No more can a person practice yoga meditation and not have his inner and outer life purified "as by fire" (I Corinthians 3:15).

And that means change–yes, continual change, for his consciousness will continually change and evolve until all change ceases in divine perfection.

Those who do not wish change–drastic change–or are not willing to pray the price for it, should never take up yoga, "lest haply, after he hath laid the foundation, and is not able to finish it, all that behold it begin to mock him, saying, This man began to build, and was not able to finish" (Luke 14:28-29). This is just the fact. For Jesus says the change will be *faneros*–open, broad, and widely known. One meaning of the word is "plainly seen and known." Negative associates (including family members) may not have an intellectual knowledge of the yogi's inner work, but will intuit it and be even more insistently and virulently opposed to it, engaging in hand-to-hand combat literally or figuratively to stop his practice. As Jesus warned: "A man's foes shall be they of his own household" (Matthew 10:36). I have observed for nearly half a century that this is true, though not inevitable, for it really depends on how much negativity is in the beginning yogi himself. Many use others as an excuse for abandoning the yoga life. I have seen some abandon it when their friends and families were actually supportive and wanting them to continue because they saw how much it was benefitting them. It all comes down to ourselves in the end–and the beginning.

But when ye pray, use not vain repetitions, as the heathen do: for they think that they shall be heard for their much speaking. Be not ye therefore like unto them: for your Father knoweth what things ye have need of, before ye ask him. Jesus is not referring to mantra japa, which is not prayer but invocation. There is a great difference between the two. Jesus is talking about people asking God for something over and over and over, as if He were deaf, forgetful (maybe even senile), or could be badgered by human beings into doing what they want. It is ridiculous, but it goes on everywhere. And it also applies to religious ceremony that goes on and on, saying and doing the same thing, with the same foolish motivation as mentioned.

Actually, Jesus is indicating in the latter part of the verse that God already knows what we need and will take care of it if we align ourselves to Him so His will can manifest in our life. It it just a matter of sympathetic vibration, which is what right prayer is. So Jesus now tells us about it.

The Lord's Prayer

> After this manner therefore pray ye: Our Father which art in heaven, Hallowed be thy name. Thy kingdom come. Thy will be done in earth, as it is in heaven. Give us this day our daily bread. And forgive us our debts, as we forgive our debtors. And lead us not into temptation, but deliver us from evil: For thine is the kingdom, and the power, and the glory, for ever. Amen (Matthew 6:9-13).

This is a model for prayer and also an outline of the spiritual perspective that each one should possess when praying. It is not just a verbal formula, it is also a pattern for living. At the same time, it is a spiritual invocation, a mantric formula whose repetition in a prayerful manner will infuse spiritual power in those that recite it. So much so, that it was often customary to recite the Lord's Prayer over and over. In later centuries it was usual for devout people to have strings of Pater Noster (Our Father) beads which were used to count the number of prayers–usually one hundred and fifty, corresponding to the one hundred and fifty psalms of the Psalter. In the original rule of the Carmelite Order a certain number of Our Father's were to be prayed at various times of the day to substitute for the formal liturgical "hours" of the Divine Office.

Our Father. In Greek and Latin it is *Pater Imon* and *Pater Noster*, so we should consider "Father" first. I have written enough about the meaning of "Father," so it can be simply said that it is a title of the Primal Godhead, the Transcendental Being known in Indian scriptures as Brahman. In Christianity whenever "God" is spoken of it usually means the Father, though it often means the entire Trinity. Being transcendent, He is also impersonal, as contrasted with "the Son" or Ishwara the Lord, the personal God.

How then is He ours in any sense of the term? Because He is our Source, or Progenitor. He did not create us–rather we derive our eternal existence from Him. We are a part of Him, incomprehensible as that may be to our presently limited minds, and are as eternal as He is. We are gods, as David and Jesus said (Psalms 82:6; John 10:34). We live in Him and He lives in us.

Which art in heaven. Since the Father is transcendent, beyond all space or place, how can He be in heaven? The word *ouranos* means the vast expanse of the sky, a symbol of Infinite Consciousness–the Chidakasha of Indian philosophy. God is never confined to any locale, nor is God contained by creation, although He pervades it. "Know me, eternal seed of everything that grows.... They are contained in me, but I am not in them.... That is why the world fails to recognize me as I really am. I stand apart from them all, supreme and deathless" (Bhagavad Gita 7:10, 12-13). We, too, are ever dwelling in the Chidakasha, but have "fallen" into the illusion of relative, mortal existence.

Hallowed be thy name. *Agiadzo* both means to make something holy and to acknowledge its holiness. The second meaning applies here. We are praying to truly and rightly acknowledge the holiness of the Name of God–which includes recognizing its identity with God. For *onoma*–name–is derived from *ginosko*, which means that which makes something known. Ordinary names are mere indicators of an object, but the Name of God *is* God–so the mystics of all religions have said, however much the exoterics of their traditions may have mocked or been outraged.

Thy kingdom come. This is the effect of hallowing the Name of God by Its continual invocation and employment as an object of meditation.

In its simplest meaning, *basileia* is the place where a king lives. God dwells in His kingdom, the *Ouranos*, the Chidakasha, the Consciousness of God. So we are praying for the advent of Divine Consciousness into our own consciousness, our transmutation into Divinity with which we are already one. *Basileia* also means dominion–rulership–and we pray that God will have absolute rule in our lives and in the world around us–not in the sense of absolute dictatorship, but rather that we and the world may be so attuned to the Divine that it will naturally manifest its will in all things.

There is also another meaning: royal power, which we pray may come to us so we may reign over all the aspects of our lives, that we may be kings in the small kingdom of our own being and the sphere of our life. That this is supposed to be, is shown twice in Revelation: "[Jesus Christ] hath made us kings" (Revelation 1:6; 5:10).

We pray that the heavenly kingdom should come. *Erxomai* means for something to come from one place to another–to arrive–for the Divine Consciousness to descend into our consciousness and assume it to itself. It also means for something to be perceived, to be recognized. In that sense we are praying to have the ever-present kingdom revealed to our inner sight, to have the Divine Vision. And finally it means for something to become permanently established so it will never go away. For this, too, we pray.

Thy will be done in earth, as it is in heaven. The Greek word for will–*thelema*–means more than a mere desire or wish. It means a determination, a setting forth of the will, to cause something to exist or occur. We therefore pray for the Divine Purpose to be realized in us and in all sentient beings– that the Divine Pattern, the blueprint of creation, be perfectly manifested.

Presently there is a dichotomy between heaven and earth, between spirit and matter, between God and humanity. We pray for this conflict and disharmony to be dissolved and for a total union in which that which is now the lower will become identical with the higher–that the distinction between low and high will vanish and absolute unity prevail. We are really praying for earth to become heaven, for their estrangement to be ended forever.

Give us this day our daily bread. Certainly *didomi* means to give something to someone, but it means both to give spontaneously and to give in response to a request. This implies that we should actively seek that for which we pray, while being aware that God wills that we should have it. It also means to show something to someone. In this verse it means that we pray for God to reveal to us that which is already at hand, which has already been provided, but which in our spiritual blindness we do not perceive. As Kabir said, we are "fish athirst in water." *Didomi* has a final means of causing something to come into being, and implies an extension of the giver. This is the most esoteric meaning: we are praying that God should impart Himself to us and cause us to live in and on Him as our Daily Bread.

"Daily" (*epiousios*) means that which is necessary and which will fulfil all necessities as they arise. Actually, it means *perpetual*–day-by-day–rather than daily in our usual English sense.

Artos is leavened bread, but means food of any kind. This petition refers to material fulfilment only secondarily. The primary intention is a petition for continual spiritual nourishment and enlivenment.

And forgive us our debts, as we forgive our debtors. There are many unfortunate mistranslations in English Bibles, and this is one of them, because it fosters the false idea that we need God to forgive us. The word *aphiemi* means to dismiss or separate from something–to send it away. The petition here is for God to free us from something, to dismiss, to remove it from our life altogether.

We are seeking freedom from our karmic debts–from our liability to the law of sowing and reaping incurred by our past actions–and from the psychic distortions that our karmas have produced in us and that may impel us to future karmas. For human beings karma is a perpetual cycle, like the serpent that eats its own tail but keeps growing so it never is consumed or quits going round and round.

There are various ways to become free of karma, yoga practice being the most effective. But Jesus points out that a definite mental state is required–that of forgiving, letting go of–the debts others owe to us. For if we hold on to the wrongs and transgressions of others, our own will cling to us. If we have wronged another, in the future we must make amends. But if we wish to be freed from that compulsion, yet are not willing to let go of the karmic debts others have incurred by wronging us, we will never be freed ourselves. It is not a matter of God insisting that we be fair and observe the golden rule, but a matter of mental magnetism.

The mind is a field of subtle energies, a kind of energy mechanism worked by our intelligence. If our mind is not cleared, neither will our karma be expunged. For in the final analysis, karma is only the conditioning of our mind. For example, if we steal we shape our mind into thief consciousness that will both impel us to future theft on our part and also to be stolen from. In the same way, if someone steals from us and we resent and brood over it, thief consciousness will also be instilled in our minds, with the same results. Being one of the pure in heart is a very exalted thing, not easily accomplished, as we can see. Dedication to watchfulness over the mind and heart are absolutely necessary.

And lead us not into temptation. This is one of the most misunderstood sentences in the Bible, for on the surface it seems to imply that God will actually cause a person to be tempted to evil. But a little analysis will show its real meaning. The word *eisphero* means to bring someone into something in the sense of bringing them *among* something. *Peirasmos* means both temptation and testing, but it also means fruitless efforts and even adversity and affliction. So in this petition we are asking that we not find ourselves beset on every side, surrounded by negative forces or objects that could lead us astray, or in the midst of trials of strength and endurance, adversity and affliction, and useless or hopeless endeavors. In other words, we ask that our life path not lead us through any such things.

But deliver us from evil. We ask for God to keep us (*rhoumai*) from–or raise us above–the paths of life which would bring us into contact with things that are *poneros*–both outright negative, or which will bring us struggles, harrassment, hardships, dangers, and troubles in general, including mental and physical suffering. The basic root of *poneros* is *penes*, which means to be poor, to lack that which is needed. We beg to be spared the situations in life which would subject us to all these things.

In essence we pray God to be led away from negativity and its attendant miseries, to be able to say with David: "He restoreth my soul: he leadeth me in the paths of righteousness for his name's sake" (Psalms 23:3). For God had centuries before given the promise through the prophet Isaiah: "I will bring the blind by a way that they knew not; I will lead them in paths that they have not known: I will make darkness light before them, and crooked things straight. These things will I do unto them, and not forsake them" (Isaiah 42:16).

This is only reasonable: to ask to be able to turn from our tangled way and move in the paths of God:

For thine is the kingdom, and the power, and the glory, for ever. Amen. To live in God is to live in His consciousness, His kingdom, where there is abundance of *dunamis*–power and strength–and *doxa*: glory, praise, and honor, splendor, and majesty–"the glorious condition of blessedness into which it is appointed and promised that true Christians shall enter" (Strong's definition). Amen–may it be so!

For if ye forgive men their trespasses, your heavenly Father will also forgive you: but if ye forgive not men their trespasses, neither will your Father forgive your trespasses (Matthew 6:14-15).

Jesus expounds only on the Lord's Prayer petition regarding forgiveness, because the ego is so prone to resentment and harboring ill will for supposed wrongs. Those who truly believe in and understand the law of karma realize that all which comes to them are merely their own past actions rebounding to them in kind. This was the first lesson I learned after awakening to the realities of karma and rebirth. In my life there had been people of exceptional cruelty and malice who had made my life truly a living hell. I had adamantly refused to brood over their words and actions, knowing that if I hated or even disliked them it would corrode me inside, producing an effect much worse than their hatred and malevolence. When I understood about karma I completely dismissed even the idea that they were at fault. Oh, yes, they were morally responsible in their personal life sphere, and had created negative karma for themselves. But they could have done nothing to me if I had not done the same things to others (perhaps even them) in a previous life. If I wanted anyone to blame it should be myself, none other. Further, since the reaping of karma is beneficial and a very necessary form of purification if we learn the necessary lessons from it, they had actually been instruments of good. I vividly remember looking at my main tormentor and thinking: "There is the 'cross that raiseth me,'" and from then on I had no trouble holding a friendly attitude toward that person, and in time we became the closest of friends, with deep love between us.

The Secret, Hidden Life of the Spirit

> Moreover when ye fast, be not, as the hypocrites, of a sad countenance: for they disfigure their faces, that they may appear unto men to fast. Verily I say unto you, They have their reward. But thou, when thou fastest, anoint thine head, and wash thy face; that thou appear not unto men to fast, but unto thy Father which is in secret: and thy Father, which seeth in secret, shall reward thee openly (Matthew 6:16-18).

We usually think of a hypocrite as someone who is insincere, pretending to be something they are not, and although that is the main meaning of *upokrites*, it also means someone who is putting on an act, literally a stage player. These kinds of people have plagued human society from the beginning, and religion is not free from them. They make sure that everyone knows all the good they do, and especially their supposed asceticism and nobility of personality. The matter of abstention from food is just an example, but Jesus has the whole range of holy show (*agia phania*) in mind.

For example, I knew a man that everyone spoke of in awe: "Why, did you know," they would say in hushed tones, "that he has given every penny he had to his children, and told them: 'Well, now I am just a charity case for you to look after or kick out if you want.'" They would just shiver when telling of this awesome renunciation. But it was all a sham. He lived in high style, drove around in the latest model Cadillac, dressed in expensive clothes, lived in a fine house, and spent huge sums of money. He had not surrendered anything to anyone, and on top of it was a drunk.

On the other hand, I knew a formerly wealthy woman in New Delhi that had truly given everything to her family, and lived in a corner of the temple room she had built at the top of the house. She had a couple of plain white saris, and sat and slept on an old-fashion canvas and wood frame army cot placed so she could always see the image of Krishna. The only thing she claimed was hers was an ancient japa mala that had belonged to her guru, and which he had given to her just before he left his body. To be in her presence was to be immersed in an atmosphere of holiness and humility. She lived in quiet simplicity with God. There are great teachers in India who do not allow anyone to even speak of their existence.

In India the religious hypocrites are especially addicted to putting on big tilaks, wearing huge beads (usually in enormous quantities), carrying around bright-colored bags with japa malas inside (which they only use, muttering mantras to themselves, when someone is looking at them) and all sorts of costumes from slick, expensive orange clothes (I saw one guru that had pierced the ends of his silk shirt-sleeves so he could put gold cufflinks in them), to disheveled rag-bag style. And the mythology about their ascetic feats is abundant. "He has drunk only Ganges water for the last forty years." "He is living on milk alone." "He only eats Neem leaves and amalaki." "He never rides in any vehicle, but only goes by foot." All the most shallow and meaningless crazes are indulged in by these people. And it is indulgence, not discipline.

Sri Ramakrishna often spoke of those who "meditate inside the mosquito net," meaning those who meditate in secret while others are sleeping. "There is the sattwa mood of devotion. The devotee of the sattwa mood meditates in great secret. He perhaps meditates inside the mosquito net. Everybody else thinks that he is perhaps sleeping, perhaps he had no sleep in the night and so is late in getting up. Further, his care for the body extends only to filling the stomach. A diet of rice and greens is good enough. No fuss about food and no ostentatiousness about dress."

The most important part of this passage from Matthew is the statement that God is "in secret." This is absolutely so: the true God is hidden in the depths of the heart, at the core of our being. And those who seek God live a hidden life. "And Jesus said, The kingdom of the Holy One is in the soul;

men cannot see it with their carnal eyes; with all their reasoning powers they comprehend it not. It is a life deep hid in God; its recognition is the work of inner consciousness" (Aquarian Gospel 75:15-16). Those who seek the Hidden God within, in a hidden manner, will find Him–also in a hidden manner.

There was a Buddhist monk whom people jokingly named Wintermelon because he seemed a completely useless blockhead. One day he left the town and was never seen again. He left behind a piece of paper on which he wrote a poem that concluded with the words: "I walk through the streets and no one guesses that Paradise [Sukhavati] is within." Once an over-educated wiseacre in China met an old woman who was walking along the road muttering the mantra of Amida Buddha. "Old lady," he sneered," are you thinking that you will go to Amida's Paradise when you die?" To his surprise, she emphatically shook her head. Being a confirmed fool, he tried another tack. "Where is your Amida Buddha, then?" She smiled, tapped her chest, and walked on.

> **Lay not up for yourselves treasures upon earth, where moth and rust doth corrupt, and where thieves break through and steal: but lay up for yourselves treasures in heaven, where neither moth nor rust doth corrupt, and where thieves do not break through nor steal: for where your treasure is, there will your heart be also (Matthew 6:19-21).**

People need to live, and there is nothing wrong with living above mere subsistence, but there is a great difference between using what we have and hoarding much more than we can ever need. This latter is foolish because it profits no one and in time will be left behind for others to (usually) fritter away. Think of the incredible amount of positive karma we can gain for ourselves if we use our excess to help others. One of my favorite stories is that of a very rich man whose will simply said: "I, being of sound mind, spent every penny I had."

All material things are subject to diminishment and disintegration, the "change and decay" of the popular hymn "Abide With Me." Therefore Jesus urges us to accumulate that wealth which is safely stored away in the higher reaches of our being (heaven) and which cannot be taken from us, especially the inner wealth of evolution in consciousness. Spiritual riches alone are a safe investment. As Jesus (Luke 10:41-42) said to Martha: "Thou art careful and troubled about many things: but one thing is needful," the treasure of the spirit.

Wherever we keep investing, there will be our heart, our center of attention, and vice versa. Since only spirit is real, it is simple practicality to keep investing in the spirit, in consciousness, through meditation and the yoga life.

> The light of the body is the eye: if therefore thine eye be single, thy whole body shall be full of light. But if thine eye be evil, thy whole body shall be full of darkness. If therefore the light that is in thee be darkness, how great is that darkness (Matthew 6:22-23).
>
> No man can serve two masters: for either he will hate the one, and love the other; or else he will hold to the one, and despise the other. Ye cannot serve God and mammon.
>
> Therefore I say unto you, Take no thought for your life, what ye shall eat, or what ye shall drink; nor yet for your body, what ye shall put on. Is not the life more than food, and the body than raiment?
>
> Behold the fowls of the air: for they sow not, neither do they reap, nor gather into barns; yet your heavenly Father feedeth them. Are ye not much better than they?.
>
> Which of you by taking thought can add one cubit unto his stature?.
>
> And why take ye thought for raiment? Consider the lilies of the field, how they grow; they toil not, neither do they spin: and yet I say unto you, That even Solomon in all his glory was not arrayed like one of these. Wherefore, if God so clothe the grass of the field, which to day is, and to morrow is cast into the oven, shall he not much more clothe you, O ye of little faith?

Therefore take no thought, saying, What shall we eat? or, What shall we drink? or, Wherewithal shall we be clothed? (For after all these things do the Gentiles seek:) for your heavenly Father knoweth that ye have need of all these things.

But seek ye first the kingdom of God, and his righteousness; and all these things shall be added unto you.

Take therefore no thought for the morrow: for the morrow shall take thought for the things of itself. Sufficient unto the day is the evil thereof (Matthew 6:16-34).

The light of the body is the eye: if therefore thine eye be single, thy whole body shall be full of light. The word translated "light" is *luchnos* which really means lamp or any device that emits light. The eye spoken of is the eye of perception, of consciousness, and includes the focus of our awareness. Jesus tells us that our eye must be "single" if our entire being, and therefore our life in general, is to be filled with light. *Haplous* means to be one in the sense of undivided, and comes from the root *pleko* which means gathered up into oneness. It is when we continually experience and perceive Unity that our life will be *photeinos*, not just full of light, but actually formed of light (*jyotirmayi*). We will see ourselves and all things as essentially Divine Light. This is a profound metaphysical principle, and just one of so many points in Jesus' teachings that prove him to be a messenger of Sanatana Dharma, having spent most of his life in India with the yogis.

But if thine eye be evil, thy whole body shall be full of darkness. If therefore the light that is in thee be darkness, how great is that darkness. The word *poneros* does not mean simple negativity, but the condition of being pulled in many directions, subject to many currents, filled with stress and even pain. It also implies a diseased or defective condition. It comes from the root word *ponos* which means intense trouble and pain. It designates the mental condition of being immersed in divided and conflicted consciousness, completely alienated from Unity and therefore plunged into an ocean of confusion and suffering. In that condition the individual is *skoteinos*, seemingly formed of darkness, blinded by ignorance. This is the opposite of the state described in the previous verse. Such a person sees himself in a completely deluded manner. If he is religious he will see himself as sinful and depraved by nature, even though the truth is he is essentially Light. Consequently "how great is that darkness" and how dark is his religion which is based on such untruth. Where will such a one find hope? Only when the liberating truths of the evolving spirit shine into his darkness can there be any hope at all.

No man can serve two masters: for either he will hate the one, and love the other; or else he will hold to the one, and despise the other. Ye cannot serve God and mammon. This is a continuation of the verses regarding the treasure of the heart and the habitual focus of consciousness. No matter what a person might say or think, dual attention is not possible: either we are intent on Spirit or on materiality (mammon). Either we value and love the one or the other. Our daily life will show which it is, not our words and ways when in spiritual situations in front of others. For example, in Indian texts we are told that we should notice what a person reflexively calls out when in sudden danger, pain, or fear, for that will be coming directly from his inner mind. But outside of that, our habitual mode of thinking, speaking and acting will give the clue. It is easy to act religious but only the genuine can truly live religiously. Most people need to heed the counsel of Swami Sri Yukteswar: "Examine your thoughts unremittingly for twenty-four hours. Then wonder no longer at God's absence" (*Autobiography of a Yogi*, Chapter Twelve). Here once more we see the value of: "Therefore, become a yogi!" (Bhagavad Gita 6:46).

Therefore I say unto you, Take no thought for your life, what ye shall eat, or what ye shall drink; nor yet for your body, what ye shall put on. Is not the life more than food, and the body than raiment? Behold the fowls of the air: for they sow not, neither do they reap, nor gather into barns; yet your heavenly Father feedeth them. Are ye not much better than they? These words have been interpreted very foolishly by many who wished to cloak their indolence with piety, faith, and supposed non-materialism. A man I knew told me that in his home town there was a neighbor who refused to do any kind of work. His wife supported him and their children by doing drudge work, mostly other people's laundries. In the good weather he sat for hours on the front porch with a Bible that had gilt edges flashing in the sunlight. He would slowly turn the pages from front to back, supposedly reading it. If his wife would call out and ask him to do the slightest thing to help her, he would smile broadly and reply: "Wife! 'Know ye not that I must be about my Father's business?'" Yet he was always in and at the table when it was time to eat.

At one time the pseudo-Franciscan "Spirituals" gave a great deal of trouble, even murdering the rich and looting their homes and businesses, claiming to follow Jesus' teaching in these verses. Yet they fully expected the "unspiritual" to work, make money, and support them in their immaterial glory. Money was a great evil only if it was not spent on them!

"Take no thought" is the translation of *me merimnao*, which means to not be anxious, troubled or worried. It does not mean to be idle and irresponsible. "Life" is a translation of *psuche* (not *dzoe*, which does mean life) which means the life of the body, literally, but also means the life-sphere of the transient personality or ego.

Jesus is telling us to not be anxious or fearful, but to do our best and realize that God will ensure that all will go well, and that includes reaping either prosperity or poverty karma. Whichever comes is the right thing for us, is our own action simply returning to us.

What we should be intent on is the life of the spirit, which extends far beyond food and clothing and beyond the life of the body, for that matter. "Behold the fowls of the air: for they sow not, neither do they reap, nor gather into barns; yet your heavenly Father feedeth them. Are ye not much better than they?" (Matthew 6:26). The creation is not haphazard or whimsical, it has a divine purpose for all sentient beings, not just humans, and it shall be fulfilled in us and all others. We are every moment living within God, and nothing can go wrong, however it may seem to our limited understanding. Even death is a minor incident. When an American disciple of Swami Chidananda of the Divine Life Society left the body, she told her friends regarding the impending departure: "Don't worry; I've done this lots of times!" And so have we.

Which of you by taking thought can add one cubit unto his stature? Worrying accomplishes nothing and changes nothing. Ever.

And why take ye thought for raiment? Consider the lilies of the field, how they grow; they toil not, neither do they spin: and yet I say unto you, That even Solomon in all his glory was not arrayed like one of these. Wherefore, if God so clothe the grass of the field, which to day is, and to morrow is cast into the oven, shall he not much more clothe you, O ye of little faith? Therefore take no thought, saying, What shall we eat? or, What shall we drink? or, Wherewithal shall we be clothed? (For after all these things do the Gentiles seek:) for your heavenly Father knoweth that ye have need of all these things. Three principles are indicated here. First, we must realize that all operates according to the Divine Law, which is the same as the Divine Will. So there is nothing to be fearful about. Second, anxiety about externals is a symptom of a consciousness separated from Spirit. And third, that all we have real need for is already on the way in the Divine Dream.

But seek ye first the kingdom of God, and his righteousness; and all these things shall be added unto you. Those who seek the inner life and conform to the Divine Order (*Ritam*) need be concerned for nothing else, all these will be supplied by the cosmos. Again, this does not mean that we need not be practical and look after things in the outer world, but we must do so in the context of spiritual life, and keep our priorities very clear and correct. Our outer life must be an expression of the inner life. Then all will be well in the fullest sense.

Take therefore no thought for the morrow: for the morrow shall take thought for the things of itself. Sufficient unto the day is the evil thereof. Without a good grasp of karma, nothing makes any sense. Everything is karma, day-to-day. A friend of mind who was much wiser than I, used to exasperate me by continually saying: "It is just their/your/our karma." But she was right. Thank you, Helen.

We cannot get around having to deal with people continually unless we are living in virtual isolation. And a lot of wise people and yogis do just that. But Jesus wants us to know how to see people clearly and understand how to deal with them according to our seeing of them.

WISE JUDGMENT

Judge not, that ye be not judged. For with what judgment ye judge, ye shall be judged: and with what measure ye mete, it shall be measured to you again (Matthew 7:1-2).

Spiritual bullies, wishing to browbeat others who can see their hypocrisies and evil ways into feeling guilty about pointing out and objecting to their wrongdoings, toss this up as a smokescreen. "Judge not lest ye be judged!" they misquote threateningly.

I knew a very intuitive young man who used to see the hidden evil within some people and condemn himself for it, since he misunderstood this verse, having heard it slung around a lot by the hypocrites in his very fundamentalist church. He told me that he used to pray and pray for God to forgive him and to clear his mind of "judging." But one day when praying again about this, suddenly two verses from the Bible popped right into his mind: "By their fruits ye shall know them" (Matthew 7:20), and "Beloved, believe not every spirit, but try the spirits whether they are of God" (I John 4:1). Now how could he do that without looking at (and in his case, into) people and coming to a conclusion about them? Of course, he could not. This was underlined a short time later when he heard a minister he admired say: "I am not a judge, but I am a fruit inspector like the Bible tells me to be." ("Ye shall know them by their fruits. Do men gather grapes of thorns, or figs of thistles? Even so every good tree bringeth forth good fruit; but a corrupt tree bringeth forth evil fruit. A good tree cannot bring forth evil fruit, neither can a corrupt tree bring forth good fruit. Every tree that bringeth not forth good fruit is hewn down, and cast into the fire. Wherefore by their fruits ye shall know them" (Matthew 7:20.) He told me that one of the greatest anxieties of his life was dispelled by those words.

So what does this verse really mean? The word translated "judge" is *krino*, which in this instance means to condemn someone and hate them, wishing harm to come upon them as punishment. It also implies a feeling that no mercy should be shown to the guilty ones. Karma being operative in every department of our life, and thoughts being real energy entities, such an attitude toward someone generates very intense and poisonous karma, for karma is mental as well as physical. If we harbor such unmerciful and vengeful attitudes, in time the same thing will be directed to us, not by God, but by human beings. For God, with "whom is no variableness, neither shadow of turning" (James 1:17), ever loves us with an eternal love. Human beings, on the other hand, do not, and they shall condemn us as we have condemned others. Also, if we are unjust in our view of others, they will view us unjustly as well. This is why Jesus said: "Blessed are the merciful: for they shall obtain mercy" (Matthew 5:7).

The second half of this verse indicates that as we treat others so shall we be treated by them. Again, it is only a matter of karma, of cause and effect. If we are fair, we shall be treated fairly; if we are generous, we shall be shown generosity; if we are honest, others shall be honest with us, or we shall be protected from the unfair, the ungenerous, and the dishonest.

And he spake a parable unto them, Can the blind lead the blind? shall they not both fall into the ditch? (Luke 6:39).

Here is the number one problem with religion: the ignorant teach their ignorance to other ignorant people and they in turn pass it on to others. Both the Roman Catholic and Eastern Orthodox churches have an unbroken history right back to Jesus and the twelve apostles. But their succession is only historical–external. They do not teach what either Jesus or the apostles taught. Their theology is spiritually invalid–blind. So from generation to generation the teachers and the taught fall into the ditch of self-satisfied and self-congratulating ignorance. And it does not stop there. Real evil begins to be done by them, persecuting, imprisoning and even killing those who do not believe or teach as they do.

Truth is not just learned, it is acted upon and embodied in genuine spiritual evolution which is the attainment of the divine consciousness of the divine Self. Consequently those who would truly follow Jesus must find and follow that which he teaches. And by the way, Jesus is citing a verse from the Katha Upanishad (1.2.5): "Abiding in the midst of ignorance, wise in their own esteem, thinking themselves to be learned, fools treading a tortuous path go about like blind men led by one who is himself blind."

The disciple is not above his master [teacher]: but every one that is perfect shall be as his master (Luke 6:40).

The disciple is not above his master. "Good Christians" are supposed to be sheep–the New Testament is full of it. But sheep are stupid–that is their main characteristic, along with the fact that they follow you everywhere you go and you can shear them and even slaughter them without their resisting or complaining. Now that is the ideal Christian of the contemporary world. They do not think or aspire to anything but being part of the herd, and you can fleece them all you want. Televangelists love them and they love televangelists.

Jesus used sheep as symbols because his hearers were familiar with them, but he did not intend for his disciples to be what I have just described. Quite to the contrary. *Mathetes* means a learner, a student, someone who uses his head and is seeking knowledge of higher life and consciousness as well as the means to attain them–not an unquestioning follower. A disciple of Jesus has intellectual ability and integrity.

I once read a book entitled *Simple Shepherd of the Simple Sheep.* That was the ideal of the author and her readers. But it is not the ideal of Christ. "Childlike saints" are the hope of the morally lax and intellectually lazy. Certainly there are guileless saints, but they are all "wise as serpents and harmless as doves" (Matthew 10:16). Otherwise they would not be saints. God is not stupid and gullible, nor was Jesus; so how could their followers be so?

The root word of *mathetes* is *manthano*, which means to understand, to increase one's knowledge, to apply oneself and become informed, to be in the habit–accustomed to–learning and seeking knowledge. That is why Saint Clement of Alexandria wrote an entire book on the ideal Christian entitled *The Gnostic*–The Knower.

Once I was looking through a very complex Eastern Orthodox website that included articles about how Christians should just mind their own little life sphere and trust God and Jesus (and the Church) to do what is needed and not to inquire too closely into the "mysteries of faith," because that always leads into pride and heresy. Sheep-wits are certainly wanted there!

Jesus promised his disciples that the Holy Spirit "shall teach you all things" (John 14:26), and "will guide you into all truth… and he will show you things to come… for he shall receive of mine, and shall shew it unto you" (John 16:13, 14). Is this part of "the Christian experience" in this world? Just the opposite. So do these people really "have" the Holy Spirit? They cannot even figure out the reality of karma, reincarnation and the evolution of consciousness–three fundamentals of earthly life itself, much less spiritual life.

When Communism dissolved in Russia, tremendous numbers of people sought baptism and confirmation (chrismation) in the Orthodox Church. But not long after that I read an article by an Orthodox priest bewailing the fact that a large percentage of those people had been influenced by the New Age and were demanding of their parish priests: "What more is there for us to learn?" But there was no "more." After all, they were "rational sheep of Christ" (no kidding, they use that expression) who did not need to think or learn any more. All they need do was hang on, not sin too much (and even then confess and be absolved) and die and go to eternal joy in heaven. The sheep have been penned up and told to be quiet.

It is the same in America. Eastern Orthodox priests are chagrined by the insistence of new converts that there has to be something more. And there is. But they do not have it. (Actually a few do, but they keep it a secret so they will not be branded a heretic and expelled from their church.) A man I knew demanded of his parish priest: "Does or does not the Orthodox Church teach reincarnation?" The priest shuffled around a bit and finally said: "Well, let's just put it this way: *At this time* it does not."

Is this what Jesus had in mind? No; because Jesus was a true *didaskalos*–a master teacher. The word does not just mean anyone who decides to teach others, but one who is qualified and competent to teach. It implies a person to whom people are drawn by their spiritual power. Nicodemus said to Jesus: "We know that thou art a teacher come from God" (John 3:2). Now here is something very interesting. The root word *didasko* means both teacher and the thing taught. That is, the teacher is a living manifestation of the teaching. I am happy to say that I have met such teachers in Hinduism, Buddhism, and Eastern Christianity. (In this latter they were extremely rare and looked on with suspicion, but they were there.)

Every one that is perfect shall be as his master. Here we see that it is Jesus' intention that his disciples should be exactly what he is–no less. Therefore the true Christian aspires to be a Christ like Jesus. Christianity went astray very early on when Christians decided to make Jesus God instead of a god. That way they could not possibly be what he was and to seek such a thing would be pride and blasphemy. Instead Jesus was a God who could dispense to his favored followers whatever they wanted. All they need do was believe and pay tribute of praise. Easy. And completely contrary to the intention of Jesus, who is "first among his brethren" by virtue of being what he intends them to be. And this is possible because it is their eternal nature and destiny to become so. That is the purpose of creation and our finding ourselves within it.

To find the teachings of Jesus we must turn to the Eternal Religion–Sanatana Dharma–of India and follow its wisdom, which is the same wisdom Jesus found there during his "lost years" and which he brought back to Israel to those very few who could grasp its meaning and follow it. And that includes the practice of Soham Yoga meditation. (Again: see *Soham Yoga: The Yoga of the Self*.)

Change Yourself

And why beholdest thou the mote that is in thy brother's eye, but perceivest not the beam that is in thine own eye? Either how canst thou say to thy brother, Brother, let me pull out the mote that is in thine eye, when thou thyself beholdest not the beam that is in thine own eye? Thou hypocrite, cast out first the beam out of thine own eye, and then shalt thou see clearly to pull out the mote that is in thy brother's eye (Luke 6:41-42).

And why beholdest thou the mote that is in thy brother's eye, but perceivest not the beam that is in thine own eye? The primary difficulty here is one of non-perception, which is what *kataneoeo* literally means. Jesus is speaking to those who cannot see their own condition at all, and who exaggerate the flaws of others.

A *karphos* is a speck; it has the connotation of being dry, the implication being that it is insubstantial. On the other hand, a *dokos* is not just a plank, the equivalent of millions of motes, it is a beam that is used as a support in building, such as holding up a roof. That is the equivalent of billions of specks of wood dust. So we have the picture of someone in tremendous spiritual trouble who is completely unaware of the fact but obsessively intent on others' very tiny faults, considering them to be mountains instead of the molehills they really are. However, sometimes this condition exists because that is the way a person hides from his own reality or keeps others from noticing his faults by constantly fussing about those of others.

One point easily overlooked is that Jesus is reminding such persons that those they are complaining about are their brothers, that no one is an outsider or stranger, but our very own.

Either how canst thou say to thy brother, Brother, let me pull out the mote that is in thine eye, when thou thyself beholdest not the beam that is in thine own eye? The word *ekballo* means to forcefully, even violently, cast something out. So there is no consideration for the feelings of the accused, or even an interest in the ultimate result of such an expulsion. And as Jesus also implies, how can a person with a huge beam in his eye possibly see how to remove a tiny speck from another's eye? We might even question whether or not he can even see a speck.

Thou hypocrite, cast out first the beam out of thine own eye, and then shalt thou see clearly to pull out the mote that is in thy brother's eye. And now the point about all this that no one has ever even hinted at in my entire life: it is possible and permissible to cast out the mote; a person just needs to be qualified and have the right motivation and the request of those with the motes. I have known people who by a few words could turn around the direction others were going in, but those people wanted to turn around. Even God never trespasses on the will of another. It is not uncommon among Vietnamese Buddhists to ask a monk to come live with them and their family for a while and then to give their opinion on how they can improve their life. So there are those who can help those with specks in their eyes if they are asked to do so. (Chances are the "beamers" cannot be helped by anybody because they like the beams.)

Whether or not we are interested in becoming spiritual ophthalmologists, it is good to be able to "see clearly." The word *diablepo* means actually "to look through; penetrate by vision." Buddha called this deep insight "penetration" and spoke of this a great deal as a necessity for all those who pursue enlightenment. We must see into things, not just observe the surface appearance.

There just comes to mind a vivid example. A friend of mine was once working in the emergency room of a Los Angeles hospital when a woman was brought in who had been stabbed by a screwdriver which was still in her back next to her spine. One of the doctors said: "Well, let's just pull it out," but my friend suddenly cried out: "No! We should x-ray her first." All the others considered this pointless, but my friend was so insistent they agreed. The x-ray revealed that the screwdriver was somehow bent around her spine, that if they had attempted to just pull it out they would have paralyzed the woman.

We must be able to see deeply into things. My friend Sri Dattabal, a yoga-siddha (adept yogi), told me: "I do not just read a person's mind. I look far beyond the mind, through the subconscious impressions (samskaras) until I see their Self (Atma)." That is why he could help people. And most of all we need to help ourselves through our own insight.

Caution and Prudence

Give not that which is holy unto the dogs, neither cast ye your pearls before swine, lest they trample them under their feet, and turn again and rend you (Matthew 7:6).

Waste of time is a manifestation of lack of understanding or a sense of responsibility. "Look before you leap" is a valuable principle to apply in spiritual life. Jesus said: "Which of you, intending to build a tower, sitteth not down first, and counteth the cost, whether he have sufficient to finish it? Lest haply, after he hath laid the foundation, and is not able to finish it, all that behold it begin to mock him, saying, This man began to build, and was not able to finish. Or what king, going to make war against another king, sitteth not down first, and consulteth whether he be able with ten thousand to meet him that cometh against him with twenty thousand?" (Luke 14:28-31).

There is a wonderful word that has dropped completely out of our vocabulary for nearly a century, but it was very common earlier, even in the Bible. That word is *circumspection*, which literally means to look around and see where we are and the nature of our surroundings. Only then should we decide upon a course of action. This is a cardinal virtue in religion, especially in dealing with people.

No spiritually sane person will concede to the bullying insistence that religion should never be brought up or discussed in conversation. For religion, our relation to God and God's relation to us, is the primary foundation of truly human thought and life. Yet intelligence and wisdom must be employed when we speak of spiritual matters, and the first thing to determine is whether we should speak. Just as a farmer does not sow seed in unprepared or unsuitable ground, neither should we sow the seeds of spiritual knowledge in the ears of those either not sufficiently evolved to comprehend our words or whose negativity will guarantee hostility and rejection in response to them. Again, it is a matter of knowing when time spent will be time wasted. As the wise Solomon said, there is "a time to keep silence, and a time to speak" (Ecclesiastes 3:7).

Cheap, shallow people have a cheap, shallow religion and continually scatter it around. Many are those that never lose a chance to "witness for Christ" or question all those they encounter about their "soul's salvation." I well remember a woman in my hometown who ran a hat shop. Anyone who bought a hat would find a "gospel tract" tucked inside it when they got it home. I myself supposedly "got salvation" when I was nine and a "gospel worker" at the Moody Bible Institute in Chicago gave me a cheap little booklet of the Gospel of John and made me sign on the inside cover that I accepted Jesus Christ as my "personal Lord and Savior." (I wish I had the proverbial dollar for every time I heard that cliché in this life!)

But those whose religion is an expression of true wisdom are not so prodigal with it. Rather, they hold it as a precious treasure to be imparted only to those who can comprehend it. It is never to be cast about without heed as to where it will end up and what the result will be.

At the time of Jesus, dogs and pigs were wild animals, repulsive, dangerous, and usually diseased, not the animals we know today. Jesus loved all mankind and gave himself in loving sacrifice for them because he saw them as errant children of God, themselves gods (John 10:24; Psalms 82:6-7). Yet he used the expressions "pigs" and "dogs" for people whose spiritual consciousness is undeveloped, who cannot comprehend real spiritual truth and consequently will despise or mock it, if they respond at all. If we held out a handful of pearls or gems to a dog or pig, the poor animal might eagerly gulp them down and be harmed or even die. We must protect both ourselves and them from such a folly. So we must not put them in a position where they will be upset, confused or hostile. That is one reason why Saint Paul said he had become "all things to all men" (I Corinthians 9:22). He spoke to people on their level, saying only what they could understand and relate to. Or, if need be, he said nothing and absented himself.

Every single action creates karma. Those who mock spiritual teaching and defame worthy spiritual teachers, even seeking to do them harm, create terrible negative karma for themselves. When they do, usually in future lives, seek out the spiritual path themselves, they run into all kinds of obstacles, not the least being people who react to them the way they had reacted previously toward those who sought the higher life. Often defamation and persecution are aimed at them relentlessly. Sometimes it deflects them from spiritual life in that and future births. Negative spiritual karma is the worst karma there is, as they find out. As I say, they should be protected by the care and wisdom of those who have traveled further along the evolutionary path.

A yogi friend of mind once begged me to come with her to visit her mother because she was afraid to see her alone. The mother truly did suffer from religious mania. At one time she had been institutionalized and had escaped and hid out near her home for several days before breaking in at night and trying to kill my friend, screaming as she was choking her that her daughter was the devil. Naturally, when she could my friend had moved to the opposite side of the country and only rarely returned for a visit, and then only when her father would be present to control her mother. But her father was in Lebanon at the time. So she wanted me to be her bodyguard. What could I do? I agreed and away we went.

Upon meeting the mother I saw that she was really in a precarious mental state. Of course she talked with me about religion and I carefully spoke with her, doing my best to draw on the spiritual wisdom I had learned from the Bhagavad Gita and the writings of Paramhansa Yogananda. (She knew I was a yogi like her daughter.) She listened very calmly and even cheerfully. Finally she played the piano and sang sentimental hymns for us. I thanked her, shook hands and left. Gia drove the car about a block and then pulled over and gave herself some time to shake off her "on guard" tension. Then she turned to me and said: "Do you know, that is the sanest I have ever seen my mother respond to anyone? I think she really learned something. Thank you." "The thanks is not to me," I told her, "but to God whom you and I prayed to for help, and to the great Master whose grace-filled words give healing to many weary and wandering souls." "Like me," commented Gia. "And me," I added. Then on we went, silently thinking of that holy Master who had told his disciples before his passing ten years before: "To those who think me near, I will be near." Gia and I knew that was true.

Sister Vijaya, one of Yogananda's monastic disciples, told me that he always spoke to people according to their level of understanding. Toward the end of his life he was in retreat at Twenty-Nine Palms dictating his Bhagavad Gita commentary. She and a few others were there with him, and they were filled with awe at his incredibly profound words on the Gita, but even more were they in awe of the Divine Presence around him as he dictated. She told me those were the holiest memories of her life. Yet at one point he was asked to speak at a Rotary club in a nearby town. So they all went with him, wondering what he would say. He told the assembled people about his hilarious misadventures during the great depression when he was trying to get a washing machine. Everyone was laughing so hard they could hardly breathe. Later she heard several people say: "I have never laughed so hard in my life." Then they returned to the desert and spent more sacred hours at the feet of him who had known just what to say to those other people with whom he had shared his mirth and joy so readily.

Yogananda had written in his autobiography that his guru, Swami Sri Yukteswar, had told him regarding his guru, Lahiri Mahasaya: "Even when Lahiri Mahasaya conversed on other than strictly religious topics, I discovered that nonetheless he had transmitted to me ineffable knowledge." Yogananda, too, did the same. Of him his hearers could truly say: "Never man spake like this man" (John 7:46). Because he was more than "man."

Rules For Living in the Spirit

Ask, and it shall be given you; seek, and ye shall find; knock, and it shall be opened unto you: for every one that asketh receiveth; and he that seeketh findeth; and to him that knocketh it shall be opened.

Or what man is there of you, whom if his son ask bread, will he give him a stone? Or if he ask a fish, will he give him a serpent? If ye then, being evil, know how to give good gifts unto your children, how much more shall your Father which is in heaven give good things to them that ask him?

Therefore all things whatsoever ye would that men should do to you, do ye even so to them: for this is the law and the prophets (Matthew 7:7-12).

There seems to be no end to learning about karma, which is no surprise since it is the basis of the universe and of our evolution. Usually the Gita or one of the Upanishads says any philosophical principle best, but Saint Paul set forth the doctrine of karma as both action and reaction better than anyone of East or West when he wrote: "Be not deceived; God is not mocked: for whatsoever a man soweth, that shall he also reap. For he that soweth to his flesh shall of the flesh reap corruption; but he that soweth to the Spirit shall of the Spirit reap life everlasting. And let us not be weary in well doing: for in due season we shall reap, if we faint not" (Galatians 6:7-8).

Action produces reaction. Karma is inevitable. The Bhagavad Gita shows the way to live and think so that no karma is being produced by action, but that requires a tremendously high level of spiritual development. So Jesus begins to teach how to make the kind of karma that will elevate us and set our feet on the path to transcend karma.

Ask, and it shall be given you; seek, and ye shall find; knock, and it shall be opened unto you: for every one that asketh receiveth; and he that seeketh findeth; and to him that knocketh it shall be opened. Materialistic people interpret even the most abstract of spiritual principles in a materialistic manner. So they always say this is a Precious Promise that whatever material thing or situation we want from God is ours just for the asking. But it is no such thing. It is instruction in how to create and increase positive karma by asking and seeking for understanding and wisdom and the grace to attain "unto the measure of the stature of the fulness of Christ: That we …may grow up into him in all things" (Ephesians 13-15). We are meant to grow up *into* Christ. That is, our entire being ("all things") is to be transmuted into Christ–into Christhood.

Can we find this truth being expressed by contemporary Christians? Why stop there? Can we find it being expressed by anyone outside the writings of those mystics who have consistently been branded as heretics by official Christianity throughout the centuries? We cannot. False, anti-Christian teachings have supplanted the original Gospel of Jesus Christ. Those who hold to Jesus' original teachings are not even persecuted anymore–just mocked and the ignored.

Jesus is telling us that the entire divine treasury of knowledge and power is available to us if we ask and seek aright. Sometimes we have to be insistent and knock, but "it shall be opened" to us.

Or what man is there of you, whom if his son ask bread, will he give him a stone? Or if he ask a fish, will he give him a serpent? If ye then, being evil, know how to give good gifts unto your children, how much more shall your Father which is in heaven give good things to them that ask him? There is a terrible flaw in human beings which enables them to doubt and even deny the unchanging good will, love and mercy of God toward them. This is both false and blasphemous and is based mostly on ignorance of the laws of karma. Believing that everything happening to us is just God's whimsical toying with us like a cat with a mouse is a terrible thing. These wrongheaded notions are part of the "works of the devil" that Jesus came to end (I John 3:8). As he said to his disciples and through them to all humanity: "Fear not, little flock; for it is your Father's good pleasure to give you the kingdom" (Luke 12:32). There is no doubt that the kingdom is already ours—we need only reach out and take it, for that is the will of God for each one of us. He intends to say to every single one: "Thou art my Son; this day have I begotten thee" (Psalms 2:7; Acts 13:33; Hebrews 1:5; 5:5).

Therefore all things whatsoever ye would that men should do to you, do ye even so to them: for this is the law and the prophets. We have already been told two chapters back: "Be ye therefore perfect, even as your Father which is in heaven is perfect" (Matthew 5:48). And here is one of the ways we manage that: by always and only doing good to others. This encompasses both the outer ("law") and inner ("prophets") realms of life which must conform to the divine patterns.

Part of taking charge of our life is taking charge of our karma, of consciously creating it rather than unconsciously putting into motion forces we are completely unaware of until they come back and hit us. No more karmic surprises! We must be masters, as God intends for us to be.

The Two Gates and Ways (Paths)

> Enter ye in at the strait gate: for wide is the gate, and broad is the way, that leadeth to destruction, and many there be which go in thereat: because strait is the gate, and narrow is the way, which leadeth unto life, and few there be that find it (Matthew 7:13-14).

Because we naturally think of the way of life implied by these words, we fail to note that each way is accessed by a gate which is of the same character as the road to which it leads. The idea is that no one should be surprised at the nature of the road, because the gate they took indicated it before they set foot on it. Look Before You Enter is a reasonable motto for the would-be traveller.

This all seems simple good sense, but few people live accordingly. For example, people make arrangements with those they know to be dishonest and then are astonished when they are cheated by them. People continually marry those that were unfaithful to their spouses (with them) and then of course are betrayed by them as well. And it goes on with many variations. What you begin with you will end up with.

So if we examine the conditions needed to begin walking a path we should be able to know what the path itself will be like as a factor in our life. It is not at all complex.

William Gray, a student of the great British esotericist, Dion Fortune, wrote an essay about how the entire drama of creation consists of two basic factors: cosmos (order) and chaos (disorder). The tension and interaction between them accounts for all the phenomena of this relative world. If we look at our personal drama of evolution at its present level we see that these two forces manifest in our lives as discipline and non-discipline; or as one source has it: governed and ungoverned. In the matter of personal evolution, "governed" means *self*-governed, otherwise development of personal will–a major factor of evolution–does not enter into it. It is perfectly appropriate, then to characterize the broad way as the path of no discipline, laxity or indulgence, and the narrow path as the path of discipline.

Because of our wandering in ignorance and delusion for countless lifetimes, the way to destruction seems easy to travel, even though it only produces conflict and misery. We are very much like an addict who only feels good or right when under the influence of deadly elements such as alcohol, drugs, etc. Addicts constantly say "I need" when they really mean "I am enslaved." This is a terrible condition to be in, and to see through it and put forth the necessary will to counteract or reverse it is virtually impossible for many. Yet eventually it must be done, and yoga is the only path that will really do the needful.

Certainly we may have awakening experiences and even divine interventions that enable us to see clearly, but since all trouble comes from the mind and ego-directed will, they are ultimately useless in extracting ourselves from the way to destruction. A kind of back-and-forth pattern can develop, but since it is not based on spirit-perception but only on the flaws of the world and the mind there can be no lasting benefit. Yoga alone puts us in direct contact with our true Self, enabling us to progress from there. Right from the first it must be a matter of opening and developing our inmost consciousness.

Certainly we work and deal with the energy side (prakriti) of our being, but we do so by putting it in direct contact with our consciousness. Just as the sun brings about the manifestation of life and growth, in the same way it is the communication of spirit-consciousness that lifts us up and enables us to escape from the broad way that leads to (and is) death. We must come to life, and spirit alone is life. The broad way by its very nature prevents us from coming to life. It is not freedom, it is bondage, it is not happiness but distraction from the truth of our condition.

Discipline producing ordered thought and action is the only path to life, to true freedom. Evolution is the effect we are after and evolution is basically the opening of higher consciousness and establishment in it. Again, yoga is an essential factor. Many things such as prayer, worship and study of spiritual texts can purify the mind and prepare it for the advent, the awakening, of higher consciousness, but yoga is the only thing that really produces it. This is why religiosity has only temporary effects, producing no lasting changes.

Exoteric religion, being shallow, can be a presence in our life from birth to death, but no actual growth takes place since it is just a static, artificial piety that satisfies the externalized ways of rootless religion. Degeneration on an inner level is inevitable, but is rarely detected beneath the veneer of religion. The only way to avoid this is to follow the basic message of the Bhagavad Gita: Become A Yogi. This may seem very narrow-minded, but it is not. Consider all that external life entails–absolute necessities for the simple maintenance of the body. It is the same with our higher self, with our interior development leading to revelation of the eternal Self. Yoga is ultimately essential; the absolute necessity for continuing life in Spirit.

"Now it came to pass that Jesus entered into a certain village: and a certain woman named Martha received him into her house. And she had a sister called Mary, which also sat at Jesus' feet, and heard his word. But Martha was cumbered about much serving, and came to him, and said, Lord, dost thou not care that my sister hath left me to serve alone? bid her therefore that she help me. And Jesus answered and said unto her, Martha, Martha, thou art careful and troubled about many things: But one thing is needful: and Mary hath chosen that good part, which shall not be taken away from her" (Luke 10:38-42).

This is depiction of external religion versus the internal cultivation of yoga. I do not think I have met a single exoteric Christian that did not balk at and reject this account. "We need Marthas as much as we need Marys!" they always protest. But Jesus clearly says that Mary is the wise one, not Martha, that Martha is scattered and obsessed with outer action. Mary, on the other hand, sits at the feet of Jesus, a yogini absorbed in the radiance of his revealed divinity, lifted into his world and leaving the world of Martha behind. Martha and Mary are poles apart: one is absorbed in time and materiality and the other is intent on the eternal matters of the spirit. Mary is seeking direct experience of higher awareness while Martha is caught in the net of pots and pans. Martha has received Jesus into her house as a guest, but Mary has received Jesus into her heart as a living spirit. It is her reception that Saint John speaks of when he says: "As many as received him, to them gave he power to become the sons of God" (John 1:12). Mary opened herself to the possibility of Christhood. It is not enough to recognize and honor the Christhood of Jesus; we must seek and attain our own Christhood. Otherwise we are not Christians, not disciples of Jesus. (Martha eventually got the idea and became a saint.)

"Then said Jesus, Verily, verily, I say unto you, I am the door of the sheep. I am the door: by me if any man enter in, he shall be saved, and shall go in and out, and find pasture" (John 10:7, 9). Jesus the Way-Shower came to show the way to "enter in" our inmost being, to discover the inner Christ and "be saved." Because of exoteric orientation everyone considers that great teachers establish religions, but that is not true: they come to show the way to God, to the revelation of our innate divinity. But few really want that narrow and strait way, so in the masters' names they create their own broad, easier path, shamefully dishonoring the great masters as they do so. That is why when Gandhi was asked what he considered the main hindrance to the spread of Christianity in India he replied: "Christians." True religion is not theology or philosophy, but The Way to the Eternal. That is why the term "Way-Shower" is exactly right. Buddha came to show us how to become Buddhas and Jesus came to show us how to become Christs. They were great perfected (liberated) yogis and they came to show others how to be just like them.

Jesus went to India and lived with the master yogis there, returning to the West to give the Good News, the Gospel of "Christ in you, the hope of glory" (Colossians 1:27), "till we all come… unto the measure of the stature of the fulness of Christ" (Ephesians 4:13). When this ideal is not set before us, we are not disciples of Jesus. As Jesus himself says a few verses further on: "Many will say to me in that day, Lord, Lord, have we not prophesied in thy name? and in thy name have cast out devils? and in thy name done many wonderful works? And then will I profess unto them, I never knew you: depart from me, ye that work iniquity" (Matthew 7:22-23). Iniquity: that is how Jesus regards exoteric Christianity.

God-consciousness is the mark of a saint, not miracle-working. To hold any other perspective is to go astray and mislead others along with us. India is not free of this materialistic superstition, either. Often the more eccentric, even psychotic, a person is the more enlightened they are considered to be. Neither the Upanishads or the Bhagavad Gita set forth any other ideal than that of total union with God. This is why Patanjali explains in the Yoga Sutras how miracles are worked–to show that no external phenomena demonstrate enlightenment. He even tells us that many "powers" come from drugs, not yoga. Insane people often manifest amazing abilities, and so do those that are possessed by spirits–especially in matters of clairvoyance.

The last thing we should look for in anyone is miraculous abilities. The great masters sometimes show us that the world is not what we think it is by manifesting wonders, but their sole worthwhile miracle is the awakening and transformation of the consciousness of those that will heed their call to higher life and become what they are: perfect yogis.

If we really apply the standards of the Upanishads, Bhagavad Gita and Yoga Sutras we will see that yoga is the only religion and yogis are the only truly religious people. The rest are engaged in self-dramatization and pious play-acting, however sincere they may be. There is more spiritual maya in this world than true religion. Religions in general are the broad and wide gates to the path of bondage and destruction. Yoga is the strait and narrow path to life.

It is true: few there be that find the way of life. But that is normal in many aspects of even ordinary life. Out of all those enrolled in school, how many will earn a doctor's degree? I knew a physician who told me that out of forty enrollees in his class in the medical school he attended only four became doctors. Always there are only a few at the very top of anything–even organized crime. So those who press forward to the top of the mountain of spiritual realization and ascend to divine consciousness are very few–at a time. But a continuous trickle do manage it.

The fact is that everyone will attain divine ascension, but it is only a comparatively few at a time. Those who need the companionship and support of others will not make it. That is why Saint Paul wrote: "Know ye not that they which run in a race run all, but one receiveth the prize? So run, that ye may obtain" (I Corinthians 9:24). "Wherefore…, let us lay aside every weight…, and let us run with patience the race that is set before us" (Hebrews 12:1). As has long been said, the path to God is "the flight of the alone to the Alone."

Let us then become "narrow" minded in the sense of dedication to following the Narrow Way That Leads To Life.

Be Cautious, Be Wary

> Beware of false prophets, which come to you in sheep's clothing, but inwardly they are ravening wolves. Ye shall know them by their fruits. Do men gather grapes of thorns, or figs of thistles? Even so every good tree bringeth forth good fruit; but a corrupt tree bringeth forth evil fruit. A good tree cannot bring forth evil fruit, neither can a corrupt tree bring forth good fruit. Every tree that bringeth not forth good fruit is hewn down, and cast into the fire. Wherefore by their fruits ye shall know them (Matthew 7:15-20).

"Behold, I send you forth as sheep in the midst of wolves: be ye therefore wise as serpents, and harmless as doves" (Matthew 10:16). This is how Jesus viewed his disciples in this world: surrounded by danger and therefore of necessity wise and perceptive, undeceived by the ploys of the world and its slaves yet perfect in harmlessness (ahimsa), causing injury to none. And he viewed their adversaries as wolves. At other times he did not hesitate to call similar people wild dogs and wild pigs. Since he felt so strongly about it, we should examine his words to us on the subject.

Beware of false prophets, which come to you in sheep's clothing, but inwardly they are ravening wolves. This is an ancient dilemma which prevails even today: mistaking evil and evil intentions for truth and honesty. But since Jesus tells us to beware he is assuming that we will have the wisdom and caution to examine all sheep that may really be wolves. And it will certainly involve "judging" on our part, which is why the wolves continually howl, "judge not, that ye be not judged" (Matthew 7:1), hoping to cow the wise into taking them and their ilk at face value and suffering the unpleasant consequences.

Ye shall know them by their fruits. Do men gather grapes of thorns, or figs of thistles? Here we have a very easy and simple rule to follow in judging the true character of any person or group: Scrutinize the effect they have in the lives of those that are associated with them and that will give you a clear insight into their true nature. Do not pay any attention to the glowing words they speak, but take a good hard look at them. What are they, really? Of course we will have to know the difference between grapes, thorns, figs and thistles. Not everyone does.

Even so every good tree bringeth forth good fruit; but a corrupt tree bringeth forth evil fruit. We need to realize that the eventual result reveals whether something is good or evil. An ancient Christian monk said, "It is not how you begin but how you end that reveals the truth."

A good tree cannot bring forth evil fruit, neither can a corrupt tree bring forth good fruit. This is such a simple principle and one that would save multitudes from grief and worse, yet how many people will adopt it? Instead, excuses and rationalizations are brought to hide and deny the true character of so much in religion.

Every tree that bringeth not forth good fruit is hewn down, and cast into the fire. Because the universe is fundamentally good, in time all that is false and negative becomes revealed and dissolved. Then human beings think of more craziness to delude themselves and others. But in time that, too, will disappear.

Wherefore by their fruits ye shall know them. This principle should be ever-present with us so we can see the real state of things. We not only need to scrutinize others, we need to scrutinize ourselves lest we be self-deluded. "Examine yourselves, whether ye be in the faith; prove your own selves" (II Corinthians 13:5).

> **A good man out of the good treasure of his heart bringeth forth that which is good; and an evil man out of the evil treasure of his heart bringeth forth that which is evil: for of the abundance of the heart his mouth speaketh (Luke 6:45).**

The word translated here as "good" is *agathos*, which means beneficial good, good that makes things better. So this is a benevolent person, not just personally good, but someone who makes his environment better for himself and others. He is a benefactor. *Thesauros* means treasure, something that is not only valued but held onto and safeguarded. This is the treasury of the individual's heart, his inmost being, which includes his karmas and samskaras. It is his personality which has grown and developed throughout the cycle of his many reincarnations.

Only what is there can be brought out, and we can be sure that what is not there cannot be brought out. We need to understand this about people. We can expect from them what is present within them and that what is present within them will be manifested eventually. On the other hand, we cannot expect that what is not in them will somehow come forth in time. Trying to convert or correct someone is completely pointless if it is not in their inner conditioning (samskaras) to do or avoid something. "Even a wise man acts according to the tendencies of his own nature. All living creatures follow their tendencies" (Bhagavad Gita 3:33). We need to gauge the nature (character) of a person to know what to expect from him. "Do men gather grapes of thorns, or figs of thistles? Even so every good (*agathos*) tree bringeth forth good fruit; but a corrupt (*sapros*: decayed, diseased) tree bringeth forth evil (*poneros*: evil; harmful; poisonous) fruit. A good tree cannot bring forth evil fruit, neither can a corrupt tree bring forth good fruit" (Matthew 7:16-18).

For of the abundance of the heart his mouth speaketh. What is inside comes out sooner or later. Moreover, the power of speech is creative vibration that emanates directly from the mind (buddhi: intellect) of a person. The words of a person carries the vibration of his mind into the ears and mind of whoever hears him speak. Therefore some speakers are highly influential for either good, folly or evil. It is possible to dominate someone through the power of speech. Hitler is a prime example. He swayed thousands with words that were stupid and insane, innoculating them with his evil.

False and Real Discipleship

And why call ye me, Lord, Lord, and do not the things which I say? (Luke 6:46).

Kurios means Lord in the sense of a person of supreme authority or a master teacher. But the title means nothing if the person is never heard, or if they are heard and not paid attention to. To call someone "Lord" who is ignored or unknown is a mockery. To say "Lord God" and not have it be so in our hearts and lives is also hypocrisy.

> Not every one that saith unto me, Lord, Lord, shall enter into the kingdom of heaven; but he that doeth the will of my Father which is in heaven.
> Many will say to me in that day, Lord, Lord, have we not prophesied in thy name? and in thy name have cast out devils? and in thy name done many wonderful works? And then will I profess unto them, I never knew you: depart from me, ye that work iniquity. (Matthew 7:21-23).

The idea that a person need only "believe in Jesus" and "confess" him before others to assure their salvation is both rank egotism and rank superstition—and a complete lack of knowledge regarding the nature of salvation. The two words used in the New Testament for salvation are *soterion* and *soteria*. They mean freedom or deliverance from bondage and imply restoration of a lost condition. The word *soter*, savior, means one who sets free. *Sozo* means to deliver, make complete and heal. And this is exactly the meaning of the Sanskrit term moksha: freedom. It is the ultimate state of evolution, the state of the sons of God, and has nothing to do with the theologizing of exoteric Christianity. That is why Jesus said: "Not every one that saith unto me, Lord, Lord, shall enter into the kingdom of heaven; *but he that doeth the will of my Father which is in heaven*" (Matthew 7:21). "Heaven" is not somewhere in the far reaches of the universe; rather, *ouranos* is the vast sky of Consciousness, the Chidakasha (etheric consciousness) which is found in every human being within the sahasrara chakra, the thousand-petalled lotus of the physical, astral and causal brain. There God dwells united with the individual spirit which is eternally one with the Father.

Many will say to me in that day, Lord, Lord, have we not prophesied in thy name? and in thy name have cast out devils? and in thy name done many wonderful works? And then will I profess unto them, I never knew you: depart from me, ye that work iniquity. Throughout the world miracles are cited by the various religions to prove that they are "true" and of God. In India it is very common that a biography of a saint is nothing but a collection of miracle stories which contain not a single word of wisdom or spiritual teaching by the saint. This is certainly a flaw of the authors of such books, but in many cases the flaw is in the supposed saint or master. In many cases they simply behaved in a chaotic and irrational manner and were therefore assumed to be enlightened–only God knows why. Mentally ill people often exhibit miraculous phenomena, I have witnessed this myself and others have told me of their experiences with insane people who foretold the future, read minds, and could transport themselves from one place to another in a flash.

Therefore Jesus says that the miracle-workers will assure him that they have prophesied correctly in his name, cast out evil spirits by the same means and worked many miracles. Yet, he tells us: "Then will I profess unto them, I never knew you: depart from me, ye that work iniquity." Their religiosity means nothing, but is declared iniquity by Jesus. The word translated iniquity is *anomia*, which means iniquitous, unrighteous, transgression of the law of God, outside the law, contempt and violation of law and lawlessness itself. That is Jesus' opinion. And it should be ours–not to judge others but to examine ourselves to determine whether or not we meet the standards of Christ.

> **Therefore whosoever heareth these sayings of mine, and doeth them, I will liken him unto a wise man, which built his house upon a rock: and the rain descended, and the floods came, and the winds blew, and beat upon that house; and it fell not: for it was founded upon a rock.**
>
> **And every one that heareth these sayings of mine, and doeth them not, shall be likened unto a foolish man, which built his house upon the sand: and the rain descended, and the floods came, and the winds blew, and beat upon that house; and it fell: and great was the fall of it. (Matthew 7:24-27).**

This parable is about the two poles of consciousness: unity and multiplicity. In yoga writings we find the expression "one-pointed" quite frequently. The Bhagavad Gita says: "'The light of a lamp does not flicker in a windless place': that is the simile which describes a yogi of one-pointed mind, who meditates upon the Atman. When, through the practice of yoga, the mind ceases its restless movements, and becomes still, he realizes the Atman. It satisfies him entirely. Then he knows that infinite happiness which can be realized by the purified heart but is beyond the grasp of the senses. He stands firm in this realization. Because of it, he can never again wander from the inmost truth of his being. Now that he holds it he knows this treasure above all others: faith so certain shall never be shaken by heaviest sorrow. To achieve this certainty is to know the real meaning of the word yoga. It is the breaking of contact with pain. You must practice this yoga resolutely, without losing heart" (Bhagavad Gita 6:19-23)

The wise man dug away the earth until he came to the rock. Then he built his house with its foundation on the rock. This is a symbol of unity in consciousness. No matter what forces beat upon the house, it was firm and immovable. In the same way the consciousness of the wise yogi is unshakeable.

The foolish man built his house on the sand. Now, sand is crushed rock, but it is countless tiny fragments. So sand represents a consciousness of multiplicity, of seeing only the many and not the underlying unity. So when the storms came the house collapsed and was completely destroyed.

The idea is simple: those with a consciousness of their union with God cannot be shaken or turned from the path. But those who have no such consciousness have no stability of mind and heart and become literal washouts.

> **And it came to pass, when Jesus had ended these sayings, the people were astonished at his doctrine: For he taught them as one having authority, and not as the scribes (Matthew 7:28-29).**

Earlier we considered how Jesus' words: "Out of the abundance of the heart the mouth speaketh" indicated that the vibration of a person's voice revealed his inner intellectual and spiritual condition. "Having authority" involves both speaking in a clear, confident and unhesitant manner and the ability to impart insight to his hearers. That is why when they had seen him after his resurrection, two of his disciples "said one to another, Did not our heart burn within us, while he talked with us by the way, and while he opened to us the scriptures?" (Luke 24:32). Jesus' authority accomplished even more: "Then opened he their understanding, that they might understand the scriptures" (Luke 24:45).

Being Worthy of Healing

Now when he had ended all his sayings in the audience of the people, he entered into Capernaum. And a certain centurion's servant, who was dear unto him, was sick, and ready to die. And when he heard of Jesus, he sent unto him the elders of the Jews [Judeans], beseeching him that he would come and heal his servant. And saying, Lord, my servant lieth at home sick of the palsy, grievously tormented (Luke 7:1-3; Matthew 8:6).

And when Jesus was entered into Capernaum, there came unto him a centurion, beseeching him, and saying, Lord, my servant lieth at home sick of the palsy, grievously tormented. And Jesus saith unto him, I will come and heal him. Although in the King James version *paralutikos* is many times rendered "palsy," it really is a generic term for any kind of paralysis. Paralysis is worse than many diseases because it is a condition of disconnection between the brain and the body. There are antidotes for many diseases, but virtually none for paralysis. So a commander of one hundred Roman soldiers came seeking healing for his paralyzed servant. By this we see his character, for he had such concern for a domestic servant that he came to Jesus for help. And this he would not have done if he had not believed that Jesus could heal the sick.

And when they came to Jesus, they besought him instantly, saying, That he was worthy for whom he should do this: for he loveth our nation, and he hath built us a syna-

gogue. And Jesus saith unto him, I will come and heal him (Luke 7:4-5; Matthew 8:7).

It is no surprise then that Jesus immediately agreed to go and heal the sick man.

> Then Jesus went with them. And when he was now not far from the house, the centurion sent friends to him, saying unto him, Lord, trouble not thyself: for I am not worthy that thou shouldest enter under my roof: wherefore neither thought I myself worthy to come unto thee: but say in a word, and my servant shall be healed. For I also am a man set under authority, having under me soldiers, and I say unto one, Go, and he goeth; and to another, Come, and he cometh; and to my servant, Do this, and he doeth it (Luke 7:6-8).

This shows that the centurion did not just have faith, he had some esoteric understanding as well. He understood that there is power in the spoken word, that those who are in complete attunement with God can by their very words make changes in the world and in others. He also understood the power of mantra, for despite its degeneration, the Greco-Roman religion had its roots in India.

The centurion's words also show that he knew Jesus was not just a good man, but one whose spiritual authority was limitless. He addressed him as *Kurios*: Lord/Master, and said: "Speak the word only, and my servant shall be healed." He knew that Jesus had such power and did not doubt his merciful good will to grant healing.

So many of the incidents in the Bible seem like fables to those who know nothing but the ignorant materialism of modern pseudo-civilization. Such things as the miracles and the miraculous character of the holy people written about there can hardly be imagined, whereas in India such miracles and miracle-workers are so common as to be the norm. This is why I think of India when I hear the hymn:

> There is a happy land, far, far away,
> Where saints in glory stand, bright, bright as day;
> Oh, how they sweetly sing, praises to our God and King,
> And make the heavens ring: praise, praise for aye.

And my heart joins with Yogananda in saying:

> Hail, mother of religions, lotus, scenic beauty,
> And sages!
> Thy wide doors are open,
> Welcoming God's true sons through all ages.
> Where Ganges, woods, Himalayan caves, and men dream God—
> I am hallowed; my body touched that sod.

In India I lived with gods. Some I found in ashrams and in temples, and others walking down the street—even in railway stations.

No wonder Yogananda also wrote in that poem:

> Though mortal fires raze all her homes
> and golden paddy fields,
> Yet to sleep on her ashes and dream immortality,
> O India, I will be there!

When Jesus heard these things, he marvelled at him, and turned him about, and said unto the people that followed him, I say unto you, I have not found so great faith, no, not in Israel (Luke 7:9).

In spiritual life the most important factor is the aspirant's samskaras. Samskaras are impressions in the mind, either conscious or subconscious, produced by actions or experiences in this or previous lives. They are also propensities of the mental residue of impressions, subliminal activators or prenatal tendencies. In the mind, which is a mass of subtle magnetic energies, samskaras of the same type join to form vasanas, subtle desires and tendencies created in a person by the doing of an action or by enjoyment. Vasanas induce the person to repeat the action or to seek a repetition of the experience. These subtle impressions in the mind are capable of developing into action, and are the cause of birth and experience in general; the impression of actions that remains unconsciously in the mind. Samskaras and vasanas determine our personality and our reactions to things. To succeed in spiritual life, and especially yoga, we must persevere in it, and that requires deep samskaras to keep us motivated. Jesus was impressed because the centurion's actions and words showed his profound samskara for spiritual matters.

> **And I say unto you, That many shall come from the east and west, and shall sit down with Abraham, and Isaac, and Jacob, in the kingdom of heaven. But the children of the kingdom shall be cast out into outer darkness: there shall be weeping and gnashing of teeth (Matthew 8:11-12).**

It is a grave mistake to consider great teachers as merely a part or product of the culture in which they are born. Certainly there will be some influence, especially in their childhood, but great ones like Buddha and Jesus are world teachers, and their wisdom is relevant to all nations. However, they are born in a country for a reason. For centuries people in Israel had looked for a great teacher to come among them and revolutionize their lives. But when he came, only a comparatively few recognized him or followed him. He was the Promised One and the Hebrews were the People of the Promise. Yet in the intervening two thousand years we see that billions throughout the world have been attracted to Jesus and his teachings, whereas only a trickle of of the People of the Promise have accepted him and followed him. As a result great confusion and suffering have resulted–not as punishment, but because great spiritual opportunities were missed. That is why the esoteric tradition in Judaism says that the Messiah will come twice: once as Son of Joseph and be rejected, and then as Son of David and will be accepted. God's love always wins in the end, even if it is in the far future.

> And Jesus said unto the centurion, Go thy way; and as thou hast believed, so be it done unto thee. And they that were sent, returning to the house, found the servant whole that had been sick (Luke 7:6-9; Matthew 8:11-13; Luke 7:10).

The centurion knew: Jesus need only speak the word and his servant would be healed. For Jesus was one with the Father (John 10:30) who said: "Let there be light: and there was light" (Genesis 1:3).

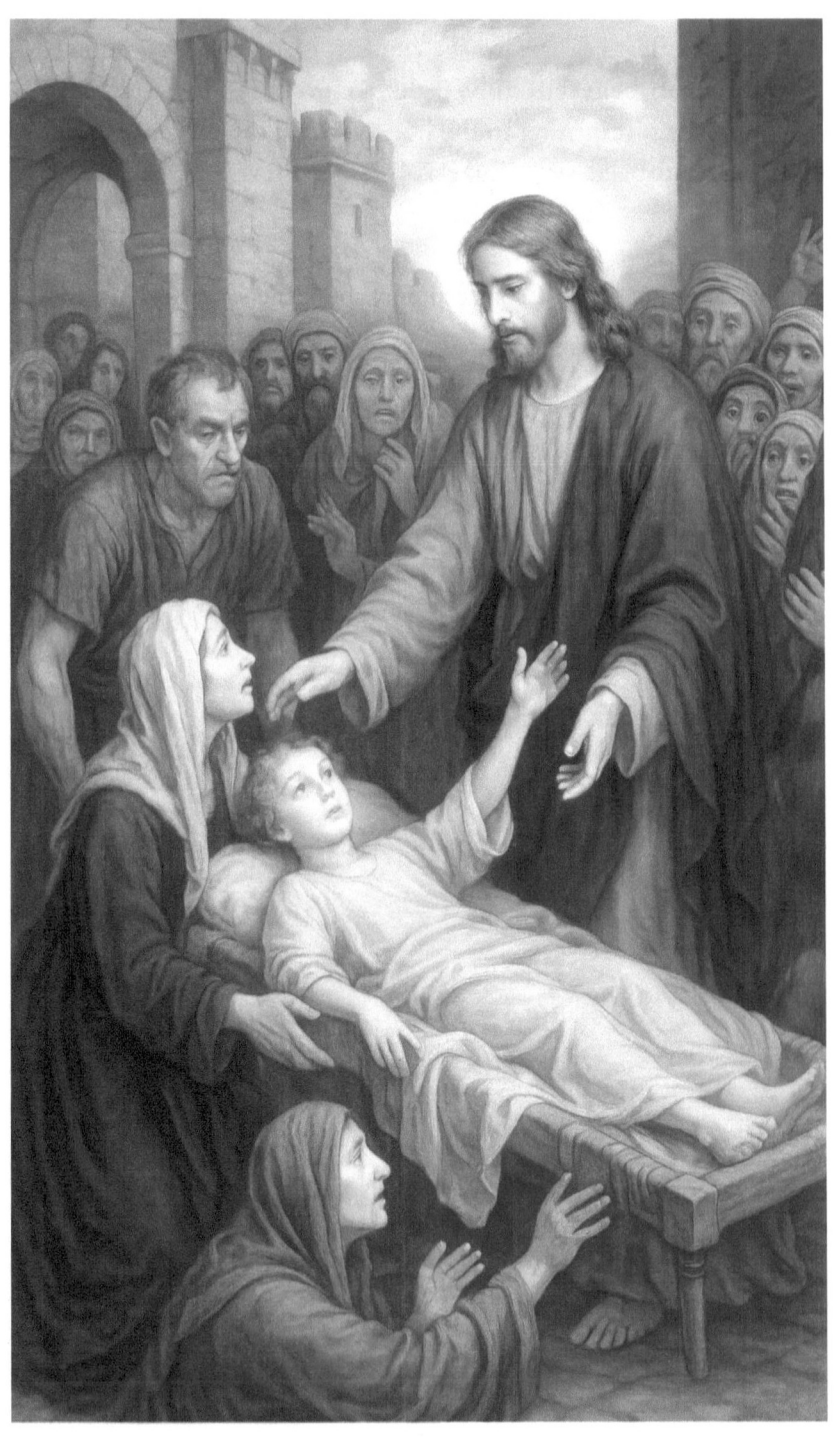

From Death To Life

> And it came to pass the day after, that he went into a city called Nain; and many of his disciples went with him, and much people.
>
> Now when he came nigh to the gate of the city, behold, there was a dead man carried out, the only son of his mother, and she was a widow: and much people of the city was with her. And when the Lord saw her, he had compassion on her, and said unto her, Weep not. And he came and touched the bier: and they that bare him stood still. And he said, Young man, I say unto thee, Arise. And he that was dead sat up, and began to speak. And he delivered him to his mother. And there came a fear on all: and they glorified God, saying, That a great prophet is risen up among us; and, That God hath visited his people.
>
> And this rumour of him went forth throughout all Judaea, and throughout all the region round about. And the disciples of John shewed [told] him of all these things (Luke 7:11-18).

I say unto thee, Arise. Egeiro means to awaken in the sense of collecting one's faculties and being fully aware. It also means to stand up. All of us who wish to rise from spiritual death and have heard the call to higher life must take every aspect of ourselves and our life in hand and enliven and unify them in the search for God-consciousness. All this must be done by us through the power of our will directed by our intelligence. No one can do this for us, not even God. We must arise into higher consciousness and life through our own will and action, both inner and outer. That is, we must come into mastery of our inner and outer life. And it is not a miracle from on high, it is an awakening and empowering from within ourselves. Our inner Christ Principle must be awakened and liberated from its sleep by our own will and effort as awakened and motivated yogis.

And he delivered him to his mother. We, too, must be returned and put into the care of the Holy Spirit, the Mother aspect of God. For the Holy Spirit is Herself the evolving principle of the universe. She brings us forth and nourishes us and sees that we reach maturity of consciousness, that we become fully awakened and empowered children of God. For this reason all mystics who are truly following the path of awakening are drawn to the Mother aspect of God and are aware of Her reality and power in their life. Wherever there is genuine, effective mysticism there we will find interaction with the Holy Spirit Mother. Soham is the breath of the Holy Spirit that has been with us always and which after so many ages must be consciously linked to our consciousness in yoga sadhana (Soham Yoga) for the completion of our evolutionary journey both in this world and beyond.

And the disciples of John shewed [told] him of all these things. Saint John was always following the ministry of Jesus through the accounts of those who had witnessed it for themselves.

Message to John the Baptist

And it came to pass, when Jesus had made an end of commanding his twelve disciples, he departed thence to teach and to preach in their cities. Now when John had heard in the prison the works of Christ, he sent two of his disciples, And said unto him, Art thou he that should come, or do we look for another? (Matthew 11:2-3).

When the men were come unto him, they said, John Baptist hath sent us unto thee, saying, Art thou he that should come? or look we for another? And in that same hour he cured many of their infirmities and plagues, and of evil spirits; and unto many that were blind he gave sight (Luke 7:20-21).

Jesus answered and said unto them, Go and shew John again those things which ye do hear and see. The blind receive their sight, and the lame walk, the lepers are cleansed, and the deaf hear, the dead are raised up, and the poor have the gospel preached to them. And blessed is he, whosoever shall not be offended in me (Matthew 11:4-6).

There are two points in this segment for us to consider. First are the things that a Messiah does, which are also the marks of the disciple of a Messiah. Second is the correct response to a Messiah.

The blind receive their sight, and the lame walk, the lepers are cleansed, and the deaf hear, the dead are raised up, and the poor have the gospel preached to them.

These are all spiritual symbols. Physical healing is wonderful, but if there is no spiritual awakening or healing, then little is accomplished. In Chapter Four of *Autobiography of a Yogi*, Yogananda recounts a conversation with Swami Kebalananda regarding a miracle of Lahiri Mahasaya. Swami Kebalananda said in conclusion: "The numerous bodies which were spectacularly healed through Lahiri Mahasaya eventually had to feed the flames of cremation. But the silent spiritual awakenings he effected, the Christlike disciples he fashioned, are his imperishable miracles." It was no different with Jesus.

It should also be pointed out that just as there can be no cure of a disease without a diagnosis, there can be no spiritual correction without acknowledgement of defects. So a true spiritual guide sees all problems the student may have and will help him to see them for himself and will give him the means to clear them up by his own efforts.

The blind receive their sight. Spirit blindness is a terrible handicap, especially since the spiritually blind are almost never aware of their condition and therefore do not seek to see in the spirit. But without that sight there is no real spiritual awareness or development. True spiritual teachers show the way to spiritual sight. Sometimes they temporarily bestow spiritual (in)sight on others, but if those so blessed do not work to preserve and increase it, they will fall back into the darkness of spiritual blindness.

The lame walk. Spiritual paralysis is another terrible condition. To walk we must have the strength and ability to walk. Within every human being there are many spiritual powers lying dormant. False teachers tell their disciples that they have done everything for them and will keep on doing so. But true teachers enable others to walk on their own. I have seen a lot of glitter gurus who could make a good impression on others, while their disciples were complete washouts. Fortunately I have met worthy teachers whose disciples were proof of their spiritual power to awaken and empower.

The lepers are cleansed. Purification is an absolute essential to fit ourselves for spiritual life, and continual purification is necessary to maintain it. Therefore an authentic teacher will teach the means to detect and eliminate all that hinders the aspirant.

The deaf hear. Spiritually speaking, most people are walking around in a coma, unable to see or hear. A fundamental condition of spiritual life is *awareness*, including the ability to hear and act on spiritual instruction. A worthy teacher knows how to get through to the sleepwalkers and help them to awake and stay awake.

The dead are raised up. The inner spiritual powers of the seeker are awakened through his sadhana. If such an awakening does not occur, then either he is not practicing, is not practicing correctly, or the methods taught him do not work. There is a lot of worthless and ineffectual "yoga" being peddled by worthless and ineffectual teachers. A man once wrote to me complaining that in nearly thirty years what he had been taught as the "highest" yoga had produced no effect.

On the other hand, there is a lot of "yoga" that does work–to the yogi's harm. One man told me that all of his guru's disciples detested one another. I was well acquainted with the "yoga" that group advocated, and the practice itself was the problem, actually making things worse for the practitioner.

One of my friends literally came to the verge of losing her mind through deep depression brought on by the negative practice she had been taught by "the only true master in the world." As soon as she stopped the practice she began recovering from its effects.

More than one person has come to me with mental and physical problems that stopped just as soon as they quit the illegitimate practices taught them by one of the best-known glitter gurus.

I knew a woman in India who was continually depressed because she believed that God hated her. I explained to her the nature of the practice her false guru had taught her, so she stopped it. A few hours later when I saw her she was smiling. "Are things better?" I asked her, and she answered: "I now know that God is with me."

The poor have the gospel preached to them. Even though yoga is a matter of interior cultivation, there must be intellectual knowledge and understanding as well. A worthy teacher gives very full and careful instruction to his students in both the methodology and the philosophy which is the basis of the yoga he teaches them. Furthermore, he points out the pitfalls, inner and outer, that they must avoid. And he will encourage them in spiritual study as a necessary part of their lives. He will not keep them in "loyal" ignorance.

And blessed is he, whosoever shall not be offended in me. The current of the world is toward bondage, so those who seek and teach the way to freedom are in conflict with the world and its ways, including the ways of the worldlings who are utterly deluded by the world–and like it. Opposition is sure to come to the aspiring yogi. The degree (intensity) of that opposition will be according to the yogi's karma. Sadly, a lot of people give in to pressure from family, friends and "society" and abandon the yoga life. So right from the beginning the aspirant must be ready for opposition and even persecution to some degree.

The word translated "offended" is *skandalizo* which means both "offend" and "make to offend." Many people are embarrassed and ashamed if others find out they are yogis. This is being offended in the search for God. Others agree to cut corners or forsake yoga altogether, and thus themselves offend. But it is their own selves they sin against, not God.

Skandalizo also means to allow oneself to be hindered or brought to a standstill, to be persuaded to turn away from the good. It also means to allow doubt and distrust to enter their hearts (regarding the higher life and its principles). It is quite common that a fallen yogi persuades himself that yoga is worthless or evil just as his opponents tell him it is. He either pretends to see and think as they do, or he really does begin to see and think in an erroneous and negative way. The "fox without a tail" syndrome is quite common.

The Greatness of John the Baptist-Elijah Reincarnated

And as they departed, Jesus began to say unto the multitudes concerning John, What went ye out into the wilderness to see? A reed shaken with the wind? But what went ye out for to see? A man clothed in soft raiment? behold, they that wear soft clothing are in kings' houses. But what went ye out for to see? A prophet? yea, I say unto you, and more than a prophet. For this is he, of whom it is written, Behold, I send my messenger before thy face, which shall prepare thy way before thee.

Verily I say unto you, Among them that are born of women there hath not risen a greater than John the Baptist: notwithstanding he that is least in the kingdom of heaven is greater than he.

And from the days of John the Baptist until now the kingdom of heaven suffereth violence, and the violent take it by force. For all the prophets and the law prophesied until John. And if ye will receive it, this is Elias, which was for to come. He that hath ears to hear, let him hear.

But whereunto shall I liken this generation? It is like unto children sitting in the markets, and calling unto their fellows, and saying, We have piped unto you, and ye have not danced; we have mourned unto you, and ye have not lamented. For John came neither eating nor drinking, and

they say, He hath a devil. The Son of man came eating and drinking, and they say, Behold a man gluttonous, and a winebibber, a friend of publicans and sinners. But wisdom is justified of her children. (Matthew 11:7-19).

And as they departed, Jesus began to say unto the multitudes concerning John, What went ye out into the wilderness to see? A reed shaken with the wind? But what went ye out for to see? A man clothed in soft raiment? behold, they that wear soft clothing are in kings' houses. But what went ye out for to see? A prophet? yea, I say unto you, and more than a prophet. For this is he, of whom it is written, Behold, I send my messenger before thy face, which shall prepare thy way before thee.

Saint John was more than a prophet, both in his spiritual attainment and in his office as *malak*, which means not just a messenger, but a representative of the One who sent him. Saint John was the true Vicar of Christ, speaking for God. In him the revelation of Jesus was begun. In a sense those who believed in and followed him were disciples of Jesus already. Seeing Saint John was seeing Jesus in a mystical way. In him the divine plan began to unfold before the manifestation of Jesus at his baptism.

Verily I say unto you, Among them that are born of women there hath not risen a greater than John the Baptist: notwithstanding he that is least in the kingdom of heaven is greater than he.

The Christians of the East have always understood that Saint John has a unique status. The present-day miracles and appearances of Saint John are many and astonishing in their magnitude. There is a reason why in the depiction known as the Deisis it is Saint John who is standing with the Virgin Mary before Jesus. And also why in icons Saint John is often depicted with angels' wings. The expression "an earthly angel and a heavenly man" was coined in reference to him.

What, then, did Jesus mean by saying: "Notwithstanding he that is least in the kingdom of heaven is greater than he"? First we must understand what is the kingdom of heaven.

Basileia, translated "kingdom" does not just mean a place, but royal power, kingship itself, dominion and rule. It also means the right or authority to rule over a kingdom.

Ouranon (ouranos) means the boundless sky which contains all things. It also implies a heaven beyond the material heaven or creation, the "heaven of heavens" which is eternal, the transcendent abode of God and all perfected beings: Satyaloka, the "world of the Real," or Siddhaloka, the world of the Perfected Ones (siddhas).

So the kingdom of heaven is obviously a spiritual level or attainment in which the individual participates in the omnipotence of God as a son of God. Jesus is not saying that any person who has been baptized and chrismated and incorporated into the Church on earth is in the kingdom of heaven and therefore greater than Saint John who was not an official "Christian" through the sacraments. Rather, he is saying that the greatest human being is not equal to a totally liberated being, a jivanmukta, a literal son of God, one with God as was Jesus and all the great masters of history.

He that is "born of woman" is a human being, however perfect. He that is "born of God" *is* god.

And from the days of John the Baptist until now the kingdom of heaven suffereth violence, and the violent take it by force. Those who are going to attain liberation from all the worlds will not do so by being "sweet" and "nice"–synonyms for being unintelligent and ineffectual (in other words, a likeable, spiritual nobody). They must be *biazo*: forceful, using their will to accomplish their goal, especially through self-discipline. The root word *biastes* implies being strong and applying that strength.

The word translated "take" is *harpazo*, which means to seize something by force and make it one's own with intense will and desire. Its root word, *haireomai*, means prefer or choose, and its root word is *airo*, which means to seize and carry away, making something one's own. It also implies to actively master and use what has been taken. The word translated "force" is also *biazo*.

We can get the idea from all this: spiritual life consists of jumping in and "winning the day" quite literally. Spiritual life and sadhana are not genteel endeavors, but real plundering, even warfare. Intensity is the word. This also implies that spiritual life and sadhana are the center of our life, that it comes first at all times and is seen as the main focus of our life. It is not an additive to our life, it *is* our life. Two of my friends who were living in a grihasta ashram in the Himalayan foothills had this motto on their wall: "I remember God and I live. I forget God and I die." It truly is a life or death matter, spiritually speaking, and we need to maintain that perspective throughout our life.

For all the prophets and the law prophesied until John. And if ye will receive it, this is Elias, which was for to come.

It is ridiculous to say that reincarnation is not in the Bible (though that would have nothing to do with it being either true or false). Here Jesus tells the disciples that Saint John the Baptist was the reincarnation of the prophet Elijah. Through the prophet Malachi God had said: "Behold, I will send you Elijah the prophet before the coming of the great and dreadful day of the Lord" (Malachi 4:5), the Messiah. That is why Jesus' "disciples asked him, saying, Why then say the scribes that Elias [Elijah] must first come? And Jesus answered and said unto them,...I say unto you, that Elias is come already, and they knew him not, but have done unto him whatsoever they listed.... Then the disciples understood that he spake unto them of John the Baptist" (Matthew 17:10, 12, 13). And we have seen that he has already said earlier in this section we are considering: "This is he, of whom it is written, Behold, I send my messenger before thy face, which shall prepare thy way before thee....And if ye will receive it, this is Elias, which was for to come."

Furthermore: "When Jesus came into the coasts of Caesarea Philippi, he asked his disciples, saying, Whom do men say that I the Son of man am? And they said, Some say that thou art John the Baptist: some, Elias; and others, Jeremias, or one of the prophets" (Matthew 16:13, 14). This is plainly evident that at the time of Jesus the people of Israel believed in reincarnation.

And even more: "As Jesus passed by, he saw a man which was blind from his birth. And his disciples asked him, saying, Master, who did sin, this man, or his parents, that he was born blind? Jesus answered, Neither hath this man sinned, nor his parents: but that the works of God should be made manifest in him" (John 9:1-3). This indicates that Jesus and his disciples believed in both karma and reincarnation. Long before that Job had said: "Naked came I out of my mother's womb, *and naked shall I return thither"* (Job 1:21). Reincarnation definitely is in the Bible, and especially in the life of Jesus. (See *May A Christian Believe In Reincarnation?*)

He that hath ears to hear, let him hear. Yes. Let him whose spiritual ears have opened hear and understand the universal laws of karma and reincarnation.

But whereunto shall I liken this generation? It is like unto children sitting in the markets, and calling unto their fellows, and saying, We have piped unto you, and ye have not danced; we have mourned unto you, and ye have not lamented. For John came neither eating nor drinking, and they say, He hath a devil. The Son of man came eating and drinking, and they say, Behold a man gluttonous, and a winebibber, a friend of publicans and sinners. Basically the idea is that people do not as a rule employ reason in their reactions to things. And certainly negative people with distorted minds reject what is true and positive, and accept what is false and negative. So it does not matter what positive people say or do–most of the world will accuse and defame them.

I experienced an example very like the one given here by Jesus. A man I knew continually griped about churches pressuring people to give them money. Once I told him about a church I knew of that was opposed to taking up collections or making any form of solicitations for money. At the back of the church building they had a box with a slot in the top and people put money in it, or did not. They asked that checks not be put in the box because they did not want to know who gave what amount–that was between them and God. The man then began bellowing about how stupid that was since churches needed money to function. I got the picture.

Also here Jesus is showing us that the world wants to control the thought and behavior of all those living in it, and woe to those who do not conform to its demands. Saint James summed it up very well: "Know ye not that the friendship of the world is enmity with God? whosoever therefore will be a friend of the world is the enemy of God" (James 4:4). There it is.

But wisdom is justified of her children. Wisdom, *sophia*, means both fully developed knowledge and understanding of that knowledge. Such knowledge is not narrow, confined to exclusively religious or philosophical subjects, but includes many diverse branches of knowledge. It includes both human and divine wisdom.

Mystical wisdom is especially indicated by sophia, so much so that in Eastern Christianity the second aspect of the Trinity, the Only-begotten Son, or Ishwara, is called The Holy Wisdom: *I Agia Sophia*. In the highest sense wisdom is God, and attaining to divine wisdom is attaining to God-realization (Brahmajnana).

Sophia also implies practical wisdom by which all can benefit, the capacity to see deeply into anything–the process Buddhism calls Penetration. Esoteric wisdom is the crowning glory of Holy Wisdom, wisdom is an attribute of God.

Sophos, the root of Sophia, especially means skilled, even expert, especially in creative matters. A wise person is a worthy scholar, not some simple-minded "man of faith." The wise do not believe, they *know*. In a filmed interview Carl Jung was asked if he believed God exists. He immediately responded: "I do not *believe* God exists; I *know* God exists."

The wise are the justification and proof of the truth and value of wisdom. We who seek higher life and consciousness should be the proof of such life and consciousness. The wise are the revelation of the ultimate Truth and Wisdom: God.

Mercy and Love

And one of the Pharisees desired him that he would eat with him. And he went into the Pharisee's house, and sat down to food. And, behold, a woman in the city, which was a sinner, when she knew that Jesus sat at food in the Pharisee's house, brought an alabaster box [jar] of ointment [perfumed oil], and stood [knelt] at his feet behind him weeping, and began to wash his feet with tears, and did wipe them with the hairs of her head, and kissed his feet, and anointed them with the ointment (Luke 7:36-38).

A woman in the city, which was a sinner. The woman is described as *hamartolos*, "full of sin." Obviously she was well-known (notorious), and her entry into the Pharisees' house would have been offensive to him and no doubt embarrassing.

At his feet. In the East the feet of holy people are bowed down to and touched because a person's biomagnetic energies or prana are strongly flowing out from his hands (which is why healing can be done by the "laying on of hands") and feet. Taking refuge in someone is said to be taking refuge "at their feet."

Weeping. Klaio does not just mean to shed tears (*dakruo*, to weep silently), it means to sob and even wail aloud, to lament. In this way she indicated her heartfelt repentance.

Kissed. Kataphileo means to kiss with great love and feeling.

Certainly the woman's actions were shocking and offensive to "the righteous" who were there. And so:

> Now when the Pharisee which had bidden him saw it, he spake within himself, saying, This man, if he were a prophet, would have known who and what manner of woman this is that toucheth him: for she is a sinner (Luke 7:39).

The word *Pharisaios* literally means "a separatist" in the sense of one who is not just exclusively religious, but religious in an exclusionary manner or attitude. That is, they believed in avoiding all contact with those who were not of their persuasion, thus keeping themselves "pure" from defilement through association. Realizing this we can see how horrified he was that the woman had even entered his house. And Jesus was allowing her to touch him and "make a spectacle of herself" right there!

In India we find the concept of "untouchability," that there are people who should not be touched or even allowed to come near those who are spiritually inclined, that their aura or personal energy field will influence and defile the auras of those they come near. "Distance pollution" is a very real concept, and in past centuries there were laws setting how much distance must be kept by an untouchable (or even a low caste person) so they would not defile someone else. In some places, the distance required indicated the social status of those they were to avoid coming near. And kings would officially grant longer and longer distances to those who were more and more prestigious. Violating the laws of distance pollution was punished with severe beating or even death. Also there were laws as to who could kill those "polluters" without being considered guilty of homicide.

I personally met two persons who told me about their experience of untouchablility. One was an Indian friend of mine who told me that attached to his Brahmin family was a family of "low caste" hereditary servants. Every day when the senior servant came to ask his father about the day's work they would stand so far apart that they would have to speak in very loud voices or even shout to hear one another. The other was more interesting. She was a European who came to India at the beginning of the Second World War to teach in a girls' school in Varanasi (Benares) attached to the Theosophical Society. Later she joined a very strict and conservative ashram where non-Indians were considered untouchable. So she not only had to observe very many do-not-touch and do-not-go-there rules, she was generally treated with disrespect and dislike. Although the rules applied to all non-Indians, she was the only one who got such unpleasant "special" treatment. This offended her very much. Then one night she had a vivid dream which she believed was a real past life recall experience. She was an Indian man riding a horse in a town when an untouchable man came up asking for alms and in the process touched him. Going into a rage, she/he beat the man to death. When she woke up she realized that it was her action in a previous life that resulted in her present situation. So she accepted it and only paid attention to her spiritual life–always a good idea.

The Pharisee, in keeping with his usual attitude, was feeling contemptuous of Jesus for not repulsing the woman and driving her away.

> And Jesus answering said unto him, Simon, I have somewhat to say unto thee. And he saith, Master [didaskalos: teacher], say on.
> There was a certain creditor which had two debtors: the one owed five hundred pence, and the other fifty. And when they had nothing to pay, he frankly forgave them both. Tell me therefore, which of them will love him most?
> Simon answered and said, I suppose that he, to whom he forgave most. And he said unto him, Thou hast rightly judged.
> And he turned to the woman, and said unto Simon, Seest thou this woman? I entered into thine house, thou gavest me no water for my feet: but she hath washed my feet with tears, and wiped them with the hairs of her head. Thou gavest me no kiss: but this woman since the time I came in hath not ceased to kiss my feet. My head with oil thou didst not anoint: but this woman hath anointed my feet with ointment. Wherefore I say unto thee, Her sins, which are many, are forgiven; for she loved much: but to whom little is forgiven, the same loveth little.
> And he said unto her, Thy sins are forgiven.

> And they that sat at food with him began to say within themselves, Who is this that forgiveth sins also?
> And he said to the woman, Thy faith hath saved thee; go in peace (Luke 7:40-50).

The Pharisee, Simon, had acted toward Jesus in an insulting manner. It was common custom that a host would greet a guest by either offering him water to wash his feet or would wash the guest's feet himself. He would then greet him with a kiss and put oil on the guest's head to alleviate the dryness of the climate. But the "sinful" woman had done all these things instead of the host. Therefore Jesus said to her, "Thy faith hath saved thee." For she trusted in the love and mercy of Jesus and knew he would not reject her.

No action is purely physical, but is also interior–mental. So what went on in the woman's soul, in her mind and heart, itself brought about a reformation which liberated her from her sinful state. For the word *sozo* means to be delivered, healed and restored. And so it was with her.

The Friends Of Jesus Think He Is Insane

And it came to pass afterward, that he went throughout every city and village, preaching and shewing the glad tidings [gospel: good news] of the kingdom of God: and the twelve were with him, and certain women, which had been healed of evil spirits and infirmities, Mary called Magdalene, out of whom went seven devils,and Joanna the wife of Chuza Herod's steward, and Susanna, and many others, which ministered unto him of their substance (Luke 8:1-3).

And the multitude cometh together again, so that they could not so much as eat bread. And when his friends heard of it, they went out to lay hold on him: for they said, He is beside himself (Mark 3:20-21).

There is a Russian proverb: "Even if you convince me, I will not be convinced." A person who is determined to misunderstand will do so, no matter what. Jesus was healing disease and delivering people from spirit possession and preaching the message of hope. So to his "friends" he was insane. (*Existemi* means to be out of one's mind or beside oneself–out of control.) They wanted to restrain him by force, put him away and end his ministry of healing and deliverance from sin and ignorance. As we so often say: With friends like that, who needs enemies? The truth being that they really were his enemies.

The Kingdom of God is Come Unto You

Then was brought unto him one possessed with a devil, blind, and dumb: and he healed him, insomuch that the blind and dumb both spake and saw. And all the people were amazed, and said, Is not this the son of David? But when the Pharisees heard it, they said, This fellow doth not cast out devils, but by Beelzebub the prince of the devils. And Jesus knew their thoughts, and said unto them, Every kingdom divided against itself is brought to desolation; and every city or house divided against itself shall not stand: And if Satan cast out Satan, he is divided against himself; how shall then his kingdom stand? And if I by Beelzebub cast out devils, by whom do your children cast them out? therefore they shall be your judges. But if I cast out devils by the Spirit of God, then the kingdom of God is come unto you. Or else how can one enter into a strong man's house, and spoil his goods, except he first bind the strong man? and then he will spoil his house. He that is not with me is against me; and he that gathereth not with me scattereth abroad (Matthew 12:22-30).

Then was brought unto him one possessed with a devil, blind, and dumb: and he healed him, insomuch that the blind and dumb both spake and saw. Because the body of a person is formed with his guidance in the womb according to his karmic patterns (configurations), when an alien spirit invades him and tries to completely possess him, it is sometimes not possible to fully do so. Therefore certain physical functions of the possessed person may be impaired, as in the case of this possessed man who was blind and mute as a result of the conflict produced in his body by the possession.

And all the people were amazed, and said, Is not this the son of David [the Messiah]? But when the Pharisees heard it, they said, This fellow doth not cast out devils, but by Beelzebub the prince of the devils. This is business as usual with the cult religionists. When something is done by their group it is proof that they are the only true group. So when the same thing is done by another group or religion it is harshly declared to be "of the devil" or the product of some kind of human or supernatural deception.

And Jesus knew their thoughts, and said unto them, Every kingdom divided against itself is brought to desolation; and every city or house divided against itself shall not stand: And if Satan cast out Satan, he is divided against himself; how shall then his kingdom stand? This is simple good reason, but we can learn a little more from Jesus' words.

First, about ourselves. If our inner kingdom is split–part positive and part negative–it will eventually come to nothing. Only if it is totally positive and consistent in all aspects will we succeed spiritually. So those with divided minds should heed the words of Saint James the Great: "A double minded man is unstable in all his ways" (James 1:8). And: "Purify your hearts, ye double minded" (James 4:8). *Dipsuchos* means "two-spirited" or vacillating. In other words, those he is speaking to are a mixture of positive and negative in their minds and wills. Part of them tends to the dark and part of them tends to the light. Only those who are single-minded will succeed. Sri Ramakrishna said that during his tapasya he once saw that two subtle forms came out of his body. Each one looked like him. One was totally dark like deep shadow and the other was totally radiant with light. He understood that one was the papa purusha, the negative side of his nature and the other was the punya purusha, the positive side of his nature. They fought and the punya purusha killed the papa purusha with a trident, the weapon of Shiva. This struggle must eventually take place in everyone and the positive must "kill" the negative by overcoming and banishing it.

Second, about others whose claims may not be so. We often find people we think are quite honest, truthful and positive–and claim to be so themselves. But then we find that although they will not advocate evil or compromise with evil personally, they will not take an active or overt stand against it. Then we know that they are really still on the other side and therefore cannot stand against it either mentally or externally. A classic example is that of a man (who later totally abandoned spiritual life) who told me, smiling all the while: "I am against abortion, but I am for choice." Not so. "He that is not with me is against me; and he that gathereth not with me scattereth abroad" (Matthew 12:30).

The enemies of Jesus did not hesitate to speak plainly and openly about Jesus, so he returns the compliment.

The Blasphemy Against The Holy Spirit

> Wherefore I say unto you, All manner of sin and blasphemy shall be forgiven unto men: but the blasphemy against the Holy Ghost shall not be forgiven unto men. And whosoever speaketh a word against the Son of man, it shall be forgiven him: but whosoever speaketh against the Holy Ghost, it shall not be forgiven him, neither in this world, neither in the world to come (Matthew 12:31-32).

Exoteric Christians have a tremendous amount of fun with these verses, usually directing them to whomever or whatever they dislike at the moment. A minister publicly declared (in her presence) that a cousin of mine had committed the sin against the Holy Spirit and could never be "saved." As a result she never went to church again, but lived the rest of her life terrified of dying and going to hell. So it is a good idea to really understand the words of Jesus concerning this.

First of all, who is he speaking about? The Holy Spirit. And not just the Holy Spirit as God–part of the Trinity–but the Holy Spirit in Her aspect of evolutionary power, which is the basis of all relative existence, and includes the stimulus or urge toward higher evolution. Just as earthly mothers conceive, bring the child to term, give it birth and nourish it from their bodies, in the same way the Holy Spirit Mother brings us into relativity, brings us many times into birth from many earthly mothers, and throughout all our subsequent lives sustains us and fosters our evolving consciousness in many ways in order to ultimately bring us to full enlightenment and the divine status meant by the words "sons of God."

Second, what is he speaking about? He is speaking about our slowing or prevention of the process of the evolution of our consciousness. This is the sin against the Holy Spirit, for besides transgression, *amartia* also means offence: rebellion against the destiny intended for us "before the world was" (John 17:5). And *blasphemia* means to disrespect and dishonor–in this case, the divine image within us which is fostered by the Holy Spirit. Therefore, our every blocking or prevention of our spiritual evolution is the Sin Against The Holy Spirit. And it is also a sin and blasphemy against ourselves–our true Atman-Self as children of God and part of God.

One usual–and very sad–effect of neglecting or being careless in spiritual discipline (for there is no spiritual life without spiritual discipline) is simply falling asleep inwardly and being unaware of it, being completely numb in intuition and conscience. Deep sleep is very comfortable, and so is deep spiritual sleep.

There is another more metaphysical aspect to this. Every moment in our life is a result of the karma we have created, either long past or only a few minutes before. To come into the orbit of spiritual truth and spiritual practice, especially yoga sadhana, takes a great positive karmic accumulation or power. Without this karmic backup, spiritual life can only be a temporary, passing phase. And neglecting or postponing spiritual life (sadhana, especially) negates that positive force, and we are in danger of losing the insight we had, and just lapsing back into spiritual unconsciousness.

For every action there is an equal and opposite reaction is the law. This means that when a door of opportunity opens, there is an equal possibility of it closing. And for many people, the door opens and closes without their even knowing it. Others know it has opened and assume that they can take all the time they want–even years–to go through it. But they are wrong, and one day it closes. Some become aware of that, and instead of doing all they can to retrace their steps and reopen it, they become depressed and sure that "it's all over" for them spiritually. And it is. Because they want it to be that way, thinking it absolves them of all responsibility for betraying the Christ in them just as Judas betrayed Jesus. They are wrong. But the deadening effect is a present reality.

I once heard a song sung in church that I never forgot even though it was over sixty years ago. It said:

> There's a line that is drawn by rejecting our Lord,
> Where the call of His Spirit is lost,
> And you hurry along with the pleasure-mad throng–
> Have you counted, have you counted the cost?

In time our inner ears become deaf to the call and it is all over for this incarnation.

This sin and blasphemy against our own spirit-Self is the most negative of all actions, and its result is the worst of all karmas since it is against both God and our Self which are one. Other karmas can be neutralized or greatly lessened by positive actions, but this is not "forgiven" in that sense. *Aphiemi* means to banish and cancel something. But the consequences of this karma must be faced either in this life or in future lives. It must be undergone by experiencing spiritual stagnation (the karma) against which we must struggle to break through and free ourselves from. This is a fully conscious act and can only take place when we realize that spiritual growth is the primary purpose of human life and when we desire it above all else and are willing to do anything to bring it about. It always entails effort, perseverance and sacrifice.

Jesus was speaking in the power and at the will of the Holy Spirit, and those who defamed him were defaming God. So he continues with what used to be called "home truths."

Evil Or Good

> Either make the tree good, and his fruit good; or else make the tree corrupt, and his fruit corrupt: for the tree is known by his fruit (Matthew 12:33).

We have already considered the state of being double-minded. There are people that vacillate (shilly-shally is a good southern term) between right and wrong, good and evil. Sometimes they are positive and sometimes they are negative–neither just one or the other. Jesus is telling his opponents to wake up and realize the real state of things and then be one or the other and so reveal their true character to themselves and others.

The major point here is our ability to make ourselves what we are, or shall be. We have to take charge of our bodies, minds and lives and put them on the path we desire: up or down. *Kalos* means morally good, virtuous and worthy. *Sapros* means corrupt, worthless, decayed and diseased. They are very distinct from one another.

The word *karpos*, fruit, is particularly appropriate here, for its root word means something that has been picked from a tree or bush. It is karma! We decide if our karma is going to be good or bad. It is all up to us. When people are going through difficulties they often lament, "It is just my karma!" And they are right. They did it. They chose it. And now they can change the quality of what they do and choose. Nobody else can do it for them. Everyone loves the idea of free will until faced with the consequences and implications. We do it to ourselves. Not God. Not others. Ourselves.

> O generation of vipers, how can ye, being evil, speak good things? for out of the abundance of the heart the

mouth speaketh. A good man out of the good treasure of the heart bringeth forth good things: and an evil man out of the evil treasure bringeth forth evil things (Matthew 12:34-35).

Our life is our own creation. No one else is involved, though we may try to excuse ourselves by blaming others. We are IT. We have considered this previously.

The Power Of Every Spoken Word

> But I say unto you, That every idle word that men shall speak, they shall give account thereof in the day of judgment. For by thy words thou shalt be justified, and by thy words thou shalt be condemned (Matthew 12:36-37).

The power of speech (logos) is what distinguishes human beings as a species. And it is power, especially to those of a more esoteric viewpoint, especially the yogis. Jesus spoke with the perspective of a yogi, saying that every word we speak has an effect on us. However, "word" here is not logos but *rhema*, which means worthless speech, either because the topic is nothing in itself or has nil value or beneficial effect. This is underscored by the word "idle" (*argos*) which means idle, barren, careless, ineffectual and useless. This can include false or baseless speech, and especially trivial or pointless speech.

It is a sobering thought that every (*pas*) such word we speak has an effect in our subtle energy levels. It may be small, but when there are hundreds or thousands of words piling up in a day, it is not to be shrugged off. As Saint James (5:12) advises us: "Let your yea be yea; and your nay, nay." In other words speak straight and to the point and let there be no doubt of your meaning. There are people who never give a clear or complete picture when they speak. No matter how much you try, you cannot get them to speak plain truth. Or when you ask them a question that can easily be answered Yes or No, they go into some ramble either to prolong the time before they finally have to speak plainly, or to avoid the truth, or to cloud the truth and create confusion and uncertainty. This is very real mental and spiritual flaw. There are people that say more than the truth and those that say less than the truth. Both are liars. As Jesus has already said: "Let your communication [logos–speech] be, Yea, yea; Nay, nay: for whatsoever is more than these cometh of evil" (Matthew 5:37).

Such insubstantial or irrelevant speech is a karmic sowing and will be reaped in some form in the future. It may in the form of being led astray by others who engage in such speaking, or in our being unable to perceive the truth of things from others' speech. Either way, the result is definitely detrimental to us. The "day of judgment" is when our speech karma comes back and we reap the result which itself is our justification or condemnation.

The True Family Of Jesus

> While he yet talked to the people, behold, his mother and his brethren stood without, desiring to speak with him (Matthew 12:46).
>
> And the multitude sat about him, and they said unto him, Behold, thy mother and thy brethren without seek for thee (Mark 3:32).
>
> But he answered and said unto him that told him, Who is my mother? and who are my brethren? And he stretched forth his hand toward his disciples, and said, Behold my mother and my brethren! For whosoever shall do the will of my Father which is in heaven, the same is my brother, and sister, and mother (Matthew 12:48-50).

Jesus was the only child of the Virgin Mary, but in the East (including India) cousins are called brothers. An Indian friend of mine had only one brother, but over time he introduced several men to me as "my brother." When I asked him about this, he said, "They are my cousin-brothers." Some of these wanting to speak to Jesus might have been children of the sister of Saint Joseph whom he had adopted after her death. Either way, it must have been a shock when he said that his disciples and all who did the will of God were his brothers and sisters and even his mother!

But it does not surprise me. About five hundred years ago in India a great scholar and devotee named Advaita Acharya felt that the only thing that could straighten out the spiritual chaos which prevailed would be an incarnation of God—the birth of an avatar. Everyone told him that the sacred books declared that at that time things were so dark spiritually that no avatar could be born—not for centuries. But he enlisted the aid of several other genuine devotees and every day each one of them did ritualistic worship and prayed specifically for the advent of an avatar. Early one morning after some years, Advaita Acharya had a vision in which a divine being told him, "You have called me, and I have come," and showed him where he had been born. Advaita told the others and they went to the place shown in his vision and found that a child had just been born there. By their spiritual eyes they could see that their prayers had been fulfilled and an avatar had come to them. The child, Nimai, grew into an astonishing spiritual person. When he was old enough he became a sannyasi with the name Krishna Chaitanya. And from childhood he used to salute Advaita Acharya and call him father because he had brought about his incarnation. In the same way, those for whose upliftment Jesus was incarnate were in a sense his parents and family.

Jesus is also showing to us that those who do the will of the Father by living in a pure way and ever seek to know God are our true family, closer to us than any blood relatives that do not seek God or even believe it is possible.

The Field Of The Heart

The same day went Jesus out of the house, and sat by the sea side (Matthew 13:1).

And when much people were gathered together, and were come to him out of every city (Luke 8:4).

He went into a ship, and sat; and the whole multitude stood on the shore (Matthew 13:2).

And he taught them many things by parables, and said unto them in his doctrine, Hearken; Behold, there went out a sower to sow (Mark 4:2-3).

And as he sowed, some fell by the way side; and it was trodden down, and the fowls of the air devoured it (Luke 8:5).

And some fell on stony ground, where it had not much earth; and immediately it sprang up, because it had no depth of earth:but when the sun was up, it was scorched; and because it had no root, it withered away. And some fell among thorns, and the thorns grew up, and choked it, and it yielded no fruit. And other fell on good ground, and did yield fruit that sprang up and increased; and brought forth, some thirty, and some sixty, and some an hundred. And he said unto them, He that hath ears to hear, let him hear.

And when he was alone, they that were about him with the twelve asked of him the parable. And he said unto them, Unto you it is given to know the mystery of the kingdom of God: but unto them that are without, all these things are done in parables (Mark 4:5-11)

For whosoever hath, to him shall be given, and he shall have more abundance: but whosoever hath not, from him

> shall be taken away even that he hath. Therefore speak I to them in parables: because they seeing see not; and hearing they hear not, neither do they understand. And in them is fulfilled the prophecy of Esaias, which saith, By hearing ye shall hear, and shall not understand; and seeing ye shall see, and shall not perceive: For this people's heart is waxed gross, and their ears are dull of hearing, and their eyes they have closed; lest at any time they should see with their eyes, and hear with their ears, and should understand with their heart, and should be converted, and I should heal them.
>
> But blessed are your eyes, for they see: and your ears, for they hear. For verily I say unto you, That many prophets and righteous men have desired to see those things which ye see, and have not seen them; and to hear those things which ye hear, and have not heard them (Matthew 13:12-17).

After these verses Jesus will explain the parable, but now he tells the apostles the way things are in relation to the ordinary people and to them. It is very important for us to realize this is not a matter of Jesus or God having favorites or that God arbitrarily chooses whom He will grace or turn away. Rather it is all according to the inner desire and disposition of each individual.

Unto you it is given to know the mystery of the kingdom of God: but unto them that are without, all these things are done in parables. The word here translated "know" is *ginosko*, which has several possible aspects. Some people know something because they allow themselves to know it, and many people do not know something because they do not allow themselves to know it: 1) by refusing to recognize the truth; 2) by just not bothering to know the truth; 3) by ignoring the existence of the truth; 4) by blinding themselves to the truth; and 5) by willfully either not understanding or misunderstanding the truth. Human beings habitually engage in all of these.

Spiritual knowledge is a mystery (*musterion*) in the sense that it is secret and hidden. But not secret because God or someone does not let us have knowledge, but because it has to be sought after and uncovered since it is not readily at sight. That means we have to know or intuit it is there and then make the effort to gain it. The Greeks had a story that the gods stole happiness from humans and consulted with each other as how they could hide it from them. One god said, "Let's hide it deep in the earth." "No," said another, "no matter how deep we hide it, they will eventually dig down to it." Another said, "Then let's hide it in the sky among the stars." "No, one day they will get to the stars." "Let's hide it in the deepest part of the sea." "They will get there, too." "Let's hide it on the highest mountain." They will climb up there one day." Then a wiser god, who understood humans better than the others, said, "I know what to do! We will hide happiness inside them–they will never think to look there." And so they did.

Jesus speaks of those "that are without." The word is *exo*, which means actually outside a place, or even simply not there–an alien or stranger. We are always in two places: outer and inner. Our body is in one place, but our mind can be in another. My maternal grandmother lived in a house on a corner. To the west of her house there lived the town grouch. Directly across the street lived the town gossip, and on the opposite corner lived a family of rich, F. Scott Fitzgerald-type drunks. The worlds her neighbors lived in were absolutely different from the supernatural world she lived in at all times. Whenever I would enter her door I was instantly in another dimension that was wondrously indescribable. No one knew that she was a great spiritual clairvoyant, spiritual visionary and healer but myself. She was In and her neighbors were Out. It was all a matter of consciousness.

"Done" is a very strange translation. *Ginomai* means told, shown or revealed. Jesus revealed the mysteries of the kingdom in symbols, *parabole*. Why did he do this? They were a test to determine who was In and who was Out. If they understood, they were In, and if they did not understand, they were Out. Jesus did not make them In or Out. That was done by them, by their own state of awareness and understanding or lack thereof.

For whosoever hath, to him shall be given, and he shall have more abundance. To really have something implies knowledge and control over it as an active part of the possessor's life. Those whose spiritual life is not just an aspiration or an idea, but a present reality which can be manifested, are those that have spiritual consciousness. And since it is the nature of living things to grow and develop, so does the life of those who are spiritually alive. *Scheo* (have) implies control and active use. Those who are in charge of their spiritual life and are evolving in consciousness as a result will by the very nature of things draw to themselves more growth and development. The word *perisseuo* does not just mean having a lot, but a continual growth–superabundance. It also means to excel and move upward without any loss or diminution. "Beyond measure" is one meaning. It is a dynamic condition. The American nun-poet Sister Maddaleva wrote:

> Know you the journey that I take?
> Know you the voyage that I make?
> The joy of it – one's heart could break.
>
> No jot of time have I to spare,
> Nor will to loiter anywhere,
> So eager am I to be there
>
> For that the way is hard and long,
> For that gray fears upon it throng,
> I set my journey to the song.
>
> And it grows wondrous happy so
> Singing I hurry on for–oh!
> It is to God, to God I go.

But whosoever hath not, from him shall be taken away even that he hath. We "have" something by being in touch with it and actively possessing it. Many times people are born with karmas and samskaras that indicate spiritual growth and insight gained in a previous life. But if in the present life that spiritual awareness is not truly possessed and expanded, then it will drain away and be lost. For that is the nature of life in this ever-changing, unstable world.

Therefore speak I to them in parables: because they seeing see not; and hearing they hear not, neither do they understand. Again, this is not a condition brought upon them by God, but by themselves. They do not wish to see, hear or understand. Jesus does not speak to them in parables because he does not want them to understand, but because he wants to reveal to them their inability to comprehend in hope that they will seek to awaken and understand.

I knew a man that went to India to meet Anandamayi Ma. He told me, "Every time I looked at Ma I could tell there was what the Bible calls 'a great gulf' between us–I might be only a few feet from Ma physically, but spiritually I was not even in the room. I prayed and prayed for that gulf to be taken away, but only after some years of struggle and undergoing tremendous adversities did it vanish and I found myself 'with' Ma always." Sadly, few are those who realize and admit the problem, and much fewer are those that get busy and overcome or remove it.

> **And in them is fulfilled the prophecy of Esaias, which saith, By hearing ye shall hear, and shall not understand; and seeing ye shall see, and shall not perceive: For this people's heart is waxed gross, and their ears are dull of hearing, and their eyes they have closed; lest at any time they should see with their eyes, and hear with their ears, and should understand with their heart, and should be converted, and I should heal them (Matthew 13:14-15).**

And in them is fulfilled the prophecy of Esaias, which saith, By hearing ye shall hear, and shall not understand; and seeing ye shall see, and shall not perceive. The word translated "understand" is *suniemi*, which means to come to a conclusion and thereby comprehend something. And it also has the implication of acting according to the understanding. Of course we cannot understand something if we do not look at it carefully and think about its implications. In other words, we have to use our intelligence. And to do that we have to care about the matter. This pretty well covers the motivation of those who bother and those who do not. There are those who hear but do not hear and see but do not see. Or we could say that they hear but do not heed and see but do not notice. As Saint Peter said (II Peter 3:5), "they willingly are ignorant."

For this people's heart is waxed gross, and their ears are dull of hearing, and their eyes they have closed; lest at any time they should see with their eyes, and hear with their ears, and should understand with their heart, and should be converted, and I should heal them. The mind is the fundamental faculty of the human being and determines the perceptions, thoughts and actions of everyone. Sri Ramakrishna often said, "The mind is everything." And Jesus feels the same: that is the problem with many people. He says that the people's minds are *pachuno*, which means coarse, dull, heavy and insensitive. They are either deaf or only partially hearing. And the eyes of their minds are closed, so they are mentally blind as well as deaf. This guarantees that they will never "see with their eyes, and hear with their ears, and understand with their heart, and be converted (*epistrepho*–turned around), and I should heal them." It is a self-imposed sentence of spiritual death.

But blessed are your eyes, for they see: and your ears, for they hear. For verily I say unto you, That many prophets and righteous men have desired to see those things which ye see, and have not seen them; and to hear those things which ye hear, and have not heard them (Matthew 13:16-17).

Those who see and hear are *makarios*: supremely blest and happy.

The Seed In The Heart

> Hear ye therefore the parable of the sower.
>
> When any one heareth the word of the kingdom, and understandeth it not, then cometh the wicked one, and catcheth away that which was sown in his heart. This is he which received seed by the way side.
>
> But he that received the seed into stony places, the same is he that heareth the word, and anon with joy receiveth it; yet hath he not root in himself, but dureth for a while: for when tribulation or persecution ariseth because of the word, by and by he is offended.
>
> He also that received seed among the thorns is he that heareth the word; and the care of this world, and the deceitfulness of riches, choke the word, and he becometh unfruitful.
>
> But he that received seed into the good ground is he that heareth the word, and understandeth it; which also beareth fruit, and bringeth forth, some an hundredfold, some sixty, some thirty (Matthew 13:18-23).

Hear ye therefore the parable of the sower. Akouo means to listen, hear and understand–all that. So-called "believing" that is nothing more than accepting something as true with no real thought about the matter is itself shameful. Jesus knows that his words must at least be understood, even if in many cases they will not be followed.

When any one heareth the word of the kingdom, and understandeth it not, then cometh the wicked one, and catcheth away that which was sown in his heart. This is he which received seed by the way side. Interestingly, "cometh" is the translation of *erchomai*, which means both come and enter. Who comes and enters? The wicked one. And who is that? Satan, the force of cosmic delusion. Quite some time back we briefly considered the subject of Satan, and I am repeating the paragraph here to make sure we are in perspective.

"In English we tend to have relatively simple words for things, mutations of either Latin or Greek words that express their nature. In some languages, though, they string together several words to get the idea across. In *The Expanded New Testament* Wuest has done this, naming Satan 'He-Who-Puts-To-The-Test-By-His-Solicitation-To-Do-Evil.' Lengthy, but accurate. Human beings have many depictions and ideas about the nature of 'the Devil,' but here we have its essential nature. Satan is the magnetic force that pulls people toward the path of evil. And evil need not be the obvious things such as lying and murder, but those things which conduce to evil or weaken us, making us susceptible to the pull of negativity. Often a thing is evil because of what it leads to, though not evil in itself. So the Satanic force draws us toward that as a step toward evil. From this we can see that virtually everything that exists has the possibility of being 'satanic.' For this reason Saint Peter wrote: 'Be sober, be vigilant; because your adversary the devil, as a roaring lion, walketh about, seeking whom he may devour" (I Peter 5:8). And he has many "mouths" with which to devour.

Satan is the cosmic force of evil and chaos. It is not a person, but a field of energy which is so large and strong that is can influence virtually anything in the material level of creation. It is not a person, but since all things are made of Intelligence, it has a kind of semi-life. And of course all those evil beings which have been to some degree absorbed or united with it can direct its power. There are, as I say, evil beings such as evil human beings, angels and archangels that live and move in the outer darkness just as the saints and angels and higher evolved beings live and move in the light and love of God. They are literally poles apart.

And then there is the much more dangerous entity: our own ego with its ignorance, greed and corrupted understanding and will. Since that is part of our very makeup it is to a great extent "us," even though it is not really our eternal, true nature which is divine spirit.

So when the light of truth comes to us, negative forces both outside and within us (our energy makeup) move into action and begin to draw us away and back into the dark, hoping to completely steal from us our understanding. In this parable the seed was not sown in prepared earth, but just incidentally by the side of the road. So it was walked upon by wayfarers and crushed into the ground and destroyed. Spiritual marauders, including our own negativity, spoil it. Often (usually) the seed does not fall into our hearts, but just into our fickle and restless minds. And there it lies to no purpose at all until wiped out.

But he that received the seed into stony places, the same is he that heareth the word, and anon [immediately] with joy receiveth it; yet hath he not root in himself, but dureth for a while: for when tribulation or persecution ariseth because of the word, by and by he is offended. This is by far the most common scenario: at first encounter receiving the truth of the spirit with *chara*–gladness and great happiness. I have found that it is not a good sign when there is great display and declarations of "home at last" and similar exuberances, rather than just quiet appreciation accompanied by serious consideration of how to apply the principles newly learned. Actually, it has been my observation that the more noise and show these people put on, the sooner will be their departure and the more negative their rejection of the truth they seemed to welcome. This is because their jubilation was to a great extent a display of egoic self-confidence and the jubilation of a child with a new toy–something to use for personal satisfaction. But when it comes time to sit down and take stock of what is required to apply the new discovery the exit begins to appeal more and more. Over the hill and far away is the result.

Jesus indicates the reason for this: shallowness and superficiality. They have no "root" within. That is, they have no background from previous lives and no depth of intention whatever. They are like a little cousin of mine about whom an aunt said to me: "He is alway 'ready to go' but never 'ready to stay.'"

The word translated "tribulation" is *thlipsis*, whose root word is pressure, and means inner trouble or pain resulting from pressure. As soon as the pressure of the need to conform to higher principles or to eliminate from their life whatever is contrary to those principles, they become unhappy, then sullen, and then defiant and finally depart, usually with as much noise as they arrived–but this time negative and critical. Their bluff has been called and their lack revealed.

"Offended" is a misleading translation of *skandalizo*, though offense is implied. It literally means "made to stumble [and fall]." This type of person ends up claiming to have been wronged, pressured or even taken advantage of. They are now offended at those they formerly thanked for the knowledge they received. They delude themselves (or others) into deciding they they have been wronged, that there was an attempt to force or control them. And so they depart in accusation and blame. In earlier centuries it was believed that when a demon was encountered it would eventually disappear, leaving behind the rotten-egg smell of burning sulphur. It is much the same with them.

He also that received seed among the thorns is he that heareth the word; and the care of this world, and the deceitfulness of riches, choke the word, and he becometh unfruitful. This is a sadder situation. The previous failure resulted from a general lack on the part of the person, but this is a person who is overcome by the things around him. The previous person is not sincere, while this person is. But he is too weak to withstand the bombardment of his environment. The snares of the world entrap him. I could not begin to list the snares of the world, because they are infinite and often tailor-made by Satan for that individual person. Sometimes they take the form of obstacles and sometimes they take the form of opportunities. I have many times seen Satan offer to someone something they have wanted for a long time and they took it and were vanquished. Sometimes Satan threatens and frightens, or entices and cajoles. But I have seen that after a seeker has turned from spiritual life and taken that object, it is very quickly lost. And he never turns back to spiritual life. So he ends up with nothing.

Sometimes worldly obligations overwhelm him. Family or friends attack his aspirations and pull him away. The delusions of happiness through material gains often ruin a person's spiritual opportunities. I have known people to be given money so they would drop their spiritual interests. Satan is still in the business of "All these things will I give thee, if thou wilt fall down and worship me" (Matthew 4:9), though in the spirit the person becomes *akarpos*, utterly barren and desolate.

But he that received seed into the good ground is he that heareth the word, and understandeth it; which also beareth fruit, and bringeth forth, some an hundredfold, some sixty, some thirty (Matthew 13:18-23). The deciding factor in this successful reception of the seed is *kalos*: good. It also means true, fitting and worthy, and these are the key to Jesus' meaning.

True. Most people do not know their own minds. Rare are those who can see themselves clearly exactly as they are, that are true in self-knowledge. Only those who have illusions about themselves fail to realize when they are not capable of something. When I was just a child I realized that accurately knowing what I could do was important, but that it was equally important for me to know what I could not do. Later on I saw all around me people who were attempting what they were incapable of successfully doing. And I saw truly gifted people who had no idea of their potential and consequently never realized it. Seeing clearly and living true to oneself is a fundamental trait of goodness. Shakespeare had it absolutely right: "To thine own self be true, and it must follow, as the night the day, thou canst not then be false to any man," including oneself.

Fitting. It is impossible to have an effective spiritual life if our outer life is not compatible with immersion in spiritual practices and the resulting higher consciousness. We have already considered this in the section about the destructive effects of putting new cloth on old cloth and new wine in old bottles. As a fundamentalist Protestant I had no idea what this meant, so I just "read and believed" like a good exoteric Christian and stayed ignorant. But when I became a yogi its meaning was clear right away, for its meaning is fundamentally related to sadhana and spiritual life.

As I say, I became a yogi and had many yogi friends and acquaintances, but I am sorry to tell you that most of them left the yoga life. Some retained the claim to being a yogi but never meditated, only going to social events sponsored by yogis or yoga organizations. In their personal, daily life they were not yogis by any stretch of the imagination. Many of them reverted to the life they lived before becoming yogis, and a large percentage actually lapsed into a condition much worse than the life they led before they took up yoga.

Some of those that had been the most serious and dedicated developed an aversion to anything spiritual. It became impossible to talk with them about spiritual things. They were like the description of Saint James: "Clouds they are without water, carried about of winds; trees whose fruit withereth, without fruit, twice dead, plucked up by the roots;… wandering stars" (Jude 12-13). "And the last state of that man is worse than the first" (Matthew 12:45; Luke 11:26). "For if after they have escaped the pollutions of the world…, they are again entangled therein, and overcome, the latter end is worse with them than the beginning" (II Peter 2:20).

Why? How did this happen? Because although they became yogis to some extent, they did not completely change their way of life and associations. They continued to live heedlessly and carelessly in their usual way. In other words, they tried to put new on old, to put new in the old. Their former lives had not been evil or criminal, but they had been devoid of spiritual consciousness, just coasting along thinking of nothing but daily life and its material ways. When they found yoga they got some spiritual books, maybe some holy pictures, yet continued to remain in the sterile mediocrity of "ordinary" and "normal" life. So after a while yoga faded out of their life–and usually so did the books and pictures which they gave or threw away. Having lived in the spirit for a while, they had died to the spirit. And as I say, many plunged into an utterly negative way of life and maintained it to the end.

One yogini I knew introduced a very good friend to yoga, and their friendship was even closer because it was based on spiritual realities. For a while her friend was very sincere and serious about living the yoga life. Then he began drifting away, slowly at first and then faster and faster. One day he was gone, having moved far away without telling anyone. My friend could not believe that he really was abandoning spiritual life, so she drove for two or three days to get where he was living. She found him running his own business–and very successfully. After a few minutes' conversation he told her that she need not bother talking about "all that stuff" (spiritual life and ideals), because only three things interested him in life: sex, drugs and money. She left and never had contact with him again, but mutual acquaintances told her that he sank further and further in the swamp of samsara, a descent that ended only with his death.

What about the yogis that persevered? They all had these things in common: 1) They moved away from their home towns if they were devoid of yogis and settled in places where other yogis were living and continually getting together for satsang (spiritual gatherings). 2) They associated with spiritually-oriented people. 3) They quit jobs that were not in conformity with yogic moral principles (yama and niyama) and got more suitable ones. 4) They were strict vegetarians, never eating meat, fish, eggs or anything containing them. (The dropouts had always boasted: "When I go to someone's house to eat I never ask them if something is vegetarian or has eggs in it. And when I go home at Thanksgiving and Christmas I eat what everyone else eats." Is it any wonder that they ended up living like "everyone else"?) 5) They read spiritual books daily. 6) They considered themselves foremost to be yogis and Sanatana Dharmis–everything else was secondary. These six points are essential for the new life necessary to persevere and succeed in yoga. It is the yoga life. Of course there was a seventh point: They meditated daily–usually twice in a day.

Worthy. Those who are True and Fitting are therefore Worthy. Spiritual life is not a cosmetic or a condiment. It is an entire lifestyle: a total immersion in spiritual consciousness which spiritualizes everything in life or else eliminates it altogether. Yogi Gorakhnath wrote: "By birth I was a Hindu; but by maturity I became a yogi." But a yogi who perfectly followed Sanatana Dharma.

Now Jesus is going to describe how it is done if we want real spiritual life.

Light In The Heart And Mind

> No man, when he hath lighted a candle, covereth it with a vessel, or putteth it under a bed; but setteth it on a candlestick, that they which enter in may see the light. For nothing is secret, that shall not be made manifest; neither any thing hid, that shall not be known and come abroad (Luke 8:16-17).

No man, when he hath lighted [kindled] a candle [lamp]. Fire is a sacred element in some religions, a symbol of the transmuting power of God. The lamp we must light, enkindle, is our own life: body, mind and spirit. The divine power must pervade our whole being. Otherwise there is no light. Fire was made in ancient times in two ways: striking a rock (flint preferred) with steel to generate a spark, or producing enough friction to generate a spark. Completely essential was the material which would catch fire when touched by the spark. Most people have no spiritual life because they are not flammable–end of story. But even if we are flammable, we have to get the spark. And the only way to do that is yoga sadhana, which is why it is called tapasya, the generation of heat–and ultimately fire.

Covereth it with a vessel. Kalupto means both to cover and to hide. Real spiritual life cannot be hidden. It comes out just like the measles. It is good for a yogi to usually keep quiet about his practice, but its results will manifest outwardly in some form.

Or putteth it under a bed. A bed is a place for sleeping–not awakening. A life of spiritual sleep cannot accommodate the light-bearing lamp of yoga sadhana that is intended to keep the yogi spiritually awake at all times.

But setteth it on a candlestick [lampstand]. Spiritual life is to be lifted up and put in its proper place on high as a necessary priority and dominant power in the yogi's entire life.

That they which enter in may see the light. The yogi does not display, boast about or babble on about his practice. (A lot of phony yogis with phony gurus, do.) But he will be seen–or rather, his life will be seen. Observers may not know he is a yogi specifically, but they will know he has something to do with God.

For nothing is secret, that shall not be made manifest; neither any thing hid, that shall not be known and come abroad. The book of Proverbs asks, "Can a man take fire in his bosom, and his clothes not be burned? Can one go upon hot coals, and his feet not be burned? (Proverbs 6:27-28). No one can correctly practice true yoga and not produce a perceptible effect. Certainly, most results will be inward and known to him alone, but his life will absolutely change and begin to reflect his inner change. The inner brings about change in the outer. Otherwise it is sham. What is inside comes out.

Ears To Hear

If any man have ears to hear, let him hear (Mark 4:23).

This is a very important verse because it reveals the way a yogi views those around him in relation to yoga. Only those who have "hearing ears" can hear. If they do not, then they will not hear. And those who do hear will not be deaf. It is all a matter of the individual's level of evolution and awakening (the same thing, really). So a yogi is never a missionary or tries to recruit others to yoga practice or Sanatana Dharma. If questioned he will speak, but the results are up to the hearers–not him. And he knows it. And leaves it to them.

Take heed therefore how ye hear: for whosoever hath, to him shall be given; and whosoever hath not, from him shall be taken even that which he seemeth to have (Luke 8:18).

Hearing/understanding are necessary abilities. So we must take heed how we go about them. For *blepo* means to scrutinize, be cautious, see the reality of something and mark it mentally and proceed in that context. All of that is needed to just be in the picture. For we must make sure of what we really possess, have really made ours, by assimilating it and making it an irrevocable part of us. Do you see what a serious thing it is to aspire to be a yogi? For if a yogi has really made the yoga life his own, his progress is assured. More shall come to him. But if he has not, then he will eventually lose what he only seems to have. Yogi no more. True hearing in the spirit is not passive but active.

The Field Of The Soul

> And he said, So is the kingdom of God, as if a man should cast seed into the ground; and should sleep, and rise night and day, and the seed should spring and grow up, he knoweth not how. For the earth bringeth forth fruit of herself; first the blade, then the ear, after that the full corn in the ear. But when the fruit is brought forth, immediately he putteth in the sickle, because the harvest is come (Mark 4:26-29).

So is the kingdom of God, as if a man should cast seed into the ground. The kingdom of God is not an abstraction or an aspiration. It is a living thing inhabited by living beings. And here is the way it all comes about.

The yogi casts the seed of divine consciousness in himself by observance of the moral principles of yama and niyama.

And should sleep, and rise night and day, and the seed should spring and grow up, he knoweth not how. Both sleeping and waking, action and inaction are part of the "doing" of the inner work of the kingdom. The yogi practices faithfully, sometimes active, sometimes passive and merely observant, but learning all the time. And the seed he has sown in himself grows and increases. Just how it grows he does not know because the process is so profound, reaching into the unknown heights and depths of his very being.

For the earth bringeth forth fruit of herself. Everything is in the yogi. All potential is there and all actualization rises from there. It is a manifesting of the eternal Self which pervades the yogi's entire being until he realizes it is his own Self. Just as the earth requires preparation, sun, rain and seed, so does the yogi, his sadhana–including yama and niyama–being all that.

First the blade, then the ear, after that the full corn in the ear. Everything goes in a definite order. First comes a little, feeble green blade, then it grows upward out of the earth into the light and sun, and it then develops the beginning of the ear of wheat ("corn" in the Bible always means grain, usually wheat), and finally it expands into the full ear, consisting of grains like the original seed which themselves are able to produce more life as did the original seed. All these stages are inherent in the seed as all the stages of yoga sadhana culminating in enlightenment are in the very beginning of the yogi's endeavors, only awaiting manifestation.

> **But when the fruit is brought forth, immediately he putteth in the sickle, because the harvest is come (Mark 4:26-29).**

And total liberation is the harvest.

> **Another parable put he forth unto them, saying, The kingdom of heaven is likened unto a man which sowed good seed in his field: But while men slept, his enemy came and sowed tares among the wheat, and went his way. But when the blade was sprung up, and brought forth fruit, then appeared the tares also. So the servants of the householder came and said unto him, Sir, didst not thou sow good seed in thy field? from whence then hath it tares? He said unto them, An enemy hath done this. The servants said unto him, Wilt thou then that we go and gather them up? But he said, Nay; lest while ye gather up the tares, ye root up also the wheat with them. Let both grow together until the harvest: and in the time of harvest I will say to the reapers, Gather ye together first the tares, and bind them in bundles to burn them: but gather the wheat into my barn (Matthew 13:24-30).**

If God is good, and his creation is good, how is it that evil is in the world, including evil people? Creation goes in cycles. The Bhagavad Gita says, "They know the true day and night who know Brahma's Day a thousand yugas long and Brahma's Night a thousand yugas long. At the approach of Brahma's Day, all manifested things come forth from the unmanifest, and then return to that at Brahma's Night. Helpless, the same host of beings being born again and again merge at the approach of the Night and emerge at the dawn of Day" (8:17-19). This is called a Kalpa, and here is how *A Basic Sanskrit Dictionary* defines it: "Kalpa: A Day of Brahma–4,320,000,000 years. It alternates with a Night of Brahma of the same length.... In the Day of Brahma creation is manifest and in the Night of Brahma is it resolved into its causal state." Elsewhere I have explained about Satan and the flawing of our part of the evolving creation. The presence of cosmic evil (negativity) in the form of Satan is being dealt with in this parable.

The kingdom of heaven is likened unto a man which sowed good seed in his field: But while men slept, his enemy came and sowed tares among the wheat, and went his way. But when the blade was sprung up, and brought forth fruit, then appeared the tares also. Satan causes negative individuals to be born in this present creation along with those who are positive–though nearly all are really a mixture of positive and negative in our type of creation. Those who are predominately negative even though they may have some positive traits or aspects, are considered negative. Those who are predominately positive even though they may have some negative traits or aspects, are considered positive. The positive use their birth to purify themselves and go higher and the negative use their birth to degrade themselves and sink lower.

It is the intention of Satan to hinder the ascent of the positive and if possible to corrupt them and make them predominantly negative so they will not be able to ascend to the next level of evolution.

So the servants of the householder came and said unto him, Sir, didst not thou sow good seed in thy field? from whence then hath it tares? He said unto them, An enemy hath done this. The servants said unto him, Wilt thou then that we go and gather them up? But he said, Nay; lest while ye gather up the tares, ye root up also the wheat with them. Let both grow together until the harvest: and in the time of harvest I will say to the reapers, Gather ye together first the tares, and bind them in bundles to burn them: but gather the wheat into my barn. The servants are both angels and highly evolved human beings who are the teachers and benefactors of humanity. The angels have the power to prevent negative people from being born into this world and to hasten their exit when they are here, but God does not permit it, for the positive people need the negative people for their further development because of karma accumulated when previously they were themselves servants of Satan. This mixed character of inhabitants is virtually unique to our world or plane of evolution, and its fate is dual. The time will come when things will have come to such a condition that the positive will have evolved to the point where they can pass upward into a higher level and the negative will have devolved to the point where they are impelled by their vibration to sink down into a lower world. And so it will be, and this stratum of creation will dissolve, being no longer needed. Please be assured that this is not reward and punishment, rather the natural sequence of evolution and devolution. Both good and evil are their own rewards. As I say, our world is virtually alone in being like this.

Again, the kingdom of heaven is like unto treasure hid in a field; the which when a man hath found, he hideth, and for joy thereof goeth and selleth all that he hath, and buyeth that field (Matthew 13:44).

The kingdom of heaven, of infinite consciousness, is hidden within each one of us. When someone discovers that he does not make a big fuss or display, but keeping quiet sets about purifying himself in various ways including eliminating from his life all that is incompatible and a hindrance to his possessing the kingdom That is his "selling." And he cultivates in himself all that which will enable him to truly possess it. That is "buying" it. He cannot buy before he sells. And he must sell everything.

The Pearl of Great Price

> **Again, the kingdom of heaven is like unto a merchant man, seeking goodly pearls: who, when he had found one pearl of great price, went and sold all that he had, and bought it (Matthew 13:45-46).**

Here we have the same requisites of selling and buying to possess the kingdom of spirit. We also find here the necessity of actively seeking spiritual life, not just waiting for it to somehow come to our attention.

To gain the kingdom we must pay a great deal (*polutimos*), for it is of infinite worth. So however great the price, it is nothing compared to the infinite gain of entering and possessing the heavenly kingdom.

Revealing That Is A Concealing

All these things spake Jesus unto the multitude in parables [as they were able to hear it—Mark 4:33]; and without a parable spake he not unto them. That it might be fulfilled which was spoken by the prophet, saying, I will open my mouth in parables; I will utter things which have been kept secret [hidden] from the foundation of the world (Matthew 13:34-35).

And when they were alone, he expounded all things to his disciples (Mark 4:34).

When we are alone with God in our heart, even though we are surrounded by many people and things, He will make clear to us whatever we need to know and understand.

The Kingdom Of Heaven Within

> Again, the kingdom of heaven is like unto a net, that was cast into the sea, and gathered of every kind: which, when it was full, they drew to shore, and sat down, and gathered the good into vessels, but cast the bad away.
>
> So shall it be at the end of the world: the angels shall come forth, and sever the wicked from among the just, and shall cast them into the furnace of fire: there shall be wailing and gnashing of teeth.
>
> Jesus saith unto them, Have ye understood all these things? They say unto him, Yea, Lord.
>
> Then said he unto them, Therefore every scribe which is instructed unto the kingdom of heaven is like unto a man that is an householder, which bringeth forth out of his treasure things new and old (Matthew 13:47-52).

Here again we have the picture of the ending of a creation when it is going to be dissolved and the positive and negative taken to their new abodes.

The kingdom of heaven is like unto a net, that was cast into the sea, and gathered of every kind. The word *genos*, translated "kind" is properly applied only to human beings. It means a nation or country. Even if it goes by stages, eventually everyone in a creation encounters the message of the kingdom of heaven.

Which, when it was full, they drew to shore, and sat down, and gathered the good into vessels, but cast the bad away. "Good" and "bad" are not references to a person's external behavior, but to the state of his inner being, his mind and soul. "Bad" is the translation of *sapros*, which we have encountered before and which means corrupt in the sense of rotten or decayed.

So shall it be at the end of the world: the angels shall come forth, and sever the wicked from among the just. Sunteleia, translated "end" is a noun, not a verb. That is, it does not refer to God or the divine powers "ending" the world in an arbitrary manner. It means completion or consummation, the purpose of something having been completed or fulfilled. *Aion*, the word translated "world," means age or eon (aeon), a span of allotted time. And it also means a level of creation, not just a planet or solar system. So this is a picture of the conclusion of the time allotted a level of creation. "Angels" (*angelos*) means messengers, not necessarily angels in our everyday sense. At the end of a creation level, God sends highly advanced souls there whose task is to *exerchomai*–go throughout that level–and separate (*aphorizo*) the evil (negative) from the good (*dikaios*–righteous or just and worthy). This does not happen in the way described by Christian evangelists, but is an orderly development. Mostly they teach, perhaps even for a long time, and those who accept their teaching are the just and those who reject their teaching are the wicked. It is their choice and their inner disposition: for or against the truth and the light.

And shall cast them into the furnace of fire: there shall be wailing and gnashing of teeth. Pur can mean either fire or fiery–having the character or effect of fire. It means an energy of purification which eventually benefits those undergoing it. But at the beginning there will be suffering. However, those in such a condition will be completely aware of what is happening and why. They will understand that it is for their good and their benefit–not punishment. But the purifying power which rejoices the positive souls who yearn for purification and enlightenment is great torment for the negative, just as light is painful for diseased eyes. So there will be *klauthmos*: lamentation, wailing or weeping–either inwardly or outwardly. *Brugmos* is an interesting word, because it means a grating or grinding of the teeth in pain or in rage. So some will be suffering and others will be hate-filled and defiant, the usual guilty ones who curse and blame the judge and the judgement, but never themselves.

> Jesus saith unto them, Have ye understood all these things? They say unto him, Yea, Lord. Then said he unto them, Therefore every scribe which is instructed unto the kingdom of heaven is like unto a man that is an householder, which bringeth forth out of his treasure things new and old (Matthew 13:51-52).

Those who follow the way of the divine kingdom become wise in themselves and bring forth from their higher mind things learned in this life (new) and wisdom acquired in previous lives (old). They literally guide and teach themselves. This is why when a visitor told Swami Sivananda that he was searching for a guru, Swamiji told him, "You are the guru."

The Storm And The Calm

> And the same day, when the even was come, he saith unto them, Let us pass over unto the other side. And when they had sent away the multitude, they took him even as he was in the ship. And there were also with him other little ships. And there arose a great storm of wind, and the waves beat into the ship, so that it was now full. And he was in the hinder part of the ship, asleep on a pillow: and they awake him, and say unto him, Master, carest thou not that we perish? And he arose, and rebuked [commanded] the wind, and said unto the sea, Peace [be silent], be still. And the wind ceased, and there was a great calm. And he said unto them, Why are ye so fearful? how is it that ye have no faith? And they feared exceedingly, and said one to another, What manner of man is this, that even the wind and the sea obey him? (Mark 4:35-41).

The apostles were afraid of the storm and even more afraid when Jesus calmed the storm. This is because when people encounter spiritual realities for the first time it disturbs them. They were comfortable "believing," but when they suddenly know for themselves it is upsetting because it means they will have to really believe, and that entails changing their perspective and very likely their thoughts and deeds—even their way of life. Such is the habit of ignorance and inexperience.

Seekers often are terrified by the prospect of finding because deep in their mind they did not believe in higher things, and want them to remain a beautiful ideal or dream. They are like a character in a motion picture that said: "Of course I believe in God; I just don't think he exists!" As

Yogananda said, "People are so skillful in their ignorance." I have seen many people run from spiritual reality in terror and aversion, though they had told themselves for years that they were seekers of truth.

Encounter With Possessing Demons

And they came over unto the other side of the sea, into the country of the Gadarenes. And when he was come out of the ship, immediately there met him out of the tombs a man with an unclean spirit, who had his dwelling among the tombs; and no man could bind him, no, not with chains: Because that he had been often bound with fetters and chains, and the chains had been plucked asunder by him, and the fetters broken in pieces: neither could any man tame him. And always, night and day, he was in the mountains, and in the tombs, crying, and cutting himself with stones.

But when he saw Jesus afar off, he ran and worshipped him, And cried with a loud voice, and said, What have I to do with thee, Jesus, thou Son of the most high God? I adjure thee by God, that thou torment me not.

For he said unto him, Come out of the man, thou unclean spirit. And he asked him, What is thy name? And he answered, saying, My name is Legion: for we are many (Mark 5:1-9).

And when he was come out of the ship, immediately there met him out of the tombs a man with an unclean spirit. There are many kinds of wandering spirits that can obsess or possess people. This one was *akathartos*, an impure, foul spirit. How this was determined we are not told.

Who had his dwelling among the tombs; and no man could bind him, no, not with chains: because that he had been often bound with fetters and chains, and the chains had been plucked asunder by him, and the fetters broken in pieces: neither could any man tame him. Unnatural strength is often employed by evil spirits. This one could literally pull apart and even smash into pieces iron restraints.

And always [continually], night and day, he was in the mountains, and in the tombs, crying, and cutting himself with stones. This is sometimes the attempt of the possessed person to drive the spirit out of his body by pain or to ground his awareness in the body when the spirit is trying to push him out and take over completely.

But when he saw Jesus afar off, he ran and worshipped him. The word translated "worship" is *proskuneo*, which means to bow down in homage or to crouch before someone asking for help or protection. So we see that the possessed person still has some degree of control over his body.

And cried with a loud voice, and said, What have I to do with thee, Jesus, thou Son of the most high God? I adjure thee by God, that thou torment me not. Now the spirit speaks. The vibration of anything or anyone that is holy and of a high spiritual vibration is actually painful to an evil spirit.

For he said unto him, Come out of the man, thou unclean spirit. So Jesus was inwardly commanding the spirit to depart.

And he asked him, What is thy name? And he answered, saying, My name is Legion: for we are many. Possessing spirits lie in various ways, including boasting of their power and numbers and giving false identities. But later we shall see there really were very many of them possessing the unfortunate man.

> Now there was there nigh unto the mountains a great herd of swine feeding. And all the devils besought him, saying, Send us into the swine, that we may enter into them. And forthwith Jesus gave them leave. And the unclean spirits went out, and entered into the swine: and the herd ran violently down a steep place into the sea, (they were about two thousand;) and were choked in the sea.
>
> And they that fed the swine fled, and told it in the city, and in the country. And they went out to see what it was

> that was done. And they come to Jesus, and see him that was possessed with the devil, and had the legion, sitting, and clothed, and in his right mind: and they were afraid. And they that saw it told them how it befell to him that was possessed with the devil, and also concerning the swine (Mark 5:11-16).

Our higher Self guides the growth of our body in the womb. So everyone's body is formed exactly according to their karma and samskara. Only that person can control it perfectly. So if an alien spirit enters the body there is great disturbance. When the spirits entered the swine they went berserk and ran blindly down into the sea and were drowned.

When this was made known and the local people came out and saw the formerly possessed man "sitting, and clothed, and in his right mind," what was their reaction? They were afraid! Just like the apostles when Jesus stilled the storm. Many people fear the prospect of people being in their right mind. Yogis discover this in the reaction of the people around them, and it can be very hostile and intense.

> Then the whole multitude of the country of the Gadarenes round about besought him to depart from them; for they were taken with great fear: and he went up into the ship, and returned back again (Luke 8:37).

Now we know something about demonic people. Just as the evil spirits could not stand the presence of Jesus, neither can evil people stand the presence of positive people, especially yogis.

Healing Touch

And when he was come into the ship, he that had been possessed with the devil prayed him that he might be with him. Howbeit Jesus suffered him not, but saith unto him, Go home to thy friends, and tell them how great things the Lord hath done for thee, and hath had compassion on thee. And he departed, and began to publish in Decapolis how great things Jesus had done for him: and all men did marvel.

And when Jesus was passed over again by ship unto the other side, much people gathered unto him: and he was nigh unto the sea. And, behold, there cometh one of the rulers [officials] of the synagogue, Jairus by name; and when he saw him, he fell at his feet (Mark 5:18-22),

For he had one only daughter, about twelve years of age, and she lay a dying (Luke 8:42).

And he besought him greatly, saying, My little daughter lieth at the point of death: I pray thee, come and lay thy hands on her, that she may be healed; and she shall live (Mark 5:23).

And Jesus arose, and followed him, and so did his disciples (Matthew 9:19).

And much people followed him, and thronged him.

And a certain woman, which had an issue [continual flow] of blood twelve years, and had suffered many things of many physicians, and had spent all that she had, and was nothing bettered, but rather grew worse, when she had heard of Jesus, came in the press behind, and touched his garment (Mark 5:24-27).

For she said within herself, If I may but touch his garment, I shall be whole (Matthew 9:21).

And straightway the fountain of her blood was dried up; and she felt in her body that she was healed of that plague. And Jesus, immediately knowing in himself that virtue [power] had gone out of him, turned him about in the press, and said (Mark 5:29-30),

Who touched me? When all denied, Peter and they that were with him said, Master, the multitude throng thee and press thee, and sayest thou, Who touched me? And Jesus said, Somebody hath touched me: for I perceive that virtue is gone out of me (Luke 8:45-46).

And he looked round about to see her that had done this thing. But the woman fearing and trembling, knowing what was done in her, came and fell down before him, and... (Mark 5:32-33).

Declared unto him before all the people for what cause she had touched him, and how she was healed immediately (Luke 8:47).

And he said unto her, Daughter, thy faith hath made thee whole [saved thee]; go in peace, and be whole of thy plague (Mark 5:34).

I pray thee, come and lay thy hands on her, that she may be healed. In this incident we are going to learn something about the subtle energies of the body. They continually flow from our hands and feet, and those whose energy levels are high and strong enough can heal by their touch.

And a certain woman came in the press behind, and touched his garment, for she said within herself, If I may but touch his garment, I shall be whole (Matthew 9:21). The highest subtle energy level known as the etheric body extends an inch all around our body. (Our "aura" consists of various other subtle energies and extends a few or even many feet around our body.) Consequently our clothing becomes saturated with it. The clothing of a great saint or master retains these vibrations and can affect the awareness or the health of whoever touches it. I have experienced this many times.

And Jesus said, Who touched me? The saints and masters can feel when their subtle vibrations pass into another.

Peter and they that were with him said, Master, the multitude throng thee and press thee, and sayest thou, Who touched me? Now that is an incredibly stupid question for his disciples, who had from the beginning witnessed his omniscience. But that is the problem with human beings. No matter what their external experiences, they lapse right back into their habitual ignorance. Only when there is deep inner change does anyone's awareness and perspective really change.

And he said unto her, Daughter, thy faith hath made thee whole [saved thee]; go in peace, and be whole of thy plague. Genuine faith produces action, as in this woman's case. Therefore she was cured.

This woman was the famous Veronica of "Veronica's veil." However, she had nothing to do with the famous veil bearing the likeness of Jesus' face. Rather, that was a cloth sent by Jesus himself to King Abgar V of Edessa. The king had written to Jesus asking him to come and heal his illness and live in his kingdom at peace and safe from his enemies. Jesus sent an answer, saying that he could not come to the king. As a gift to the king, Jesus wiped his face with a cloth and it bore his photographic likeness. That was taken to the king, and its touch healed his illness.

In gratitude for her healing, Veronica had a statue of Jesus made and placed it in front of her house. We do not know her actual name, but Veronica means "True Image," referring to the statue. Eventually that statue was taken to Constantinople and kept in the treasury of the great Agia Sophia cathedral. When Constantinople was overrun by the Moslems the statue was lost.

Death, Blindness and Muteness Vanquished

While he yet spake, there came from the ruler of the synagogue's house certain which said, Thy daughter is dead: why troublest thou the Master any further? (Mark 5:35).

But when Jesus heard it, he answered him, saying, Fear not: believe only, and she shall be made whole (Luke 8:50).

And he cometh to the house of the ruler of the synagogue, and seeth the tumult, and them that wept and wailed greatly (Mark 5:38).

And when he came into the house, he suffered no man to go in, save Peter, and James, and John, and the father and the mother of the maiden (Luke 8:51).

And when he was come in, he saith unto them, Why make ye this ado, and weep? the damsel is not dead, but sleepeth (Mark 5:39).

And they laughed him to scorn, knowing that she was dead (Luke 8:53).

But when he had put them all out, he taketh the father and the mother of the damsel, and them that were with him, and entereth in where the damsel was lying. And he took the damsel by the hand, and said unto her, Talitha cumi; which is, being interpreted, Damsel, I say unto thee, arise (Mark 5:40-41).

And her spirit came again, and she arose straightway (Luke 8:55).

> And he charged them straitly that no man should know it; and commanded that something should be given her to eat (Mark 5:43).
>
> And the fame hereof went abroad into all that land).
>
> And when Jesus departed thence, two blind men followed him, crying, and saying, Thou Son of David, have mercy on us. And when he was come into the house, the blind men came to him: and Jesus saith unto them, Believe ye that I am able to do this? They said unto him, Yea, Lord. Then touched he their eyes, saying, According to your faith be it unto you. And their eyes were opened; and Jesus straitly charged them, saying, See that no man know it.
>
> But they, when they were departed, spread abroad his fame in all that country.
>
> As they went out, behold, they brought to him a dumb man possessed with a devil. And when the devil was cast out, the dumb spake: and the multitudes marvelled, saying, It was never so seen in Israel.
>
> But the Pharisees said, He casteth out devils through the prince of the devils (Matthew 9:26-34).

Jesus healed and raised the dead because of his love and compassion, and even more because he showed by it that sickness and death are but dreams. Even though those he helped should have been grateful enough to honor his request to keep it quiet, they did not and the tumult began. If in your sadhana you develop any special abilities, keep it quiet absolutely, otherwise you will be besieged by those who want you to work some kind of miracle for them. And of course there are also the modern Pharisees who will denounce you as a fraud or insane.

In The Synagogue at Nazareth

And he went out from thence, and came into his own country; and his disciples followed him (Mark 6:1).

And he came to Nazareth, where he had been brought up: and, as his custom was, he went into the synagogue on the sabbath day, and stood up for to read. And there was delivered unto him the book of the prophet Esaias. And when he had opened the book, he found the place where it was written, The [Holy] Spirit of the Lord is upon me, because he hath anointed [consecrated] me to preach the gospel to the poor; he hath sent me to heal the brokenhearted, to preach deliverance [freedom] to the captives, and recovering of sight to the blind, to set at liberty them that are bruised, to preach the acceptable year of the Lord.

And he closed the book, and he gave it again to the minister, and sat down. And the eyes of all them that were in the synagogue were fastened on him. And he began to say unto them, This day is this scripture fulfilled in your ears. And all bare him witness, and wondered at the gracious words which proceeded out of his mouth. And they said, Is not this Joseph's son? (Luke 4:16-22).

And he came to Nazareth, where he had been brought up: and, as his custom was, he went into the synagogue on the sabbath day, and stood up for to read. As I have said before, if a firstborn child was male, he was considered Levi–a Levite, a member of the tribe of Levi, the hereditary priestly class. This was the case with Jesus, and we see that he was freely allowed to teach in the synagogues on the Sabbath.

> And there was delivered unto him the book of the prophet Esaias. And when he had opened the book, he found the place where it was written, The [Holy] Spirit of the Lord is upon me, because he hath anointed [consecrated] me to preach the gospel to the poor; he hath sent me to heal the brokenhearted, to preach deliverance [freedom] to the captives, and recovering of sight to the blind, to set at liberty them that are bruised, to preach the acceptable year of the Lord.
> And he closed the book, and he gave it again to the minister, and sat down. And the eyes of all them that were in the synagogue were fastened on him. And he began to say unto them, This day is this scripture fulfilled in your ears. (Luke 4:16-21).

On this very day the prophecy of Isaiah was fulfilled and the gates of the heavenly kingdom were opened to those who would see and enter in.

> And many hearing him were astonished, saying, From whence hath this man these things? and what wisdom is this which is given unto him, that even such mighty works are wrought by his hands? Is not this the carpenter, the son of Mary, the brother of James, and Joses, and of Juda, and Simon? and are not his sisters here with us? And they were offended at him (Mark 6:2-3).

"Offended" is a very poor translation of *skandalizo*, which means to be scandalized or shocked at someone or something which literally causes them to stumble and fall. Shallow as it was, just because they had known him in his youth they could or would not believe in his virtue and wisdom, though they were witnessing it for themselves. As I have cited before, the

Russian proverb says, "Even if you convince me, I will not be convinced." Such is the plight of the deluded mind.

> And he said unto them, Ye will surely say unto me this proverb, Physician, heal thyself: whatsoever we have heard done in Capernaum, do also here in thy country (Luke 4:23).
>
> A prophet is not without honour, but in his own country, and among his own kin, and in his own house (Mark 6:4).
>
> But I tell you of a truth, many widows were in Israel in the days of Elias, when the heaven was shut up three years and six months, when great famine was throughout all the land; but unto none of them was Elias sent, save unto Sarepta, a city of Sidon, unto a woman that was a widow. And many lepers were in Israel in the time of Eliseus the prophet; and none of them was cleansed, saving Naaman the Syrian.
>
> And all they in the synagogue, when they heard these things, were filled with wrath, and rose up, and thrust him out of the city, and led him unto the brow of the hill whereon their city was built, that they might cast him down headlong. But he passing through the midst of them went his way (Luke 4:25-30).
>
> And he could there do no mighty work, save that he laid his hands upon a few sick folk, and healed them. And he marvelled because of their unbelief. And he went round about the villages, teaching (Mark 6:5-6).

The power of faith is great, but so also is the power of unbelief. As I mentioned earlier, Max Heindel wrote in *The Rosicrucian Cosmo-Conception* that unbelief is the most negative condition the human being can fall into.

Sending The Apostles On His Mission

> And Jesus went about all the cities and villages, teaching in their synagogues, and preaching the gospel of the kingdom, and healing every sickness and every disease among the people.
>
> But when he saw the multitudes, he was moved with compassion on them, because they fainted, and were scattered abroad, as sheep having no shepherd. Then saith he unto his disciples, The harvest truly is plenteous, but the labourers are few; pray ye therefore the Lord of the harvest, that he will send forth labourers into his harvest.
>
> And when he had called unto him his twelve disciples, he gave them power against unclean spirits, to cast them out, and to heal all manner of sickness and all manner of disease (Matthew 9:35-3; 10:1).

It is easy to just think of this as a kind of miracle campaign, even a kind of publicity stunt. But exorcism and healing have the same intent: setting things back into their natural, original way so the individuals benefitted can enter into the supernatural way and pursue their own self-revelation. Determining the value (and therefore ultimate reality) of a spiritual experience or a miraculous event is very simple: Is the benefitted person awakened and empowered to progress spiritually? And do they so progress? If not, the event was of no value to them.

Throughout the world people are following worthless spiritual teachers, often because they claim they had "wonderful experiences" upon meeting them or in continued contact with them. However Jesus said: "But one thing is needful [necessary]" (Luke 10:42); and that is knowledge–knowledge of our Self (Atman) and the Supreme Self (Paramatman). Astounding experiences, development of various psychic powers, and receiving of divine revelations mean absolutely nothing–especially since they are usually either false or pathological in nature. As the Chandogya Upanishad says to the seeker: "That which is the subtle essence, this whole world has for its Self. That is the true. That is the Self. That you are" (6.10.1).

> **And he began to send them forth by two and two (Mark 6:7) to preach the kingdom of God (Luke 9:2), saying, Go not into the way of the Gentiles, and into any city of the Samaritans enter ye not: But go rather to the lost sheep of the house of Israel. And as ye go, preach, saying, The kingdom of heaven is at hand. Heal the sick, cleanse the lepers, raise the dead, cast out devils: freely ye have received, freely give. Provide neither gold, nor silver, nor brass in your purses, nor scrip for your journey, neither two coats, neither shoes, nor yet staves: for the workman is worthy of his food.**
>
> **And into whatsoever city or town ye shall enter, enquire who in it is worthy; and there abide till ye go thence. And when ye come into an house, salute it. And if the house be worthy, let your peace come upon it: but if it be not worthy, let your peace return to you (Matthew 10:5-13).**
>
> **And whosoever shall not receive you, nor hear you, when ye depart thence, shake off the dust under your feet for a testimony against them. Verily I say unto you, It shall be more tolerable for Sodom and Gomorrha in the day of judgment, than for that city (Mark 6:11).**

Go not into the way of the Gentiles, and into any city of the Samaritans enter ye not.... And into whatsoever city or town ye shall enter, enquire who in it is worthy; and there abide till ye go thence. Spiritual association (satsang) is an essential in spiritual life. It is noteworthy that Sri Ramana Maharshi said that the two absolute essentials in genuine sadhana are satsang and a vegetarian diet. We must know whom to associate with and whom to avoid; what to eat and what to not eat. This is a necessity at the very beginning of our spiritual endeavor and throughout. For as Yogananda often said, "Company is greater than will power."

And when ye come into an house, salute it. And if the house be worthy, let your peace come upon it: but if it be not worthy, let your peace return to you. And whosoever shall not receive you, nor hear you, when ye depart thence, shake off the dust under your feet for a testimony against them. Verily I say unto you, It shall be more tolerable for Sodom and Gomorrha in the day of judgment, than for that city (Mark 6:11). This is not a grumpy threat, but a fact I have observed for many years. When a person engages in sadhana and progressively increases the energy levels of his entire being, the karma of those who interact with him is correspondingly increased in effect. Those who act toward him in a positive manner experience a positive reaction in their life. And those who are negative toward him experience a negative reaction. It is not reward or punishment but simply a matter of karmic reaction.

Wisdom To The Wise

Behold, I send you forth as sheep in the midst of wolves: be ye therefore wise as serpents, and harmless as doves.

But beware of men: for they will deliver you up to the councils, and they will scourge you in their synagogues; and ye shall be brought before governors and kings for my sake, for a testimony against them and the Gentiles.

But when they deliver you up, take no thought how or what ye shall speak: for it shall be given you in that same hour what ye shall speak. For it is not ye that speak, but the Spirit of your Father which speaketh in you.

And the brother shall deliver up the brother to death, and the father the child: and the children shall rise up against their parents, and cause them to be put to death. And ye shall be hated of all men for my name's sake: but he that endureth to the end shall be saved.

The disciple is not above his master, nor the servant above his lord. It is enough for the disciple that he be as his master, and the servant as his lord. If they have called the master of the house Beelzebub, how much more shall they call them of his household?

Fear them not therefore: for there is nothing covered, that shall not be revealed; and hid, that shall not be known.

What I tell you in darkness, that speak ye in light: and what ye hear in the ear, that preach ye upon the housetops (Matthew 10:16-27).

Spirit and Life

Behold, I send you forth as sheep in the midst of wolves: be ye therefore wise as serpents, and harmless as doves. Ego is always a problem because it is presenting to us false or mistaken views and assumptions that can really be harmful to us if accepted and acted upon. One of the worst is the idea that because we are trying to live and perfect our spiritual life we are therefore superior to "ordinary people." Feeling that we are God's special and chosen ones is a terrible delusion that besets many religious people. At the same time, the yogi is already living in a world apart from the rest of humanity–not because he is better, but because he is wiser and consciously changing (evolving) himself. And for that he should be grateful.

Those who would live in kindness, mercy and harmlessness (ahimsa) really are "in the midst of wolves" in the sense of a world and a society based on the dog-eat-dog philosophy. The general current of this world is downward, and the sadhaka strives upward. In the Vedas the world is shown as divided into two kinds of people: aryas and vritras. Aryas are those who strive upward toward enlightenment, and Vritras are those who burrow downward into the earth away from the light and into the darkness of ego, greed, ignorance and delusion. Obviously they are not compatible, and the vritras often despise and oppose the aryas. Conflict is sometimes inevitable. So Jesus tells us to be wise. *Phronimos* means to be thoughtful, sagacious and discreet. Its root word, *phren*, means self-controlled and clear-sighted and therefore understanding. We need not be geniuses, but we must be intelligent in all aspects of our life. Yogananda said that stupid people do not find God. Serpents, *ophis*, means someone who has sharpness of vision (perception) and is skillful in action and thought–as Buddha often recommended. Since a serpent (really Lucifer in a serpent form) deceived Adam and Eve, we must possess "counter-intelligence" in order to not be deceived.

At the same time we must be harmless, *akeraios*, which means harmless, innocent and guileless. It also means "unmixed" in the sense that we are to be totally pure of heart and of good intention toward all. This does not mean that we are to be guileless fools, though the world will view us as that. Remember Sri Ramakrishna's parable about the snake that learned to hiss. We are not supposed to be doormats for anyone to walk over. I was raised in a pacifist church. We would not only not go to war, we would not even go to court to defend ourselves. As a child I used to let bullies beat me up and never react or even resist. But when I became a yogi that changed–much to my amazement–and I realized it was no virtue to let evil have its way, that to do so was to collaborate with evil. I did not "fight back" but just walked away or firmly said No when it was needed. I never argued or accused, but made it clear that I would not back down.

But beware of men: for they will deliver you up to the councils, and they will scourge you in their synagogues; and ye shall be brought before governors and kings for my sake, for a testimony against them and the Gentiles. Now we have come to a part of Jesus' teaching that is virtually unique in world religion. It is the norm to assure people that if they do what is right and follow "the teachings" their future will be all roses and light, and that will be the proof of their being on the right path. I have heard and read this all my life, and that includes oriental religions, as well. But in contrast Jesus tells his disciples the full truth as to what their loyalty and discipline will provoke from "the world."

But when they deliver you up, take no thought how or what ye shall speak: for it shall be given you in that same hour what ye shall speak. For it is not ye that speak, but the Spirit of your Father which speaketh in you. This is a remarkable promise, but consider the future that is going to call it forth! Saint Paul wrote very openly to Saint Timothy: "All that will live godly in Christ Jesus shall suffer persecution" (II Timothy 3:12). *Dioko* (persecution) means to undergo great pressure continuously, to be hounded, pursued with malice and malicious intent. This awaits those who devote themselves to the attainment of the highest consciousness. And it is necessary for them so they may become strong in their resolve and successful in their resistance to all that would hinder them. One of the ways you can know you are on the right way is the objection and persecution from those around you, including those you thought loved you "unconditionally."

And the brother shall deliver up the brother to death, and the father the child: and the children shall rise up against their parents, and cause them to be put to death. And ye shall be hated of all men for my name's sake: but he that endureth to the end shall be saved.

The disciple is not above his master, nor the servant above his lord. It is enough for the disciple that he be as his master, and the servant as his lord. If they have called the master of the house Beelzebub, how much more shall they call them of his household? Beelzeboul is actually a Chaldean word, seemingly a mocking mutation of *Baal*, Lord of the Flies, and literally means "Dung God." It obviously is an expression of profound contempt. If we follow the way of the great masters (siddhas), why do we suppose that we will avoid the reaction the world had for all of them? What Great One was not hated, mocked and the target of violence? Every avatar has had attempts made on his life. Every one was denounced as fraudulent, crazy and evil. In the *Ramayana* of Valmiki we find entire tirades against Rama by Ravana, and they all sound very reasonable and just. But they were lies. How peculiar that people worship these avatars and expect them to deliver them from their troubles, when their lives were nothing but troubles! Their lives show what this world is: the incarnation of adharma. It is the primal and continuing enemy of light and truth. When someone asked Yogananda if he believed in hell, he smiled and asked: "Where do you think you are?" It was no joke. He knew. So should we.

Fear them not therefore: for there is nothing covered [hidden; secret], that shall not be revealed; and hid [kept secret], that shall not be known [perceived; understood]. Often people suffer greatly because the truth is not known and false things are spoken of them. But in time everything is revealed–this is a cosmic law. For truth is the essential nature of all things and must eventually emerge and be recognized. This is also a profound metaphysical principle. Ignorance cannot always prevail. The mists of confusion and illusion by their nature cannot persist forever. The old adage is true: Truth Will Out.

What I tell you in darkness, that speak ye in light: and what ye hear in the ear, that preach [proclaim] ye upon the housetops. Children like secrets. (Remember the annoying ones from your childhood that liked to chant, "I know something you don't know"?) So childish teachers and religions like to have secrets known only by the chosen few. But Jesus, like Buddha, says that anything he taught should be openly revealed. No true teacher keeps anything back from his students. The Chandogya Upanishad (4.9.3) tells us that when Satyakama asked his teacher for instruction, "To him, he then declared it. In it nothing whatsoever was left out, yea, nothing was left out."

The Way of Discipleship

And fear not them which kill the body, but are not able to kill the soul: but rather fear him which is able to destroy both soul and body in hell.

Are not two sparrows sold for a farthing? and one of them shall not fall on the ground without your Father. But the very hairs of your head are all numbered. Fear ye not therefore, ye are of more value than many sparrows.

Whosoever therefore shall confess me before men, him will I confess also before my Father which is in heaven. But whosoever shall deny me before men, him will I also deny before my Father which is in heaven.

Think not that I am come to send peace on earth: I came not to send peace, but a sword. For I am come to set a man at variance against his father, and the daughter against her mother, and the daughter in law against her mother in law. And a man's foes [enemies; adversaries] shall be they of his own household.

He that loveth father or mother more than me is not worthy of me: and he that loveth son or daughter more than me is not worthy of me.

And he that taketh not his cross, and followeth after me, is not worthy of me.

He that findeth his life shall lose it: and he that loseth his life for my sake shall find it.

He that receiveth [accepteth] you receiveth me, and he that receiveth me receiveth him that sent me.

He that receiveth a prophet in the name of a prophet shall receive a prophet's reward; and he that receiveth a righteous man in the name of a righteous man shall receive a righteous man's reward.

And whosoever shall give to drink unto one of these little ones a cup of cold water only in the name of a disciple, verily I say unto you, he shall in no wise lose his reward (Matthew 10:28-42).

Fear not them which kill the body, but are not able to kill the soul: but rather fear him which is able to destroy both soul and body in hell. The body can be killed by physical forces, including other human beings, but the subtle astral and causal bodies, formed of astral and causal energies, cannot be killed by any material forces. The word translated "hell" in this passage is Gehenna. Gehenna, the Valley of Hinnom, was really the garbage dump of Jerusalem where perpetual fires burned. Jesus used Gehenna as a symbol of the astral and causal hells where pain and misery are experienced in the subtle bodies.

It is tragic that exoteric Christianity tells people that God is the one who destroys body and soul. Never. God is Life and only gives and sustains life. It is negative forces instilled in the human being by their own negative thoughts, words and deed that alone can destroy the body and soul either here or in the astral and causal worlds. Negativity of any form is to be feared and avoided absolutely.

Are not two sparrows sold for a farthing? and one of them shall not fall on the ground without your Father. But the very hairs of your head are all numbered. Fear ye not therefore, ye are of more value than many sparrows. Part of God's omniscience is experiencing everything every sentient being is experiencing. A sparrow does not fall to the ground without God experiencing it, and as a part of God's infinite Life the sparrow cannot even fall without it ultimately being an action of God. It is the same with us. God does indeed know how many hairs are on our head. We are of infinite value because we are potentially infinite.

Whosoever therefore shall confess me before men, him will I confess also before my Father which is in heaven. Homologeo means to make profession of something, to form a covenant with someone, acknowledge someone, accept obligation to someone or something and to promise something. Its root word, *homou*, mean to unite with someone and be with them. All these things apply to the spiritual aspirants and the Universal Christ with Whom they intend to unite themselves through the revelation and entry into their own inherent Christhood. It is easy to see that this is a far cry from just saying, "I believe in Jesus Christ as my Savior." This is a matter of transmutation from humanity to divinity–as Jesus has done before us. It also implies keeping out minds on high with Christ. As Saint Paul exhorts us: "If ye then be risen with Christ, seek those things which are above, where Christ sitteth on the right hand of God. Set your affection on things above, not on things on the earth. For ye are dead, and your life is hid with Christ in God. When Christ, who is our life, shall appear, then shall ye also appear with him in glory" (Colossians 3:1-4).

But whosoever shall deny me before men, him will I also deny before my Father which is in heaven. Arneomai means to deny, reject, contradict, disavow and banish from one's life and mind. All this is meant in relation to the Cosmic Christ and our own personal Christhood.

Think not that I am come to send peace on earth: I came not to send peace, but a sword. Eirene means peace, but it also means rest, quiet and reconciliation. So none of these things are intended for us by Christ in relation to evil and ignorance! Think of all the Peace On Earth and Prince Of Peace Christmas cards! No such thing. Rather, Jesus offers us a sword (*machaira*) with which to make spiritual war, which sometimes manifests on the physical level.

For I am come to set a man at variance against his father, and the daughter against her mother, and the daughter in law against her mother in law. Dichazo means to cause a division, to divide and cut off and to set at variance. There is no doubt that the taking up of dedicated spiritual life can cause conflict and dissension in the aspirant's household, both inner and outer. Even the closest of family and friends may become alienated from us because they oppose our new life. But it is a sure thing that inwardly we will have to reject and war against our past ignorance and spiritual laziness and weakness and overcome our present karmas–all of which have brought us into earthly birth and are therefore our spiritual parents.

And a man's foes [enemies; adversaries] shall be they of his own household. The word translated "household" is *oikiakos*, which means both relatives and whoever lives with someone (in older days that included live-in servants or companions). As above, this refers to both human beings and to the flaws in our own makeup which go to make up the "family" of our own personality, including our karma.

He that loveth father or mother more than me is not worthy of me: and he that loveth son or daughter more than me is not worthy of me. Those who are going to succeed in spiritual life prize the attainment of supreme consciousness over anything in this world, whether people or our own samsaric personality. There is nothing wrong in loving others, but above all we must be loving God and God Consciousness.

And he that taketh not his cross, and followeth after me, is not worthy of me. It is interesting that Jesus is referring to the cross here in the beginning of his ministry. Obviously the "cross" is the process of deification (*theosis*), which is torture and death to the lower self and peace, joy and liberation to the higher Self. If we do not tread the same path to deification that Jesus followed, then we are unworthy of both Jesus as teacher and our inner Christ as Savior.

Lambano (take up) means to lay hold of and wield: the sword of spiritual truth and wisdom and inner spiritual strength with which we conquer all obstacles and "lay hold on eternal life" (I Timothy 6:12, 19).

Akoloutheo, translated "follow" has interesting side meanings. One is to to be walking in the same way as someone, to accompany them. Here is a confirmation of the truth that we must travel the same way Jesus travelled from humanity to divinity, not just worship him. It also means to eventually reach the one who is followed. To become a Christ is the true Christianity.

He that findeth his life shall lose it: and he that loseth his life for my sake shall find it. The only true life is the life of the spirit. *Heurisko* means to find, obtain and perceive. All these apply. Real spiritual life is something dynamic and transforming. The word translated "life" is not the word *zoe* which literally means life, but *psuche*–psyche which means our psychic aspect: mind, intellect and intuition as well as those subtle bodies in which those things exist. For unless we can get hold of and purify those levels and use them for further evolution, we have not made even the first step in spiritual life. For the yogi his psychic anatomy is much more important than his physical anatomy, which is why I included an entire chapter, "The Yogi's Subtle Anatomy," in *Soham Yoga: The Yoga of the Self*.

He that receiveth [accepteth] you receiveth me, and he that receiveth me receiveth him that sent me. There is a hierarchy of being in creation, and by one level at a time we can ascend to the higher levels. By mastery of our entire being we can ascend to the levels of the great Siddhas, and from further mastery as a Siddha into the Infinite Being of the Supreme Self, the Paramatman.

He that receiveth [accepteth] a prophet in the name of a prophet shall receive a prophet's reward; and he that receiveth [accepteth] a righteous man in the name of a righteous man shall receive a righteous man's reward. He who accepts a prophet as truly being a prophet–one who speaks by divine inspiration–receives a prophet's reward (benefits), and he who accepts a righteous man as truly righteous receives a righteous man's reward (benefits). The word *dikaios* means equitable: fair in his dealings. It also means being just, worthy and of right character. So when we acknowledge and respect a virtuous person we begin to reflect their good qualities. It is their silent blessing upon us.

And whosoever shall give to drink unto one of these little ones a cup of cold water only in the name of a disciple, verily I say unto you, he shall in no wise lose his reward. In a hot climate like that of Israel, giving someone not just water, but cool or cold water, was a great benefaction. And giving such to someone because they are considered a disciple of Christ, one who is learning to become a Christ himself, however little he may be in the view of others or how small in attainment so far, will gain the giver the blessings of discipleship. It is a matter of historical record that in the early days of Christianity the non-Christians used to say to one another in admiration: "See how these Christians love one another."

The Death Of John The Baptist

[At that time] Herod himself sent forth and laid hold upon John, and bound him in prison for Herodias' sake, his brother Philip's wife: for he had married her. For John had said unto Herod, It is not lawful for thee to have thy brother's wife.

Therefore Herodias had a quarrel against him, and would have killed him; but she could not: for Herod feared John, knowing that he was a just man and an holy, and observed him; and when he heard him, he did many things, and heard him gladly.

And when a convenient day was come, that Herod on his birthday made a supper to his lords, high captains, and chief estates of Galilee; and when the daughter of the said Herodias came in, and danced, and pleased Herod and them that sat with him, the king said unto the damsel, Ask of me whatsoever thou wilt, and I will give it thee. And he sware unto her, Whatsoever thou shalt ask of me, I will give it thee, unto the half of my kingdom.

And she went forth, and said unto her mother, What shall I ask? And she said, The head of John the Baptist. And she came in straightway with haste unto the king, and asked, saying, I will that thou give me by and by in a charger the head of John the Baptist.

And the king was exceeding sorry; yet for his oath's sake, and for their sakes which sat with him, he would not reject her. And immediately the king sent an executioner, and commanded his head to be brought: and he went and beheaded him in the prison, and brought his head in a charger, and gave it to the damsel: and the damsel gave it to her mother.

And when his disciples heard of it, they came and took up his corpse, and laid it in a tomb (Mark 6:17-29).

Here we have one of the great tragedies of the Gospels. King Herod greatly respected Saint John the Baptist, considering him a holy person, and he liked to listen to him and followed much of his spiritual advice. Yet he put him in prison because his wife hated Saint John. Here is a case where one of Herod's household proved to be his spiritual enemy and brought him to spiritual destruction. We must beware of this common failing: neglecting or turning from spiritual life because of the wishes and influence of someone close to us and for whom we have affection. Just think! Herod killed a man he considered holy because his wife wanted him to. This is moral enslavement of the worst type. I have seen men who abandoned spiritual life under the influence of their wives and women who abandoned spiritual life under the influence of their husbands. And some who abandoned spiritual life under the influence of their parents. And many who were drawn away from spiritual life by their friends. As Jesus said: "Beware of men *[anthropos*: human beings]!" (Matthew 10:17).

But this is more than it appears. It is an example of reincarnation and the influence of past lives on a person's latest life. This incident is a continuation of the Prophet Elijah's life, showing how the human drama can be played out over the "acts" of several births on the stage of this world. (This example, by the way, was pointed out to me by Bess Hibarger, a Presbyterian Sunday School teacher of long standing and great popularity, who at least once a year devoted one Sunday class to the subject of reincarnation.)

Ahab, the king of Israel, married Jezebel, who was a Gentile and an idolater. For these reasons, Elijah the prophet came to Ahab and challenged him, demanding that he rid himself of Jezebel. As could be expected, Jezebel decided that either Elijah or she had to go–and she preferred that it be

Elijah. Though she had squadrons of soldiers searching for the prophet to kill him, he managed to elude them, and departed from this world still in hiding. Later, Jezebel died, but with the desire for the death of Elijah burning in her heart. Thus was the sowing; then came the reaping.

As the Lord Jesus said (Matthew 11:14), Elijah was born again as John the Baptist. Ahab was reborn as Herod, and Jezebel as Herodias, the wife of Herod's brother. Herod broke the Law by marrying Herodias illegally, thus committing the double crime of adultery and incest. Just as in the previous lifetime, John came to Herod and demanded that he get rid of Herodias. Herod had respect for John, and so tried to simply ignore him. Finally, at the insistence of Herodias he imprisoned John, and ultimately Herodias got John's head on a platter, fulfilling her desire of centuries.

The Word Goes Out

And it came to pass, when Jesus had made an end of commanding his twelve disciples, he departed thence to teach and to preach in their cities (Matthew 11:1), and healing every where (Luke 9:6).

And they went out, and preached that men should repent. And they cast out many devils, and anointed with oil many that were sick, and healed them Mark 6:12-13).

Now Herod the tetrarch heard of all that was done by him: and he was perplexed, because that it was said of some, that John was risen from the dead, and of some, that Elias had appeared; and of others, that one of the old prophets was risen again. And Herod said, John have I beheaded: but who is this, of whom I hear such things? And he desired to see him (Luke 9:7-9).

And the apostles gathered themselves together unto Jesus, and told him all things, both what they had done, and what they had taught. And he said unto them, Come ye yourselves apart into a desert place, and rest a while: for there were many coming and going, and they had no leisure so much as to eat. And they departed into a desert place by ship privately (Mark 6:30-32).

And the people saw them departing, and many knew him, and ran afoot thither out of all cities, and outwent them, and came together unto him (Mark 6:33), because they saw his miracles which he did on them that were diseased (John 6:2).

And Jesus went up into a mountain, and there he sat with his disciples. And the passover, a feast of the Jews [Judeans], was nigh (John 6:3-4).

And they… anointed with oil many that were sick, and healed them. Jesus showed the disciples how to infuse oil with healing vibrations, and the touch of that oil healed the sick. In sacramental Christianity such oil is still blessed and used to anoint the sick. It is very important to understand that material objects can become vehicles of subtle, spiritual vibrations. This is possible because all things are made of divine creative energy.

Now Herod the tetrarch heard of all that was done by him: and he was perplexed, because that it was said of some, that John was risen from the dead, and of some, that Elias had appeared; and of others, that one of the old prophets was risen again. And Herod said, John have I beheaded: but who is this, of whom I hear such things? And he desired to see him. This desire will not be fulfilled until the arrest of Jesus by the soldiers of the Sanhedrin.

And he said unto them, Come ye yourselves apart into a desert place, and rest a while. Meditation in solitude and silence is indispensable for recharging our spiritual bodies after intense spiritual activity.

Compassion And Care

And Jesus, when he came out, saw much people, and was moved with compassion toward them, because they were as sheep not having a shepherd: and he began to teach them many things (Mark 6:34), and spake unto them of the kingdom of God, and healed them that had need of healing (Luke 9:11).

And when the day was now far spent, his disciples came unto him, and said, This is a desert place, and now the time is far passed (Mark 6:35). But Jesus said unto them, They need not depart; give ye them to eat (Matthew 14:16). And they say unto him, Shall we go and buy two hundred pennyworth of bread, and give them to eat? (Mark 6:37). He saith unto Philip, Whence shall we buy bread, that these may eat? (And this he said to prove him: for he himself knew what he would do.) Philip answered him, Two hundred pennyworth of bread is not sufficient for them, that every one of them may take a little (John 6:5-7).

He saith unto them, How many loaves have ye? go and see (Mark 6:38).

One of his disciples, Andrew, Simon Peter's brother, saith unto him, There is a lad here, which hath five barley loaves, and two small fishes: but what are they among so many? (John 6:8-9). He said, Bring them hither to me (Matthew 14:18).

And he commanded them to make all sit down by companies upon the green grass. And they sat down in ranks, by hundreds, and by fifties. And when he had taken the five loaves and the two fishes, he looked up to heaven, and blessed, and brake the loaves, and gave them to his disciples to set before them; and the two fishes divided he among them all. And they did all eat, and were filled (Mark 6:39-42).

When they were filled, he said unto his disciples, Gather up the fragments that remain, that nothing be lost. Therefore they gathered them together, and filled twelve baskets with the fragments of the five barley loaves, which remained over and above unto them that had eaten (John 6:12-13). And they that had eaten were about five thousand men, beside women and children (Matthew 14:21).

Then those men, when they had seen the miracle that Jesus did, said, This is of a truth that prophet that should come into the world. When Jesus therefore perceived that they would come and take him by force, to make him a king (John 6:14-15), straightway he constrained his disciples to get into the ship, and to go to the other side before unto Bethsaida, while he sent away the people. And when he had sent them away, he departed into a mountain to pray (Mark 6:45-46).

He saith unto Philip, Whence shall we buy bread, that these may eat? (And this he said to prove him: for he himself knew what he would do.) It is very important for us to realize that throughout our journey in and beyond this world we will come to testing points. They are not to show the omniscient God or a perfected Master what we will do, but to show us by our reaction what is our inner disposition. The word *peirazo* means to scrutinize, examine and determine the quality or character of something. One of the words Strong uses is "assay," the word used for determining an ore sample to see if it is truly gold and its quality.

And when he had taken the five loaves and the two fishes, he looked up to heaven, and blessed, and brake the loaves, and gave them to his disciples to set before them; and the two fishes divided he among them all. Please note that Jesus blessed the bread, but not the fish. Since he knew the people would not understand the need for a vegetarian diet he allowed it to be given them. But it was an extension of the fish the young boy had brought and did not entail killing the fish. Later on, after the Resurrection, we will encounter fishing and fish and its result.

He sent away the people. And when he had sent them away, he departed into a mountain to pray. Again the need for solitude and meditation. If they were necessary for Jesus, a siddha-purusha, how much more it is necessary for us.

Storm and Doubt

And entering into a ship, they went over the sea toward Capernaum. And it was now dark, and Jesus was not come with them. And the sea arose by reason of a great wind that blew (John 6:17-18).

But the ship was now in the midst of the sea, tossed with waves: for the wind was contrary [blowing against them]. And in the fourth watch of the night Jesus went unto them, walking on the sea (Matthew 14:24-25).

And he saw them toiling in rowing; for the wind was contrary unto them: and he would have passed by them (Mark 6:48).

And when the disciples saw him walking on the sea, they were troubled, saying, It is a spirit; and they cried out for fear.

But straightway Jesus spake unto them, saying, Be of good cheer; it is I; be not afraid.

And Peter answered him and said, Lord, if it be thou, bid me come unto thee on the water.

And he said, Come. And when Peter was come down out of the ship, he walked on the water, to go to Jesus. But when he saw the wind boisterous, he was afraid; and beginning to sink, he cried, saying, Lord, save me.

And immediately Jesus stretched forth his hand, and caught him, and said unto him, O thou of little faith, wherefore didst thou doubt?

And when they were come into the ship, the wind ceased.

Then they that were in the ship came and worshipped

him, saying, Of a truth thou art the Son of God (Matthew 14:26-33).

And they were sore [greatly] amazed in themselves beyond measure, and wondered. For they considered not the miracle of the loaves: for their heart was hardened (Mark 6:51-52).

And when Peter was come down out of the ship, he walked on the water, to go to Jesus. But when he saw the wind boisterous, he was afraid; and beginning to sink, he cried, saying, Lord, save me. Hudor is not just water, it is water that is being agitated by the rain and therefore choppy and uneven, heaving and subsiding. Walking on such a surface naturally bewilders and confuses the walker and frightens him. Taking his eyes off Jesus, Peter begins to sink because of his fear. It is the same in spiritual life. If we take our eyes off the Divine Goal and look at the world around us we will become unsure, ourselves agitated and fearful, and so will lose control and focus and begin to sink. Our only salvation will consist in our fixing our mind on the Infinite as our Help and Refuge.

And immediately Jesus stretched forth his hand, and caught him, and said unto him, O thou of little faith, wherefore didst thou doubt? "Little faith" is a translation of *oligopistos*, which means unbelieving, lacking confidence and lacking continuity of will and faith. *Distazo* means to waver, doubt and ultimately be of two contradictory minds–believing and unbelieving. Saint James calls it "double-minded" (*dispsuchos*), and says, "A double minded man is unstable in all his ways" (James 1:8). It is natural for the spiritual seeker, especially in the beginning, to experience this mental conflict. For without definite experience of the reality of so much in spiritual life, what else could result? So we should not blame ourselves when this conflict and doubt arises, but strengthen our resolve and press on looking neither to the right nor the left, but forward and upward. In time our own experience will confirm us in faith and confidence, *knowing* where before we only hoped or believed.

And when they were come into the ship, the wind ceased. Once we center ourselves in the life of the spirit, which is the yoga life, then all instability and doubt fades away (it is a gradual process) and we are at peace.

Then they that were in the ship came and worshipped him, saying, Of a truth thou art the Son of God. They bowed down and declared "Thou art the Son of God," but the Gospel account continues, saying:

And they were sore [greatly] amazed in themselves beyond measure, and wondered. For they considered not the miracle of the loaves: for their heart was hardened. They did not take into account their own past experiences with Jesus and the continual manifestation of his divine status. For they lacked understanding. Their hearts were *poroo*, which means blinded or insensitive–and so unresponsive. But there should be no pessimism, for Saint John in his Gospel says this very significant thing:

> **Then they willingly received him into the ship: and immediately [shortly after] the ship was at the land whither [towards which] they went (John 6:21).**

When we establish ourselves in the yoga life with our inner Christ as our companion and guide, it will not be long before we find ourselves on the safety and stability of land away from the storm and fluctuations of the samsaric sea. As Buddha said: "Turn around and lo! the Other Shore." For it is always true: The Kingdom Is At Hand.

Continuing Grace

And when they had passed over, they came into the land of Gennesaret, and drew to the shore. And when they were come out of the ship, straightway they knew him, and ran through that whole region round about, and began to carry about in beds those that were sick, where they heard he was. And whithersoever he entered, into villages, or cities, or country, they laid the sick in the streets, and besought him that they might touch if it were but the border of his garment: and as many as touched him were made whole (Mark 6:53-56).

And as many as touched him were made whole. The word *haptomai* means "touch," but its primary meaning it "to attach oneself to." Those who will unite themselves to their own Christhood will then be "made whole." *Sozo* means to be saved in the sense of being delivered from something as well as to be protected, preserved, healed and made complete. This last is the most important. When we are no longer fragmented and scattered in our makeup, but gathered together and made one, then we are truly healed of the disease of samsara.

Some Plain Speaking

The day following, when the people which stood on the other side of the sea saw that there was none other boat there, save that one whereinto his disciples were entered, and that Jesus went not with his disciples into the boat, but that his disciples were gone away alone. (Howbeit there came other boats from Tiberias nigh unto the place where they did eat bread, after that the Lord had given thanks.)

When the people therefore saw that Jesus was not there, neither his disciples, they also took shipping, and came to Capernaum, seeking for Jesus. And when they had found him on the other side of the sea, they said unto him, Rabbi, when camest thou hither?

Jesus answered them and said, Verily, verily, I say unto you, Ye seek me, not because ye saw the miracles, but because ye did eat of the loaves, and were filled. Labour not for the food which perisheth, but for that food which endureth unto everlasting life, which the Son of man shall give unto you: for him hath God the Father sealed.

Then said they unto him, What shall we do, that we might work the works of God?

Jesus answered and said unto them, This is the work of God, that ye believe on him whom he hath sent. (John 6:22-29).

Ye seek me, not because ye saw the miracles, but because ye did eat of the loaves, and were filled. It is necessary for truth to be spoken if those to whom it is spoken are to hear and understand and act and live accordingly. So

Jesus spells it all out to them. Their motives were totally material and personal. They wanted something for nothing–a lot of something, indeed–and wanted to do nothing to deserve it, but only have it given to them. The idea of the Welfare State is not new. Here it is on the shores of Galilee. Something For Nothing has an almost mystical attraction for most people. People will do almost anything and go almost anywhere to get something for nothing.

The fact that Jesus worked miracles did not attract them, for they were blind and deaf to the supernatural, being immersed in the material side of existence. This was a natural consequence of the quality of the energy of their minds. In essence we are spirit, but we are encased in many layers of vibrating energy, from most subtle to the most gross (material). The quality or nature of what we identify with will determine what we are spontaneously interested in. The entire range of vibratory creation is called prakriti: energy. The Bhagavad Gita tells us, "One acts according to one's own prakriti–even the wise man does so. Beings follow their own prakriti; what will restraint accomplish? (3:33). There is absolutely no use in trying to interest someone in anything other than what is compatible with and a part of the level or band of energy in/on which he lives. It is a matter of magnetism, of magnetic attraction. Jesus knew the prakriti of those he was speaking to. But him they did not know.

Labour not for the food which perisheth, but for that food which endureth unto everlasting life, which the Son of man shall give unto you: for him hath God the Father sealed. The food of earth passes away, but the food of spirit lasts and leads us to life that has no end. The Masters of Wisdom point us to the source of this food, but we must take and assimilate it ourselves.

In past times people kept seals which were their legal signature. One purpose was to establish ownership or approval of something. Those who attain to perfect liberation on all levels are sealed by God with his own Consciousness.

Then said they unto him, What shall we do, that we might work the works of God? Jesus answered and said unto them, This is the work of God, that ye believe on him whom he hath sent. God sends many messengers to us throughout our lives. Their purpose is to put us on the path to total awakening in spirit. The wise heed all of them and so make themselves capable of receiving further and higher messengers. The ultimate messenger is our own divine Self in which our faith prepares us for the final revelation of our Self within the Supreme Self. All genuine spiritual teaching points to this, not to dependence on anything lesser than our Self. Teachers and teachings that just lead us to them are deadly snares. Being servants of, or "taking refuge" in, anything but the Self is to be a slave in the darkness of ignorance.

The Journey Continues

Spirit and Life is not merely a book to be read—it presents a path to be walked. This first volume contains the early teachings and revelations of Jesus the Christ, leading us into the heart of his illumined wisdom.

But the story—and the transformation—does not end here.

Volume Two: The Way of Liberation continues to illumine the later teachings, parables, miracles, and final revelations of the Gospels. In its pages, you will encounter:

- The deeper meaning of the Kingdom of Heaven
- The inner teachings behind Jesus' parables
- The mysteries of death, resurrection, and divine union
- The path of awakening he set before each of us

Now available wherever you found this volume.

Did you enjoy reading this book?

Thank you for taking the time to read *Spirit and Life*. If you found it meaningful, or if it inspired you, or simply gave you something worth pondering, we invite you to leave a short review on Amazon, Goodreads, or anywhere books are shared.

Word of mouth is one of the greatest gifts you can offer to independent publishers, and helps keep this work in motion.

Continue Your Journey Within:
GET YOUR FREE MEDITATION GUIDE

Sign up for the Light of the Spirit Newsletter and get *The Pathway to Awakening: Three Essentials for a Successful Spiritual Life*

Get free updates: newsletters, blog posts, and podcasts, plus exclusive content from Light of the Spirit Monastery.

Visit: https://ocoy.org/signup

Glossary

Abhaya(m): "Without fear;" fearlessness; a state of steadfastness in which one is not swayed by fear of any kind.

Adharma: Unrighteousness; demerit, failure to perform one's proper duty; unrighteous action; lawlessness; absence of virtue; all that is contrary to righteousness (dharma).

Adharmic: Having the character of, or producing, adharma.

Adhikari(n): An eligible or qualified person; a worthy person. It implies both fitness and capability.

Advaita: Non-dualism; non-duality; literally: not [a] two [dvaita].

Ahimsa: Non-injury in thought, word, and deed; non-violence; non-killing; harmlessness.

Ajapa Japa: A yogic term that means the natural, spontaneous sound of the breath that goes on perpetually through the simple act of breathing. This sound is extremely subtle, and though non-verbal is the highest form of mantra. The Mantra "So'ham" (I am That) which is produced by the breath itself, without any conscious effort at repeating it: the inhalation sounding 'So' and the exhalation 'ham.'

Akasha: Ether; space; sky; literally: "not visible." The subtlest of the five elements (panchabhuta), from which the other four arise. It is all-pervading, and is sometimes identified with consciousness–chidakasha. It is the basis of sound (shabda), which is its particular property.

Amrita: That which makes one immortal. The nectar of immortality that emerged from the ocean of milk when the gods churned it.

Ananda: Bliss; happiness; joy. A fundamental attribute of Brahman, which is Satchidananda: Existence, Consciousness, Bliss.

Anandamayi Ma: One of the major spiritual figures in twentieth-century India, first made known to the West by Paramhansa Yogananda in his *Autobiography of a Yogi*.

Anatma(n): Not-Self; insentient.

Antahkarana: Internal instrument; the subtle bodies; fourfold mind: mind, intellect, ego and subconscious mind.

Arya(n): One who is an Arya–literally, "one who strives upward." Both Arya and Aryan are exclusively psychological terms having nothing whatsoever to do with birth, race, or nationality. In his teachings Buddha habitually referred to spiritually qualified people as "the Aryas." Although in English translations we find the expressions: "The Four Noble Truths," and "The Noble Eightfold Path," Buddha actually said: "The Four Aryan Truths," and "The Eightfold Aryan Path."

Ashram(a): A place for spiritual discipline and study, usually a monastic residence.

Ashramite: Resident of an ashram.

Asmita: I-ness; the sense of "I am;" "I exist;" sense of individuality.

Atma: See Atman.

Atmabala: Soul-force.

Atma-bhava: The nature of the Self; awareness of the self; feeling: "I am the Self."

Atma-bodha: Knowledge of the Self; also a work of that name by Sri Sankara.

Atmachaitanya: The consciousness of the Self: the awareness of the Self as an object, the awareness that one is the Self, and the actual consciousness that is the Self.

Atma-cintana: Reflection on the Self or the Atman.

Atma-darshan: The seeing or sight of the Self (atma); the vision of the Self; knowledge of the Self through direct vision or knowing; the vision of seeing everything as the Self.

Atma-drishti: Atma-darshan.

Atmajnana: Direct knowledge of the Self; Brahma-Jnana.

Atma(n): The individual spirit or Self that is one with Brahman. The true nature or identity.

Atmasakshatkara: "Direct sight of the Self;" realization of the true nature of the Self; Self-realization.

Atmavidya: Teaching about the Self and its reality; knowledge of the Self.

Atmic: Having to do with the atma–spirit or Self.

Avatar(a): A fully liberated spirit (jiva) who is born into a world below Satya Loka to help others attain liberation. Though commonly referred to as a divine incarnation, an avatar actually is totally one with God, and therefore an incarnation of God-Consciousness.

Avidya: Ignorance; nescience; unknowing; literally: "to know not." A Sakti or illusive power in Brahman which is sometimes regarded as one with Maya and sometimes as different from it. It forms the condition of the individual soul and is otherwise called Ajnana or Asuddha-maya. It forms the Karana Sarira of the Jiva. It is Malina or impure Sattwa. Also called ajnana.

Bhagavad Gita: "The Song of God." The sacred philosophical text often called "the Hindu Bible," part of the epic Mahabharata by Vyasa; the most popular sacred text in Hinduism.

Bhava: Subjective state of being (existence); attitude of mind; mental attitude or feeling; state of realization in the heart or mind.

Brahma: The Creator (Prajapati) of the three worlds of men, angels, and archangels (Bhur, Bhuwah, and Swah); the first of the created beings; Hiranyagarbha or cosmic intelligence. See Kalpa for an explanation of the Days and Night of Brahma and the length of his term as Creator.

Brahmajnana: Direct, transcendental knowledge of Brahman; Self-realization.

Brahmamuhurta: "The muhurta of Brahman." The period of one and a half hours before sunrise, which is said to be the best time for meditation and worship.

Brahman: The Absolute Reality; the Truth proclaimed in the Upanishads; the Supreme Reality that is one and indivisible, infinite, and eternal; all-pervading, changeless Existence; Existence-knowledge-bliss Absolute (Satchidananda); Absolute Consciousness; it is not only all-powerful but all-power itself; not only all-knowing and blissful but all-knowledge and all-bliss itself.

Buddhi: Intellect; intelligence; understanding; reason; the thinking mind; the higher mind, which is the seat of wisdom; the discriminating faculty.

Chidakasha: "The Space (Ether) of Consciousness." The infinite, all-pervading expanse of Consciousness from which all "things" proceed; the subtle space of Consciousness in the Sahasrara (Thousand-petalled Lotus). The true "heart" of all things. Brahman in Its aspect as limitless knowledge; unbounded intelligence. This is a familiar concept of the Upanishads. It is not meant that the physical ether is consciousness. The Pure Consciousness (Cit) is like the ether (Akasa), an all-pervading continuum.

Chit: Consciousness (that is spirit or purusha); "to perceive, observe, think, be aware, know;" pure unitary Consciousness. The principle of universal intelligence or consciousness.

Darshan: Literally "sight" or "seeing;" vision, literal and metaphysical; a system of philosophy (see Sad-darshanas). Darshan is the seeing of a holy being as well as the blessing received by seeing such a one.

Dharma: The righteous way of living, as enjoined by the sacred scriptures and the spiritually illumined; law; lawfulness; virtue; righteousness; norm.

Dharmashala: A place for pilgrims to stay, either free of charge or at a minimal cost.

Dharmi: One who follows dharma–specifically, Sanatana Dharma.

Dharmic: Having to do with dharma; of the character of dharma.

Dukha(m): Pain; suffering; misery; sorrow; grief; unhappiness; stress; that which is unsatisfactory.

Ganapati: "Lord of the Ganas" (the spirits that always accompany Shiva). See Ganesha.

Ganesha: The elephant-headed son of Shiva and Parvati; the remover of obstacles; lord (pati) of the ganas (spirits that always accompany Shiva); god of wisdom; god of beginnings; the granter of success in spiritual and material life; in ritual worship he is worshipped

first, and is therefore known as Adi-deva, the First God.
Gita: The Bhagavad Gita.
Gotra: Clan; family; lineage.
Hridaya: Heart; essential center or core of something; essence; the Self; a special mantric formula that is felt to embody the very being of the deity specially worshiped by the devotee.
Hridayaguha: The cave or chamber of the heart.
Ishwara: "God" or "Lord" in the sense of the Supreme Power, Ruler, Master, or Controller of the cosmos. "Ishwara" implies the powers of omnipotence, omnipresence, and omniscience.
Japa: Repetition of a mantra.
Japa Mala: A string of beads, usually one hundred and eight, on which repetitions (japa) of a mantra are kept count of, or used just to help the yogi remember to do japa. Though one hundred and eight is the usual number of beads, smaller malas can be used when more convenient, especially since they can be put around the wrist when not in use. The beads can be of any substance, whatever is convenient or preferred.
Jiva: Individual spirit.
Jivatman: Individual spirit; individual consciousness.
Jnana: Knowledge; knowledge of Reality–of Brahman, the Absolute; also denotes the process of reasoning by which the Ultimate Truth is attained. The word is generally used to denote the knowledge by which one is aware of one's identity with Brahman.
Jnani: A follower of the path of knowledge (jnana); one who has realized–who knows–the Truth (Brahman).
Jyotirmaya/Jyotirmayi: Full (mass) of light.
Kali: "The Black One;" the black-skinned goddess who emerged from the body of Goddess Durga to defeat the demons that were attacking her. She wears a garland of skulls (or severed heads) around her neck and a skirt of severed arms–both symbolizing the sense of egotism. In one hand she wields the sword of spiritual wisdom (prajna) and in the other carries a severed head (ego). Despite her fearsome appearance, her two other hands are held in the gestures

(mudras) that indicate: "Fear not" and "Draw near."

Kalpa: A Day of Brahma—4,320,000,000 years. It alternates with a Night of Brahma of the same length. He lives hundred such years. Brahma's life is known as Para, being of a longer duration than the life of any other being, and a half of it is called Parardha. He has now completed the first Parardha and is in the first day of the second Parardha. This day or Kalpa is known as Svetavarahakalpa. In the Day of Brahma creation is manifest and in the Night of Brahma is it resolved into its causal state.

Karma: Karma, derived from the Sanskrit root *kri*, which means to act, do, or make, means any kind of action, including thought and feeling. It also means the effects of action. Karma is both action and reaction, the metaphysical equivalent of the principle: "For every action there is an equal and opposite reaction." "Whatsoever a man soweth, that shall he also reap" (Galatians 6:7). It is karma operating through the law of cause and effect that binds the jiva or the individual soul to the wheel of birth and death. There are three forms of karma: sanchita, agami, and prarabdha. Sanchita karma is the vast store of accumulated actions done in the past, the fruits of which have not yet been reaped. Agami karma is the action that will be done by the individual in the future. Prarabdha karma is the action that has begun to fructify, the fruit of which is being reaped in this life.

Kirtan(a): Singing the names and praises of God; devotional chanting.

Kosha: Sheath; bag; scabbard; a sheath enclosing the soul; body. There are five such concentric sheaths or bodies: the sheaths of bliss, intellect, mind, life-force and the physical body—the anandamaya, jnanamaya, manomaya, pranamaya and annamaya bodies respectively.

Krishna: An avatar born in India about three thousand years ago, Whose teachings to His disciple Arjuna on the eve of the Great India (Mahabharata) War comprise the Bhagavad Gita.

Krishna Chaitanya, Sri; Chaitanya Mahaprabhu: A leading devotee of Krishna in the sixteenth century, the founder of the Bhakti Movement in Bengal. Considered an avatar by many Vaishnavas.

Loka: World or realm; sphere, level, or plane of existence, whether physical, astral, or causal.

Mahasamadhi: Literally "the great union [samadhi]," this refers to a realized yogi's conscious departure from the physical body at death.

Mahashakti: The Great Power; the divine creative energy.

Mahatma: Literally: "a great soul [atma]." Usually a designation for a sannyasi, sage or saint.

Mahavakya: Literally: "Great Saying." The highest Vedantic truth, found in the Upanishads expressing the highest Vedantic truths or the identity between the individual soul and the Supreme Soul. There are four Mahavakyas: 1) Prajñanam Brahma–"Consciousness is Brahman" (Aitareya Upanishad 3.3); 2) Ayam Atma Brahma–"This Self is Brahman" (Mandukya Upanishad 1.2); 3) Tat Twam Asi–"Thou art That" (Chandogya Upanishad 6.8.7); 4) Aham Brahmasmi–"I am Brahman" (Brihadaranyaka Upanishad 1.4.10).

Mala : Rosary (japa mala).

Manas(a): The sensory mind; the perceiving faculty that receives the messages of the senses.

Mantra(m): Sacred syllable or word or set of words through the repetition and reflection of which one attains perfection or realization of the Self. Literally, "a transforming thought" (manat trayate). A mantra, then is a sound formula that transforms the consciousness.

Mara: The embodiment of the power of cosmic evil, illusion, and delusion; Satan.

Maya: The illusive power of Brahman; the veiling and the projecting power of the universe, the power of Cosmic Illusion. "The Measurer"–a reference to the two delusive "measures," Time and Space.

Moksha: Release; liberation; the term is particularly applied to the liberation from the bondage of karma and the wheel of birth and death; Absolute Experience.

Mukta: One who is liberated–freed–usually in the sense of one who has attained moksha or spiritual liberation.

Mumukshutwa: Intense desire or yearning for liberation (moksha).

Muni: "Silent one" (one observing the vow of silence–mauna); sage; ascetic.

Nirguna: Without attributes or qualities (gunas).

Nirguna Brahman: The impersonal, attributeless Absolute beyond all description or designation.

Niyama: Observance; the five Do's of Yoga: 1) shaucha–purity, cleanliness; 2) santosha–contentment, peacefulness; 3) tapas–austerity, practical (i.e., result-producing) spiritual discipline; 4) swadhyaya–self-study, spiritual study; 5) Ishwarapranidhana–offering of one's life to God.

Om: The Pranava or the sacred syllable symbolizing and embodying Brahman.

Omkara: Om.

Om Tat Sat: A designation of Brahman; used as a benediction, a solemn invocation of the divine blessing.

Papa(m): Sin; demerit; evil; sinful deeds; evil deeds; trouble; harm; anything which takes one away from dharma.

Parambrahman: Supreme Brahman.

Param[a]purusha: The Supreme Spirit; Supreme Person. See Purusha.

Paramatman: The Supreme Self, God.

Paramhansa Yogananda: The most influential yogi of the twentieth century in the West, author of *Autobiography of a Yogi* and founder of Self-Realization Fellowship in America.

Patanjali: A yogi of ancient India, a Nath Yogi and the author of the Yoga Sutras.

Pradhana: Prakriti; causal matter.

Prajapati: Progenitor; the Creator; a title of Brahma the Creator.

Prajna: Consciousness; awareness; wisdom; intelligence.

Prakriti: Causal matter; the fundamental power (shakti) of God from which the entire cosmos is formed; the root base of all elements; undifferentiated matter; the material cause of the world. Also known as Pradhana. Prakriti can also mean the entire range of vibratory existence (energy).

Prakritilaya: Absorbed or submerged in Prakriti; the state of yogis who have so identified with the cosmic energy that they are trapped in it as though in a net and cannot separate themselves from it and evolve onwards until the cosmic dissolution (pralaya) occurs in which the lower worlds of men, angels, and archangels (bhur, bhuwah and swar lokas) are dissolved.

Prana: Life; vital energy; life-breath; life-force; inhalation. In the human body the prana is divided into five forms: 1) Prana, the prana that moves upward; 2) Apana: The prana that moves downward, producing the excretory functions in general. 3) Vyana: The prana that holds prana and apana together and produces circulation in the body. 4) Samana: The prana that carries the grosser material of food to the apana and brings the subtler material to each limb; the general force of digestion. 5) Udana: The prana which brings up or carries down what has been drunk or eaten; the general force of assimilation.

Pranam: "To bow;" to greet with respect. A respectful or reverential gesture made by putting the hands together palm-to-palm in front of the chest.

Pranava: A title of Om, meaning "Life-ness" or "Life-Giver." Om is the expression or controller of prana—the life force within the individual being and the cosmos.

Punya: Merit; virtue; meritorious acts; virtuous deeds.

Purna: Full; complete; all-encompassing; infinite; absolute; Brahman.

Purna Yoga: Complete yoga.

Purna Yogi: A full-blown Yogi.

Purusha: "Person" in the sense of a conscious spirit. Both God and the individual spirits are purushas, but God is the Adi (Original, Archetypal) Purusha, Parama (Highest) Purusha, and the Purushottama (Highest or Best of the Purushas).

Purushottama: The Supreme Person; Supreme Purusha; the Lord of the universe. (See Purusha.)

Rama: An incarnation of God—the king of ancient Ayodhya in north-central India. His life is recorded in the ancient epic Ramayana.

Ramakrishna, Sri: Sri Ramakrishna lived in India in the second half of the nineteenth century, and is regarded by all India as a perfectly enlightened person—and by many as an Incarnation of God.

Ramana Maharshi: A great twentieth-century sage from Tamil Nadu, who lived most of his life at or on the sacred mountain of Arunachala in the town of Tiruvannamalai.

Rishi: Sage; seer of the Truth.

Rita(m): Truth; Law; Right; Order. The natural order of things, or Cosmic Order/Law. Its root is ri, which means "to rise, to tend upward." It is said to be the basis for the Law of Karma.

Rudraksha: "The Eye of Shiva;" a tree seed considered sacred to Shiva and worn by worshippers of Shiva, Shakti, and Ganesha, and by yogis, usually in a strand of 108 seeds. Also used as a rosary to count the number of mantras repeated in japa.

Sadhaka: One who practices spiritual discipline–sadhana–particularly meditation.

Sadhana: Spiritual practice.

Sadhana-chatushtaya: The fourfold aids to spiritual practice: 1) Viveka, the ability to discriminate between the transient and the eternal (nitya-anity-astu-viveka); 2) Vairagya, the absence of desire for securing pleasure or pain either here or elsewhere (iha-anutra-artha-phala-vairagya); 3) Shad-Sampat (The Sixfold Virtue): Sama, the serenity or tranquillity of mind which is brought about through the eradication of desires; Dama, the rational control of the senses; Uparati, satiety or resolutely turning the mind away from desire for sensual enjoyment; Titiksha, the power of endurance (an aspirant should patiently bear the pairs of opposites such as heat and cold, pleasure and pain, etc.; Shraddha, intense faith, lasting, perfect and unshakable; Samadhana, fixing the mind on Brahman or the Self, without allowing it to run towards objects; 4) Mumukshutwa, the intense desire for liberation.

Sadhana Shakti: Both the power to successfully engage in sadhana, the the power that accrues within the sadhaka from his practice of sadhana.

Sadhu: Seeker for truth (sat); a person who is practicing spiritual disciplines; a good or virtuous or honest man, a holy man, saint, sage, seer. Usually this term is applied only to monastics.

Saguna: Possessing attributes or qualities (gunas).

Saguna Brahman: Brahman with attributes, such as mercy, omnipotence, omniscience, etc.; the Absolute conceived as the Creator, Preserver, and Destroyer of the universe; also the Personal God according to the Vedanta.

Sahasrara: The "thousand-petalled lotus" of the brain. The highest center of consciousness, the point at which the spirit (atma) and the bodies (koshas) are integrated and from which they are disengaged.

Samadhi: The state of superconsciousness where Absoluteness is experienced attended with all-knowledge and joy; Oneness; here the mind becomes identified with the object of meditation; the meditator and the meditated, thinker and thought become one in perfect absorption of the mind.

Samsara: Life through repeated births and deaths; the wheel of birth and death; the process of earthly life.

Samsari: The transmigrating soul.

Samsaric: Having to do with samsara; involved with samsara; partaking of the traits or qualities of samsara.

Samsarin: One who is subject to samsara–repeated births and deaths–and who is deluded by its appearances, immersed in ignorance.

Samskara: Impression in the mind, either conscious or subconscious, produced by action or experience in this or previous lives; propensities of the mental residue of impressions; subliminal activators; prenatal tendency. See Vasana.

Sanatana: Eternal; everlasting; ancient; primeval.

Sanatana Dharma: "The Eternal Religion," also known as "Arya Dharma," "the religion of those who strive upward [Aryas]." Hinduism.

Sanatana Dharmi: One who follows Sanatana Dharma.

Sankalpa: A life-changing wish, desire, volition, resolution, will, determination, or intention–not a mere momentary aspiration, but an empowering act of will that persists until the intention is fully realized. It is an act of spiritual, divine creative will inherent in each person as a power of the Atma.

Sannyasi(n): A renunciate; a monk.

Sat: Existence; reality; truth; being; a title of Brahman, the Absolute or

Pure Being.

Satchidananda: Existence-Knowledge-Bliss Absolute; Brahman.

Satsang(a): Literally: "company with Truth." Association with godly-minded persons. The company of saints and devotees.

Satya Loka: "True World," "World of the True [Sat]", or "World of Truth [Satya]." This highest realm of relative existence where liberated beings live who have not entered back into the Transcendent Absolute where there are no "worlds" (lokas). From that world they can descend and return to other worlds for the spiritual welfare of others, as can those that have chosen to return to the Transcendent.

Shabda: Sound; word.

Shabda Brahman: Sound-God; Brahman in the Form of Sound; Soham; the Vedas.

Shaiva/Shaivite: A worshipper of Shiva; pertaining to Shiva.

Shakti: Power; energy; force; the Divine Power of becoming; the apparent dynamic aspect of Eternal Being; the Absolute Power or Cosmic Energy; the Divine Feminine.

Shankara: Shankaracharya; Adi (the first) Shankaracharya: The great reformer and re-establisher of Vedic Religion in India around 500 B.C. He is the unparalleled exponent of Advaita (Non-Dual) Vedanta. He also reformed the mode of monastic life and founded (or regenerated) the ancient Swami Order.

Shankaracharya: The title of the head of one of the major monasteries (maths) of the Swami Order founded by Shankara. There are four maths in the four quarters of India: Sringeri, Dwaraka, Badrinath and Jagannath Puri.

Shiva: A name of God meaning "One Who is all Bliss and the giver of happiness to all." Although classically applied to the Absolute Brahman, Shiva can also refer to God (Ishwara) in His aspect of Dissolver and Liberator (often mistakenly thought of as "destroyer").

Shiva Linga: A column-like or egg-shaped symbol of Shiva, usually made of stone. The column-like linga represents the central axis of creation which was seen by Brahma and Vishnu as a column of Light that had no top or bottom, but out of which Shiva emerged and explained that he was the source–indeed the totality–of creation. To yogis it represents the sushumna nadi which embodies the Consciousness that is Shiva. The egg-shaped (garbha) linga represents Shiva as the germ or seed of the universe out of whom all things have come to be as his manifestation. It is often to considered to represent the universe itself which is identical with Shiva.

Siddha: A perfected–liberated–being, an adept, a seer, a perfect yogi.

Siddha Purusha: A perfectly enlightened being.

Siddhaloka: The highest realm of existence in which the fully liberated (siddhas) live. (However, wherever a siddha is, that place is siddhaloka.)

Siddhi: Spiritual perfection; psychic power; power; modes of success; attainment; accomplishment; achievement; mastery; supernatural power attained through mantra, meditation, or other yogic practices. From the verb root sidh–to attain.

Soham: "That am I;" the ultimate Atma mantra, the mantra of the Self; the Ajapa Gayatri formula of meditation in which "So" is intoned mentally during natural inhalation and "Ham" is intoned mentally during natural exhalation. Soham is pronounced "Sohum," as the short "a" in Sanskrit is pronounced like the American "u" in "up."

Soham Bhava: The state of being and awareness: "THAT I am." Gorakhnath says that So'ham Bhava includes total Self-comprehension (ahamta), total Self-mastery (akhanda aishwarya), unbroken awareness of the unity of the Self (swatmata), awareness of the unity of the Self with all phenomenal existence–as the Self (vishwanubhava), knowledge of all within and without the Self–united in the Self (sarvajñatwa).

Sri Yukteswar Giri, Swami: The guru of Paramhansa Yogananda.

Sukha(m): Happiness; ease; joy; happy; pleasure; pleasant; agreeable.

Sudarshana: Sudarshana Chakra.

Sudarshana Chakra: The invincible weapon of Lord Vishnu which is able to cut through anything, and is a symbol of the Lord's power of cutting through all things which bind the jiva to samsara. Thus it is the divine power of liberation (moksha).

Tapasya: Austerity; practical (i.e., result-producing) spiritual discipline; spiritual force. Literally it means the generation of heat or energy, but is always used in a symbolic manner, referring to spiritual practice and its effect, especially the roasting of karmic seeds, the burning up of karma.

Tat: That. A neuter pronoun expressing the indescribable Absolute. (See Tat Twam Asi).

Tat Twam Asi: "Thou art That." The Mahavakya (Great Saying) of the Chandogya Upanishad.

Tilak: A sacred mark made on the forehead or between the eyebrows, often denoting what form of God the person worships.

Turiya: The state of pure consciousness. *A Ramakrishna-Vedanta Wordbook* defines it as: "The superconscious; lit., 'the Fourth,' in relation to the three ordinary states of consciousness—waking, dreaming, and dreamless sleep—which it transcends."

Turiya-Turiya: "The consciousness of Consciousness;" the Absolute Consciousness of God, the Consciousness behind our individualized consciousness (turiya).

Upanishads: Books (of varying lengths) of the philosophical teachings of the ancient sages of India on the knowledge of Absolute Reality. The upanishads contain two major themes: (1) the individual self (atman) and the Supreme Self (Paramatman) are one in essence, and (2) the goal of life is the realization/manifestation of this unity, the realization of God (Brahman). There are eleven principal upanishads: Isha, Kena, Katha, Prashna, Mundaka, Mandukya, Taittiriya, Aitareya, Chandogya, Brihadaranyaka, and Shvetashvatara, all of which were commented on by Shankara, Ramanuja and Madhavacharya, thus setting the seal of authenticity on them.

Vairagya: Non-attachment; detachment; dispassion; absence of desire; disinterest; or indifference. Indifference towards and disgust for all worldly things and enjoyments.

Vak: Speech.

Vakya: Word or statement.

Vasana: Subtle desire; a tendency created in a person by the doing of an action or by experience; it induces the person to repeat the action or to seek a repetition of the experience; the subtle impression in the mind capable of developing itself into action; it is the cause of birth and experience in general; an aggregate or bundle of samskaras–the impressions of actions that remain unconsciously in the mind.

Vasana(s): A bundle or aggregate of such samskaras.

Vedas: The oldest scriptures of India, considered the oldest scriptures of the world, that were revealed in meditation to the Vedic Rishis (seers). Although in modern times there are said to be four Vedas (Rig, Sama, Yajur, and Atharva), in the upanishads only three are listed (Rig, Sama, and Yajur). In actuality, there is only one Veda: the Rig Veda. The Sama Veda is only a collection of Rig Veda hymns that are marked (pointed) for singing. The Yajur Veda is a small book giving directions on just one form of Vedic sacrifice. The Atharva Veda is only a collection of theurgical mantras to be recited for the cure of various afflictions or to be recited over the herbs to be taken as medicine for those afflictions.

Vedic: Having to do with the Vedas.

Vijnana: The highest knowledge, beyond mere theoretical knowledge (jnana); transcendental knowledge or knowing; experiential knowledge; a high state of spiritual realization–intimate knowledge of God in which all is seen as manifestations of Brahman; knowledge of the Self.

Vishishtadvaita Vedanta: The philosophy of Qualified Non-Dualism formulated by Sri Ramanuja.

Vishwaprana: The universal life force (prana).

Vishwarupa: Cosmic form; multiform having all forms.

Vivekananda (Swami): The chief disciple of Sri Ramakrishna, who brought the message of Vedanta to the West at the end of the nineteenth century.

Vritra: One who hates the light and burrows into the dark; a symbolic term used in the Vedas for those of low and bound consciousness who are the opposite of the Aryans.

Yadava: "Descendant of Yadu" an ancient Indian king; the Yadavas, a clan of India, were descended from King Yadu; a title of Krishna, since he was part of the Yadava clan. Swami Bhaktivedanta, founder of the Hare Krishna movement in the West, as well as some anthropologists, believed that the Yadava clan, who disappeared from India shortly after Krishna's lifetime, emigrated to the middle east and became the people we know today as the Jews, Abraham having been a Yadava.

Yajna: Sacrifice; offering; sacrificial ceremony; a ritual sacrifice; usually the fire sacrifice known as agnihotra or havan.

Yama: Restraint; the five Don'ts of Yoga: 1) ahimsa–non-violence, non-injury, harmlessness; 2) satya–truthfulness, honesty; 3) asteya–non-stealing, honesty, non-misappropriativeness; 4) brahmacharya–continence; 5) aparigraha–non-possessiveness, non-greed, non-selfishness, non-acquisitiveness. These five are called the Great Vow (Observance, Mahavrata) in the Yoga Sutras.

Yama-Niyama: The "Ten Commandments of Yoga" outlined in the Yoga Sutras. See Niyama and Yama.

Yoga: Literally, "joining" or "union" from the Sanskrit root yuj. Union with the Supreme Being, or any practice that makes for such union. Meditation that unites the individual spirit with God, the Supreme Spirit. The name of the philosophy expounded by the sage Patanjali, teaching the process of union of the individual with the Universal Soul.

Yoga Siddha: One who is perfected in yoga and therefore totally liberated and united with Brahman.

Yoga Sutras: The oldest known writing on the subject of yoga, written by the sage Patanjali, a yogi of ancient India, and considered the most authoritative text on yoga. Also known as Yoga Darshana, it is the basis of the Yoga Philosophy which is based on the philosophical system known as Sankhya.

Yogananda (Paramhansa): The most influential yogi of the twentieth century in the West, author of *Autobiography of a Yogi.*

Yogi(n): One who practices Yoga; one who strives earnestly for union with God; an aspirant going through any course of spiritual discipline.

Yuga: Age or cycle; aeon; world era. Hindus believe that there are four yugas: the Golden Age (Satya or Krita Yuga), the Silver age (Treta Yuga), The Bronze Age (Dwapara Yuga), and the Iron Age (Kali Yuga). Satya Yuga is four times as long as the Kali Yuga; Treta Yuga is three times as long; and Dwapara Yuga is twice as long. In the Satya Yuga the majority of humans use the total potential–four-fourths–of their minds; in the Treta Yuga, three-fourths; in the Dwapara Yuga, one half; and in the Kali Yuga, one fourth. (In each Yuga there are those who are using either more or less of their minds than the general populace.) The Yugas move in a perpetual circle: Ascending Kali Yuga, ascending Dwapara Yuga, ascending Treta Yuga, ascending Satya Yuga, descending Satya Yuga, descending, Treta Yuga, descending Dwapara Yuga, and descending Kali Yuga–over and over. Furthermore, there are yuga cycles within yuga cycles. For example, there are yuga cycles that affect the entire cosmos, and smaller yuga cycles within those greater cycles that affect a solar system. The cosmic yuga cycle takes 8,640,000,000 years, whereas the solar yuga cycle only takes 24,000 years. At the present time our solar system is in the ascending Dwapara Yuga, but the cosmos is in the descending Kali Yuga. Consequently, the more the general mind of humanity develops, the more good can be accomplished by the positive, and the more evil can be accomplished by the negative. Therefore we have more contrasts and polarization in contemporary life than previously before 1900.

About the Author

Swami Nirmalananda Giri (Abbot George Burke) is the founder and director of the Atma Jyoti Ashram (Light of the Spirit Monastery) in Cedar Crest, New Mexico, USA.

In his many pilgrimages to India, he had the opportunity of meeting some of India's greatest spiritual figures, including Swami Sivananda of Rishikesh and Anandamayi Ma. During his first trip to India he was made a member of the ancient Swami Order by Swami Vidyananda Giri, a direct disciple of Paramhansa Yogananda, who had himself been given sannyas by the Shankaracharya of Puri, Jagadguru Bharati Krishna Tirtha.

In the United States he also encountered various Christian saints, including Saint John Maximovich of San Francisco and Saint Philaret Voznesensky of New York.

For many years Swami Nirmalananda has researched the identity of Jesus Christ and his teachings with India and Sanatana Dharma, including Yoga. It is his conclusion that Jesus lived in India for most of his life, and was a yogi and Sanatana Dharma missionary to the West. After his resurrection he returned to India and lived the rest of his life in the Himalayas.

He has written extensively on these and other topics, many of which are posted at OCOY.org.

Atma Jyoti Ashram
(Light of the Spirit Monastery)

Atma Jyoti Ashram (Light of the Spirit Monastery) is a monastic community for those men who seek direct experience of the Spirit through yoga meditation, traditional yogic discipline, Sanatana Dharma and the life of the sannyasi in the tradition of the Order of Shankara. Our lineage is in the Giri branch of the Order.

The public outreach of the monastery is through its website, OCOY.org (Original Christianity and Original Yoga). There you will find many articles on Original Christianity and Original Yoga, including *The Christ of India*. *Foundations of Yoga* and *How to Be a Yogi* are practical guides for anyone seriously interested in living the Yoga Life.

You will also discover many other articles on leading an effective spiritual life, including *Soham Yoga: The Yoga of the Self* and *Spiritual Benefits of a Vegetarian Diet*, as well as the "Dharma for Awakening" series—in-depth commentaries on these spiritual classics: the Bhagavad Gita, the Upanishads, the Dhammapada, the Tao Teh King and more.

You can listen to podcasts by Swami Nirmalananda on meditation, the Yoga Life, and remarkable spiritual people he has met in India and elsewhere, at http://ocoy.org/podcasts/

Join over 33,000 subscribers and watch over 300 videos on these topics and more, including recordings of online satsangs where Swami Nirmalananda answers various questions on practical aspects of spiritual life. A new series of talks on the Bhagavad Gita has also been added.

Visit our Youtube channel here:
Youtube.com/@lightofthespirit

Reading for Awakening

Light of the Spirit Press presents books on spiritual wisdom and Original Christianity and Original Yoga. From our "Dharma for Awakening" series (practical commentaries on the world's scriptures) to books on how to meditate and live a successful spiritual life, you will find books that are informative, helpful, and even entertaining.

Light of the Spirit Press is the publishing house of Light of the Spirit Monastery (Atma Jyoti Ashram) in Cedar Crest, New Mexico, USA. Our books feature the writings of the founder and director of the monastery, Swami Nirmalananda Giri (Abbot George Burke) which are also found on the monastery's website, OCOY.org.

We invite you to explore our publications in the following pages.

Find out more about our publications at
lightofthespiritpress.com

Books on Meditation

Soham Yoga
The Yoga of the Self

A complete and in-depth guide to effective meditation and the life that supports it, this important book explains with clarity and insight what real yoga is, and why and how to practice Soham Yoga meditation.

Discovered centuries ago by the Nath yogis, this simple and classic approach to self-realization has no "secrets," requires no "initiation," and is easily accessible to the serious modern yogi.

Includes helpful, practical advice on leading an effective spiritual life and many Illuminating quotes on Soham from Indian scriptures and great yogis.

"This book is a complete spiritual path." –Arnold Van Wie

Light of Soham
The Life and Teachings of Sri Gajanana Maharaj of Nashik

Gajanan Murlidhar Gupte, later known as Gajanana Maharaj, led an unassuming life, to all appearances a normal unmarried man of contemporary society. Crediting his personal transformation to the practice of the Soham mantra, he freely shared this practice with a small number of disciples, whom he simply called his friends. Strictly avoiding the trap of gurudom, he insisted that his friends be self-reliant and not be dependent on him for their spiritual progress. Yet he was uniquely able to assist them in their inner development.

The Inspired Wisdom of Gajanana Maharaj
A Practical Commentary on Leading an Effectual Spiritual Life

Presents the teachings and sayings of the great twentieth-century Soham yogi Gajanana Maharaj, with a commentary by Swami Nirmalananda.

The author writes: "In reading about Gajanana Maharaj I encountered a holy personality that eclipsed all others for me. In his words I found a unique wisdom that altered my perspective on what yoga, yogis, and gurus should be.

"But I realized that through no fault of their own, many Western readers need a clarification and expansion of Maharaj's meaning to get the right understanding of his words. This commentary is meant to help my friends who, like me have found his words 'a light in the darkness.'"

Inspired Wisdom of Lalla Yogeshwari
A Commentary on the Mystical Poetry of the Great Yogini of Kashmir

Lalla Yogeshwari was a great fourteenth-century yogini and wandering ascetic of Kashmir, whose mystic poetry were the earliest compositions in the Kashmiri language. She was in the tradition of the Nath Yogi Sampradaya whose meditation practice is that of Soham Sadhana: the joining of the mental repetition of Soham Mantra with the natural breath.

Swami Nirmalananda's commentary mines the treasures of Lalleshwari's mystic poems and presents his reflections in an easily intelligible fashion for those wishing to put these priceless teachings on the path of yogic self-transformation into practice.

Dwelling in the Mirror
A Study of Illusions Produced By Delusive Meditation And How to Be Free from Them

Swami Nirmalananda says of this book:

"Over and over people have mistaken trivial and pathological conditions for enlightenment, written books, given seminars and gained a devoted following.

"There are those who can have an experience and realize that it really cannot be real, but a vagary of their mind. Some may not understand that on their own, but can be shown by others the truth about it. For them and those that may one day be in danger of meditation-produced delusions I have written this brief study."

BOOKS ON YOGA & SPIRITUAL LIFE

An Eagle's Flight
A Yogi's Spiritual Autobiography

Swami Nirmalananda Giri shares with rare honesty the struggles, insights, and blessings that have shaped his spiritual life.

Written with his usual insight, vividness, and humor, this book presents stories of his encounters with Anandamayi Ma, Swami Sivananda of Rishikesh and many other saints and yogis.

Satsang with the Abbot
Questions and Answers about Life, Spiritual Liberty, and the Pursuit of Ultimate Happiness

The questions in this book range from the most sublime to the most practical. "How can I attain samadhi?" "I am married with children. How can I lead a spiritual life?" "What is Self-realization?" "How important is belief in karma and reincarnation?"

In Swami Nirmalananda's replies to these questions the reader will discover common sense, helpful information, and a guiding light for their journey through and beyond the forest of cliches, contradictions, and confusion of yoga, Hinduism, Christianity, and metaphysical thought.

Foundations of Yoga
Ten Important Principles Every Meditator Should Know

An introduction to the important foundation principles of Patanjali's Yoga: Yama and Niyama

Yama and Niyama are often called the Ten Commandments of Yoga, but they have nothing to do with the ideas of sin and virtue or good and evil as dictated by some cosmic potentate. Rather they are determined by a thoroughly practical, pragmatic basis: that which strengthens and facilitates our yoga practice should be observed and that which weakens or hinders it should be avoided.

Yoga: Science of the Absolute
A Commentary on the Yoga Sutras of Patanjali

The Yoga Sutras of Patanjali is the most authoritative text on Yoga as a practice. It is also known as the Yoga Darshana because it is the fundamental text of Yoga as a philosophy.

In this commentary, Swami Nirmalananda draws on the age-long tradition regarding this essential text, including the commentaries of Vyasa and Shankara, the most highly regarded writers on Indian philosophy and practice, as well as I. K. Taimni and other authoritative commentators, and adds his own ideas based on half a century of study and practice. Serious students of yoga will find this an essential addition to their spiritual studies.

The Benefits of Brahmacharya
A Collection of Writings About the Spiritual, Mental, and Physical Benefits of Continence

"Brahmacharya is the basis for morality. It is the basis for eternal life. It is a spring flower that exhales immortality from its petals." Swami Sivananda

This collection of articles from a variety of authorities including Mahatma Gandhi, Sri Ramakrishna, Swami Vivekananda, Swamis Sivananda and Chidananda of the Divine Life Society, Swami Nirmalananda, and medical experts, presents many facets of brahmacharya and will prove of immense value to all who wish to grow spiritually.

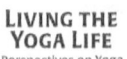

Living the Yoga Life
Perspectives on Yoga

"Dive deep; otherwise you cannot get the gems at the bottom of the ocean. You cannot pick up the gems if you only float on the surface." Sri Ramakrishna

In *Living the Yoga Life* Swami Nirmalananda shares the gems he has found from a lifetime of "diving deep." This collection of reflections and short essays addresses the key concepts of yoga philosophy that are so easy to take for granted. Never content with the accepted cliches about yoga sadhana, the yoga life, the place of a guru, the nature of Brahman and our unity with It, Swami Nirmalananda's insights on these and other facets of the yoga life will inspire, provoke, enlighten, and even entertain.

Spiritual Benefits of a Vegetarian Diet

The health benefits of a vegetarian diet are well known, as are the ethical aspects. But the spiritual advantages should be studied by anyone involved in meditation, yoga, or any type of spiritual practice.

Diet is a crucial aspect of emotional, intellectual, and spiritual development as well. For diet and consciousness are interrelated, and purity of diet is an effective aid to purity and clarity of consciousness.

The major thing to keep in mind when considering the subject of vegetarianism is its relevancy in relation to our explorations of consciousness. We need only ask: Does it facilitate my spiritual growth–the development and expansion of my consciousness? The answer is Yes.

BOOKS ON THE SACRED SCRIPTURES OF INDIA

The Bhagavad Gita for Awakening
A Practical Commentary for Leading a Successful Spiritual Life

Drawing from the teachings of Sri Ramakrishna, Jesus, Paramhansa Yogananda, Ramana Maharshi, Swami Vivekananda, Swami Sivananda of Rishikesh, Papa Ramdas, and other spiritual masters and teachers, as well as his own experiences, Swami Nirmalananda illustrates the teachings of the Gita with stories which make the teachings of Krishna in the Gita vibrant and living.

From *Publisher's Weekly*: "[The author] enthusiastically explores the story as a means for knowing oneself, the cosmos, and one's calling within it. His plainspoken insights often distill complex lessons with simplicity and sagacity. Those with a deep interest in the Gita will find much wisdom here."

The Upanishads for Awakening
A Practical Commentary on India's Classical Scriptures

The sacred scriptures of India are vast. Yet they are only different ways of seeing the same thing, the One Thing which makes them both valid and ultimately harmonious. That unifying subject is Brahman: God the Absolute, beyond and besides whom there is no "other" whatsoever. The thirteen major Upanishads are the fountainhead of all expositions of Brahman.

Swamiji illumines the Upanishads' value for spiritual seekers from the unique perspective of a lifetime of study and practice of both Eastern and Western spirituality.

The Bhagavad Gita–The Song of God

Often called the "Bible" of Hinduism, the Bhagavad Gita is found in households throughout India and has been translated into every major language of the world. Literally billions of copies have been handwritten or printed.

The clarity of this translation by Swami Nirmalananda makes for easy reading, while the rich content makes this the ideal "study" Gita. As the original Sanskrit language is so rich, often there are several accurate translations for the same word, which are noted in the text, giving the spiritual student the needed understanding of the fullness of the Gita.

All Is One
A Commentary On Sri Vaiyai R. Subramanian's Ellam Ondre

Swami Nirmalananda's insightful commentary brings even further light to Ellam Ondre's refreshing perspective on what Unity signifies, and the path to its realization.

Written in the colorful and well-informed style typical of his other commentaries, it is a timely and important contribution to Advaitic literature that explains Unity as the fruit of yoga sadhana, rather than mere wishful thinking or some vague intellectual gymnastic, as is so commonly taught by the modern "Advaita gurus."

Sanatana Dharma
The Eternal Religion

Sanatana Dharma, commonly called Hinduism, is not just beautiful temples, colorful festivals, gurus and unusual beliefs. It is, simply put, "The Way Things Are" on a cosmic scale. It is the facts of existence and transcendence.

Swami Nirmalananda has edited for the modern reader a book originally printed nearly one hundred years ago in Varanasi, India, for use as a textbook by students of Benares Hindu University. Its original title was *Sanatana Dharma, An Advanced Text Book of Hindu Religion and Ethics*.

A Brief Sanskrit Glossary
A Spiritual Student's Guide to Essential Sanskrit Terms

This Sanskrit glossary contains full translations and explanations of hundreds of the most commonly used spiritual Sanskrit terms, and will help students of the Bhagavad Gita, the Upanishads, the Yoga Sutras of Patanjali, and other Indian scriptures and philosophical works to expand their vocabularies to include the Sanskrit terms contained in these, and gain a fuller understanding in their studies.

Vivekachudamani The Crest-Jewel of Discrimination For Awakening
A Commentary on Shankara's Classic on Advaita Vedanta

Beyond theory, this commentary offers practical insights for those seeking true spiritual growth, making it an essential guide for both beginners and advanced practitioners of Vedanta.

Whether you are a seasoned yogi or new to the path of spiritual awakening, this book will illuminate your journey, helping you discern the path to higher awareness amidst the clutter of modern spiritual clichés.

Dive into this classic text reimagined for contemporary seekers and transform your understanding of self and reality.

BOOKS ON ORIGINAL CHRISTIANITY

The Christ of India
The Story of Original Christianity

"Original Christianity" is the teaching of both Jesus and his Apostle Saint Thomas in India. Although it was new to the Mediterranean world, it was really the classical, traditional teachings of the rishis of India that even today comprise the Eternal Dharma, that goes far beyond religion into realization.

In *The Christ of India* Swami Nirmalananda presents what those ancient teachings are, as well as the growing evidence that Jesus spent much of his "Lost Years" in India and Tibet. This is also the story of how the original teachings of Jesus and Saint Thomas thrived in India for centuries before the coming of the European colonialists.

May a Christian Believe in Reincarnation?

Discover the real and surprising history of reincarnation and Christianity.

A growing number of people are open to the subject of past lives, and the belief in rebirth–reincarnation, metempsychosis, or transmigration–is commonplace. It often thought that belief in reincarnation and Christianity are incompatible. But is this really true? May a Christian believe in reincarnation? The answer may surprise you.

"Those needing evidence that a belief in reincarnation is in accordance with teachings of the Christ need look no further: Plainly laid out and explained in an intelligent manner from one who has spent his life on a Christ-like path of renunciation and prayer/meditation."—Christopher T. Cook

The Unknown Lives of Jesus and Mary
Compiled from Ancient Records and Mystical Revelations

"There are also many other things which Jesus did, the which, if they should be written every one, I suppose that even the world itself could not contain the books that should be written." (Gospel of Saint John, final verse)

You can discover much of those "many other things" in this unique compilation of ancient records and mystical revelations, which includes historical records of the lives of Jesus Christ and his Mother Mary that have been accepted and used by the Church since apostolic times. This treasury of little-known stories of Jesus' life will broaden the reader's understanding of what Christianity really was in its original form.

The Gospel of Thomas for Awakening
A Commentary on Jesus' Sayings as Recorded by the Apostle Thomas

When the Apostles dispersed to the various area of the world, Thomas travelled to India, where evidence shows Jesus spent his Lost Years, and which had been the source of the wisdom which he had brought to the "West."

The Christ that Saint Thomas quotes in this ancient text is quite different than the Christ presented by popular Christianity. Through his unique experience and study with both Christianity and Indian religion, Swami Nirmalananda clarifies the sometimes enigmatic sayings of Jesus in an informative and inspiring way.

The Odes of Solomon for Awakening
A Commentary on the Mystical Wisdom of the Earliest Christian Hymns and Poems

The Odes of Solomon is the earliest Christian hymn-book, and therefore one of the most important early Christian documents. Since they are mystical and esoteric, they teach and express the classical and universal mystical truths of Christianity, revealing a Christian perspective quite different than that of "Churchianity," and present the path of Christhood that all Christians are called to.

"Fresh and soothing, these 41 poems and hymns are beyond delightful! I deeply appreciate Abbot George Burke's useful and illuminating insight and find myself spiritually re-animated." –John Lawhn

The Aquarian Gospel for Awakening (2 Volumes)
A Practical Commentary on Levi Dowling's Classic Life of Jesus Christ

Written in 1908 by the American mystic Levi Dowling, The Aquarian Gospel of Jesus the Christ answers many questions about Jesus' life that the Bible doesn't address. Dowling presents a universal message found at the heart of all valid religions, a broad vision of love and wisdom that will ring true with Christians who are attracted to Christ but put off by the narrow views of the tradition that has been given his name.

Swami Nirmalananda's commentary is a treasure-house of knowledge and insight that even further expands Dowling's vision of the true Christ and his message.

Robe of Light
An Esoteric Christian Cosmology

In *Robe of Light* Swami Nirmalananda explores the whys and wherefores of the mystery of creation. From the emanation of the worlds from the very Being of God, to the evolution of the souls to their ultimate destiny as perfected Sons of God, the ideal progression of creation is described. Since the rebellion of Lucifer and the fall of Adam and Eve from Paradise flawed the normal plan of evolution, a restoration was necessary. How this came about is the prime subject of this insightful study.

Moreover, what this means to aspirants for spiritual perfection is expounded, with a compelling knowledge of the scriptures and of the mystical traditions of East and West.

Wandering With The Cherubim
A Commentary on the Mystical Verse of Angelus Silesius–The Cherubinic Wanderer

Johannes Scheffler, who wrote under the name Angelus Silesius, was a mystic and a poet. In his most famous book, "The Cherubinic Wanderer," he expressed his mystical vision.

Swami Nirmalananda reveals the timelessness of his mystical teachings and The Cherubinic Wanderer's practical value for spiritual seekers. He does this in an easily intelligible fashion for those wishing to put those priceless teachings into practice.

"Set yourself on the journey of this mystical poetry made accessible through this very beautifully commentated text. It is text that submerges one in the philosophical context of the Advaita notion of Non Duality. Swami Nirmalananda's commentary is indispensable in understanding higher philosophical ideas, for Swami's language, while readily approachable, is rich in deep essence of the teachings." –Savitri

Christian Non-Dualism
A Commentary on Theologia Germanica

What if the roots of Christian mysticism held teachings as profound as those found in the East? What if a single medieval text, long forgotten by mainstream theology, offered a clear and proven path to inner union with God?

Christian Non-Dualism is a revelatory commentary on *Theologia Germanica*, a 14th-century mystical masterpiece that has gone through nearly 200 editions but is almost unknown today. With depth, clarity, and spiritual authority, Swami Nirmalananda Giri unveils the text's rich insights into ego-surrender, divine grace, and the path to inner revelation.

Spirit & Life–The Four Gospels for Awakening
A Practical Commentary on the Life and Teachings of Jesus Christ

Spirit & Life offers a powerful, practical commentary on a harmony of the Gospels, and is not a mere biography but a spiritual revelation consisting of both the life and the teachings of Jesus.

Far from being a conventional or doctrinal study, this book invites readers into the inner life of the soul, where Jesus is not only the Master Teacher, but the awakened Self within. With clarity and reverence, the author examines the inner meaning of the canonical Gospels, unveiling their universal message of illumination, liberation, and union with God.

A two volume set, beautifully illustrated.

BOOKS ON BUDDHISM & TAOISM AND MORE

The Dhammapada for Awakening
A Commentary on Buddha's Practical Wisdom

Swami Nirmalananda's commentary on this classic Buddhist scripture explores the Buddha's answers to the urgent questions, such as "How can I find find lasting peace, happiness and fulfillment that seems so elusive?" and "What can I do to avoid many of the miseries big and small that afflict all of us?" Drawing on his personal experience, the author sheds new light on the Buddha's eternal wisdom.

"Swami Nirmalananda's commentary is well crafted and stacked with anecdotes, humor, literary references and beautiful quotes from the Buddha. I have come to consider it a guide to daily living." –Rev. Gerry Nangle

The Tao Teh King for Awakening
A Practical Commentary on Lao Tzu's Classic Exposition of Taoism

"The Tao does all things, yet our interior disposition determines our success or failure in coming to knowledge of the unknowable Tao."

Lao Tzu's classic writing, the *Tao Teh King*, has fascinated scholars and seekers for centuries. Swami Nirmalananda offers a commentary that makes the treasures of Lao Tzu's teachings accessible and applicable for the sincere seeker.

Bio-Magnetic Therapy
Healing in Your Hands

In *Bio-Magnetic Therapy* Swami Nirmalananda teaches the techniques to strengthen your vitality and improve the body's natural healing ability in yourself and in others with specific methods that anyone can use.

Bio-Magnetic Therapy is a simple and natural way to increase the flow of life-force into the body for general good health and to stimulate the supply and flow of life-force to a troubled area that has become vitality-starved through some obstruction. It does not cure; it simply aids the body to cure itself by supplying it with curative force.

How to Read the Tarot
A Practical Method Using the Rider-Waite Deck

Discover Swami Nirmalananda's unique method of reading the Tarot specifically for use with the Rider-Waite deck, with detailed instructions on how to use the cards to develop your intuition for understanding the meanings of the cards. Illustrated with color plates of each of the cards of the Rider-Waite deck with full explanations of their symbolism.

Light on the Path for Awakening
A Commentary on Mabel Collins' Spiritual Classic

In the last quarter of the nineteenth century, Mabel Collins printed a small book on the beginnings of the spiritual quest entitled Light On The Path. She did not consider herself the author but only the transmitter.

This commentary carefully analyzes her transcription, for those who would make the Great Journey must know both the path and how to travel upon it.

Light on the Path explains the nature of discipleship and the qualities of a worthy disciple. The master of such a disciple is the disciple's own divine Self which draws its existence from the Supreme Self: God.

More Titles
Light from Eternal Lamps
Psychic Defense for Yogis

www.ingramcontent.com/pod-product-compliance
Lightning Source LLC
Chambersburg PA
CBHW020046170426
43199CB00009B/190